Jira Work Management Basics

A Beginner Guide for Novice Jira Administrators

Cloud Version

Jira is a fantastic software product that helps organizations manage Tasks, Processes, and Projects.

Jira Work Management Basics is written for business users who want the fundamentals of Jira Work Management explained in easy to understand, non-technical language.

The book delivers a comprehensive description of the Jira elements, includes exercises for hands-on experience, and provides 'How to' scripts to help you customize Jira Work Management to meet your organization's needs.

Jira Work Management Basics

A Beginner Guide for Novice Jira Administrators

Cloud Version

Rynder Roy Klomp

KRS
Publishing

Published by

KlompRS Publishing

Toronto, Canada

ISBN 978-1-988018-21-8

Dedication

As always, to my beloved wife Anna.

And to Philipp Sendek. Great advisor, and even better friend. Thank you for your support and for your invaluable guidance.

Table Of Contents

Jira Work Management Basics

Introduction

Hello, and welcome to **Jira Work Management Basics: A Beginner Guide for Novice Jira Administrators – Cloud version**.

I am excited to introduce you to Jira Work Management (JWM), an amazing product that helps organizations and users manage their tasks, processes, and projects.

In today's business world where employees are asked to do more, in less time, and with fewer resources there is a need to "automate" and simplify wherever possible. JWM meets those requirements perfectly.

I stumbled across Jira when looking for software I could use for a project I was building. I wanted software that would let me 1) manage tasks, 2) allow field agents to complete the project's status forms remotely, and 3) have automated responses based on a condition in a status form (e.g. an automated emergency email to the business owner if the status form indicated the project would not meet its deadline). Basically, I wanted something that would let me manage the project from a beach in Bora Bora. While JWM isn't yet able to do the last item, it does extremely well at delivering on the first three, and that is why I got involved with it. And I am glad I did; I was able to build a JWM project that allows a client to rollout a new product nationwide faster, at a lower cost, and with fewer challenges than the previous manual process.

Who Should read this Book

There are a number of books and articles aimed towards the Jira users. While most of them are quite good, they are almost all written by Information Technology (I.T.) professionals targeting I.T. readers. In those books and documents, it is common to read something like, *"Next, compact the parsnipial environment using a compound ambidextrous stacking algorithm. Here is a short 761 line example of how to do that using Bilingua Ascii Code. For your added enjoyment we have written the code in an obscure Western Mongolian Dialect that hasn't actually been spoken in 450 years."* This is great for I.T. individuals, but what about the rest of us?

Jira Work Management Basics is written for business team members who don't have I.T. backgrounds. It is written in non-I.T. language and is geared towards the business team member who either wants to work with Jira Work Management or has been instructed to work with JWM (*"Sam, we've just bought 300 Jira Work Management licenses to improve our processes. Figure out how it works and build us a solution. Oh yeah, and do it by next Tuesday."*). So, if you are I.T. and are looking for help to manage JWM coding or databases; or, if you are searching for specific questions regarding macros or specialized installations, etc., this book is NOT for you. Of course, you are more than welcome to read the book, you may find it helpful.

What is Jira Work Management?

Atlassian (the parent company) created Jira as a way to track issues related to "bugs" within software projects. It wasn't long before additional features were added and it grew into a project management program with the ability to "automate" a lot of the work that is necessary but provides little customer value, such as emailing or phoning a work colleague when a task is done.

Introduction

Fundamentally, Jira Work Management (JWM) is an application that helps organizations manage their tasks, processes, and projects. Additionally, it is "smart software" because much of the tedious but necessary stuff related to tasks, or processes, or project management, can be automated fairly easily. Let's look at two examples. First, let's say you need to approve a product or document (as part of your work process) You can set the process up in JWM, so the approver just needs to click the "approved" button and messages are automatically sent to whom-ever needs to be informed of the approval. If it is not approved, the approver can select from a predefined list of reasons for the rejection or can write an explanation, and again those messages are sent to the necessary individuals automatically.

In our second example, we will look at a work process (called a "workflow" in JWM). Let us say your work is part of a process crossing several departments. When you are finished your step in the process, you simply click a button and the next department or person in the process gets an automated notification that your step is done, and it is ready for them to start their work.

So what, you ask. I can do that already with emails or phone calls. Yes, you can. However, how many times have you intended to immediately write that email or make that phone call, only to be interrupted by life? Maybe you remembered a few hours later, or at the end of the day, that you needed to write that email. How many times did you recall it the next day, or forget completely until someone reminded you? Well, the benefit of JWM is that it is your silent "admin assistant"; and it automatically takes care of those tasks for you.

Processes and Procedures

JWM excels at repeatable *processes and procedures*. A process is a series of activities or tasks required to accomplish a goal. In other words, it describes *What* needs to be done. A procedure, in business, is the set of instructions which provides the steps and describes *How* to execute the steps necessary to complete the process (not to be confused with an I.T. procedure which simply lists the detailed steps).

Many processes and procedures require checks (quality control or approvals), as well as handoffs to whomever is next involved in the process. These are often time consuming, and in the case of checks, provide no value-added to the customer. It is probably fair to say that in many situations as much time is spent transferring a task for a check or handoffs as is spent working on the task itself. Anything that can be done to reduce the time spent on these activities is of great value. On top of managing the task, JWM with its workflow component, is outstanding at managing the checks and handoff transfers.

JWM has grown into a highly flexible and customizable tool to manage work activity. In addition, there are many 'apps' you can purchase at very reasonable prices that plug into JWM and offer specialty solutions to specific challenges.

For more business examples please go to the 'Which Project Type to Select' section in Chapter 3.

The Three Jira Amigos

Over time, Atlassian has "calved" Jira into three interactive applications: Jira Work Management, Jira Service Management, and Jira Software. I call them "the three amigos" (after the movie, of course). These three are interactive because you need to have JWM for Jira Service Management and Jira Software to work.

Jira Work Management

JWM started life as a means of helping software developers manage any software bugs that would show up while writing a program. Any time the developer ran into a bug, s/he would create a JWM "Issue" (a bug to be fixed). This formed the basis for JWM; and slowly this evolved into the robust Jira Work Management program that can be used to manage tasks and processes.

You must purchase Jira Work Management licenses if you want to use Jira Service Management or Jira Software. That's because Jira Work Management is the "engine" allowing Jira Service Management and Jira Software to work.

Jira Service Management

Jira Service Management helps you manage a "ticketing" process. Ticketing is any sort of work that involves a constant flow of incoming individual tasks that must be assigned to a pool of resources.

A perfect example is an I.T. help desk. Any organization having more than three computers has an I.T. help desk. In small companies it may be Sam, and you get his attention by yelling across the room, "Hey, Sam, my printer has stopped working again." But, in large organizations there is usually a department dedicated to help employees with their I.T. issues. Whenever a help call comes in, a "ticket" is created to track the issue until it is resolved. Jira Service Management handles this sort of thing perfectly. Tickets (called Issues) can be created and assigned by a manager or can be created by any team member receiving a call or email.

Many organizations use "ticketing" procedures where there is a constant flow of customer requests that need to be assigned to workers. Insurance claims, delivery orders, taxi pickups, appliance repairs, dry cleaning, etc. are examples.

With Jira you can also categorize your ticketing. Your I.T. help desk can create customized Issues (Tickets) for Printer Issues, PC Issues, Log on Issues, etc. In a transportation ticketing system two different types of Issues might be created depending on whether the product to be delivered needs a refrigerated truck or not.

Jira Work Management Basics

Jira has developed the Jira Service Management program for companies needing a ticketing solution. But to work with Jira Service Management, you must first install Jira Work Management.

Jira Software

Many projects or processes involve accomplishing numerous related tasks within a defined time frame. You may have a list of 100 tasks needing to be accomplished. A pool of six team members decides, for example, they can accomplish *these* 17 (of the 100) items in the next 30 days. Each team member grabs one of the 17 items and works on it. Once complete s/he goes back to the pool and takes another of the remaining items and then works on that item; this continues until the workload of 17 items is complete. At which point they plan their next block of work. This is called Agile Project Management.

The example above may be similar to the opening of a new store where 400 product categories (e.g. Dry Pasta) must be set up by a pool of 40 employees in 40 days. Each employee takes one category and when that product line is displayed properly s/he goes back and grabs the ticket for another category. Using the Jira program, the project manager can easily track the progress of the complete project.

Jira has developed the Jira Software program for companies needing an Agile project management delivery solution (and it is called Jira Software, because it is mostly used by Software teams). But, again, you need Jira Work Management for Jira Software to work.

The Cloud Environment

If you are new to Atlassian or are moving over from the Jira Server version, it is critical you understand the Atlassian Cloud Environment and how that environment affects JWM.

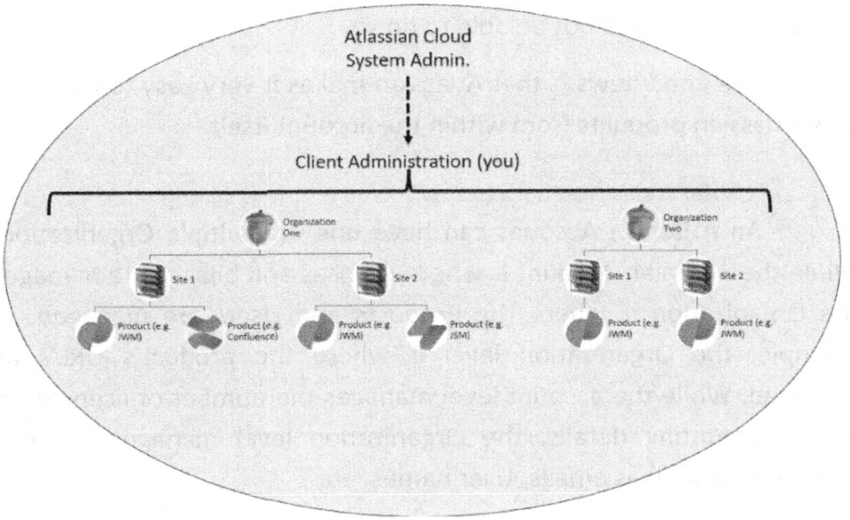

Your Atlassian Cloud environment

Your Atlassian Cloud Environment is set up as a hierarchy: Account > Organization > Site > Atlassian Product (e.g. JWM).

Your Atlassian Account

When you first start to download an Atlassian product, such as JWM, you will be asked to create an Atlassian account. Your Atlassian account is where you enter your company name, credit card, email address, licensing, etc., everything related to billing and administrative stuff. Here is the important thing: **your email address is used as the basis for your identification**. Why is this important? Let's say that at some time in the future you decide to download another Atlassian product (e.g. Confluence, Jira Service Management, etc.). When this happens, you will be asked for an email address. If you use an email address different from the one you used to set up the first account, Atlassian will set you up in an entirely new Atlassian account. Maybe that is what you want. But if you wanted to manage everything within one account, you will not be able to do so.

The good news is that Atlassian makes it very easy to download new Atlassian products from within the account itself.

YOUR ATLASSIAN ORGANIZATION

An Atlassian Account can have one or multiple Organizations. While the Atlassian Account is where licenses and billings are managed, the Organization is where the Products and Users are managed; for example, the Organization level is where the product's URL's are managed. While the account level manages the number of licenses and other accounting details, the Organization level manages the User specific data such as emails, User names, etc.

Why would you need more than one organization? There are a number of reasons, but the three most common are: business structure, region, and confidentiality.

You may want to have one Account for the entirety of your business but have an Organization for each business unit.

You may also want to have a different organization for different geographical regions (e.g. states, or countries) or languages.

You may want to have different organizations if there is a risk that there may be confidentiality breaches. For example, you may have as clients two competitors. In this case you may want to set up an organization for each competitor client. Or you may have a "top secret" division within your company. It may be easier to set up a "Top Secret" Organization.

Each Organization can have one or more "Sites".

YOUR ATLASSIAN SITES

Your Organization's site is the container for your Atlassian products. A site can hold one or more Atlassian products (e.g., JWM, Jira

Software, Confluence, etc.). In addition, you can have multiple sites within an Organization. For example, you may have two sites within your Organization, each containing JWM. However, you cannot have more than one of the same product in a single site. The table below provides some examples of what is, and what is not, allowed with multiple sites within one Organization.

Site	Allowed	Not Allowed
Site A	JWM	JWM JWM
Site B	JWM Jira Service Management	JWM Jira Service Management Jira Service Management
Site C	JWM Jira Service Management Jira Software Confluence	No Products

Why would you want multiple sites? You are likely to want multiple sites for the same reason you want multiple Organizations. It simply comes down to how you want to structure your Atlassian Cloud environment (or how your customers want it set up).

Just remember that if you assign the same User to multiple sites, you will need a separate license for that User for each site (unless you purchase the Enterprise license plan).

Which brings us to the final point. Because licenses are based on Users associated with a Site, your billing will be based on the Site. For example, if you have three Sites, you will receive three bills each month (assuming you have the Standard or Premium plans).

Now, if you are a small organization where budgets are very tight, you are probably thinking that if billing is based on Site User count you can simply create a bunch of Sites and populate each with JWM and use the free license plan. Sorry, remember that User count is aggregated at the Administration level and if your total User count exceeds the free plan limit, you will receive an email stating that you will either need to reduce your User count or pick a paid plan. To use our previous example, let's say you have three sites with each site having a JWM product and each having a free plan. Let's say that each site has 4 Users (remember that you can have up to 10 Users in the free plan), for a total User count of 12. Because the aggregated total is greater than the 10 User free plan, you will need to purchase a Standard or Premium plan.

PRODUCTS

An Atlassian product is an application. Examples are: JWM, Jira Service Management, Jira Software, Confluence, Statuspage, Opsgenie, etc. You can have multiple versions of a product within your Atlassian Environment. For example, you may have three instances of JWM. But if you have multiple instances of the same product, you will need a separate site for each instance.

Products are automatically and constantly updated by Atlassian. So, don't be surprised when you sign in one morning and your product is a little bit different from your previous session.

JWM ADMINISTRATORS

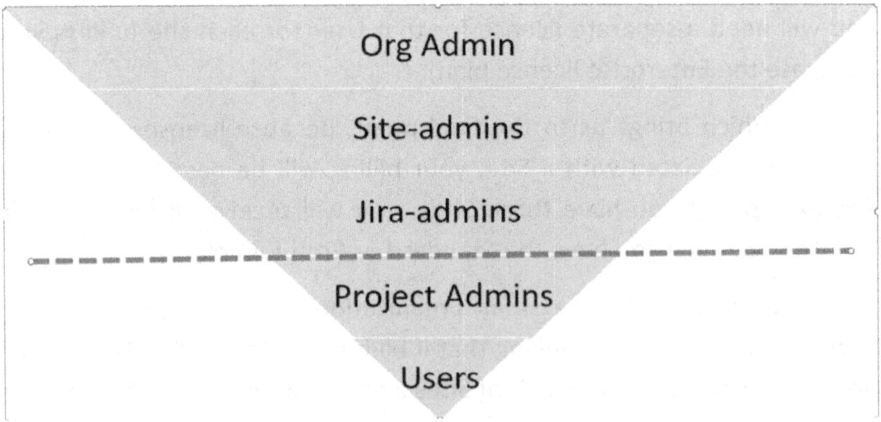

Let's next look at JWM Administrators. One unfortunate habit of Atlassian is to constantly use the term "Administrator" for almost every aspect of your Atlassian environment. Therefore, it is helpful to start with a good understanding of the various levels.

Jira Work Management has numerous security levels that allows or prevents access to different aspects of JWM. At the highest level is the **Organization Administrator** (Org Admin). This individual is primarily focused on the managing of Users and Bills, but technically has access to all Atlassian applications. As a general rule, the Org Admin is typically the person whose email address or credit card was used to create the Atlassian account.

Next is the **Site Administrator.** These folks can manage all Atlassian products within the Site. For example, if a Site contains JWM, Jira Service Management, Jira Software, and Confluence, then the Site Administrator can manage every Product within that site. In addition, they can (with permissions) create Projects, Workflows, Issue Types, Custom Fields, etc. They can also manage the Users and Bills within that site.

Next is the **Jira Administrator**. These people have the same abilities as the Site Administrator, but they are limited to working with JWM only.

Then we have the **JWM Project Administrator**. This person is limited to managing a Project, but s/he cannot create "company-managed" Projects, or Workflows, Issue Types, Custom Fields, etc. They are generally restricted to adding and managing Users within a Project. I would think of these people as more like a super-User and not so much as an Administrator.

Users are licensed to use the software, but do not have permission to modify the software. In other words, they typically are restricted to viewing, entering, and editing data within their project or projects. The whole purpose of JWM is to permit Site Admins and Jira Admins to build customized applications to be operated by USERS. Most of this book deals with areas that the Project Admin and USER cannot access; therefore, team members in those roles will probably find that other than the first couple of chapters the book is of limited value in their current role.

It will get quite tedious to constantly refer to "Org-admins, Site-admins, and Jira-admins" in this book. We will collectively call these three levels of admins as "Site-admins" (unless otherwise stated).

NOTE: This book assumes you already have JWM Cloud installed. If it is not, the good news is that JWM Cloud is extremely easy to install, even for non-I.T. users. If you do want to install JWM Cloud yourself, please go to "Chapter 14: How to..." where you will find basic instructions on how to do so.

WHY THIS BOOK?

'Process oriented' probably best describes me. Most of my work involves designing and implementing solutions for large companies. I love to design and build process solutions to a problem. While I have worked with a lot of software and I.T. people, I am not "I.T".

You know by now that there is often an "understanding gap" between IT professionals and business-people. Why? The terms and definitions that IT people use, on many occasions have slightly different meanings than those used by non-IT individuals. For example, in everyday life you would not have any difficulty understanding what a Project is, or Issue, or Schemes. But you will be very surprised how those terms are defined in JWM. I find that I.T. folks, like any specialized work group, tend to speak their own unique language. While this specialized language is necessary, it doesn't translate well for those of us who are not I.T.

Additionally, I find much of the existing JWM documentation is written by I.T. professionals for I.T. professionals, which kind of leaves the rest of us in the dark. Finally, I find that JWM documentation, while quite good at describing individual steps, tends to lack an easy-to-understand overview of JWM.

That's why I decided to write this book. I wanted to understand how JWM works and how all the JWM pieces fit together; and I wanted to describe it in a language for those of us who are NOT in I.T. can easily comprehend.

Structure of the Book

Earlier I discussed the different permission levels within JWM. This book is meant for Novice Site-admins. As stated earlier, to make life easier, I will simply use the term Site-admin and that will include the Org Administrator, Site Administrator, and Jira Administrator unless specifically noted otherwise.

The goal of the Site-admin is to make the JWM elements as simple as possible for the Users. If the Accounts Payable clerk (a User) only needs to see three fields on a task screen, then don't show him eight. If the Salesperson (a User) only needs to see five fields on her specific task screen, then there is no need to show her nine.

The Site-admin needs to make the project (a folder to hold similar Jira tasks) and its screens as simple as possible for two reasons. First, you do it because there is no sense to buy software that makes life more difficult for the Users. Second, you do it to avoid resistance. Anything that makes life more difficult for a User is going to cause resistance. And continuous resistance results in failure. There are two main causes of resistance to a software application: the Users don't see how the product benefits them; or they see the product as too complicated to use. So, while JWM can be used out of the box with its defaults, you probably will need to modify it (i.e. specialize and simplify) to make it succeed within your organization.

As just mentioned, you can start using Jira Work Management as soon as you download it. Jira Work Management comes with enough defaults that you can create projects and tasks quite rapidly. As a matter of fact, I would recommend you do so. Try setting up a trial project just using the defaults and invite a couple of volunteers to participate. As you work with your project and tasks you may find the defaults work fine for your situation. Which is fantastic, why create unnecessary work if you don't need to. However, after a while you will probably realize the defaults need to be modified slightly, or a lot, to meet your business requirements or to make it more efficient. This ability to bespoke the software into just about any imaginable configuration and meet almost any situation, is the true value of JWM.

Jira Work Management Basics: Beginner Guide for Novice Jira Administrators will:

- Walk you through the creation of a simple project using the JWM's defaults
- Explain the most common screens in Jira Work Management and how they work
- Describe the various JWM elements (what I call the "puzzle pieces"), and show how they fit together
- Modify the project we have built by creating some specialized screens and fields
- Provide a "cheat sheets" section with scripts for most of the standard activities.

When finished, you will have a good understanding of how JWM works and having built your first JWM business project you also will be able to move forward confidently on your own.

What you won't find

Since this is a Beginner's Guide dedicated to the business user you will not find:

- I.T. terms and details
- Programming language
- Topics I consider to be of Intermediate or Advanced level
- Jira Service Management or Jira Software topics

Assumptions

In writing this book we assume the following about you:

- You are a beginner to Jira Work Management
- You are a "business" user, not an I.T. professional
- You have a copy of Jira Work Management already licensed for your computer. If you do not, and want to try installing it yourself, go to "Chapter 14: How to..." for instructions on installing and configuring JWM
- You have been given Site-admin rights. These Administrator rights mean you can make changes to the application. If not, make sure you get it right away, you will need it to make modifications to the program.

Formatting

To try and make it easier for you to make sense of everything the following formats will be used in this book.

CAUTION: Indicates a warning or caution.

NOTE or TIP: Indicates a Note or Helpful Tip.

Jira Work Management Basics

Regular font (like this) will be used for normal text.

1. SMALL CAPITAL FONT WILL BE USED AS AN INSTRUCTION FOR YOU TO FOLLOW (E.G. CLICK **ADD**).

Bold Font will indicate an element in JWM such as a button, link, a field, screen, etc. Also, it will emphasize some important messages.

Italic font will specify a term used by JWM such as Step, Status, etc., or it will be the information that you might be asked to enter into a JWM field.

The word "**view**" will mean something the **User** will see when working with an Issue or Project. A **User** has very few rights and is typically limited to entering or editing data, necessary to complete his or her tasks.

Is it easy to work in JWM? No, it takes practice. But I would strongly argue that it is not the software that is difficult. The reality is that designing a process or project can be, by itself, a very difficult exercise, irrespective of the software used. If looked at from that perspective I believe JWM to be the easiest process/project software to work with. They have really worked hard over the years to translate a difficult topic into an application that is as intuitive as possible.

The good news is that within a fairly short time it does indeed become quite instinctive to use. I recommend you practice by creating a fiction project first, draw it on the paper and play with it in JWM to "feel" how all JWM elements fit together. I did it, and so can you.

What does Jira mean?

In case you are wondering what Jira means, here is the explanation as quoted from the Atlassian Jira website.

"Like all good names in the software industry, it started as an in-house code name.

We originally used Bugzilla for bug tracking and the developers in the office started calling it by the Japanese name for Godzilla, Gojira (the original black-and-white Japanese Godzilla films are also office favorites). As we developed our own bug tracker, and then it became an issue tracker, the name stuck, but the Go got dropped - hence Jira!

Further investigation into the name has revealed that Gorira is Japanese for "gorilla", whilst Kujira is Japanese for "whale". So Gojira is roughly translated to mean "gorilla the size of a whale"! (Thanks to yusuke_arclamp — Oct 2002)".

Chapter 1 - Create Your First Jira Work Management Project

To avoid confusion, in this book the term "Site-admin" includes "Org-admin, Site-admin, and Jira-admin" unless specifically noted otherwise.

NOTE: Only Site-admins can create a JWM company-managed project. Project Admins and Users can create team-managed projects. Since team-managed projects are very limited in functionality, we will not be discussing them in this book.

CHAPTER OBJECTIVES

Logically we should start this book by explaining the technical elements of Jira Work Management and how they all work together. However, if you are like most people, you probably want to get started as quickly as possible. So, in this chapter you will:

- **understand the meaning of Jira Projects and Jira Issues**
- **create your first Project**
- **create your first Issue within that project**
- **take a quick tour of the task you just created.**

NOTE: The chapters following this one will answer most of your questions as to 'how does it work', or, 'where can I find this'.

Create your first JWM Project

But first...

Let's start with a brief explanation of Issues and Projects. A Jira Work Management *Issue* is something that needs to be done, fixed, or resolved. In other words, it is a 'packet of work', a task.

An Issue **must** reside within a Project. More importantly **Issues can only be created within a Project**.

I used to call a Jira Project as a "file folder containing Jira Issues". That was back in the days when a Project was a simple container for Issues. But today, when you create a project, Jira automatically creates a whole bunch of stuff (called "schemes") that determine who can work on the Issues in your project, and what those people can and cannot do. Just as importantly, the schemes define how the Issues will work. Those topics are covered in later chapters.

Before you can create your first Issue, you must first create a Project. We will do that now.

Create a Project

Exercise: Create your First Project

To create your first project, follow these instructions:

1. On the Navigation Bar click **Projects**
2. In the Projects menu select **Create Project**

CAUTION: If you are a JWM User, you cannot create a project. Even if you are a Project-admin on another project you cannot create a project. Only Site-admins can create projects.

After you click "Create Project", the **Create Project** wizard opens:

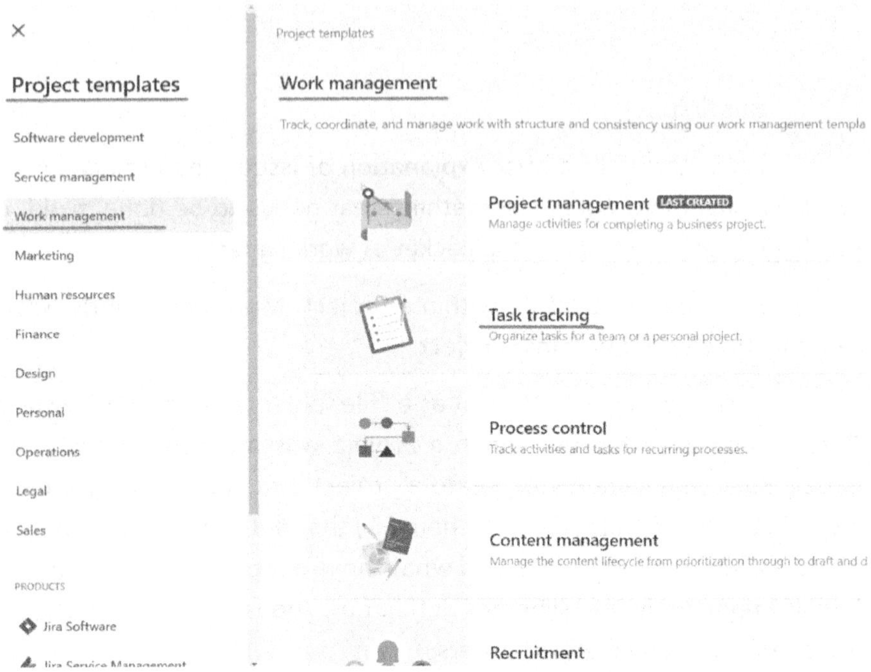

3. IN THE SIDEBAR MAKE SURE **WORK MANAGEMENT** IS SELECTED
4. IN THE WORK MANAGEMENT SCREEN SELECT **TASK TRACKING**

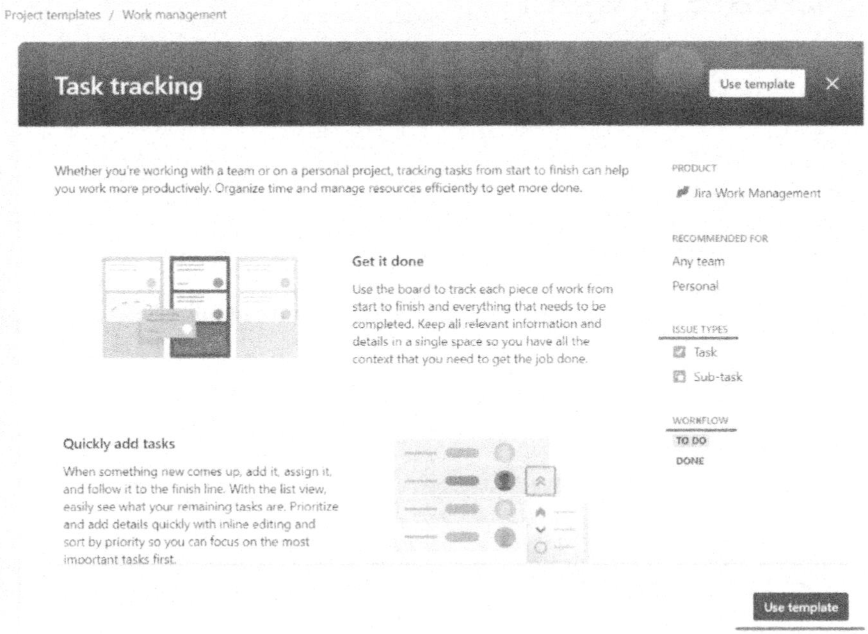

This pop-up provides an overview of the **Task tracking** Project Type. It shows that two **Issue Types** are available to you, and it shows the **Workflow** that operates with this choice. We will discuss Issue Types and Workflows very soon, but for now...

5. CLICK USE TEMPLATE

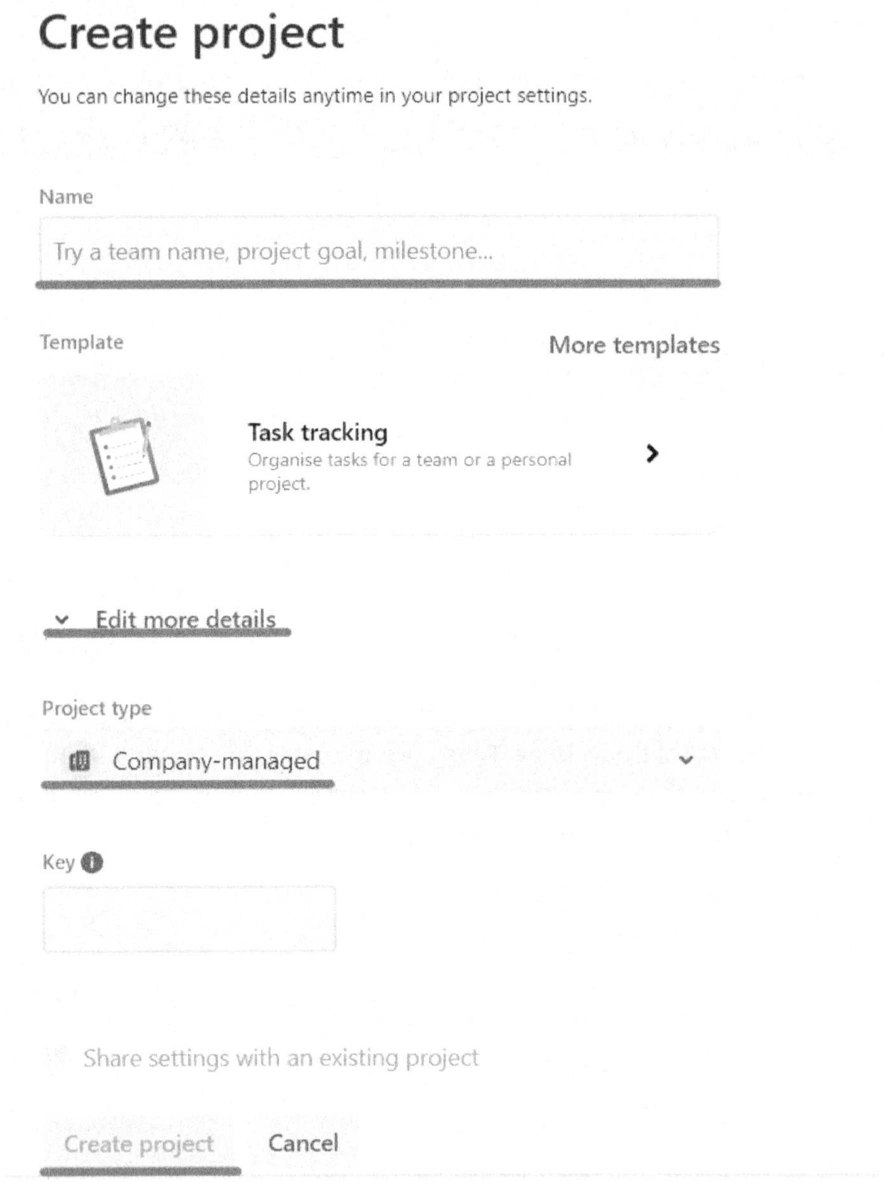

This is where you name, select project type, and create your project.

6. IN THE **NAME** FIELD TYPE "*WEEKEND ACTIVITIES*"

7. CLICK THE EDIT MORE DETAILS LINK*
8. IN THE **PROJECT TYPE** DROP DOWN SELECT "*COMPANY-MANAGED*"

*NOTE: Steps 7 and 8 are critical, if you don't select "Company-managed", you will end up with a "Team-managed" project which has limited functionality.

Notice that as you typed in the Name of the project the **Key** field automatically filled with some Capital letters. The **Project Key** performs two functions. First, this is how Jira identifies your project in its internal database. This key field creates a unique combination of letters that will differentiate your current project from any other project. Second, anytime you create an Issue, or task, in this project, Jira will assign to that Issue an Issue key number that begins with your project key (e.g. WA – 001, WA – 002, etc.). You can change the project key but that is not a very easy or wise thing to do.

9. CLICK CREATE PROJECT

Congratulations, you have just created your first project in Jira Work Management, and you should now be in the project's **List** view. This is where all your project's Issues will be shown after you create them. But since you have not yet created any, the view looks like this:

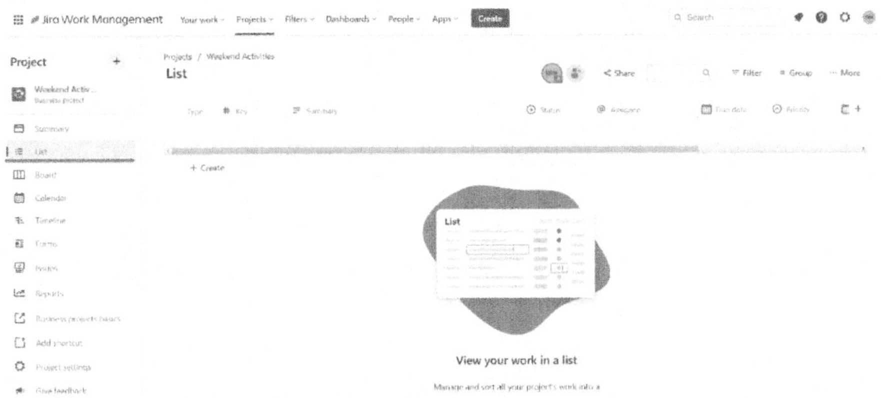

We will explore the List view in more detail in a later chapter as well as show you how to make some changes, but for now let's create your first Issue in the **Weekend Activities Project**.

CREATE AN ISSUE

EXERCISE: CREATE YOUR FIRST ISSUE

We have created a project; now it is time to create our first Issue in this project.

1. ON THE NAVIGATION BAR CLICK **CREATE:**

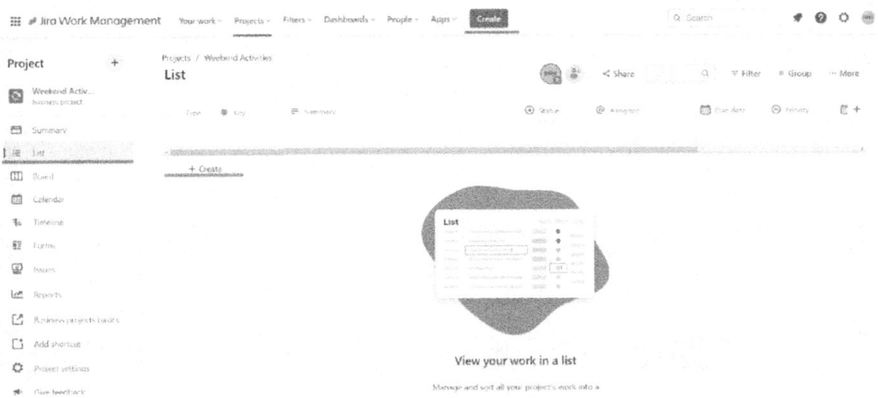

NOTE: you can also click on the +Create link in the Board view, but the blue Create button is available all the time.

The **Create Issue View** popup appears:

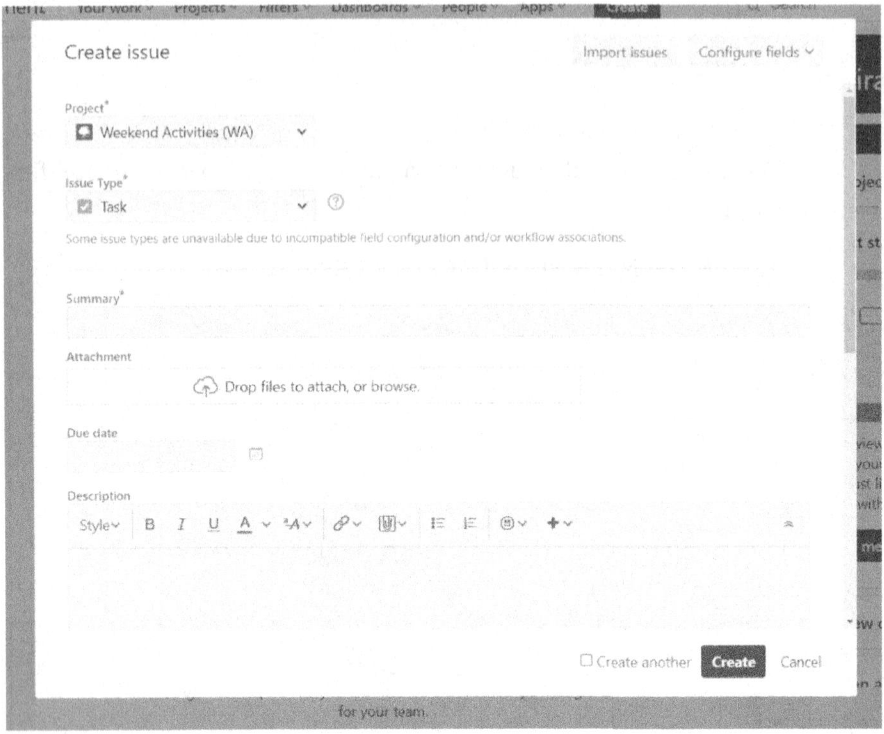

2. In the **Project** field select *Weekend Activities (WA)* project if it is not already selected
3. In the **Issue Type** field select *Task* if it is not already selected
4. In the **Summary** field type '*New Weekend Chore*'
5. In the **Due Date** field choose the end of the Year
6. In the **Description** field you can type a description of your newly created project and choose a style, font, size, insert link or/and attachment, etc. by selecting the relevant icon on the toolbar above your text
7. Scroll down, the **Reporter** field should already contain your name; if not, go ahead and enter your User name
8. In the **Assignee** field click on the <u>Assign to me</u> link below the field

9. In the **Priority** field select *High* by clicking on the drop-down arrow
10. In the **Labels** field type in or select from the drop-down list an appropriate label (or key word) for the issue
11. In the **Start Date** field, select today's date
12. Click **Create**

Woo Hoo! You have just created your first issue, and here it is highlighted in your work Board:

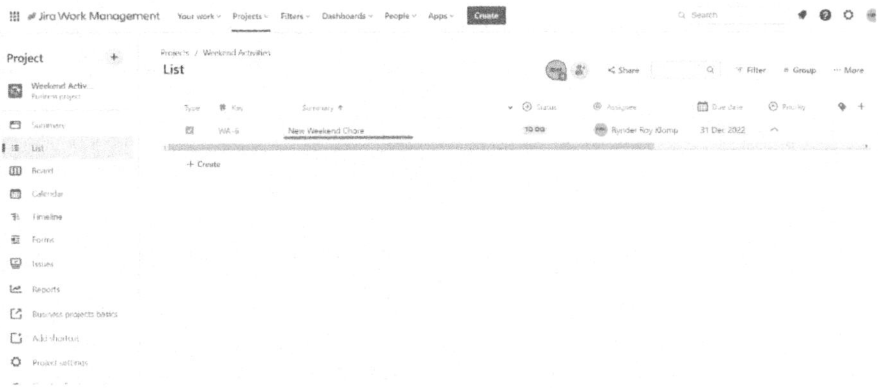

Let's look at it in more detail.

The Issue View

On the **Navigation Bar** click on **Projects** and select your newly created **New Weekend Chore**. Clicking on the **Key** will bring you to the **Issue View**:

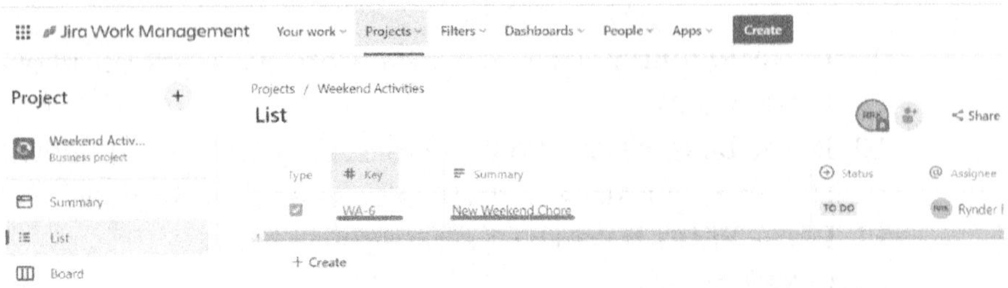

This is called the **Issue View** and shows the details of your issue:

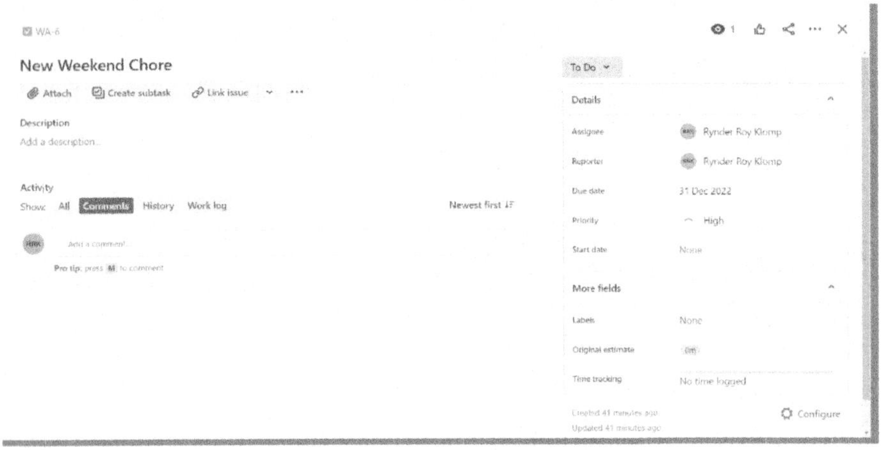

Wow, quite a busy view isn't it! If you want to know what's happening with your Issue, here is where you go. All the information you entered when you created the Issue is right here.

This will be your most used view; so, while it might seem overwhelming you will soon get used to it. Since it is your most critical view, let's take a quick look at it (we will discuss each part in more detail later in the book).

One last thing before we start. The Issue view shown above is the **default** view for the **Task** type of work. Different types of work in your organization will most likely result in different fields and different field layouts.

General Layout

The default layout for a JWM Issue view is two columns. However, if you are viewing JWM on a mobile device or other small screen you will likely be seeing the Issue in a single column view. To make things easier we will work with the standard two column view in this book.

Issue Header

The Issue Header contains two items: the Issue Key and the Issue Summary.

The issue key - **WA-6** in this example is autogenerated - and displayed for you (highlighted in the image below):

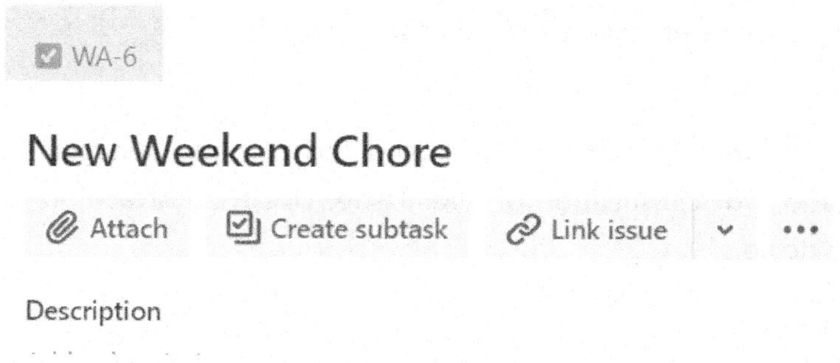

The Issue Key is automatically created, is unique, and is what Jira uses to identify your Issue.

Next is the **Summary** of the Issue ("New Weekend Chore"):

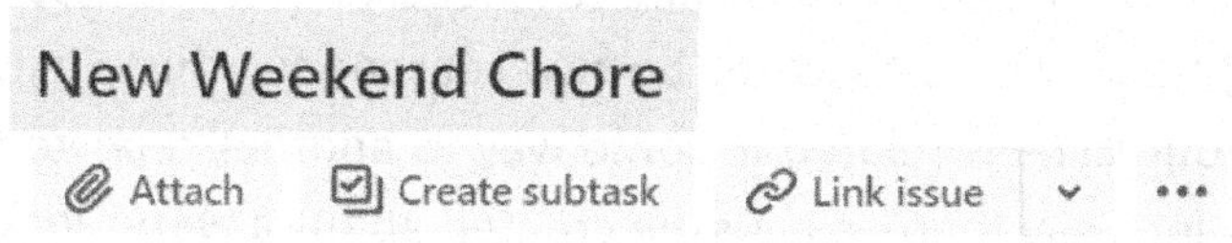

When I first started working with Jira software, "Summary" was the one thing that confused me the most. I kept looking for a place to enter the name or title of the Issue, and I could not find it. I have no idea why they just don't call it Issue Name or something that we, regular folks, would understand. But it's their product and they can do as they wish, so let's live with it.

LEFT COLUMN

Let's first look at the Issue parts located in the left column of the Issue.

QUICK-ADD BUTTONS

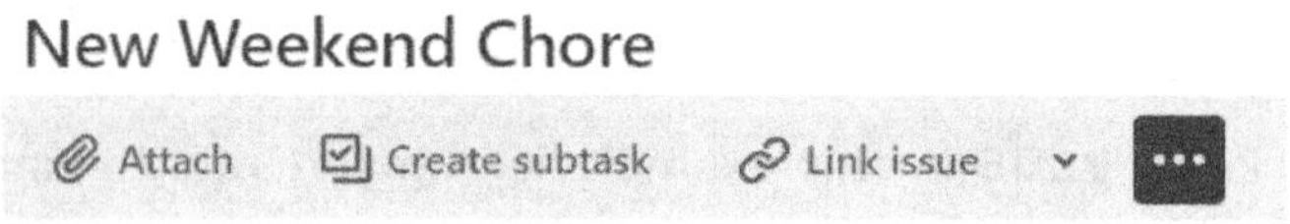

Below the Summary there is what Atlassian defines as "quick-add buttons". These buttons allow you to:

ATTACH

Often you will find the need to include image(s) or documentation for clarification of your Issue. Use the "Attach" (a file) function to do so.

CREATE SUBTASK

One of the many great things about JWM is the ability to break an Issue down into smaller pieces of work called "Subtasks". That is what the Create subtask button is used for. Subtasks are explained in more detail in "Chapter 5: JWM Issue Types".

LINK ISSUE

It is not uncommon to discover that you need to link one Issue to another existing Issue. There tends to be two reasons for this. First, you discover that your Issue is related in some way to another reported Issue. For example, let's say there is an Issue created about a water leak in room 501. You later discover that the room 501 leak relates to a previously reported water leak in room 601. You can link the two Issues together as they are clearly part of one problem. The second most common reason is that the two Issues are operationally related. For example, you may create two Issues: one to deal with dry walling a room, and another for painting the room after the dry wall work is complete. The two Issues clearly related to one another, so it makes sense to link them. Issue Linking is discussed in more detail in "Chapter 8: Fields".

DROPDOWN

The down arrow opens a menu with more quick-add buttons. The default item is the button to add a web link to your Issue.

... (MORE)

The last quick add button is the More menu (the three dots) which contains a link to the Atlassian Marketplace. Here you can find apps designed for specific purposes. Some are free, most require a quite reasonable fee. Adding an app typically requires Site-admin permission. Once an app is added, it will appear in the More drop-down menu.

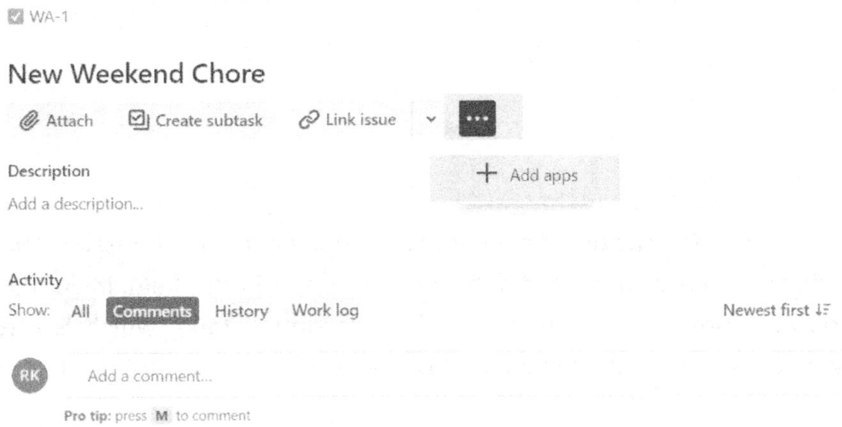

TABS

Some types of Issues will include tabs (not unlike what you will see in your browser). Tabs are typically used for two reasons. First, your Issue has so many fields that it makes it easier to manage them by placing them in separate tabs. Second, the fields might be grouped (in tabs) based on the phases of a workflow; for example: Customer Details, Problem Details, Diagnosis Results, Repair Details, Customer Billing. Fields are placed in each tab based on the information needed for that step in the process.

In the image below you will see the arrow pointing at an empty space. This is the area where Issue tabs will appear if your Issue has tabs:

DESCRIPTION

The **Description** field contains the overview of the Issue. There is no limit to the amount of detail you can enter in this field. In addition, you can format the contents of the Description field, which is often helpful if you have a large amount of content.

ACTIVITY

This area has four sections: All, Comments, History, and Work log.

All

This section shows all the details from the Comments, History, and Worklog tabs. If your Issue does not have a lot of activity, it is often easier to view the All section. Conversely, if you have a lot of activity, it is often easier to go to the specific Activity section.

Comments

This section allows you to add comments as you are working on the Issue. Comments are helpful to other team members who may be working on the Issue later, or Issue watchers who need to be informed about the Issue. Users must have permission to add, edit, or delete comments.

History

Anything that happens with the Issue will be automatically recorded and displayed here. If you need to audit an Issue or understand what happened with the Issue, this is where you will find the details as to what happened with the issue.

Log Work

If you are logging work on an Issue, this is where you do so. Logging work, estimating work, and time tracking are discussed in more detail in "Chapter 10: Managing Time".

Right Column

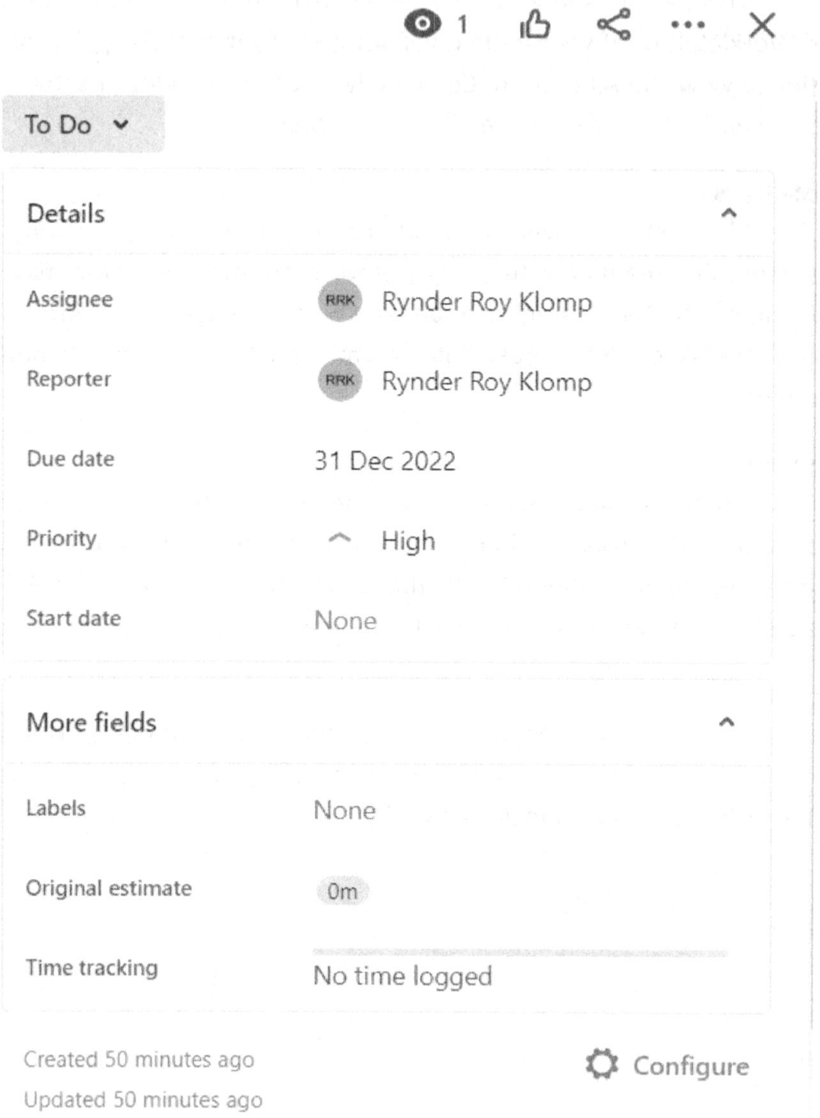

Actions Bar

The first row in the right side of the Issue view contains the action bar:

Here you can:

Watch Issues

Often there will be those who, while not directly working on the Issue, have a need or interest in watching its progress. Managers and customers are two examples. Any time something happens with the Issue, the Issue watcher(s) will be notified.

You can let people see the Issue but restrict them from working with the Issue or its data.

Vote on the Issue

There may be times when an Issue is used to solicit feedback. For example, an Issue may be about pursuing a specific course of action. People can vote as to whether they support (like) or don't support the proposal put forward by the Issue.

Share the Issue

You can share Issues with others (who have permission to see the Issue). These can include a Jira user, a Jira team member, or even an email address.

... (More)

Clicking on the three dots in the Actions bar brings up a menu of items you can use. If you can see the menu item, it means you have permission to work with it. If you cannot see it (for example, the Delete action item), that means you don't have permission to action that item.

Close Popup

The last Action Bar item is the "X". As you might guess, this is used to close the popup view. It will not delete the Issue.

Workflow Buttons

Every Issue has a predefined number of process steps. These steps in the process (Jira calls it a "workflow") will vary depending on the type of Issue you are working on. This Issue's process involves only two steps: To Do, and Done.

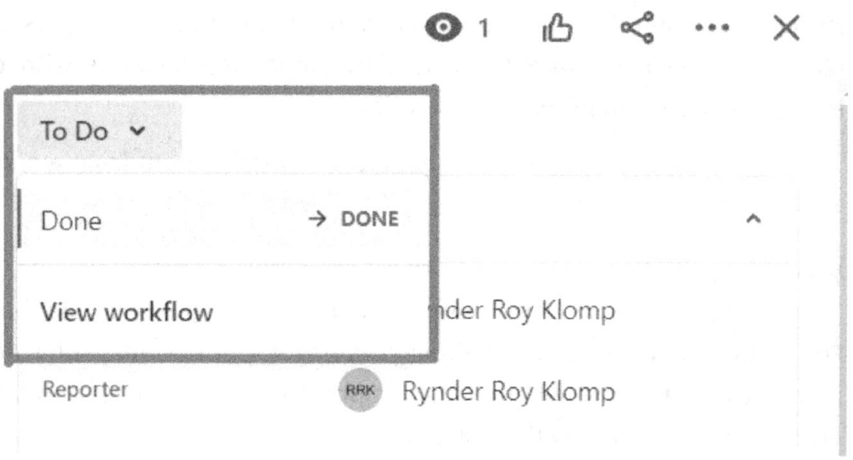

Once you are finished with a particular workflow step, simply open the workflow menu and click on the next step to proceed. Workflows are integral to Issues and are discussed in more detail in "Chapter 6: Workflows".

Assignee

The assignee is the person responsible for working on the Issue at the current time. Only one person can work on an Issue at any time. You can change assignees, which is very common if your Issue needs to be worked on by several departments or individuals.

Reporter

If you remember, Jira started as a means of managing bugs in a software project. When a bug was identified, it was "reported" using

Jira. This is where the term “reporter” comes into use. Reporter is almost exclusively the individual who “created” the Issue. Typically, they also tend to be the Issue “owner”.

Due Date

Due date is just that, the date the Issue is due to be completed.

Priority

Next, we have the priority of the Issue. Jira comes with five default priorities (Highest, High, Medium, Low, Lowest), but you can also define and create your own priority list if you need to.

Start Date

Usually, an Issue will start when a User starts working on it. However, there may be times when you want work to start on a specific date. You can enter that here.

More fields

One of the more recent features of JWM is to try and make the Issue view much cleaner and simpler. As a result, fields that are judged (by Atlassian) as not of critical importance are hidden. Clicking the arrow in the “More fields” drop-down menu shows those fields.

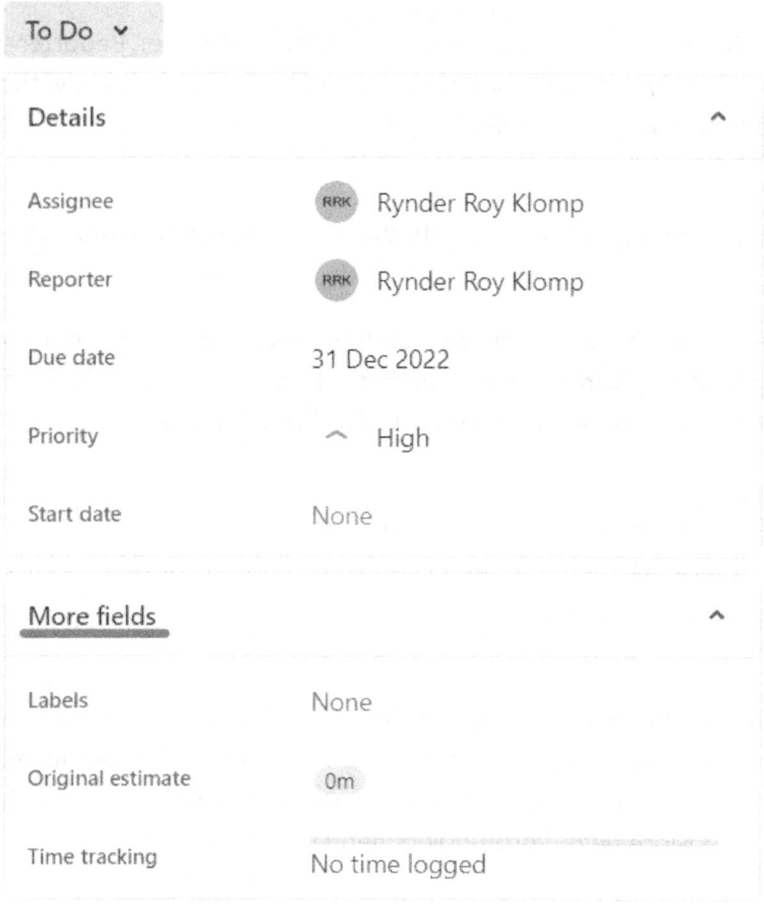

To close the expanded view, simply click the "Show less" button.

Configure

One of the other newer features in JWM is the ability to configure the layout of your Issue view. You can move fields up or down, and you can move fields from the right column to the left column and vice versa.

We will discuss how to configure the Issue view in more detail in "Chapter 7: Screens".

Chapter 2 - A Tour of Jira Work Management

To avoid confusion, in this book the term "Site-admin" includes "Org-admin, Site-admin, and Jira-admin" unless specifically noted otherwise.

Chapter Objectives

In this Chapter we will walk you through each item of the Jira Work Management Navigation bar.

At the end of this chapter you will:

- **be able to navigate the software**
- **understand who can see the navigation bar menu items (e.g. User, Project Admin, Site-Admin)**
- **understand the purpose of the menu items**

NOTE: The easiest way to work with this chapter is to have a copy of the software open and follow along as we discuss each menu item.

I am going to assume that you have Jira Work Management installed, have been assigned a **User Name** and **Log In,** and that have Jira Admin or Site Admin permissions.

Log In to Jira Work Management using the following view:

Once you have logged in, you will be transferred to your home screen. This view will depend on what your company has set up for you, but I am going to start with the Project view which is the most common set up:

NAVIGATION BAR

The navigation bar guides you throughout Jira and serves to perform actions.

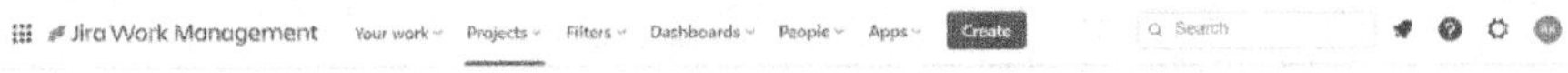

Users, Project Admins, and Site-admins will generally always see this menu bar regardless of where they are in Jira Work Management. Having said that, depending on your permission or security level, you may not see all the menu items. For example, Users and Project Admins will not see all the elements in the Settings COG.

Let's take a quick tour of the navigation bar items.

SWITCH TO

On the far left of the Navigation bar you will notice this "Switch to…" icon: 

Depend on your Jira permissions (your assigned security level within Jira) you will see different views when you click on the icon.

Jira Work Management Basics

SITE-ADMIN VIEW:

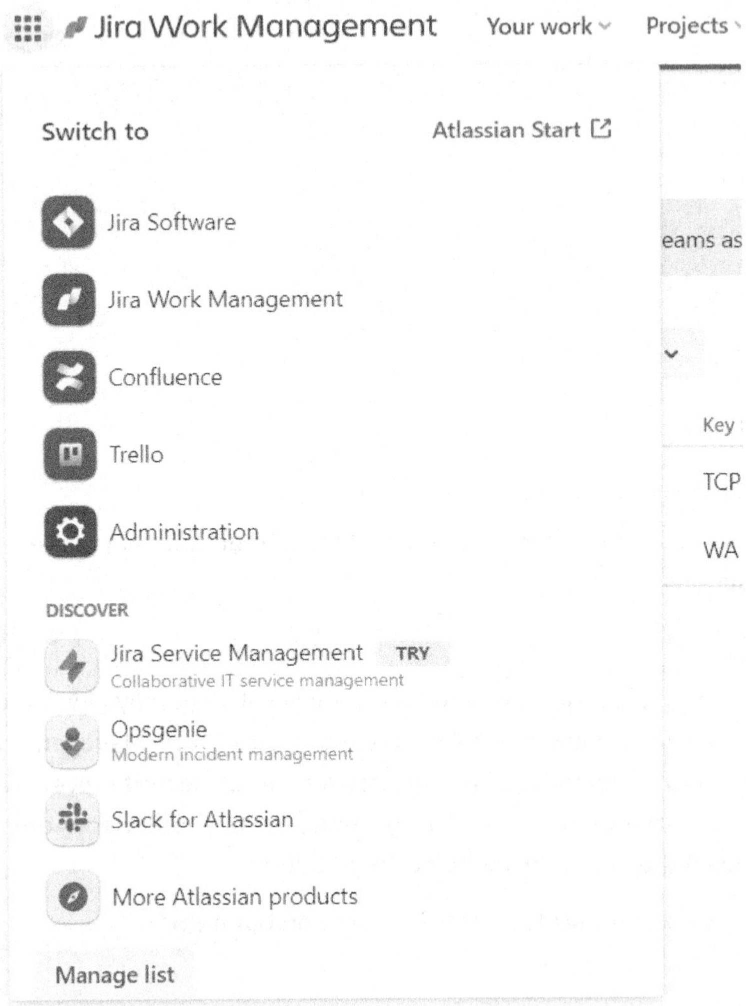

Jira-admin View:

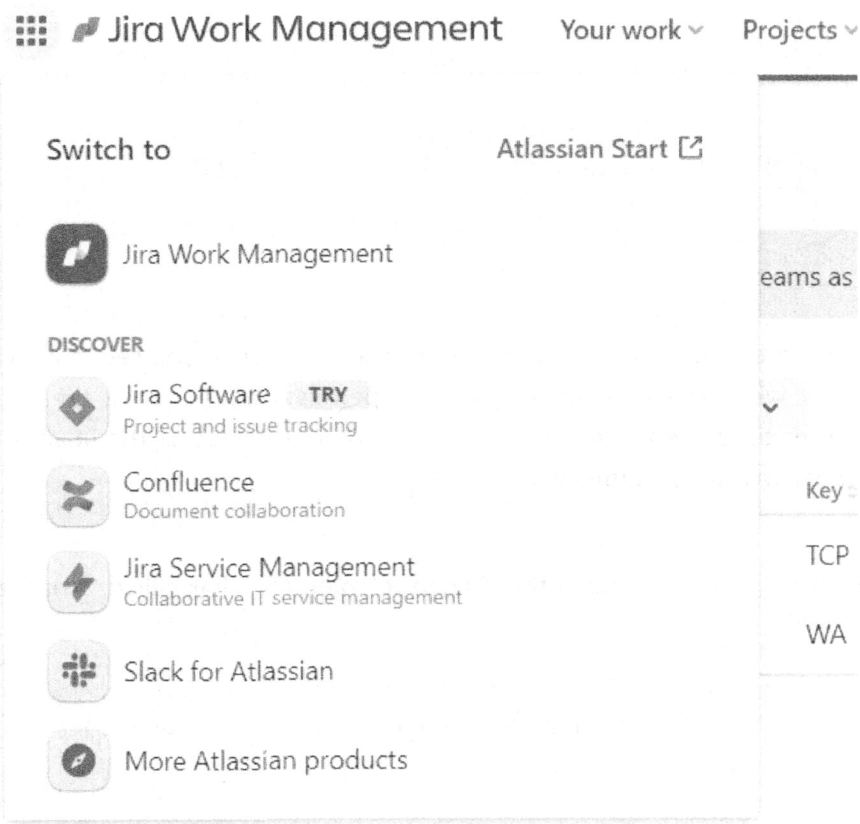

USER VIEW:

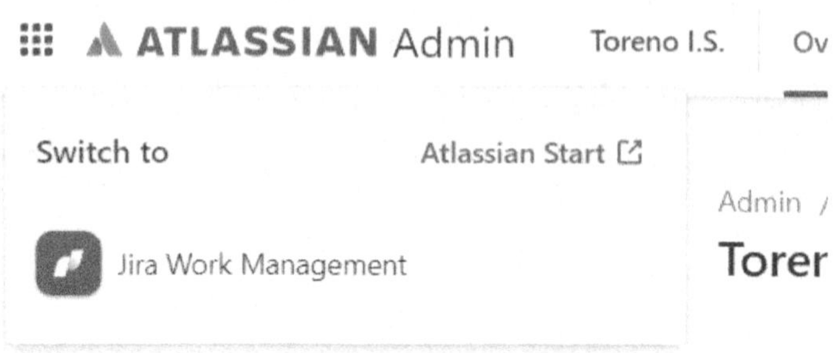

The three views you just saw demonstrate that what you see in a JWM view will often depend on your Jira permissions. To make the book easier to follow we will, unless stated otherwise, restrict the images to those that a Site-admin will see.

ATLASSIAN START

The first thing in the 'Switch to" menu is a link called "Atlassian Start":

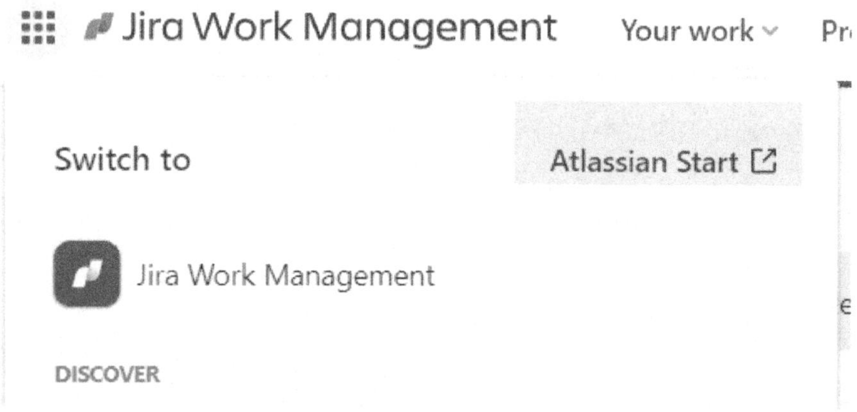

Clicking on this link will take you to several other links.

The first icons contain links to Atlassian products for which you have licenses. In this case, the User "Henry Plummer" has only one license and that is for JWM.

Account settings will take you to your profile page where you can edit your personal information and set personal preferences. We will look at Account settings in more detail when we get to the Profile section of this chapter.

Most of the links connect you with sites where you can get information or help about Atlassian products. These are Atlassian Support, Atlassian Community, and Atlassian Documentation.

You may, or may not, see the self-managed licensing link depending on your permissions. This area, as you may guess, allows you to manage your product licenses (renewals, cancelations, etc.). If you are part of an organization that has purchased the license you are working with, you will not see any license details (i.e. you will only see, "You do not have any product licenses).

The final link is to the main Atlassian.com home site.

For most Admins and Users the main Switch to menu will contain links to either Atlassian products you are licensed to use (such as Jira Software, Jira Service Management, Confluence, etc.) or to Atlassian products you might wish to purchase (in the Discover section). Most of these products will give you a free trial period if you don't already have a license. The important thing to remember is that you must be a Site-admin to be able to purchase additional licenses. And the only two ways you can become a Site-admin is to be assigned one by an existing Site-admin, or by going out and purchasing a separate, personal, JWM license. This personal license will not be affiliated with your organization's JWM.

ORGANIZATION NAME

The next item you will probably see on the Navigation Bar is "Jira Work Management" and its icon (**Avatar**), or it may have already been changed to show your organization's logo and name. Jira is the default. Clicking on it brings you to your default home page (usually the **Projects** page), which is helpful if you are somewhere deep in the Jira Work Management software and want to return to the default view quickly.

You can change the Jira logo and product name in the > **System** settings, which are discussed later in this chapter.

YOUR WORK

The next item on the Navigation Bar is "Your work", which is self-explanatory.

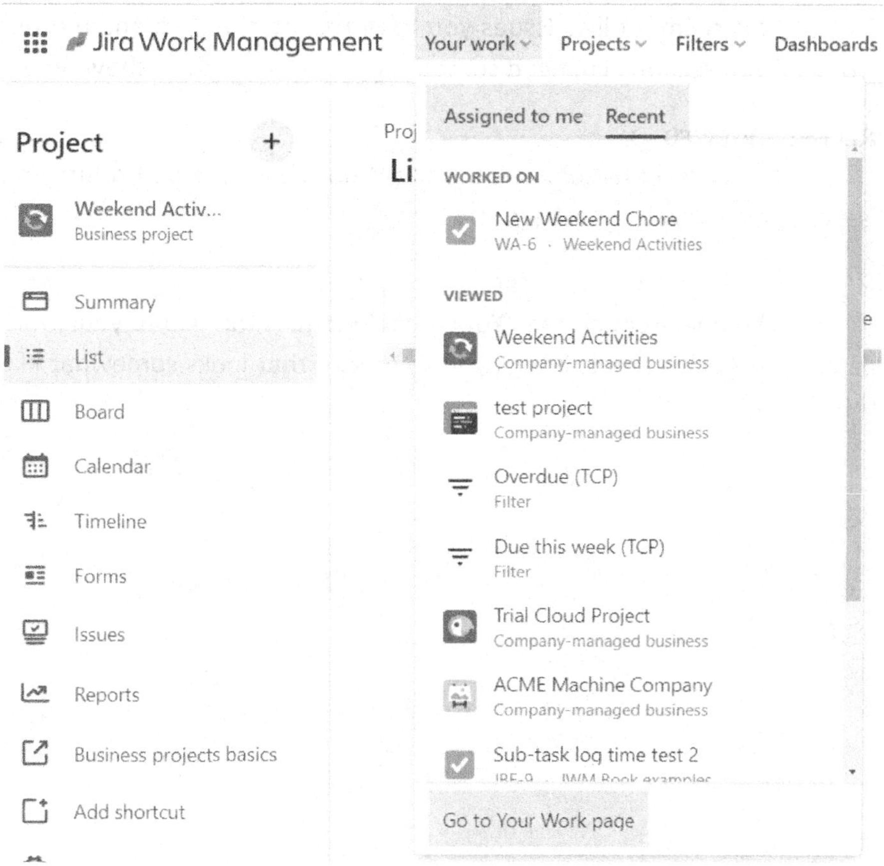

Open the "Your work" menu and you should see two tabs at the top: **Assigned to me**, and **Recent.**

Assigned to me

You should only see the **Assigned to me** tab if you actually have Issues assigned to you. The Issues shown in this section will be sorted by their status (e.g. In Progress, Waiting for approval, etc.).

Recent

The Recent tab will show the Issues you have either worked on, or viewed, recently.

Recent – Worked on

This segment lists Issues you have recently worked on. In other words, if you recently changed something in the Issue it will show here.

Recent – Viewed

If you recently looked at, but did not change, a board, project, Issue, or filter it will show here.

Go to your work page

The final item on the "Your work" menu is the "Go to your work page" link. Clicking on it brings you to a page that looks somewhat like this:

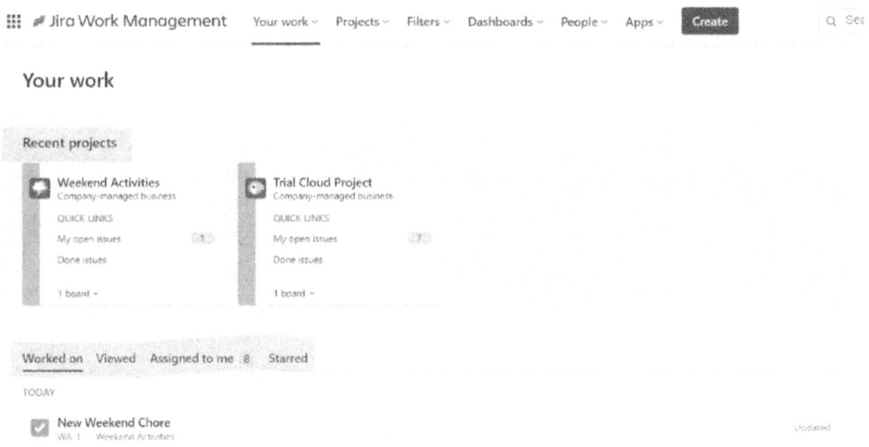

This view will show **Recent projects** you have worked on, or what is basically a repeat of the **Recent** tab in the **Your work** menu.

PROJECTS

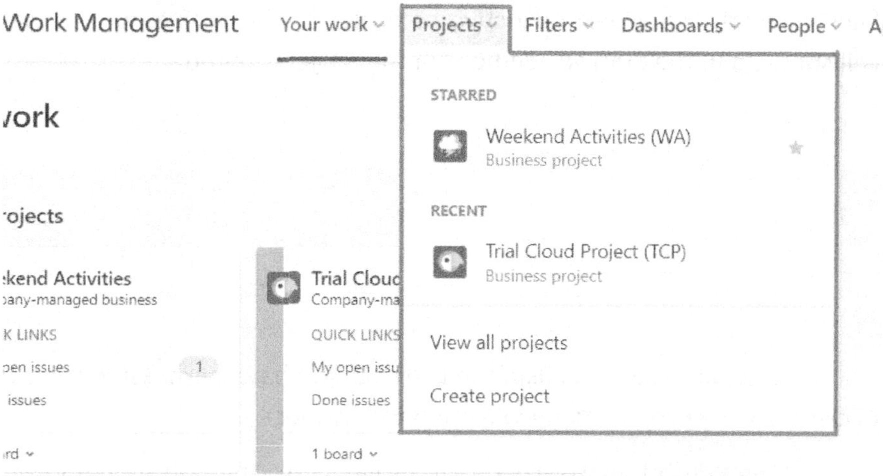

The **Projects** menu has four segments. The first "**Starred**" segment shows those projects you have designated as most important to you. You "star" projects in the "View all projects" segment of the Projects menu.

The **Recent** segment shows those projects you worked on "recently". Recent really means the projects you last opened, regardless of how long ago that was. Starred projects will not appear in this list.

Next is the "**View all projects**" link. This page is covered in more detail in "Chapter 3 – JWM Projects", so we will simply take a quick look at this time.

The **Projects** view starts with the Star column. If you want to identify a project as essential, simply click the star button so that it is filled (as with the Weekend Activities project). Any project with a star will show up in the Starred segment of the Projects menu.

The Name column lists the projects you have permission to see. Clicking on any project name will open that project.

The Key column contains the project key. This is the unique set of characters that JWM uses to identify that particular project.

The Type column indicates whether the project is a Company-managed project (i.e. a project created by a Site-admin and that has full JWM functionality), or a Team-managed project (i.e. a project created by a User or Project Admin, and that has limited JWM functionality).

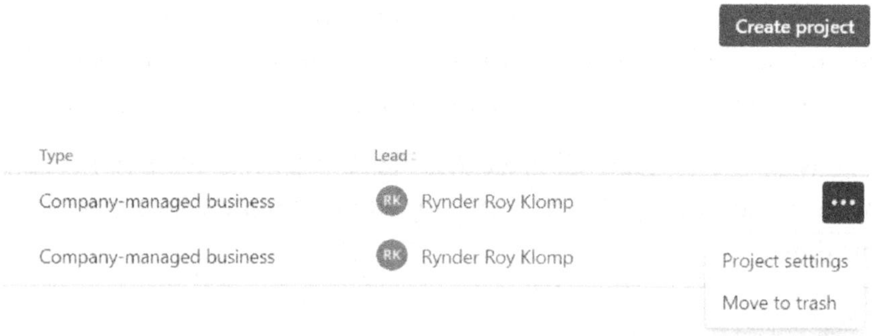

After Type is the **Lead** column. This column shows who controls the project.

The **… (MORE)** column has two menu items: Project Settings is where you can change the configuration of your project, while "Move to Trash" is where you delete the project.

The final aspect of the Projects menu is the **Create project** link. You can do nothing practical in Jira until you create a project. To be more specific, **you can only create and work on tasks/issues within a project.** You may create a project in two ways: by clicking the **Create Project** link, which brings you to a wizard where you will indeed create a project; or, by clicking the **Import your work** link. This is where you can import projects from another source. I can already hear you thinking, "Hey, cool, I can *easily* import my Excel or Microsoft Project file and get started." While the import function is indeed straightforward it is certainly not "easy". To do so you must first convert them to a CSV file format. This option is not for beginners.

FILTERS

The next item on the Navigation bar is **Filters**. The first time you open Filters in a new JWM site, you will see this:

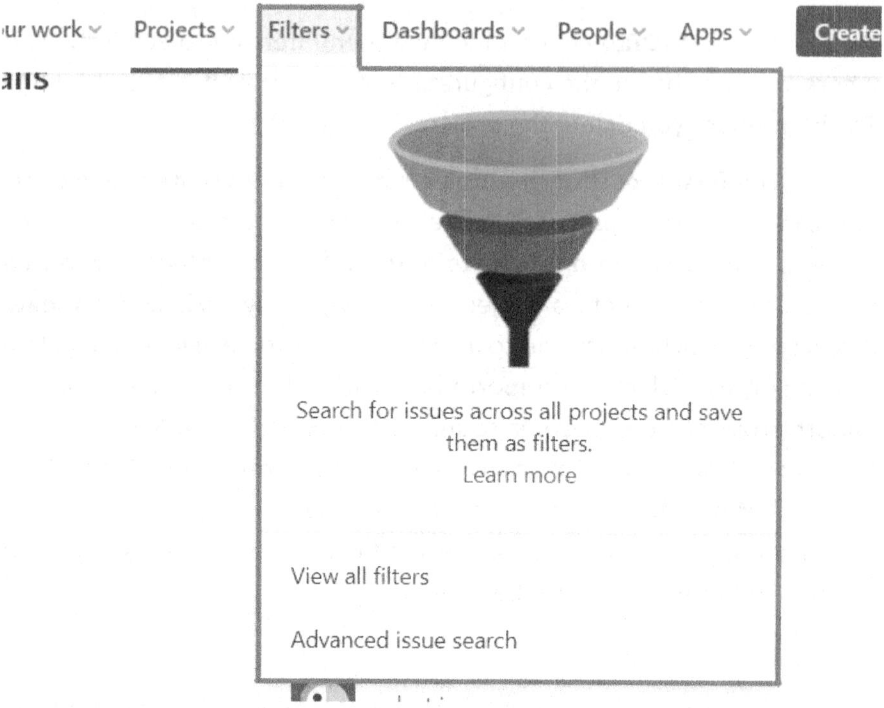

The filter image contains a link to help you learn more about how to create and manage filters.

Filters are discussed more thoroughly in “Chapter 12- Filters and Reports”. For now, we will simply take a quick tour.

Once you actively start working with Filters, your view will change to something like this:

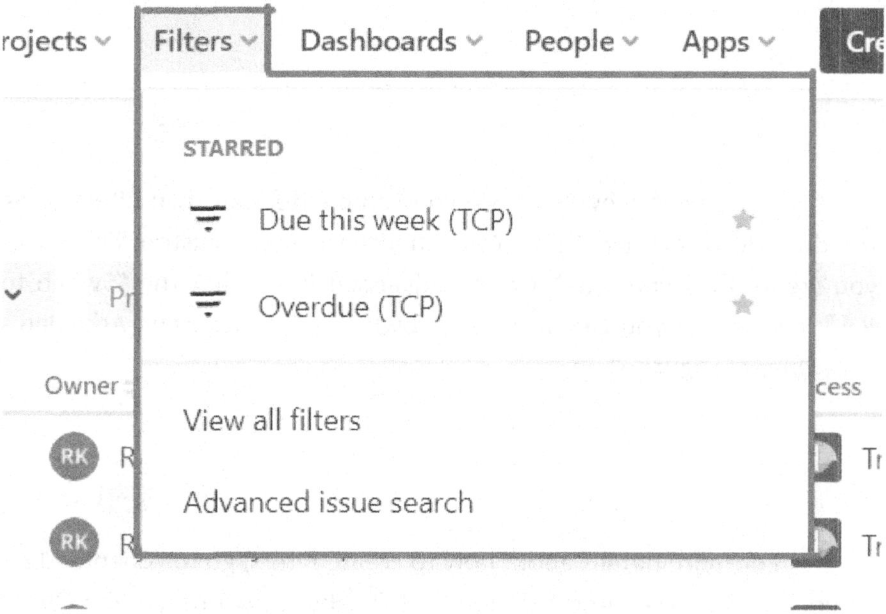

Once you create a favorite filter it will be placed in the Starred section (replacing the original "Learn more" funnel filter image).

Starred filters are created in the "View all filters" section.

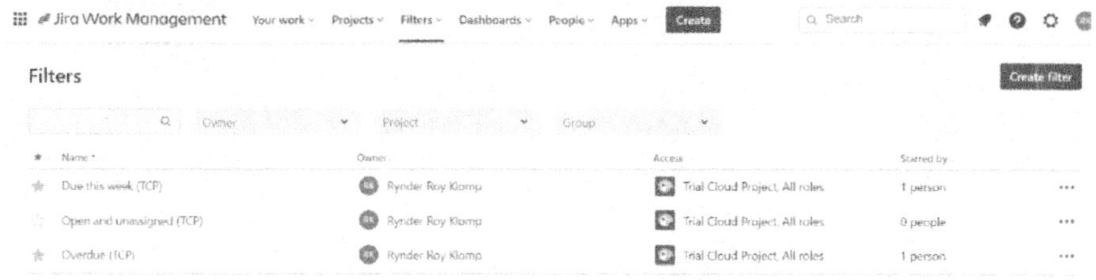

Here is a list of all filters you have permission to see. You can also use this view to create your own custom filters.

Solid stars signify favorite filters. Simply click on a star outline to make it a favorite.

The last item in the Filters' menu is "Advanced issue search".

The Search view is where you can create your own filters using the drop-down menus' items. You can also save your custom filter after you create it. If you need a more advanced filter, click the "Switch to JQL" link, where you can write your own Jira Queries using Atlassian's "Jira Query Language".

For more details about how to create filters, go to "Chapter 12 – Filters and Reports". And for more details about how to use Jira Query Language, please buy my Jira best-selling book: "Jira JQL Basics and Reference Guide" available at Amazon in both paperback and eBook versions.

DASHBOARDS

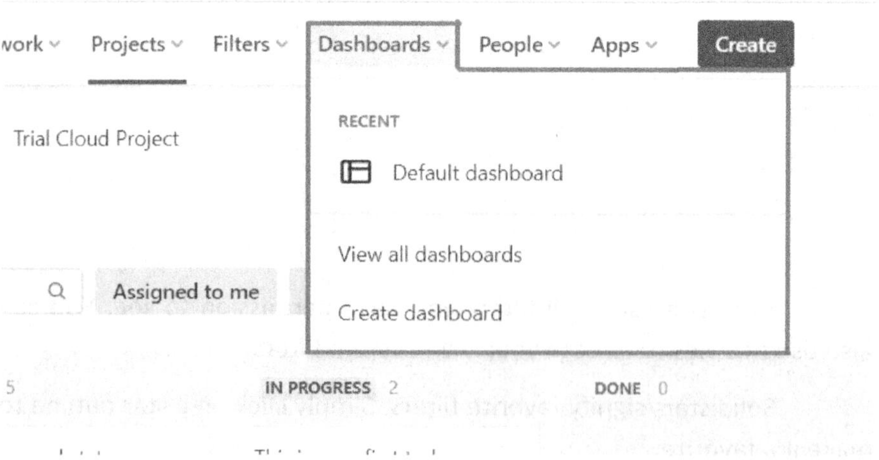

A **Dashboard** is a collection of reports or tools usually arranged around a specific theme.

Click the down arrow on the Dashboard menu item and you see that the menu is divided into four links.

The first item is the "Starred" segment which contains all your favorite Dashboards. It includes the system **Default Dashboard** (or you might see **View System Dashboard**; regardless, they are both the same) and clicking on it will open the **Default Dashboard**:

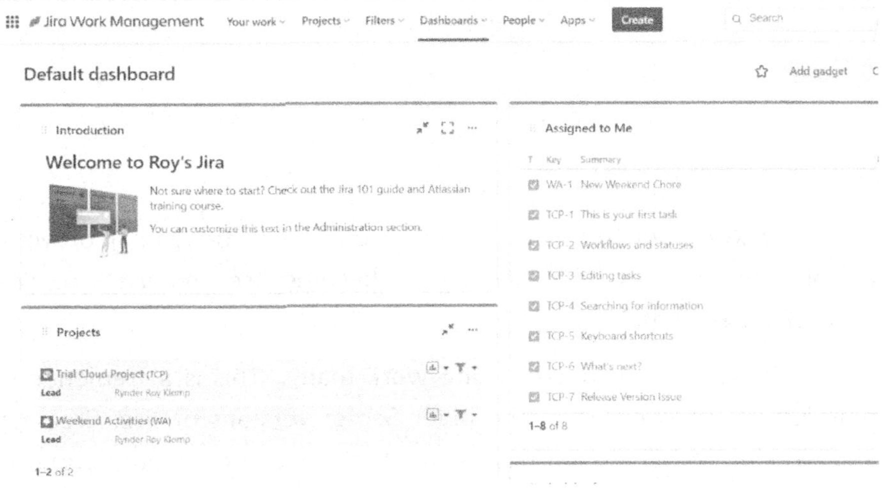

The second item is the **Recent** link and it lists all your dashboards you opened recently.

Next is "**View all dashboards**". This will bring up a list of all dashboards you have permission to see. This is where you can "star" your favorite dashboards.

The final menu item is the "**Create dashboard**" link. Clicking on it will take you to the section in Jira Work Management where you can create new dashboards or alter current dashboards to suite your needs.

Dashboards are covered in more detail in the "Chapter 11 – Dashboards" chapter.

PEOPLE

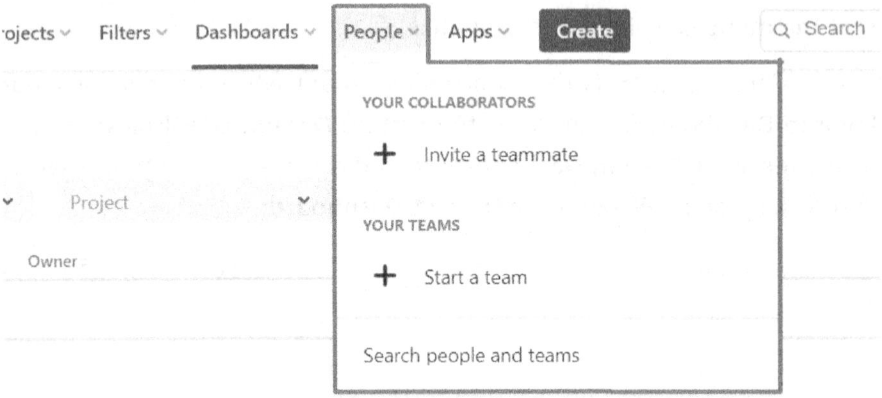

Next on our tour is the People menu. Here, depending on your permissions, you can invite people to become licensed users of Jira Work Management.

In addition, you can create work teams. This is a tremendous new feature unavailable in the older Server versions of Jira. Creating and working within a team environment allows you to communicate to the team more successfully, while enabling more effective teamwork.

Finally, you can use this menu to search for Users and Teams, which is very handy if your organization has many JWM licensed users.

This menu is covered in more detail in "Chapter 9 – Users, Roles, and Groups".

APPS

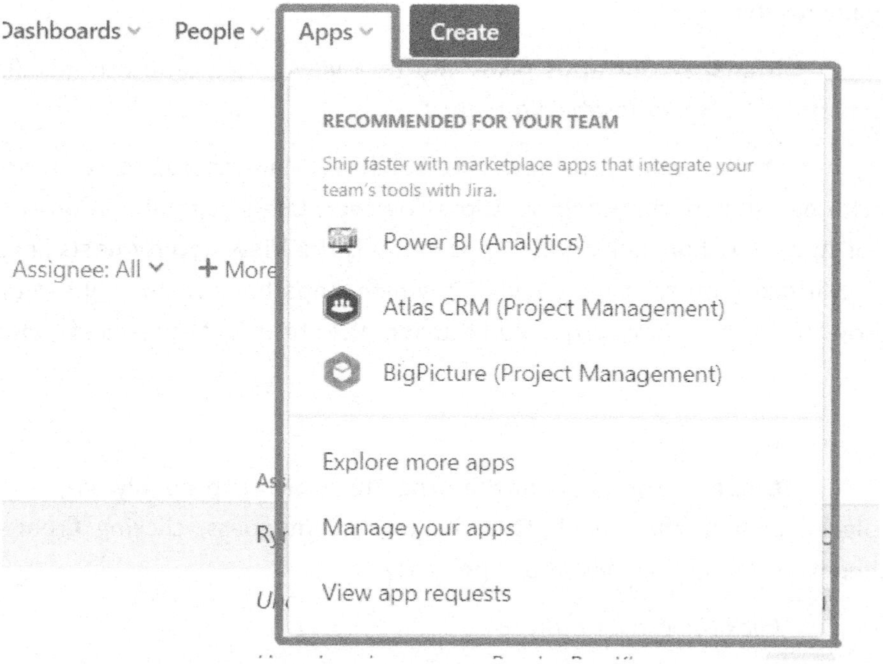

Jira has a great number of add-on applications (apps) available. These apps focus on specific features such as exporting reports or importing projects; workflow enhancements; forms and custom fields; creating charts and diagrams; roadmaps; planners, etc. They are all managed through the Atlassian Marketplace, which is where the "Explore more apps" link sends you. Remember that you need to have permission (typically Site-admin permissions) to purchase an Atlassian app.

These apps are very reasonably priced. Atlassian makes sure that all apps work with Jira, but that's not the same as saying they provide good value. That's why there is also a four-star rating system where customers can rate the product.

Explore more apps contains links to, you guessed it, featured apps. Clicking any of the featured apps' links will send you to a signup page for that app.

Manage your apps takes you to a view where you can install, update, activate, or disable your apps.

While Users can view the Atlassian Marketplace, only those with permission can purchase Apps. However, Users can put in requests for Apps. The final link on the Apps menu is the **View app requests** link. It will take you to a page showing which Apps have been requested, how many Users have requested the app, the status of the requests, etc.

CREATE

Create is the heart of the program, which is probably why it is placed in a bright blue button. As you might guess, clicking **Create** begins the "create a new Issue" process.

Click the Create button:

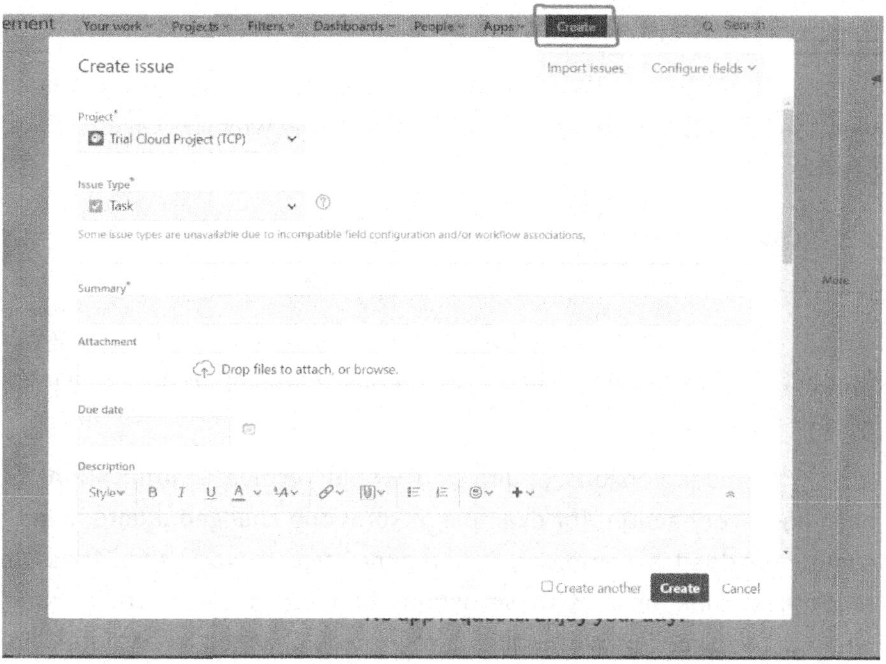

You will see a pop-up window appear with several fields. We covered creating an Issue in the previous chapter; so, there is no need to go further into the topic again. CLICK CANCEL in the lower right corner of the Create Issue pop-up to exit this view and let's move on to the next item on the menu bar.

QUICK SEARCH

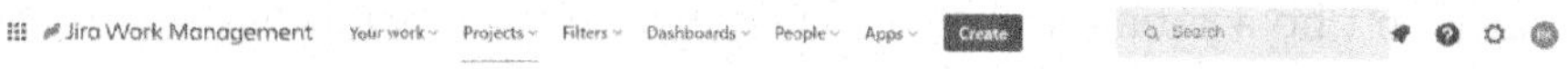

You have undoubtedly seen Search boxes in other software; so, we don't need to spend a lot of time with this item. Quick Search allows you to find Issues, recently worked on items, projects and boards. If you are going to search for specific text, be aware that Jira will only look in the Summary, Description, and Comments fields. No other fields will be checked.

You can also preface your search with specific Jira query terms for specific fields (check Atlassian documentation for those terms).

I tend to use this search box rather than going to the Search view, as I find it a little faster. Which is probably why it is called 'Quick' Search.

NOTIFICATIONS

"Notifications" are automated messages from Jira informing you that activity has occurred on Issues you are watching or are associated with in some way.

In older versions of Jira you would receive a notification for each and every action; for example, if someone changed a date field, if someone added a comment, if someone logged work, etc. Atlassian recognized that most of these actions happen in quick surges. Now, when a User goes in and makes a few quick changes to an Issue, Jira consolidates these change notices into one "single summary email". This is a fantastic upgrade! It was incredibly annoying to be constantly bombarded with notifications about this field change, that field change, this comment, that comment; to the point that I (and many others) simply turned off notifications. The summary is a most welcome feature.

Having said that, be aware that the summary email means that a notification notice may be delayed up to ten minutes. In most cases, that won't be a problem, but it may matter if your Issues are extremely time sensitive.

You can manage your Notifications in the Personal Settings area, covered in more detail later in this chapter.

Jira Help

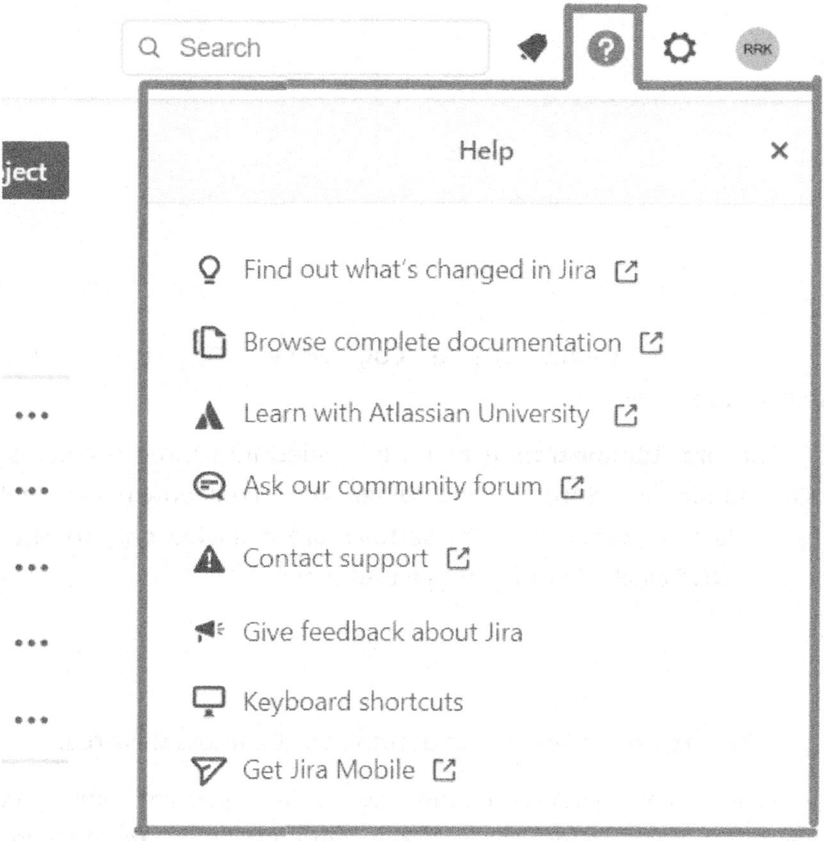

Here we have the Jira Help menu which has links to assist in numerous areas. These links are helpful to both novice and expert Jira users.

Cog Wheel

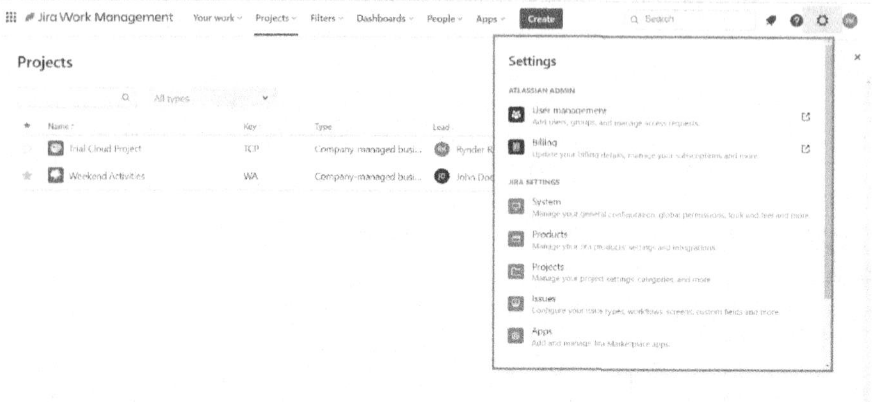

Next, you should see a **Cog** wheel. This is the **Jira Administration** menu.

The **Jira Administration** menu is divided into three segments: Atlassian Admin, Jira Settings, and (when you scroll down) Personal Settings. Atlassian Admin and Jira Settings are available only to Site-admins (i.e. NOT available to Jira Project Admins).

Atlassian Admin

NOTE: You need Site-admin permissions to access this area.

When you click on the User Management link, an Administration page opens. The Atlassian Administration area includes User Management and Billing. This area is restricted to Site-admins because the two menu items involve licenses and that means the expenditure of money (hence the restriction).

User Management

Clicking the User management link brings you to the Users view. This view shows you a list of all your licensed users. It displays a number of things such as **Username**, the full name of the individual and his/her email addresses, login details of the user, the groups the User belongs to, applications the User uses, in which directory the User details can be found, and the actions you can perform such as revoking their site access, adding them to a group, or showing which Atlassian products they are able to access.

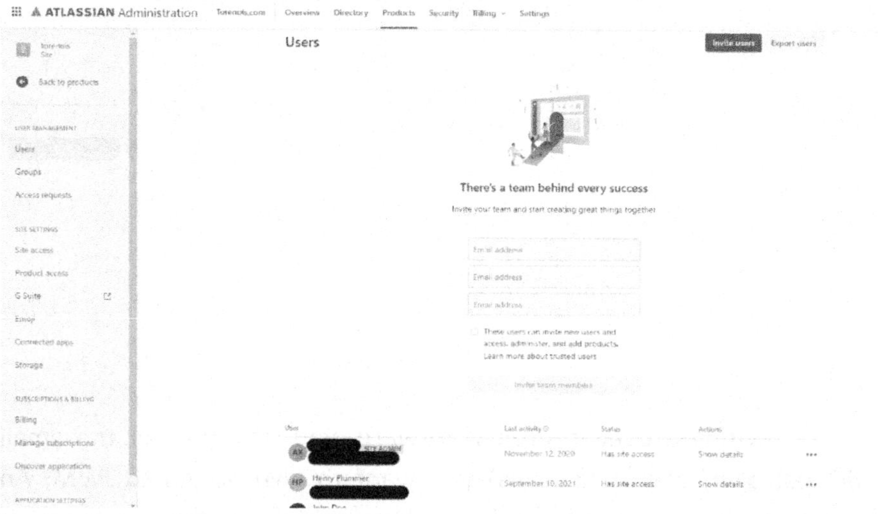

In this Users page you can also **Invite Users.**

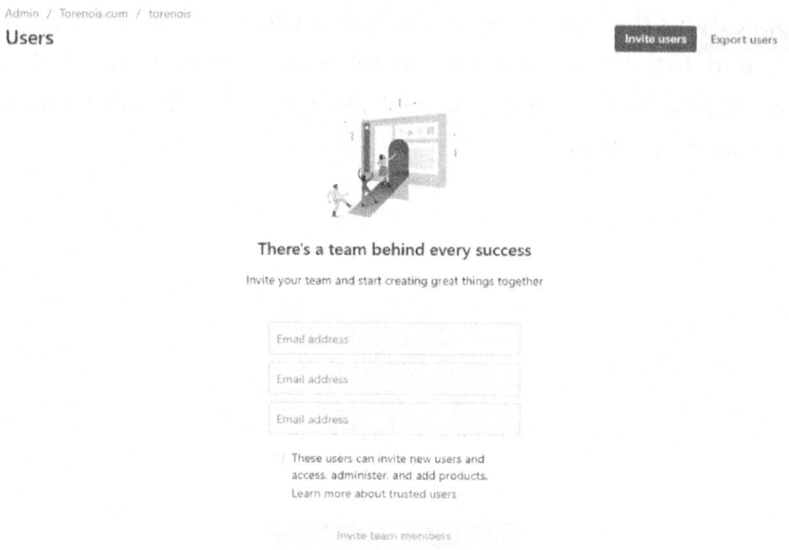

Inviting a User is straight forward; you simply enter the email address(es) of the individual(s) you want to give access to JWM. An invitation is then sent to them. If they have an existing Atlassian account, they are then given access to JWM. If not, the invitee is guided through an account set-up process.

When inviting a new User, you also determine which Atlassian product they will have access to, and their security/access level (Basic, Jira-admin, etc).

Groups

On the left side of the User management view you see a sidebar providing more options in addition to the current User view.

The User Management sidebar menu also contains a link to the **Groups** view, where you will be able to Add or Edit groups (among other things).

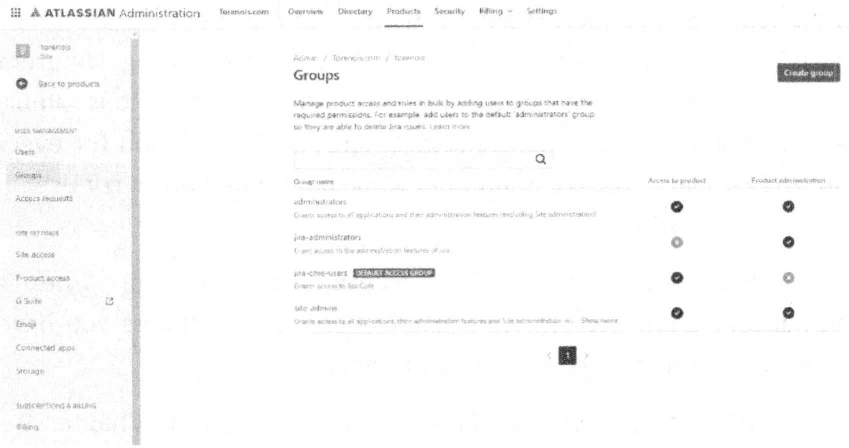

Jira sorts people into three categories: **Users, Roles, and Groups.**

A **User** is someone licensed to use Jira. For example, Jane Doe is a User.

A **Role** is a project specific assignment. Users are typically assigned to these project Roles. Quality Control Analyst in the ACME Project is an example of a Role. A User can be assigned to one or to multiple Roles. Roles have security permissions only for the project(s) designated. While there are some system provided roles (Developers for example), most roles are created by the Site-admin for specific purposes and projects.

A **Group** in Jira might be best defined as Users performing a similar function or task: a Financial Analyst Group may be a good example. Groups, unlike project roles, are global in nature; meaning they are not bound to any one project.

Why use Groups or Roles? First, **it is easier to assign permissions and security rights to the group/role than to individuals.** If the individual leaves the organization or changes job position, you just delete him/her from the group/role, and they no longer have permissions. Otherwise, you need to manually delete all the permissions from the outgoing User and manually add those same permissions to the new User. You can add a User to as many groups/roles as you wish, with each group/role having different permissions. The second reason for groups/roles is that it is simply easier to manage. It is much simpler to create a permission for every group/roles, than it is to recreate that same permission for every User in every project in JWM.

When an Invited User accepts the invitation, s/he is automatically added as a Jira-workmanagement-user, unless you have already placed them in an Administrator group.

User Management is covered in more detail in "Chapter 9 – Users, Roles, and Groups."

BILLING

Clicking on **Atlassian administration > Billing** will open this view:

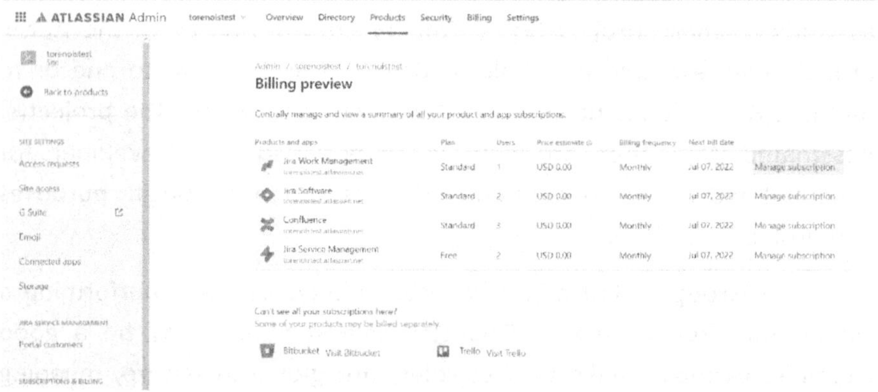

This is the **Billing preview**. You will find here your Atlassian products, the License plan associated with each product, the total billing estimate, how often you will be billed, when your next bill will be sent, and a link to **Manage your subscriptions**.

If you click on **Manage your subscriptions**, you will see something like this:

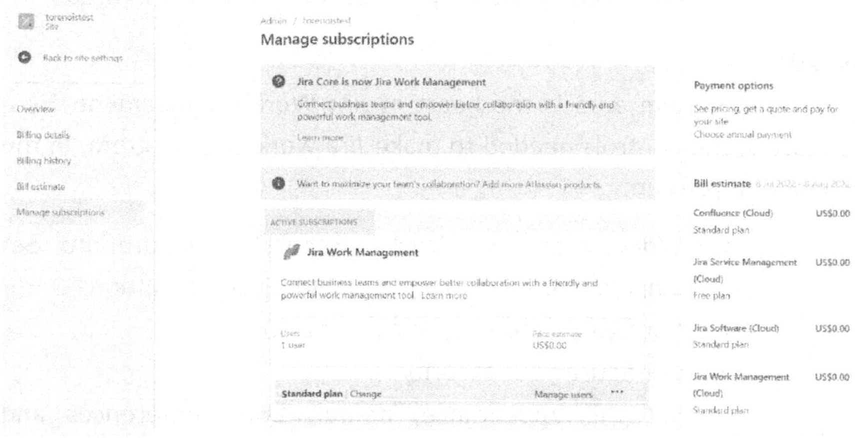

This is the **Manage subscriptions** view. All your product subscriptions will be listed here. Each product has its own separate area where you can see how many User licenses are associated with that product, and an estimate of how much you will pay. The bottom of each product area will show you which plan you are using, provide a link to allow you to change your plan, a link to manage your Users, and with the More (...) link allow you to either Delete this product or contact Atlassian for Support.

The Sidebar also contains a number of links. The Overview link will bring you to a view, where you can see your total bill estimate (for all your products) and billing history, where you can change your payment details and the billing contact information. The sidebar also includes links to a more detailed view of your billing details, billing history, and bill estimate.

Jira Settings

NOTE: You need Site-admin permissions to access this area.

System

The System area is the heart of Jira Work Management. Here are most of the controls needed to make Jira work as a program. In the System area you can:

- Work with the JWM's General configuration: Set language, time, and set a great number of options
- Configure your audit log (paid plan only)
- Configure your security
- Set the appearance, default User preferences and dashboard
- Import and Export Issue data
- Configure your mail settings
- Share filters
- Work with advanced settings, such as attachments, events, Webhooks, etc.
- Create Automation rules to run mundane tasks routinely

System Settings are dealt with in more detail in "Chapter 13 – System Settings".

Products

Clicking on the Products link opens the page where you can configure your Jira applications and integrate JWM with other applications:

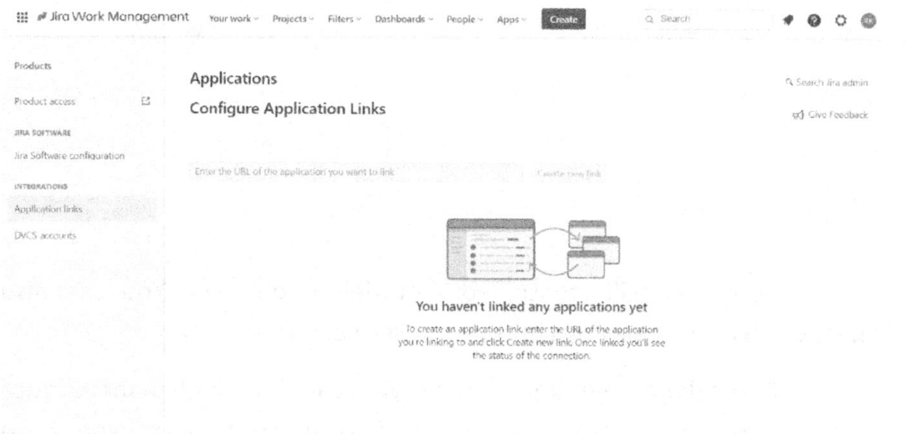

Product access

This section is where you determine which Jira groups have access to JWM. The default access group is jira-workmanagement-users-<sitename>, meaning that any new licensed JWM User must be assigned to the jira-workmanagement-users group to work with JWM.

You must have Site-admin permissions to access this area.

Links tother Atlassian products

If you have **other Atlassian products** (e.g. Jira Software or Jira Service Management) you can use the links in the sidebar to configure or work with those product.

Integrations

These links allow you to integrate with other Jira products or external applications. This is an advanced topic.

PROJECTS

Clicking on **Projects** will land you on **Manage projects**:

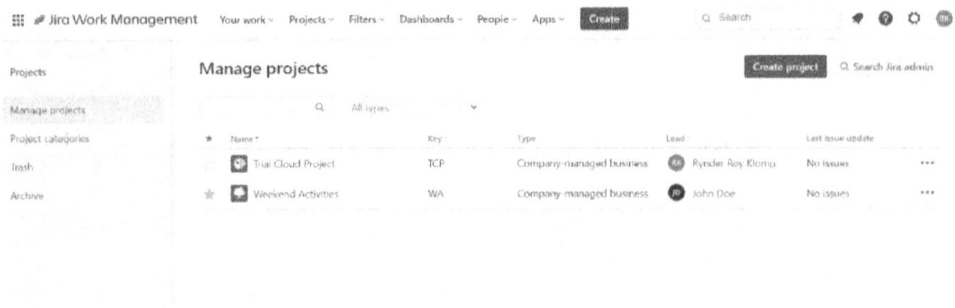

Here you will create, edit, or delete projects. You can also change the project settings in the **...** (More) column.

The sidebar has links where you can find and manage your projects, manage project categories, find those projects you have deleted (trash), and those projects you have archived.

"Chapter 3 – JWM Projects" covers these topics in more details.

ISSUES

Issues will become your most important view when you start to bespoke your project. It is the coordination hub for all defaults and modifications done in Jira. Here you make changes to your project's **Issue Types, Workflows, Screens, Fields, Priorities, Issue Features, Issue Attributes, Security, Notifications,** and **Permissions**.

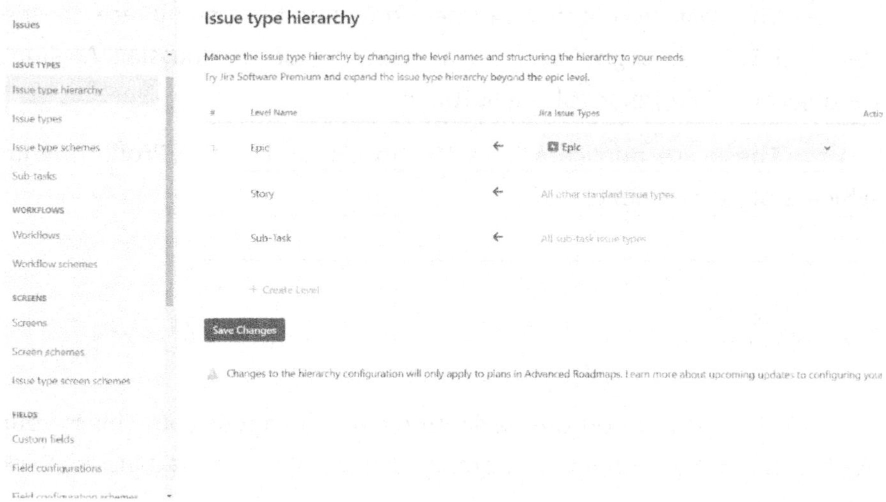

We will cover most of these items in following chapters, so, for now let's move on to our next COG menu item.

CAUTION: Just one word of caution! You may be tempted to start making changes on your own. I strongly discourage doing so until you have read the remainder of the book. **Changing any of the defaults will affect the entire program and is often difficult to reverse. If you are going to change anything, first, copy one of the Jira's existing defaults (e.g. Issue Type, Screen Scheme, etc.), rename it, and then edit it.** You can always delete your copy with no damage to the Jira defaults.

APPS

This is another link to take you to the Atlassian Marketplace where you can (with permissions) purchase and install new apps. As you may recall, we already covered this topic earlier in the chapter.

Personal Settings

The last two items in the administration menu are in the Personal Settings segment. They are your personal Atlassian Account Settings and your Personal Jira Settings.

These are duplicate links to those found in the Profile menu, which is discussed next.

Profile

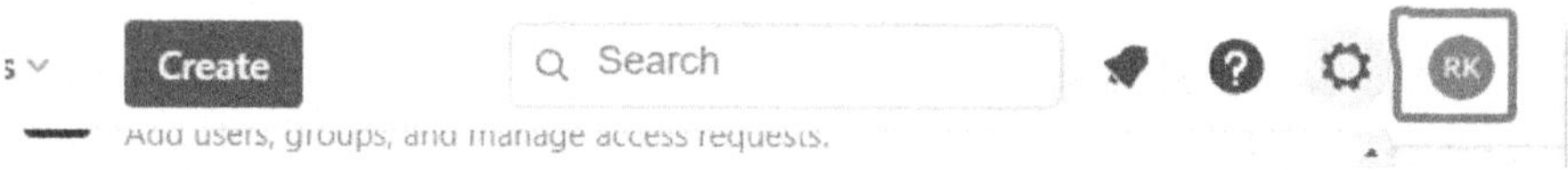

The last item on the navigation bar is all about you. This is your **Profile** menu. You should see a small circle with your initials inside. Click on this icon:

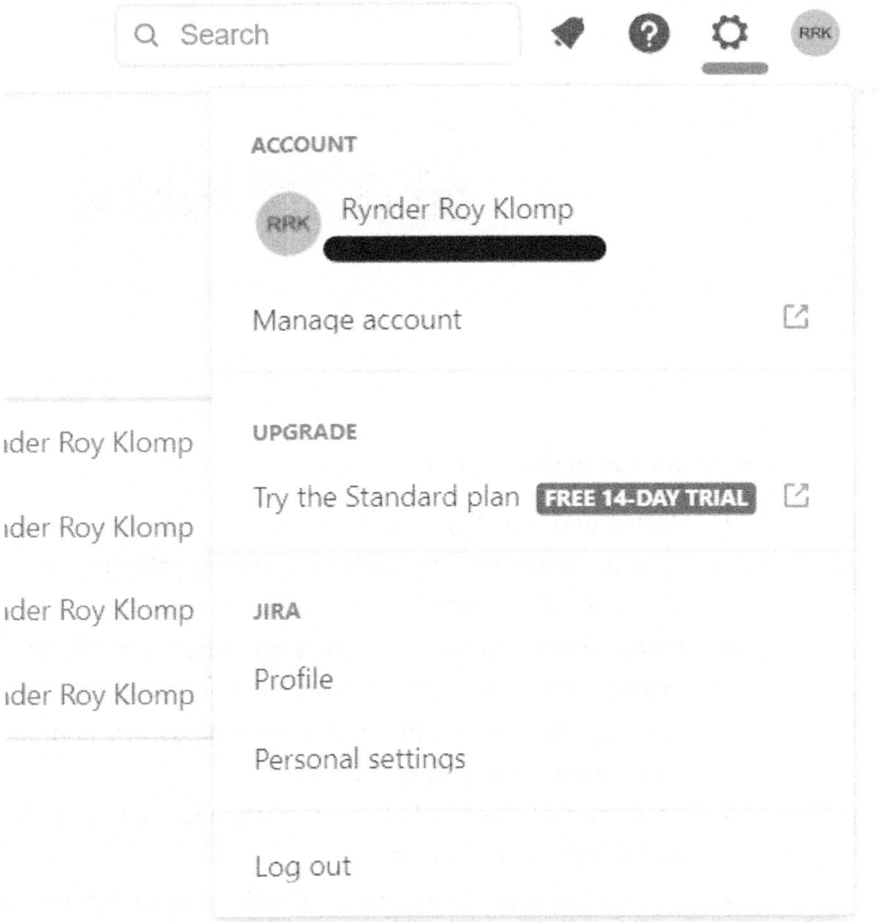

The **Profile** menu has three sections: Account, Jira, and Log out.

Account

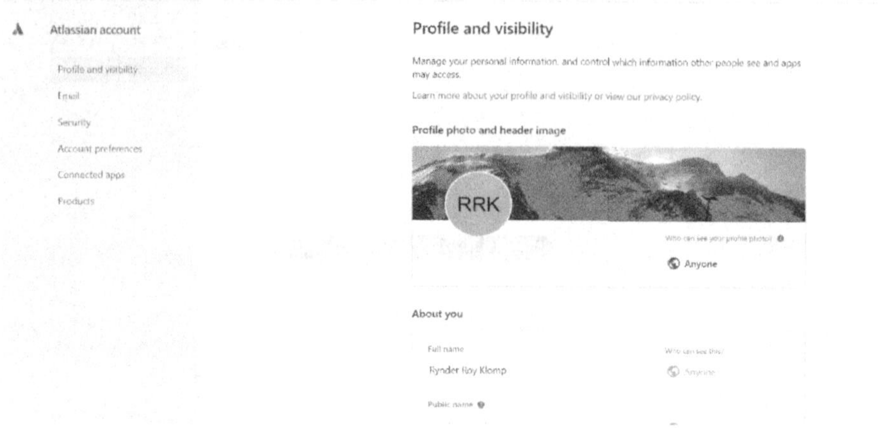

The Account view sidebar has links to:

- Profile and visibility: This is where you edit your profile. It also contains the settings that configure what elements of your profile are visible and to whom
- Email: Here you can change your email address and manage the emails you get from Atlassian products
- Security: Here you can change your password and set up additional security measures
- Account preferences: Set up your language & Time zone, and delete your account
- Connected apps: Contains details about apps (Atlassian and Atlassian 3rd party)
- Products: Here you can configure the most common Atlassian settings (language, time zone, etc.) for all your Atlassian products

Jira

The Jira section is made up of Profile and Personal Settings.

Profile

The profile contains your profile details that others will see. To change your profile details and visibility click on the **Manage your account** link.

It also shows you Issues you have worked on in the last 90 days, projects or spaces you worked in, and the teams you have worked with.

Personal Settings

The Jira personal settings page is where you configure Jira to your needs. Here you will set your time zone and language. You can also configure the following:

Watch your issues

This setting needs some explanation. In every Jira Issue there is a "switch" that allows you to watch that Issue. After that, any time there is activity with the Issue, you will receive an email (unless you turn off that setting; described a little later). However, there is a way to automatically turn on watching of Issues. That is by clicking the "Enabled" option in the drop-down menu. But using this setting only happens in two ways: when you create an Issue, or when you add a comment to an Issue (any Issue).

You can turn off this setting by clicking the "Disabled" option.

Your Site-admin can configure fields in an Issue that can be used to automatically turn on **watch your Issues**. For example, they may decide that adding a comment should not be a watch your Issue trigger. When they make these changes, it affects all Users in the organization. That is the purpose of the "Inherit from global settings" option.

Your Jira homepage

The Jira homepage is the page you see when you first log in or when you click on the Jira logo. You can select one of three Jira home pages. You can choose the projects "directory", "your page", or the "dashboards" page.

Email notifications for issue activity

By default, you receive emails when activity occurs on Issues you are watching. Many Users like this feature. Many others do not. To turn off this function, simply click the "Don't send me email notifications".

You may say, but I want to be notified about some activities although not others. The good news is that there are a great many ways to customize Issue activity notifications and they are covered in more detail in the "Watching Issues" section of "Chapter 14 – How to..."

Get email updates for Issue activity when:

This section includes several email update settings you can toggle. By default, you will not receive email updates for Issue activity when you make changes. That's because Jira assumes you know what you did and don't need to be told about it. So why this setting? You may want to receive email updates for your own activity because you need to forward that email to someone else (not a Jira User) as a confirmation. The second common reason is that you use the emails for proof of work, typically required for billable hours or detailed time tracking.

Email notifications format

You can use this drop-down to determine if you want to receive your email notifications in Text or HTML format.

Log Out

This is the final menu item and appropriately enough you use it to Log Out of the program.

Chapter 3 – Jira Work Management Projects

To avoid confusion, in this book the term "Site-admin" includes "Org-admin, Site-admin, and Jira-admin" unless specifically noted otherwise.

Chapter Objectives

By the end of this chapter you will be able to:

- **navigate the various Project views**
- **understand the Project elements**
- **make some minor changes to a Project**

Additionally, you will understand the differences between the Jira Work Management Project types.

The Project Navigation view

Jira has numerous views dedicated to managing a project or projects. In this section we will take a closer look at the Project Navigation view and its constituents. Let's start with a project we already created.

As you recall, in Chapter 1 we created a Task management project called Weekend Activities. We will use that project as the basis for our tour.

1. On the Navigation Bar select **Projects** > *Weekend Activities (WA)*:

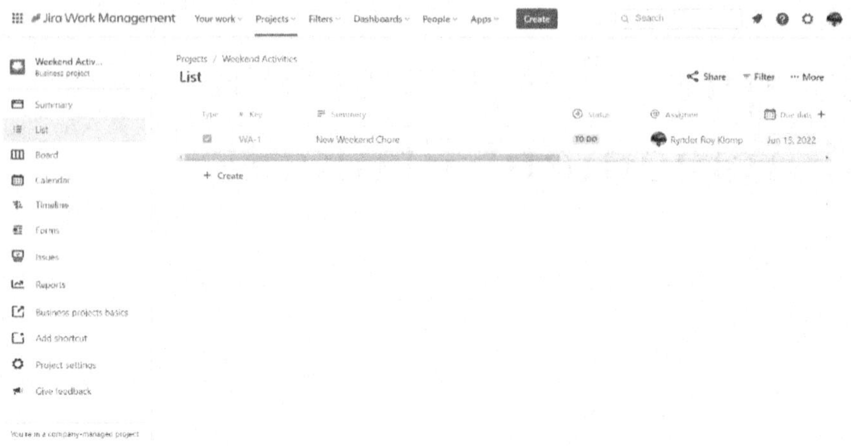

You should now be seeing the **Project Navigation** view. The view has two parts: Project Navigation Sidebar and Main View (by default you will see the project List view, as in the image above).

Project Navigation Sidebar

The Project Navigation Sidebar is located on the left side of the Project Navigation view:

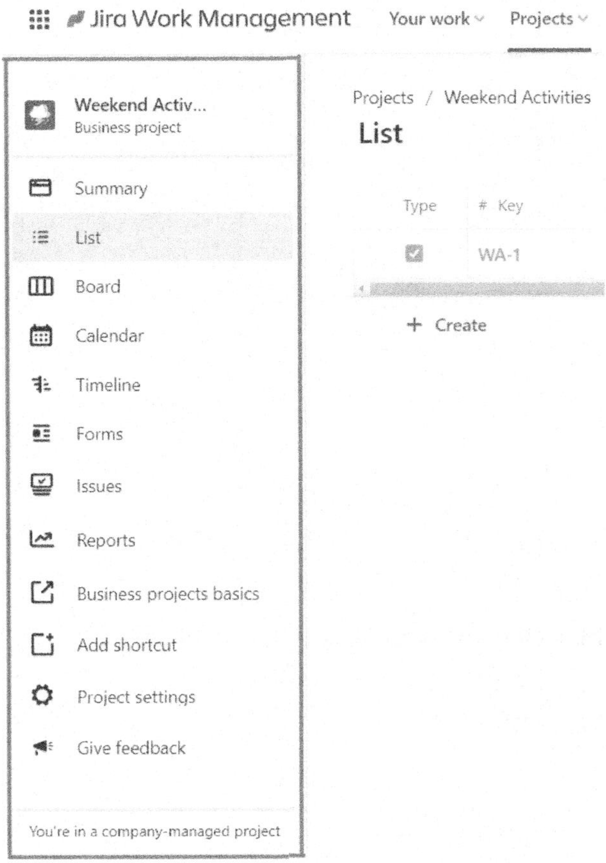

The purpose of the sidebar is to help the User or Admin quickly access specific views related to the project.

If you have a lot of detail on the main view, it is sometimes convenient to hide the sidebar.

Hover your mouse arrow over the dividing line between the sidebar and main view. Click on the left-facing arrow that appears to hide your sidebar:

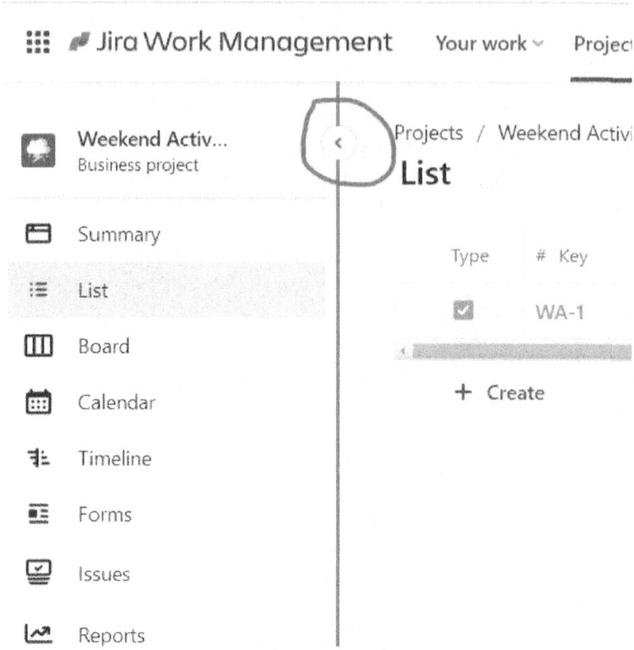

Click on the right-facing arrow to expand the sidebar:

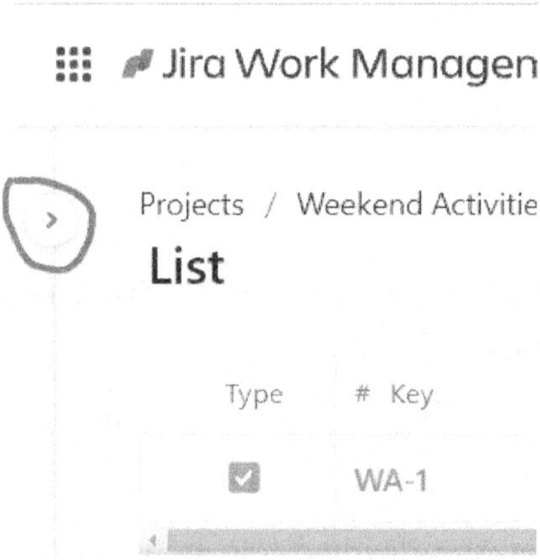

The Project Navigation sidebar has at least 14 options: **Project Title, Summary, List, Board, Calendar, Timeline, Forms, Pages, Issues,**

Reports, Business projects basics, Add shortcut, Project settings, Give feedback, and **project class.**

PROJECT TITLE

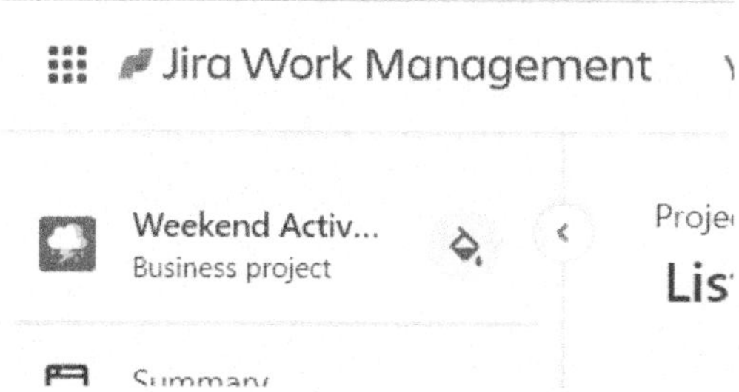

The project title shows you the name of the project and the project type. The project type is based on the project template you selected when you created the project. We will come to the Project type section later in this chapter.

When you hover the mouse over the project title, a paint icon will appear. Clicking on this icon allows you to change the background colour of your project:

SUMMARY

Clicking the **Summary** link in the Project Navigation sidebar will open the Project Summary Activity view:

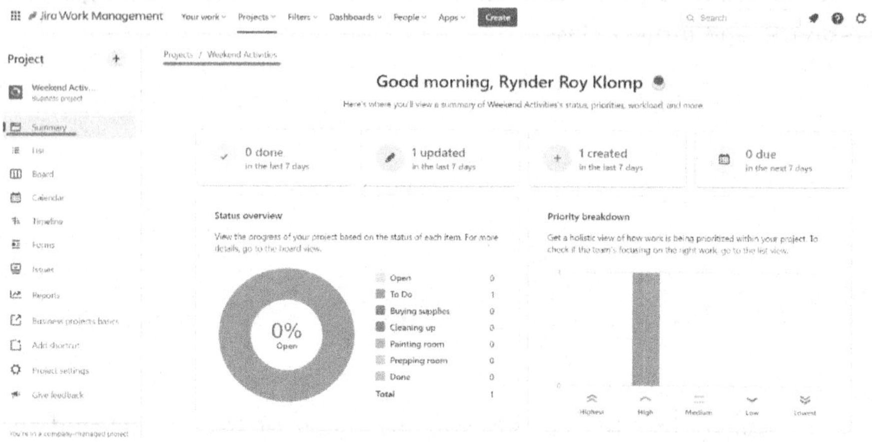

This view looks like a dashboard and provides an Issues and workload summary of the project.

List, Board, Calendar, Timeline

The next four items in the project sidebar provide links to different views of your Issues: List (table) view, Board view, Calendar view, and Timeline (Gantt) view:

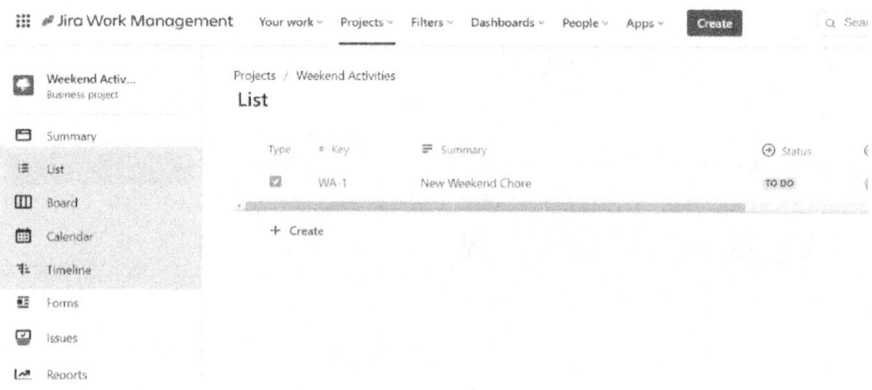

When you open a Jira project, you will see the List view as the default.

Forms

Forms is a nice new feature in Jira. It allows you to create simple forms to collect information and share that collected information with your team. For example, you can build a form that asks stakeholders for their business requirements for a specific piece of software. Or you can build a form with questions to help you find the root cause of an organizational problem.

Forms is not a core function of Jira, so is out of scope for this book. But I recommend you explore this feature at your leisure.

Pages

Often a project will need a little, or a lot, of documentation. Many companies use Atlassian's Confluence to manage this documentation. The pages link lets you connect your project to Confluence. Of course, you will need Confluence licenses to use this feature.

Issues

The Project's **Issues** view shows only those Issues associated with the project and that you have permission to see. For example, since we opened *Weekend Activities* project, we will see only *Weekend Activities* issues. Right now, we have only one issue, and it is *New Weekend Chore WA-1* (see image above).

While there are a number of ways of seeing issues in your JWM site, I like this particular view as it allows me to focus on a **particular project**.

You have the option of two ways of seeing Issues in this view: The List view or Detail View. You can switch between the views by clicking either button located in the upper right corner of the view.

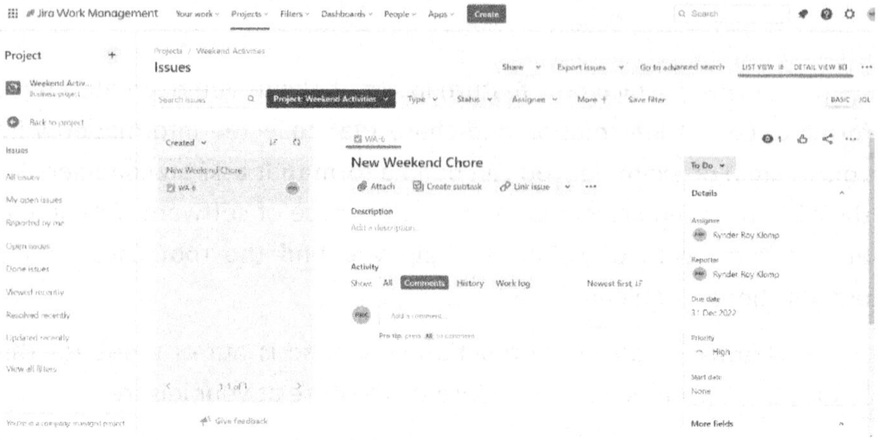

If you wish to open an issue in the full screen, click the Issue Key:

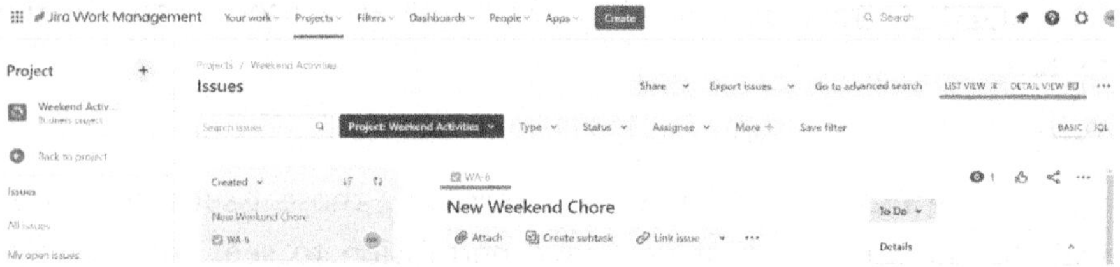

Reports

The **Reports** link in the project's sidebar gives you access to predefined reports **for that project**.

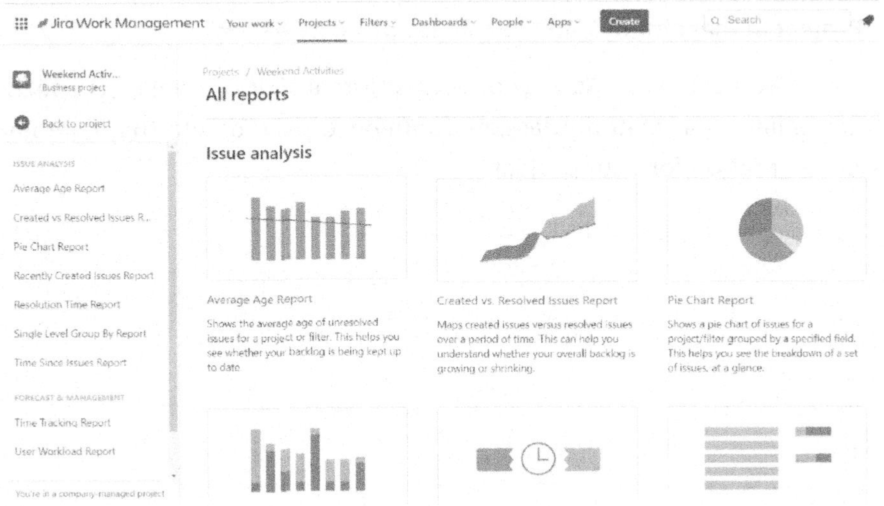

Clicking on any of these reports sends you to a 'Configure' page where you can modify the design of that report to some degree. For example, the Average Age Report shows the average age of your project's unresolved issues. You can specify the period (Hourly, Daily, Weekly, Monthly, Quarterly, Yearly) as well as the number of days to be shown in the graph.

To answer your next question, Jira does give you the ability to create your own reports based on Jira elements (issues, projects, users, issue types, etc.). However, if you want to create reports based on custom fields you have created, that is more challenging. Go to "Chapter 12 – Filters and Reports" for more details about building custom reports.

Additional Links

You may have additional links in this section of the sidebar depending on your software set up, installed Jira Apps, and some other conditions. For example, if you open the "Trial Cloud Project" you probably have links to instruction pages containing information about "**Project management**", and "**Business projects basics**".

You can also "Add" your own shortcut. For example, you might want a link to a related Atlassian Confluence page or site that contains documentation for your project.

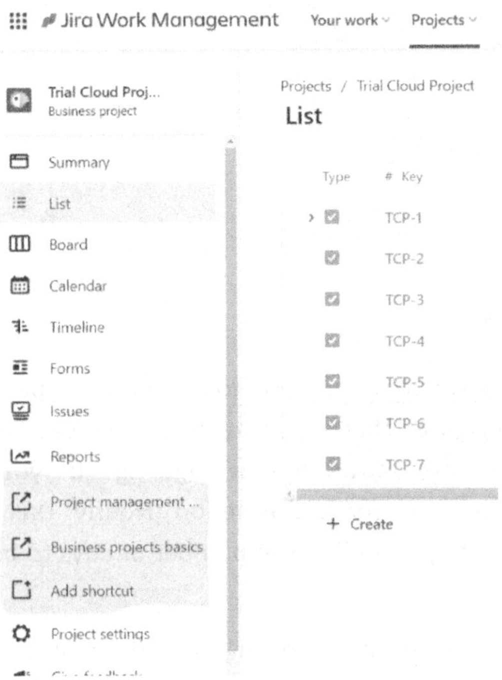

We are going to skip over Project Settings for the moment, as it is such a large aspect of the Project sidebar that it will take over the bulk of the remainder of this chapter.

Give Feedback

One nice feature about Atlassian is that they are always looking for customer feedback about their products. This is the link to do so.

Company-managed or Team-managed projects

At the very bottom of the sidebar is a line of text that says either, "You're in a company-manage project." Or, "You're in a team-manage project". What does that mean?

A team-managed project is a basic, and simplified, Jira project. A team-managed project can be created, and managed, by any Jira User (i.e. it doesn't need a Site-admin to set it up). It comes with standard features with little ability to change anything. A team-managed project cannot interact with other projects, it is isolated.

A team-managed project is great for teams that need a basic, simple project that is limited to their team.

A company-managed project is a robust, and customizable, Jira project. It must be set up by a Site-admin. It also allows just about any aspect of the project to be customized. A company-managed project can also interact with other Jira projects.

A company-managed project is perfect for teams that need a customized solution that allows the team to work with Issues in other projects or Jira applications (such as Jira Software or Jira Service Management).

This book will be restricted to company-managed projects. In other words, team-managed projects are out of scope.

Project Settings

Near the bottom of the Project Navigation Sidebar is the "Project settings" link:

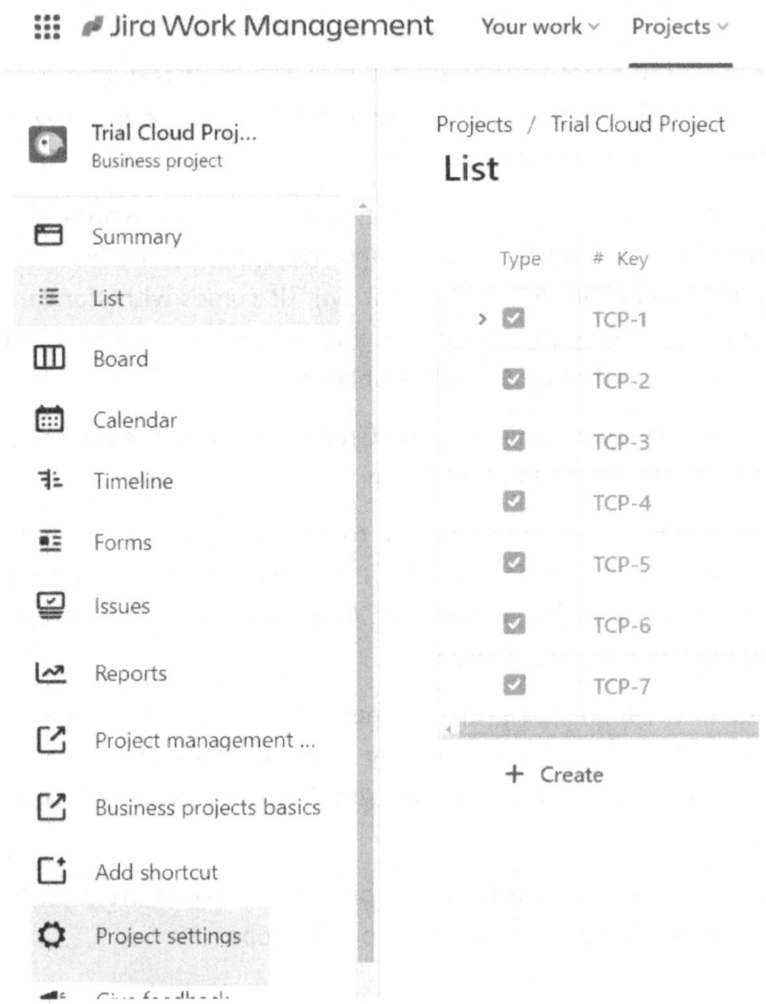

Both Site-admins and Jira Project Admins have access to this link.

Clicking **Project settings** carries you to a view displaying the various puzzle pieces that make your project work and that you can modify or configure. But it is important to remember that while the Project Admin can make some minor modifications to the Project settings, the bulk of major modifications such as creating new Issue Types, workflows, custom fields, custom screens, etc. can only be done by Site-admins and are done in the Site-administration area (the Cog).

Project Settings View

1. Click On The **Project settings** Link To Open that Project's Settings view:

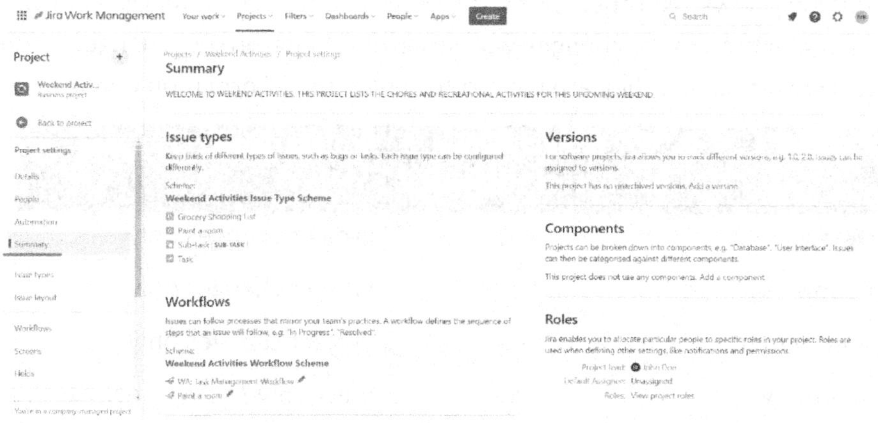

When creating or customizing a project, I cannot think of any single area in Jira more important than the **Project Settings' Summary area**. I must admit, when I started to build my first project in Jira, it took me a while to realize the essential role this view plays. It should be the number one view you constantly visit when developing your project.

Why? First, it provides the necessary information about the Jira elements (issue types, workflows, screens, fields, priorities, project's components, users and roles, permissions and notifications, etc.) you are using in this particular project; and second, it acts as a portal to each of those elements in the event you want to make changes.

PROJECT SETTINGS' VIEW PERMISSIONS

As stated above, what you can see and interact with depends on your JWM permissions. The table below provides a list of all possible views in the Project settings sidebar. All these views are available to Site-admins.

Site-admins can make significant changes in these Project settings' views.

Project Admins will have no visibility to some of these Project settings views. In other cases, Project Admins will have visibility but their ability to make changes will vary from major project changes to no changes at all (i.e. they are limited to seeing the information only).

View	Project Admin Access to view?	Project Admin Changes?
Details	Yes	Project changes only
People	Yes	Project changes only
Automation	Yes	Project changes only
Summary	Yes	View only / minor changes*
Issue types	No	None
Issue layout	Yes	Project changes only
Workflows	Yes	View only
Screens	Yes	View only
Fields	Yes	View only
Versions	Yes	Project changes only
Components	Yes	Project changes only
Permissions	Yes	View only
Issue Security	Yes	View only
Notifications	Yes	View only

Issue Collectors	Yes	Project changes only
Slack Integration	Yes	Project changes only

*You must have a paid version of Jira Work Management in order for Project Admins to work with Project Roles and Project Permissions.

These various Jira elements, which I call the puzzle pieces, are described in more detail in the next Chapters.

Project Settings Sidebar and Main area

The Project Settings view is divided into two segments: Project Settings sidebar and Main area.

Project Settings sidebar elements

Below is a more detailed description of each of the sidebar elements in your Project Settings.

Project Settings: Details

Site-admin can view and make changes
Project Admin can view and make some changes

Details contains the high-level information about your project, such as: Project name, project key, project type, category, avatar (project image), project description, Project lead, etc.

Exercise: View Project's Details

1. Click on **Details** on the Project settings sidebar:

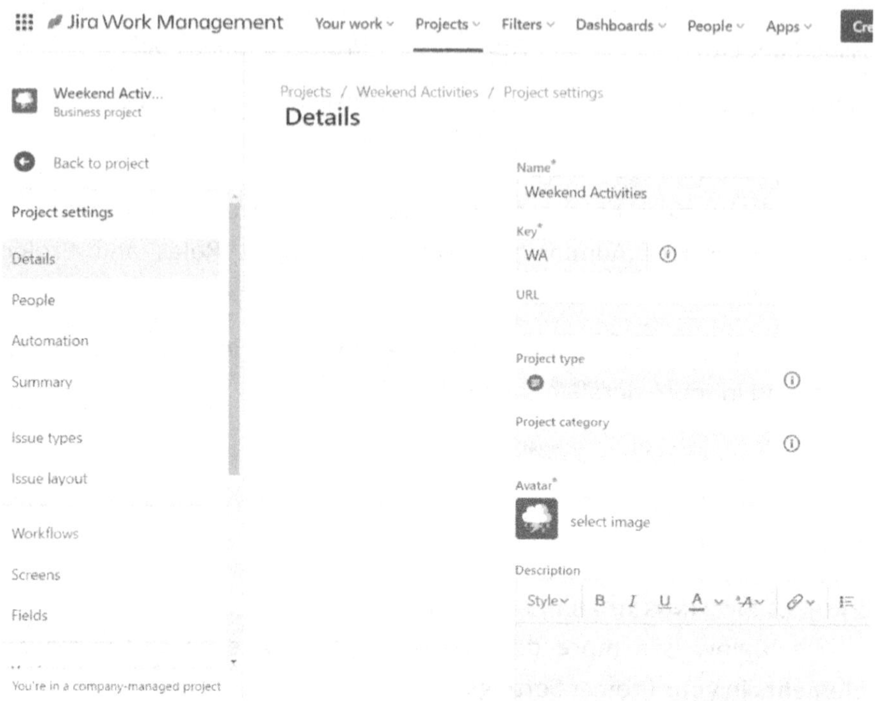

Here you can edit the project. For example, you can change the name of the project. Changing the **Project name** will NOT change the **Key**. If you really want to change the project key (**not recommended**), click on the Information icon right beside the Key field and press the "Learn more about project keys" link.

You can change your **URL** if you are so inclined.

You can change **Project type** to a *Software project* type or *Service Management project* type, assuming you have the license to do so. Why would you want to change project type? Well, first, there may be workflows available in these other project types that are not available in the Business project type. Second, it will give you access to other functions not possible in Business. For example, you can manage Agile and Epics in a Software project type, or the Service Management shell in a Service Management project type (don't worry if you don't know what I am referring to (Agile or Service Management), as it's not important for this book).

To change a project type, the Site-admin must first create a new project (in the appropriate project type) and then bulk move all the Issues to the new project. Project Admins cannot change project type.

You can also change the **Project category**. Project categories are simply a means for you to organize related projects. For example, you might have several "product design", or "product rollout", or "public relations" projects. Organizing them into categories (that you create) makes these projects easier for your teams to access.

If you have not created any Project Categories, click on the Information icon right beside the Project category field and click the "Add a new project category" link. You can also change your Project **Avatar**. I personally like to use unique avatars for each project, as this makes it a little easier to keep track of them and their related issues. Why don't we do that now.

2. CLICK ON **SELECT IMAGE** LINK:

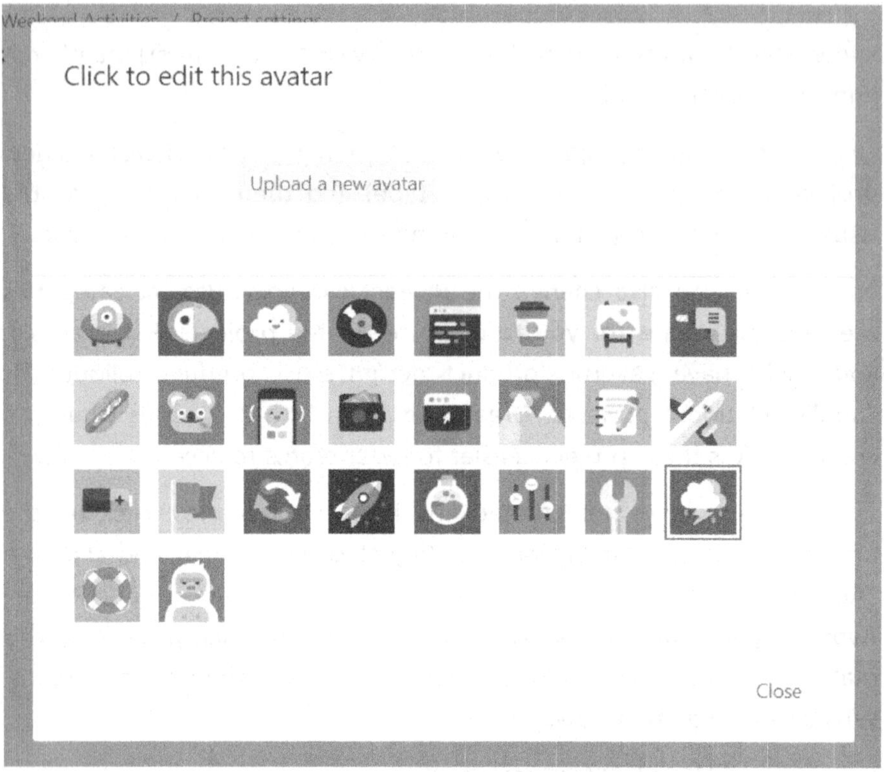

You have a couple of options: you can select from a predefined set of icons, or you can browse your files for an image you like. If you are going to upload a file to use as an avatar, remember that the image size cannot be larger than 2000px x 2000px.

As Weekend Activities is generally a repeating set of activities, let's select the circular arrows icon. As soon as you click on the icon you are brought back to the **Details** area and your new icon should be showing.

Next is the **Description** field.

3. TYPE IN SOMETHING LIKE "WELCOME TO WEEKEND ACTIVITIES. THIS PROJECT LISTS THE CHORES AND RECREATIONAL ACTIVITIES FOR THIS UPCOMING WEEKEND."

The description area will take wiki markup. It also allows you to make font and formatting changes in the description area (such as adding hyperlinks), but let's stay away from that right now.

Next is one of the most important fields in the details area: the **Project lead**. The project lead is the Project Admin. When the project is being created, the Site-admin is assigned as the project lead by default. Once the project is created, the Site-admin can access the Project Details view and assign a new project lead. Project leads cannot change the Project lead field.

The final field is the **Default assignee** for this project. The default assignee is the individual automatically assigned to any Issue created in this project. If you don't want a default assignee, simply choose the "Unassigned" option. Both the Site-admin and Project Admin can assign a default assignee.

4. IF YOU LIKE THE CHANGES, CLICK **SAVE DETAILS**.

Project Settings: People

Site-admin can view and make changes
Project Admin can view and make some changes

This is where you can add licensed Jira Work Management Users to your project. Simply enter their name in the search box, and then select a project role for them. A Jira role is a pre-defined "job description", such as "product designer", or "accounts payable", or "field rep". Each role is created for a particular project (or projects) and has specific permissions. Roles can only be created and assigned to projects by Site-admin. Once a role is assigned to a project, the Project Admin can assign Users to the appropriate role. Users and Roles are discussed in detail in "Chapter 9 – Users, Roles, and Groups".

Project Settings: Automation

Site-admin can view and make changes
Project Admin can view and make some changes

Automation is an incredibly powerful tool in Jira Work Management. It allows you to build "rules" that will automatically cause something to happen when the terms of the rule are met. This lets your team members perform more value-added work while the important but mundane tasks in your Jira project execute automatically. For example:

- when the priority field changes to "high", automatically send an email to the supervisor
- when the workflow status changes to "pending", automatically assign "John Doe" to the task
- when the value in the "estimate" field is updated, automatically notify the customer

We will not be covering Automation in this book as it falls outside the scope of "basics". If you are interested in this topic, I recommend you read my book "Jira Core Workflows" where I cover Automation in detail. "Jira Core Workflows" is written for the Server version of Jira but is applicable for Jira Work Management.

Project Settings: Summary

Site-admin can view and make changes
Project Admin can view and make some changes

A Jira Work Management project is comprised of numerous schemes. A scheme is a structure or system that helps make the project work as designed. Think of schemes as infrastructure. They are like the plumbing, electrical, communication systems in your home. But instead of a plumbing system, your Jira will have a Screens scheme. Instead of an electrical system, your Jira will have an Issue Types scheme. Instead of a communication system, your Jira will have a Workflows scheme. And because different homes have different plumbing, electrical, and communication layouts, so your project will likely need different Screen, Issue Type, and Workflow schemes from other projects. For that reason, each project will have its own set of unique schemes. That way, if you make a change to something in your project's screen scheme, that change won't affect any other project.

Below is a table detailing all the items shown in the Summary view. Most of the Summary Items are covered in much more detail later in the book.

Site-admin can make changes in each of these areas. The "Project Admin" column will show if the Project Admin can make changes or is limited to "view only".

Summary Item	Project Admin access
Issue Types	View only
Workflows	View only
Screens	View only
Fields	View only
Settings	Can make changes
Versions	Can make changes
Components	Can make changes
Roles	Can make changes
Permissions	View only
Notifications	View only
Issue collectors	Can make changes
Slack integration	Can make changes

Project Settings: Issue Types

Site-admin can view and make changes
Project Admin cannot view and cannot make changes

This view shows the Issue Types associated with the project. An Issue Type is just that, it is the type of work you need to do. "Hire a new employee" and "Fire an employee" are two examples of Issue Types.

Project Settings: Issue layout

Site-admin can view and make changes
Project Admin can view and make some changes

The Issue layout setting allows both the Site-admin and Project Admin to:

- change the order of the fields in the Issue layout
- hide some fields not necessary for that Issue
- hide other fields if they are empty (i.e. if there is no value in the field)

If you want to change the order of a field, simply click on it, and then drag it to its new location.

Project Settings: Workflows

Site-admin can view and make changes
Project Admin can view but cannot make changes

A workflow describes the process steps (called "statuses" in Jira) an Issue or Task typically will go through in its lifecycle. If a project has more than one Issue Type, then it may also have more than one workflow. Workflows in a project are managed by the Workflow Scheme. Project Admins can view the workflow scheme but must request the Site-admin to make changes to it.

Project Settings: Screens

Site-admin can view and make changes
Project Admin can view but cannot make changes

Screens are made up of an assortment of fields. These are the fields necessary for your team to work with on a particular Issue Type. Screens within a project are managed by an Issue Type Screen Scheme.

Project Admins can view the Issue Type Screen Scheme but must request the Site-admin to make changes to it.

Project Settings: Fields

Site-admin can view and make changes
Project Admin can view but cannot make changes

The fields necessary for your project are managed through a Field Configuration.

Project Admins can view the Field Configuration, but if they need to add, delete, or edit those fields they must request the Site-admin to make changes to the project's Field Configuration.

Project Settings: Versions

Site-admin can view and make changes
Project Admin can view and make some changes

Often Jira projects deal with product releases. For example, software releases of version 1.1, version 1.2 etc. However, there may also be a need for product releases related to product models, years, seasons, language, Country, Region, etc.

The Versions settings area allows Site-admins and Project Admins to create their own Versions. Doing so augments the planning and execution of the products' version releases or rollouts.

Project Settings: Components

Site-admin can view and make changes
Project Admin can view and make some changes

Components allows you to organize Issues within a project into categories. For example, you may have a project related to the rollout of a product across North America. You may want to create Mexico, USA, and Canada components in order to track Issues in each of those countries.

The Components settings area allows Site-admins and Project Admins to create their own Components.

Project Settings: Permissions

Site-admin can view and make changes
Project Admin can view but cannot make changes

Permissions are the rules that determine what, based on their project role, the team members on your project can and cannot do. Permissions are managed through a permission scheme.

Project Admins can view their project's Permission scheme but must request the Site-admin to make any changes.

Project Settings: Issue Security

Site-admin can view and make changes
Project Admin can view but cannot make changes

Permissions are based on people, in other words who can and who cannot do or see things in Jira. Conversely, Issue Security is based on Issues, who can and cannot view specific Issues. For example, you may have an Issue about the plan to fire Bernard. You probably don't want Bernard, or Bernard's friends, finding out about this, so you need to put Issue Security in place. Issue Security is managed through an Issue Security scheme.

Project Admins can view their project's Issue security scheme but must request the Site-admin to make any changes.

Project Settings: Notifications

Site-admin can view and make changes
Project Admin can view but cannot make changes

Notifications lets Jira inform others of things that have happened with Jira Issues or Projects. For example, if an Issue is edited, then anyone Watching the Issue will get a notification of the edit. Notifications are managed through a Notification scheme.

Project Admins can view their project's Notification scheme but must request the Site-admin to make any changes.

Project Settings: Issue Collector

Site-admin can view and make changes
Project Admin can view and make some changes

The Issue Collector function is a fantastic Jira tool. It allows you to set up a mini-app in any website (with that website owner's permission, of course). This mini-app collects "feedback" (problems, complaints, compliments, etc.) and converts each into a Jira Issue to be addressed.

Site-admins and Project Admins can create an Issue Collector by clicking the "+ Add issue collector" button and filling in the form that appears. Once complete Jira automatically creates a javascript for that Issue Collector that can be copied and embedded in the appropriate website.

Project Settings: Slack integration

Site-admin can view and make changes
Project Admin can view and make some changes

Slack is a tool that let's teams communicate more effectively. It is not an Atlassian product but is closely integrated with it. You must have a Slack license in order to use Slack.

More Projects menu items

So far, in the Navigation Bar's Projects' menu we have been looking at specific projects. However, there are two other menu items that we want to discuss in more detail: **View All Projects**, and **Create Project**.

There are two ways of viewing your list of projects depending on what you want to do and what **Permissions** you have.

View all projects

On the Navigation bar select **Projects** > **View all projects**:

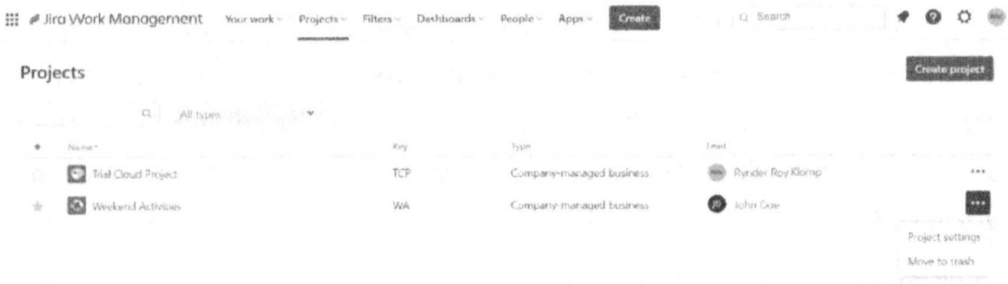

Here you will see a list of **All Project Types – All Categories** projects which you have permission to see and browse. Clicking on any of the project names will open that project.

If you are a Site-admin, you will see everything in the view above.

If you are a Project Admin or Jira User, you will see everything above except for the "Create project" button, and the "Move to trash" link.

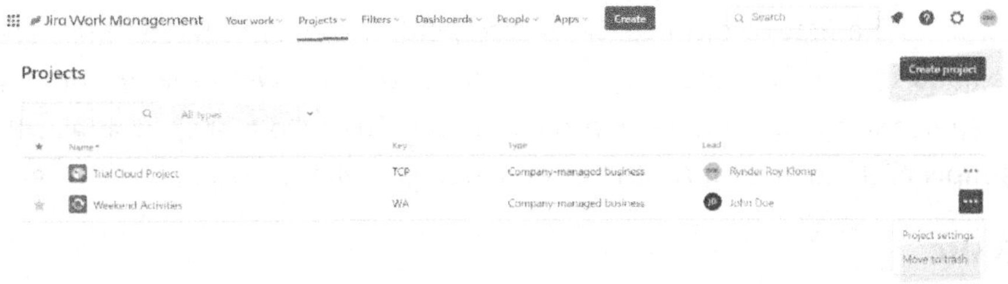

SITE-ADMINS' VIEW OF MANAGE PROJECTS

EXERCISE: VIEW PROJECTS

1. ON THE NAVIGATION BAR SELECT **SITE-ADMINISTRATION** (THE COG WHEEL) > **PROJECTS**

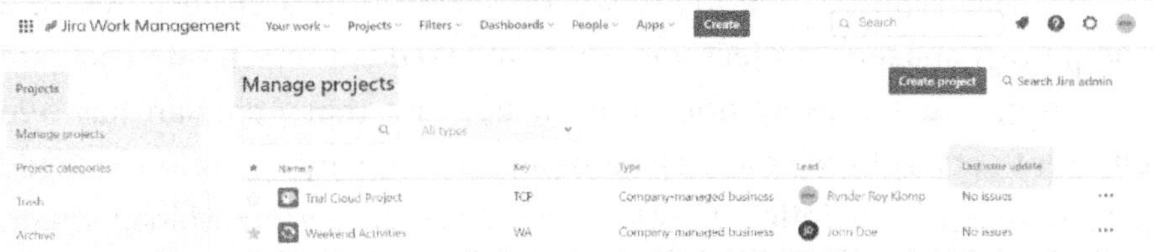

This **Administration (COG) "Manage Projects"** view is similar to the **Projects** view found in the Projects menu but with one major difference. Because it is meant for those with Site-admin access, its Projects sidebar includes four links to related views:

- Manage projects (the default view)
- Project categories
- Trash
- Archive

MANAGE PROJECTS VIEW

The Manage Projects view contains seven columns.

Jira Work Management Basics

Favorites

The first column contains stars, either empty or filled. If the star is filled that means the project is a "favorite" and will show in the first area of the Navigation Bar's project menu. To make a project a favorite simply click on an empty star. That action will fill the star.

Name

This is the name of the project. It is also a link to the project.

Key

This column contains the key to the project. This is the unique identifier Jira Work Management uses to distinguish that project and its contents.

Type

The Type column identifies what kind of Jira project this is, a company-managed project or team-managed project. If you are confused, you are likely not alone. It appears that Atlassian has two different sets of Project Types: to define a company or team managed project type; or, to define an Atlassian product (Jira Work Management, Jira Service Management, or Jira Software project type).

Lead

This column shows who is the project's lead (Proj-admin).

Actions

Actions (the last) column is where the Site-admin can change the **Project Settings** or Delete the project by clicking the **Move to trash** link.

Create Project

The **Create Project** button on the upper right corner of the Project List works the same as **Create Project** from the Browse Projects view.

Go to the "JWM Project Templates" section later in this chapter for more details about which Jira Project Template to select when creating a Jira Work Management project.

Project Categories

1. While still in the **Administration > Manage projects** view, Click on the **Project Categories** Link in the sidebar:

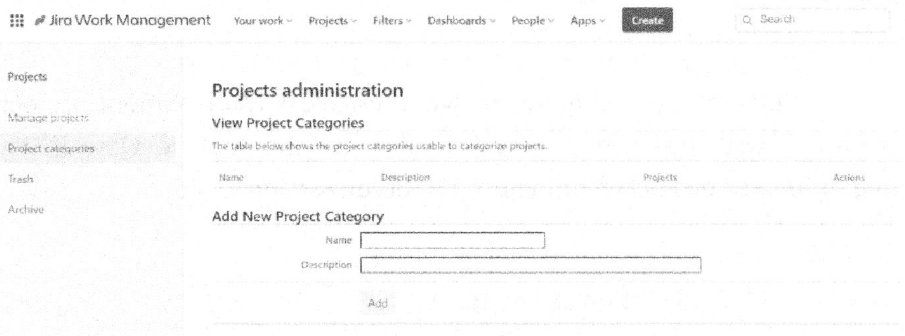

The **Project Categories** view allows you to create new project categories. Why do you need this capability? In some cases, you may have hundreds of projects within your organization, each one representing some sort of issue or group of issues. Many of these projects may belong to particular departments or may belong to cross functional process such as Supply Chain or Marketing. Categorizing makes it easier to associate and keep track of your projects.

Trash

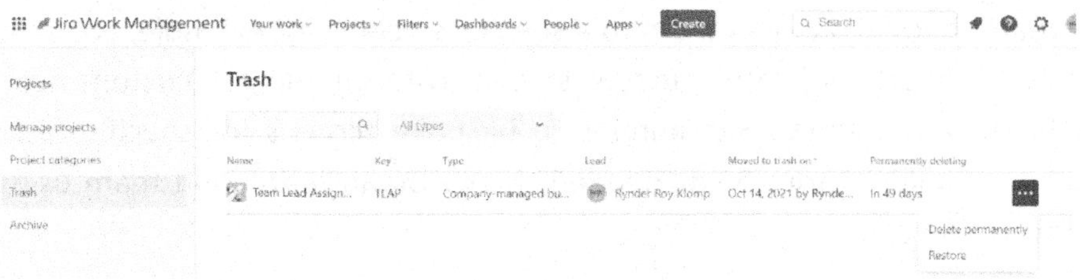

When you click the "Move to trash" link in the Manage Projects view, this is where those projects go. The trash view is where you send projects you want to permanently delete. Any project moved to this view will automatically and permanently delete after 60 days. Or you can permanently delete them immediately by clicking the **Delete permanently** link in the "more" column.

On those rare occasions when you have moved a project to trash in error, you can make it active again by clicking the **Restore** link in the "more" column. This will move the project back to the **Manage projects** view.

Archive

Currently, you cannot archive a Jira Work Management project. However, you may see archived projects in the Archive view if you migrated over projects from your Jira Server version.

JWM Project Templates

As you remember, when you clicked on the **Create Project** from the Projects on the Navigation Bar, you were taken to the **Create project** wizard pop-up, where you were asked to select from one of many template options. Let's look at those in more detail as to what exactly a template project is, because it often confuses new users.

Fundamentally, a project is composed of screens, fields, and workflows working together in one or more Issues. A screen is a collection of fields. Some fields are "system" fields, meaning they come with the software. Other fields are "custom" in that a Site-admin can create them and assign them to a specific screen. For example, you may have a "work estimate" custom screen, with an "hours" custom field. This function allows Site-admins to bespoke screens for specific tasks and to build custom fields needed by the organization and team using the screen.

In addition to the screen/field combination, there is a workflow. A workflow is a work process, the steps the User or team go through to complete their work. Jira calls these steps "Statuses". For example, a simple workflow may have three statuses: To Do (not started), In Progress, and Done.

A Jira project template is a combination of specific screens/fields and workflows customized to complete related tasks.

Once upon a time in the far distant past, Jira had three Business project type options: **Task management**, **Project management,** or **Process management.** Those three basic "generic" options are still available. Your choice will depend on the complexity of the tasks within your project.

Let's look at these three options more closely.

Task Management

Let's say you want to create a project that deals with basic action items or simple To Do activities such as: Send file to Barry, Sign approval form, Check with Dave on Option B, Phone Mom, Pick up Milk on the Way Home.

Each of these activities are 'checklist' items. They tend to be completed very quickly. In these cases, all you need is a workflow that has two steps or statuses: To Do and Done.

Project Management

Next is the Project Management option. Where the Task Management project type works well with simple, quick checklist tasks, Project Management works best with straightforward tasks that need a significant amount of time to complete. Examples might be: ship product from Germany to USA, grow a crop of corn, pour concrete for a building foundation. If you have tasks where a supervisor or customer may phone you up a few times and ask, "Is it done yet?", then those are eligible to be project management type tasks. To manage these types of tasks, the Project Management project type has a three-status workflow: To Do, In Progress, and Done.

Process Management

The Process Management project type is designed for tasks or processes that have an approval step. As seen in the image below, the steps have several options available for the user to select, based on conditions within the task or process. For example, when a task is **In Progress** it can either be sent to an **Under review** status or the task can be **Cancelled**.

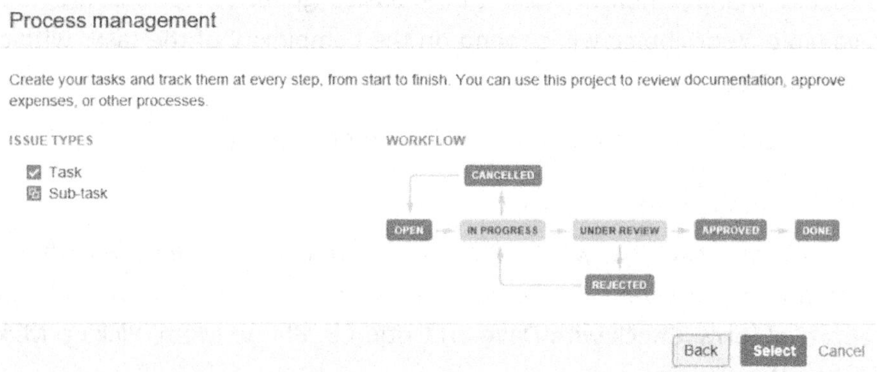

Category Templates

At the time of writing Jira has a portfolio of 33 templates, each focused on a specific aspect of business. 9 of these templates are meant for Jira Software or Jira Service Management projects and are out of scope for this book. That, currently, leaves 24 unique Jira Work Management templates in eight categories:

Category	Templates
Marketing	• Project management • Content management • Email campaign

	• Event planning • Go-to-Market • Campaign management
Human Resources	• HR service management • Recruitment • New employee onboarding • Policy management • Performance review
Finance	• Month-end close • Budget creation • RFP process
Design	• Project management • Web design process • Asset creation
Personal	• Project management • Task tracking • Personal task planner
Operations	• Process control • Procurement • RFP process
Legal	• Legal service management • Document approval • IP infringement
Sales	• Lead tracking • Sales pipeline

NOTE: if you counted the number of templates, you will realize that there are 28 listed, whereas I stated earlier there are 24. That's because there are some duplicate templates shown in different categories. For example, Project management is listed in three different categories (Marketing, Design, and Personal).

These templates generally contain workflows designed specifically for each template. You may need to modify them for your organizations' distinct needs, which your Site-admin can do.

WHICH TEMPLATE TO CHOOSE?

So? Which template to choose? Einstein once said, "Everything should be as simple as possible, but not simpler." Or, put another way, how long is a piece of string? One consistent observation I have made is that teams tend to over complicate things they start working with Jira. If the screen has 5 fields, the team wants to add 10 more. Why? Because they *might* be needed. If a workflow has 4 statuses, the team wants to add 7 more. Why? Because it seems logical to do so. They soon come to one of two conclusions. First, they really don't need all those additional fields and statuses. Most of those additional fields and steps aren't necessary; indeed, all they do is add unnecessary time to the entire process. The next thing they find, after working with the template for a while, is that instead of the fields and steps they added, different fields and steps are needed. So, an entire rework of the template is required.

My advice is this. Choose the simplest template you can find that most closely matches your needs. Don't do anything to the template for a reasonable amount of time. Instead let the team work with the template and build up a list of "change requests". After a few months, sit the entire team down, go through the change requests, identify those that are truly necessary and then modify your template.

Chapter 4 – The Jira Work Management Puzzle Pieces

To avoid confusion, in this book the term "Site-admin" includes "Org-admin, Site-admin, and Jira-admin" unless specifically noted otherwise.

Chapter Objective

In this Chapter you will gain an understanding of the Jira Work Management elements (puzzle pieces) and how they interact.

In this chapter we want to take a high-level overview of the various elements that make up a Jira project. They are **Issue Types, Workflows, Screens, Fields, Schemes, Roles, Permissions, Notifications**, etc. These elements (I call them the 'Puzzle Pieces') form the structure that makes Jira work. You need to understand them in order to customize your Jira project.

Setting the context

Before diving into the details of all the Jira Work Management puzzle pieces let's take a brief step back and look one more time at the three major Jira components: **Projects, Issues,** and **Issue Types.**

Project, Issues, and Issue Types

Projects

The foundation of Jira is **Projects**. Without a project you cannot create an Issue.

Jira Work Management Basics

To slightly paraphrase the Oxford dictionary, its definition of a project is a unique 'something' that must be completed by a certain date. However, it is probably more accurate to think of a Jira Project as a file folder which contains one or more files (the Issues) needing completion. While I suppose it is technically possible to create one big project called, "Stuff We Need To Do", most people create Jira Projects based upon work themes or similar activities.

You can create projects manually, or you can import projects from other sources.

Issues

In Jira, an Issue is a piece of work to be completed. It may be easier to think of an Issue as a "task". It's as simple and as complex as that. An Issue can stand alone (within a project), or it can have Sub-tasks associated with it. Sub-tasks cannot have their own Sub-tasks. In other words, Issues can only include two levels: Task and Sub-tasks.

With company-managed projects, Issues can also be linked or associated with other Issues, either in the existing project or with other projects.

Just as a Process requires People, and Technology, Issues require the same People-Process-Technology components to work. These can be categorized as: **Issue Types** and **Workflows** (the Process), **Screens** and **Fields** (the Technology), and **Users/Roles** (the People).

Issue Types

Most of us tend to categorize work. We may have Action Items, To Do lists, Approval tasks, or specific processes in departments such as Marketing, Accounts Payable, Receiving, Repair, Delivery, etc. We categorize them because the work process, or type of work required, in each of these categories is similar.

Jira calls each of these work categories an **Issue Type**. An Issue Type may represent a very simple single-operation 30-second task, or a complicated work type (e.g. "Hire a new employee" procedure) that can require a number of steps and take a month or more to complete. Regardless, an Issue Type is something most of us would recognize as a single deliverable.

How the three work together

When you first create an issue, you will notice the two fields at the top of the Create Issue pop up. These two fields ask you to select the Project and Issue Type for this issue. Many folks skip over these two fields rather quickly and don't understand the full importance of them. Here's **why they are important**: when you select the Project and Issue Type, you also (behind the scenes) define ALL the following:

- Users who are authorized to view, edit, and work with the issue
- Screens and Fields the Users will see and use
- Workflow steps the process will take
- Rules the Issue will follow

If, when creating an Issue, you didn't select a Project or Issue Type, the software wouldn't know what to provide you for that Issue.

The need for Change

In the previous chapters we demonstrated how to work with Jira Work Management Projects and Issues using the default settings. Indeed, it is recommended you continue to work with default settings until you develop a good working knowledge of the program and gain experience. As the saying goes, 'practice makes perfect'.

Like most of you, I started with the basic assumption that all I needed to do was create an Issue or Task and everything would be fine. And indeed, in many cases the default settings are good enough. Jira has done a really great job at making a 'Swiss Army Knife' that meets most requirements right out of the box. If you want to build a simple project where all you ask of a User is to mark an Issue as complete when it is done, then the Jira Work Management program with its prebuilt defaults will work fine for you. And often, that is all you need. Why over complicate things?

Yet, in today's business world where employees are asked to do more, in less time, there is a need to 'automate' and simplify wherever possible. For example, what happens if a User has a question related to her Issue? How can we help improve the Issue process if there is an approval step? What can we do to make the User's screen as simple and as useful as possible? How do we manage things if we need to reopen the Issue because of a quality control problem?

Sooner or later, you will undoubtedly find that you need to modify your project, issues, screens, the fields on those screens, workflows, etc. These modifications can be categorized in two ways: Customization and Simplification.

CUSTOMIZATION

Users will often ask for the creation of bespoke fields or screens tailored towards specific business requirements. For example, someone may need a custom field where a User can select from a list of options. This field needs to be created AND it needs to be placed on a specific screen. Additionally, Users may ask for explicit project roles to be created. These roles will be given precise permissions as to what the User assigned to that new role can and cannot see and what s/he can and cannot change or edit. These are just a few examples of customization requests.

SIMPLIFICATION

When creating a standard, default Task Issue, Jira may include fields you don't need in your particular Jira project. Users often become confused as they are unsure what to do with those fields. As a Site-admin one of your responsibilities is to create screens focused on a single type of User and include on that screen only those fields necessary for the User to complete his or her issue. That may mean simplifying a project by removing fields.

Customization and Simplification both have the same goal: to build explicit screens and fields for specific User roles based on the work that is to be performed. This is not a simple undertaking, and it explains why there are so many complex elements in Jira that must be addressed when bespoking the software.

Overview of The Jira Puzzle Pieces

The diagram below indicates, to some degree, the complexity of a Jira Project:

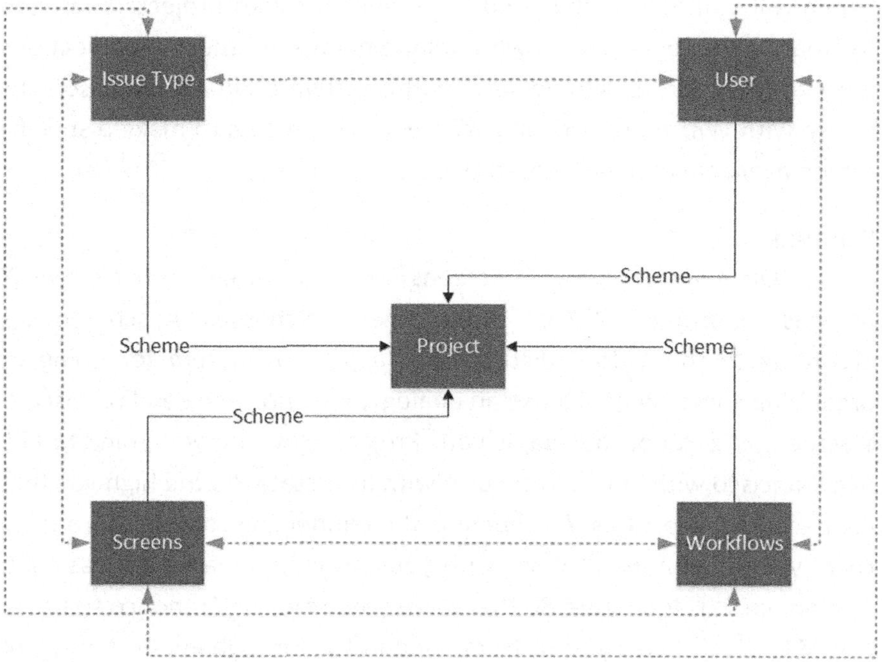

Jira Work Management Basics

If you are going to modify a project, you need to consider things such as:

- what type of work (Issue Type) will be done?
- what User's permissions and job rules will you need?
- what Screens and Fields will the User need for the type of work to be done?
- how will the work progress through the Issue life cycle (the Workflow)?

When you customize any of these four things you also make significant changes to the application. For example, if you are going to modify one of the screens (**a screen is a group of fields**), you don't just change the default, you should create a new screen with a new name. You do this because the default screen may still be in use on another project, or you may need that default screen somewhere else. What happens if you decide you need six screens for your project? You need to create six unique screens with unique names. All these modifications must to be recorded somewhere so the software knows *What* screens to use with *Which* Projects and *Where* in the process to make a specific screen available to a designated User.

SCHEMES

Once you create your screens how will Jira know that screen X belongs to project Y? That is the role of **Schemes**. A scheme is – according to the Oxford dictionary - "a plan or system for doing or organizing something." To use an analogy, let's pretend San Francisco is a Screen, and Reno, Nevada, is your Project. How are you going to link San Francisco with Reno? You do so with Interstate 80, the highway that connects the two cities. A scheme is the connecting road. If there is no road, your screen won't work with your project; it's as simple as that. And notice, it is Interstate 80 that takes you from San Francisco to Reno. Not M1, which takes you to from London to Nottingham. Certainly not E26, which runs from Berlin to Hamburg. Just like you need to know the specific road to take to go from city to city, Jira also needs to know the same thing. This is why you are required to build roads (schemes) with unique names.

Often you must take more than one road to go from city A to City B. Such is occasionally the case with Jira. If I want to drive from Toronto, Canada to Miami, USA, I will take Highway 401 to the U.S. Border at Detroit Michigan. There I need to go through Customs, and then get on Interstate 75 which will take me to Miami. There are occasions in Jira where you need to take similar multiple roads, and these routes and actions (such as clearing the border) must all be rigorously defined and recorded, otherwise you end up in Fargo, North Dakota, or you don't get out of Toronto at all.

Schemes let Jira know which **Issue Types, Workflows, Screens, Fields, Permissions,** and **Notifications** work with your **Project**. Without schemes how would the software know to open your "Select my Weekend Activities" screen, or your "Make a Peanut Butter and Jam Sandwich" workflow?

There are a number of different schemes in a Jira Project. These are Issue Type Scheme, Screen Scheme, Issue Type Screen Scheme, Workflow Scheme, Field Configuration Scheme, Permissions Scheme, and Notification Scheme. Each tie an element to your project.

The image below is a diagram of the Jira Work Management elements and the schemes with which they are associated.

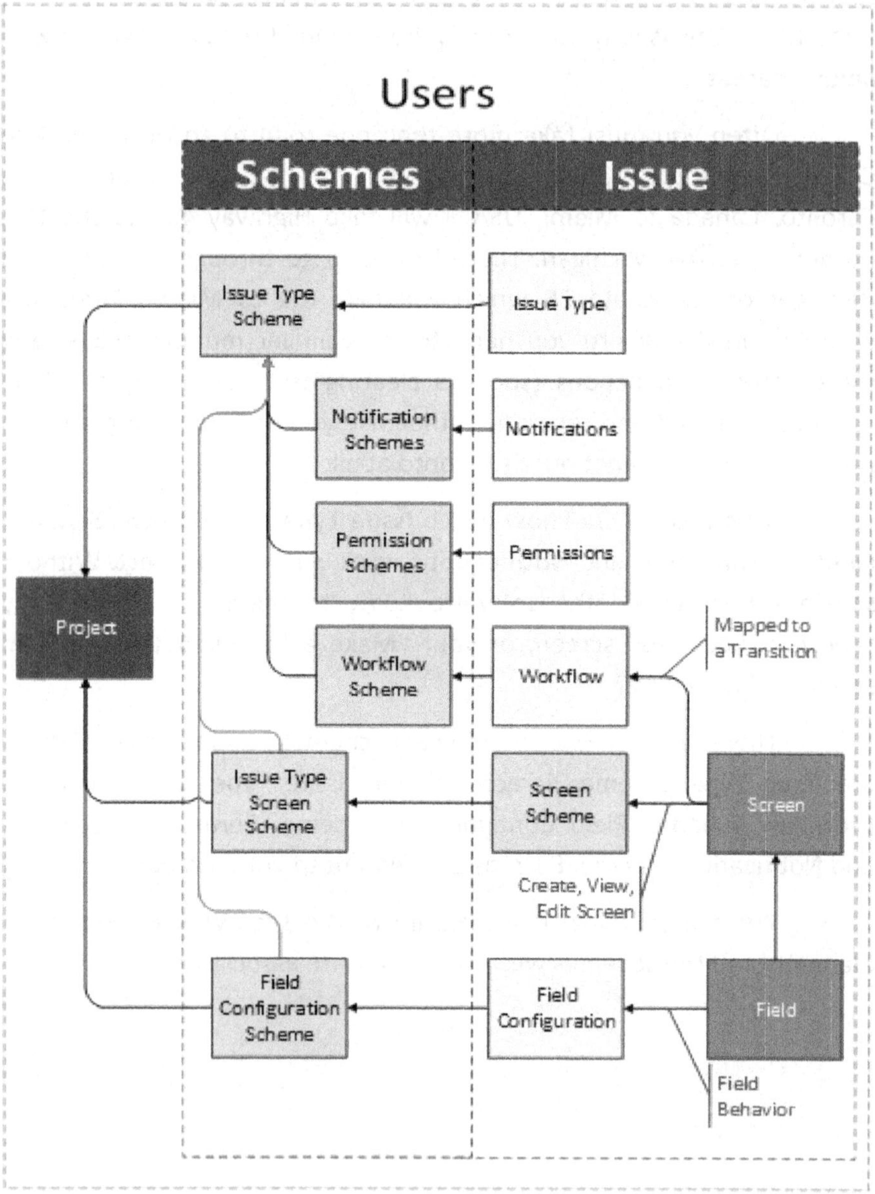
Users
Schemes
Issue
Issue Type Scheme
Issue Type
Notification Schemes
Notifications
Permission Schemes
Permissions
Project
Mapped to a Transition
Workflow Scheme
Workflow
Issue Type Screen Scheme
Screen Scheme
Screen
Create, View, Edit Screen
Field Configuration Scheme
Field Configuration
Field
Field Behavior

The JWM Puzzle Pieces

"Why does it need to be so complicated", I can hear you asking. If you have ever designed a process, you know that in addition to the *process* itself you must consider the *people* who will be involved, as well as the *technology* to be used (technology can be something as simple as a pencil or as complex as the Large Hedron Collider). The interaction with People and Technology is essential to the successful implementation of any Process; and I believe Jira Work Management is the best software for managing this People, Process, Technology (PPT) interaction. We will cover these People, Process, Technology components: **Issue Types, Workflows, Screens, Fields, Permissions and Notifications, Users, Roles, and Groups** in more detail in the next five chapters.

The collaboration of customized screens, fields in the screens, workflows, and User roles (I collectively call them a 'process') is what makes Jira such a strong product.

The challenge is that a Jira process with all its puzzle piece elements is complex. And that's because it's very complicated to build a process in the first place, regardless of whether you are using Jira or not. You will immediately relate to this if you have ever sat in a meeting (or many meetings) trying to design, or improve, a work process. Like I said, it's very complicated, but we do it because the benefits are substantial.

Jira recommends, and I whole heartedly agree, that you design your process on paper and then build it in Jira.

So far, we have been talking in theory about our roadmap. Let's look at it in reality. The diagram below shows a typical project structure. We have the elements (the cities) and the schemes (the connecting roads). While this diagram certainly isn't complete, it will give you very good idea of how all the Jira elements, the puzzle pieces, fit together.

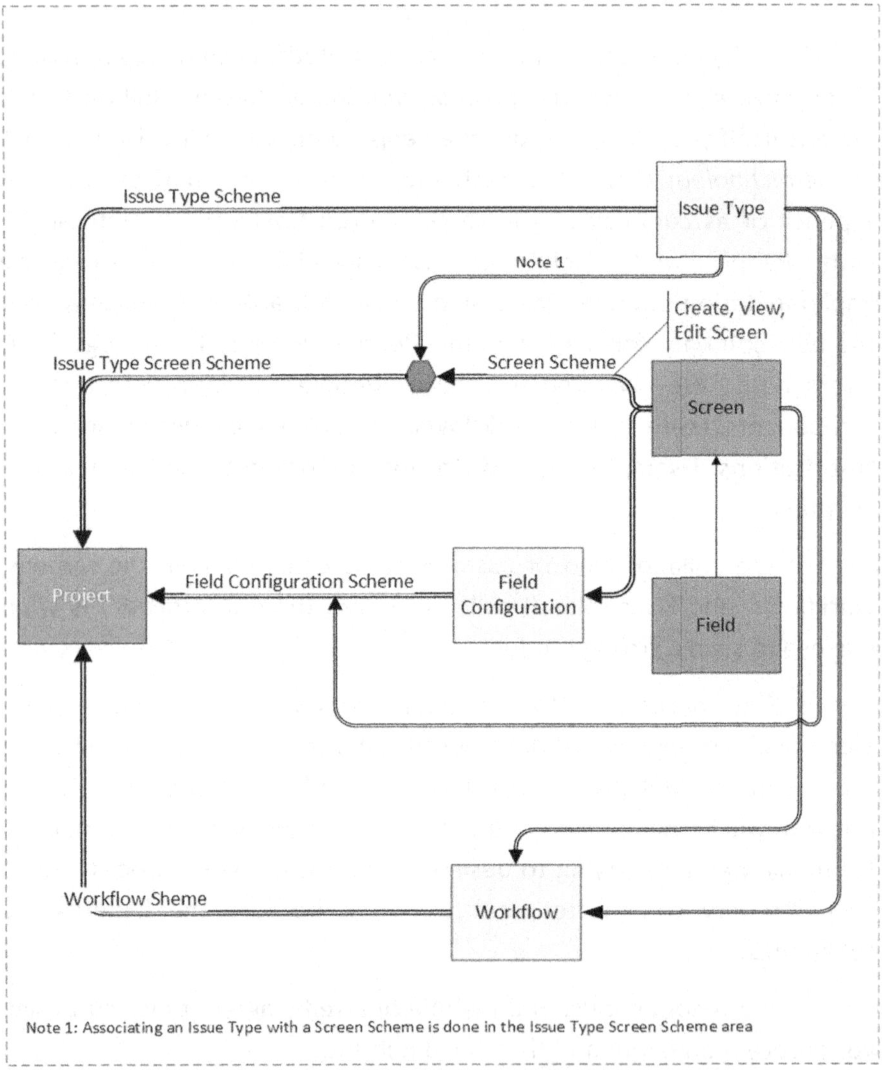

Jira comes with default schemes, depending on the project template you use. Typically, the only major difference between them is the type of workflow used and a few different fields. The important thing to remember is that every time you create a new project, Jira builds a new set of unique schemes for your project. These schemes are all copies of Jira's default schemes; however, they have unique identifications. So, any time you make a change to a scheme in your project, you will not affect any other schemes in other projects.

The remainder of the book will discuss the various elements and schemes in much greater detail.

Chapter 5 – JWM Issue Types

To avoid confusion, in this book the term "Site-admin" includes "Org-admin, Site-admin, and Jira-admin" unless specifically noted otherwise.

Chapter Objectives

In this Chapter you will:

- **gain a deeper understanding of Issue Types, Issue Type Schemes, and Sub-Task Issue Types**
- **create your first Issue Type and Issue Type Scheme**

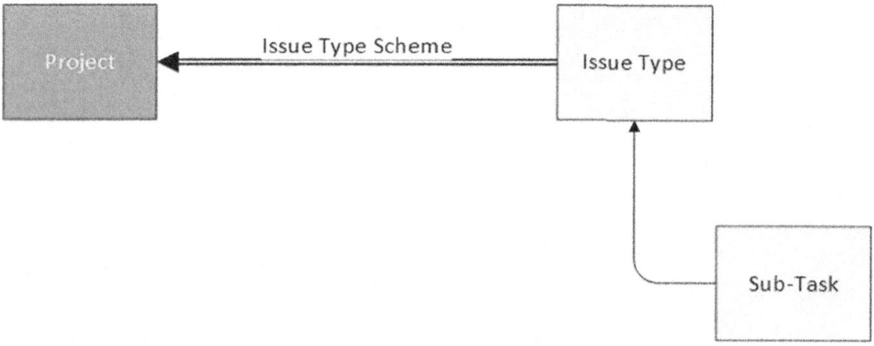

Issue Types and Schemes

Issue Types

An **Issue Type** in JWM is the specific nature of work to be performed. For example, most Human Resource departments have defined processes for "Hire a new employee", "Annual employee review", and "Terminate an employee". Those HR processes require unique steps, forms, approvals, etc. Each of these examples could be Issue Types (custom built) in Jira.

Jira comes with two default Issue Types: **Task** and **Sub-task**.

An Issue Types acts as a linchpin to - directly or indirectly - connect most of the Jira elements (Users, workflows, screens, fields, etc.) required to complete an Issue.

Whenever you create an Issue one of the first fields you are required to complete is to select the Issue Type you are going to use for that Issue.

You can add (or create) your own Issue Type. You might want to make a "Design Package" Issue Type, or you might want to build a "Peanut Butter and Jam Sandwich" Issue Type. If you believe you are going to perform a certain task repeatedly, it is recommended you add your own Issue Type (if the defaults aren't exactly what you want).

Let's see how to add an Issue Type.

In the COG Administration drop-down list, click on Issues to open the Administration Issues view:

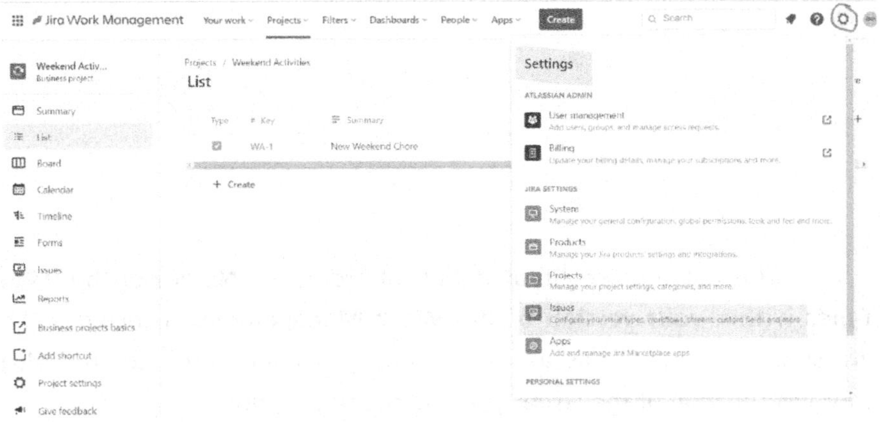

NOTE: There are two ways to access the administration Issues view. The first is to click on the **Summary** link in the **Project settings** sidebar. This will allow the Site-admin to edit the Issue Types scheme and Issues related to that project. The second route is to use the **Administration Cog > Issues** method. This will allow the Site-admin to create new Issue Types and Issue Type schemes unrelated to any project. I recommend you use the project settings approach if all you want to do is edit the element or scheme of an existing project. Otherwise use the Admin Cog route.

In this book we will use the **Admin Cog** method, unless specifically stated otherwise.

The **Administration > Issues > Issue Types** view contains four columns: **Name, Type, Related Scheme,** and **Actions:**

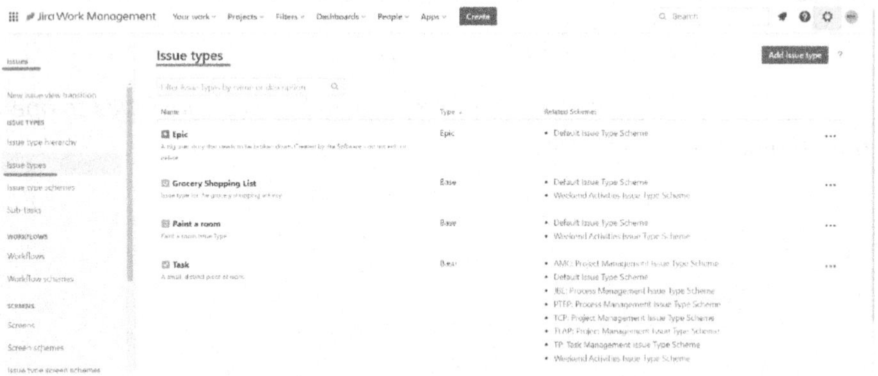

NAME

This column lists, in alphabetical order, the **Names** of the **Issue Types within your version of Jira Work Management**. It includes the Jira supplied Issue Types as well as any you added. The column also contains the Icon of the Issue type and the description.

TYPE

The next column indicates if it is an **Epic, Base,** or **Sub-task** Issue Type. This is very simple, if an Issue Type is not a Sub-task, then it is a Base Issue Type (also called **Standard Issue Type** in some screens). The **Epic** Issue type is used by Jira Software licensed Users.

RELATED (ISSUE TYPE) SCHEME

An **Issue Type Scheme** connects the **Issue Type** to your Project. Put another way, it controls which Issue Types a Project is permitted to use. Let's say you have 13 Issue Types available in your Jira Work Management program (the three default Issue Types supplied by Jira and 10 Issue Types created by your organization), but you want only four of these Issue Types associated with your project. You do this using the Issue Type Scheme. Basically, when you create an Issue Type Scheme, it asks you the name of the project and which Issue Types are permitted to be used in that project.

You associate an Issue Type to an Issue Type Scheme in the Issue Type Scheme screen. Issue Type Schemes is discussed in more detail later in this chapter.

ACTIONS

The Actions column allows you to **Edit**, **Delete**, or **Translate** the Issue Type.

EDIT

In the Edit Issue Type page, you can:

- Change the name of the **Issue Type**
- Change the **Description**
- Change the **Avatar**

DELETE

An Issue Type can be deleted. But be aware, Jira may not allow you to delete an Issue Type if there are Issues, Workflows, Schemes, etc.

associated with your Issue Type. You will need to delete or modify those first.

> CAUTION: It is highly recommended you NOT delete an Issue Type if it is associated with Workflow Scheme(s), Field Configuration Scheme(s), or Screen Scheme(s), as doing so will really, really, *really* mess up your project(s). If the Issue Type is associated with any of these schemes you will need to move them to a new Issue Type.

TRANSLATE

In the Issue Type Translation page you can add a translation of your Issue Type Name and Description. Note that Jira will NOT do the translation for you. To use the translation function, you first select the language you are going to use from the drop-down list. At this time Jira supports 24 languages (or language dialects). Next, you enter the translated Name and Description in the translation fields.

What's the point, you may ask, if Jira doesn't translate the language for you? It's very simple. You may build a project where Users are in different countries, thereby requiring you to work with multiple languages. You insert the appropriate translated text, and the User in the other country will see the translated text (after they select their language choice when configuring their version of Jira). That is why Jira provides the Translation function.

Let's start by creating an Issue Type that we will use later in the book.

EXERCISE: ADD NEW ISSUE TYPE

1. SELECT NAVIGATION BAR >  > **ISSUES**
2. THE **ISSUE TYPES** VIEW SHOULD BE OPEN. IF NOT, ON THE SIDEBAR CLICK ON **ISSUE TYPES**
3. IN THE UPPER RIGHT CORNER OF THE ISSUE TYPES VIEW CLICK ON THE **ADD ISSUE TYPE** BUTTON

4. IN THE ADD ISSUE TYPE POP-UP:
    i. IN THE **NAME** FIELD ENTER "*PAINT A ROOM*" FOR THE ISSUE TYPE (REQUIRED)
    ii. IN THE **DESCRIPTION** FIELD ENTER "*PAINT A ROOM ISSUE TYPE*"
    iii. WHEN ASKED TO SELECT THE TYPE OF ISSUE, CHOOSE *STANDARD ISSUE TYPE*
5. CLICK **ADD**

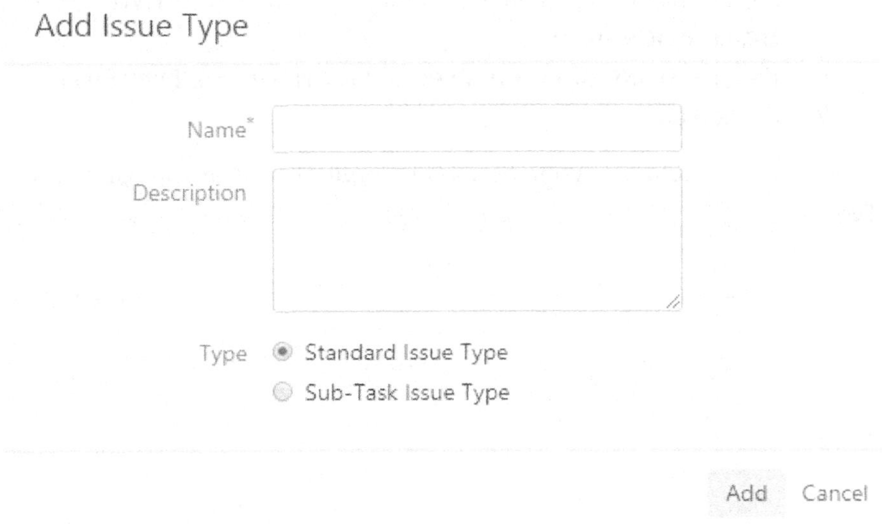

As you can see it is very easy to add an Issue Type. You simply fill in the name of your new Issue Type, add a Description and select whether it is a Standard or Sub-Task Issue Type.

Let's create another Issue Type that we will use in our Weekend Activities project later in the book.

EXERCISE: Add another new Issue Type

In this exercise you will:

- Create a new **Issue Type**

1. Select Navigation Bar >  > **Issues**
2. The **Issue Types** view should be open. If not, on the Sidebar click on **Issue Types**
3. Click on **Add issue type** button in the upper right corner of the Issue Types view
4. In the **Add Issue Type** Pop-up enter *'Grocery Shopping List'* in the **Name** field
5. Enter 'Issue Type for the Grocery Shopping Activity' in the **Description** field
6. Ensure **Standard Issue Type** is selected in the **Type** Field
7. Click **Add**

You should see your new Issue Type appear in the list of Issue Types.

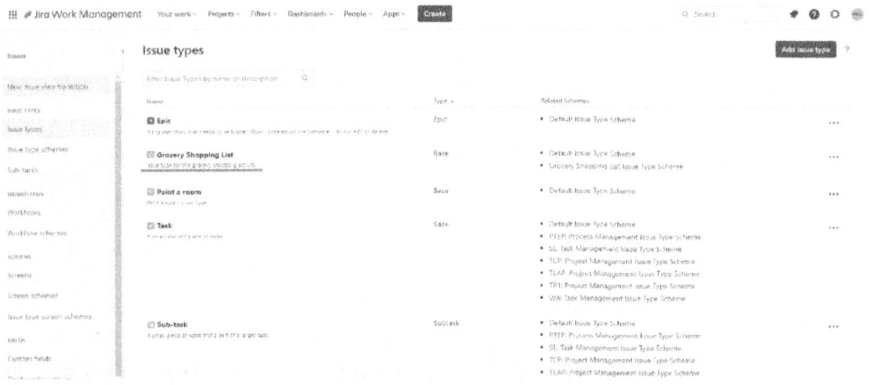

Issue Type Schemes

The **Issue Type Scheme** is what links the **Issue Type(s)** to your **Project**. Just as importantly, it prevents all the other unnecessary Issue Types from interfering with your Project and causing confusion. If you are creating a project about weekend household tasks, why would you want an Issue Type that is meant for software Bugs?

JWM Issue Types

A project can have as many Issue Types as you need, but a project can have only one Issue Type scheme.

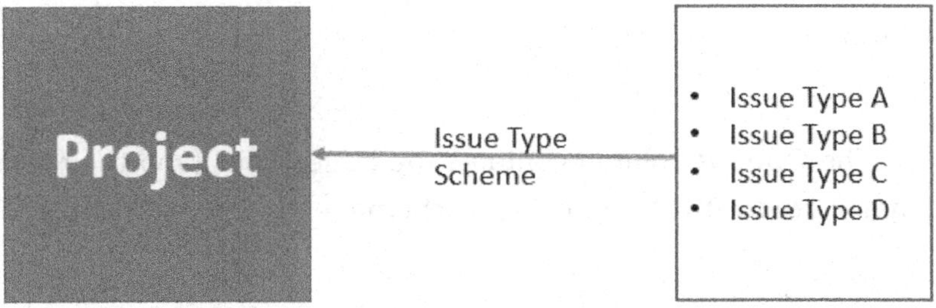

An Issue Type Scheme can be reused with different projects, but if you make a change to the scheme for Project X, then any other projects using that same scheme will also see the same change. That's why I recommend you always use unique schemes for every project, so that your project won't be negatively impacted if someone makes a change to your scheme in another project.

Let's look at the Issue Type Scheme view.

1. SELECT NAVIGATION BAR >  > **ISSUES**
2. IN THE SIDEBAR CLICK ON **ISSUE TYPE SCHEMES**

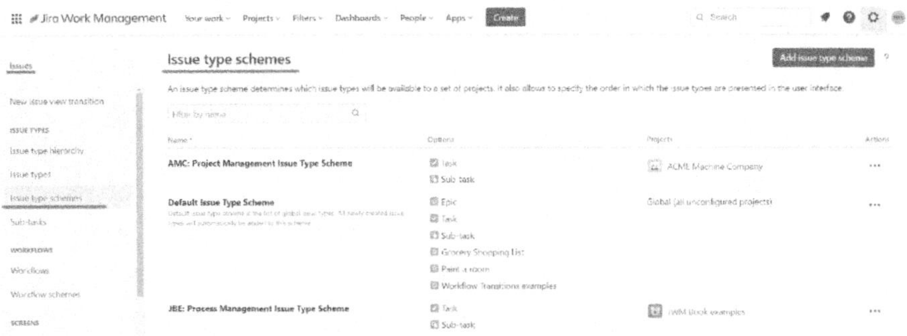

The Issue Type Schemes view contains four columns: **Name, Options, Projects,** and **Actions**.

Name

Here is the listing of all your Issue Type Schemes. They are listed alphabetically.

Options

The Options column contains the Issue Types (and their related Icon) associated with the Issue Type Scheme.

Projects

This column shows all Projects associated with the Issue Type Scheme.

You associate a Project to an Issue Type Scheme in the **Actions** column. You will learn how to do this a little later.

Actions

Finally, in the Actions column you can **Edit, Associate, Copy,** and **Delete** an Issue Type Screen Scheme.

Edit

Click on the Edit link of any Issue Type Scheme (except the Default Scheme) to open the Modify Issue Type Scheme view:

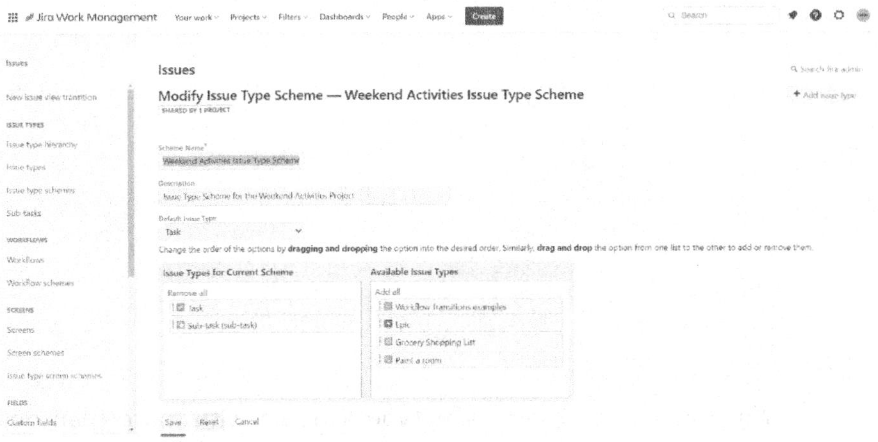

In the **Modify Issue Type Scheme** view you can change the

- **Name** of your Issue Type Scheme
- **Description**
- **Default Issue Type** (i.e. the Issue Type which is shown first in the Issue Type drop down list when you create an Issue in a Project)
- **Issue Types for Current Scheme or Available Issue Types** by dragging and dropping or removing them from one column to the other.

CAUTION: It is highly, highly, and even more highly recommended you NOT edit the Default Scheme.

In addition, you can – except with the Default Scheme – add a new Issue Type through this page by clicking on the **Add Issue Type** button at the upper right corner.

Associate

The **Associate Issue Type Scheme** page is where you link your **Issue Type Scheme** to your **Project**(s).

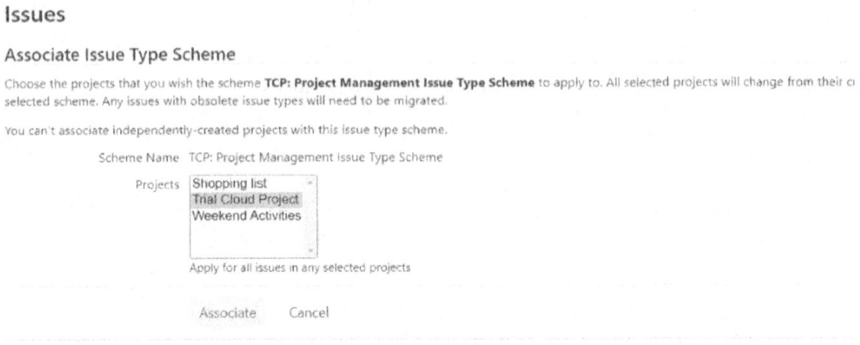

You can associate an Issue Type Scheme with more than one project by holding down the **Control** button on your keyboard and selecting the projects you want to associate with your Issue Type.

Copy

Let's say you want to create a new Issue Type Scheme. It is often better to copy and rename an existing Issue Type Scheme if it has most of the features and Issue Types you are looking for in your new Scheme. You can then modify the copied scheme to meet your new needs, which is much easier than building an entirely new Scheme.

Delete

Lastly, you can delete an Issue Type scheme (except the Default Scheme) by accessing the **Delete Issue Type Scheme** page. Before you can delete a scheme, you must first remove any Projects associated with the Issue Type scheme. You do so through the **Project(s)' Administration Issue Types** view by changing the current Issue Type Scheme to a different one.

Exercise: Create new Issue Type Scheme

In this exercise you will:

- create a new **Issue Type Scheme**

- associate both of our new **Issue Types** to the **Issue Type Scheme**, and
- associate the **Issue Type Scheme to** the *Weekend Activities* **Project**

1. Select Navigation Bar >  > **Issues**
2. In the Administration view Select **Issue Type Schemes** on the sidebar
3. In the Issue Type Schemes view click on **Add Issue Type Scheme** button
4. In the Add Issue Type Scheme view:
    i. Enter "Weekend Activities Issue Type Scheme" in the **Scheme Name** field
    ii. Enter "Issue Type Scheme for the Weekend Activities Project" in the **Description** field
    iii. Skip Default Issue Type for now
    iv. If there are any Issue types in the **Issue Types for Current Scheme** field, click **Remove All** link
    v. Find *Grocery Shopping List* in the **Available Issue Types** list
    vi. Select and Drag *Grocery Shopping List* to the **Issue Types for Current Scheme** Field
    vii. Select and Drag *Paint a room* to the **Issue Type for Current Scheme** Field
    viii. In the **Default Issue Type** Field Select *Grocery Shopping List* (It should be your only option)
5. Click on **Save** at the bottom of the view

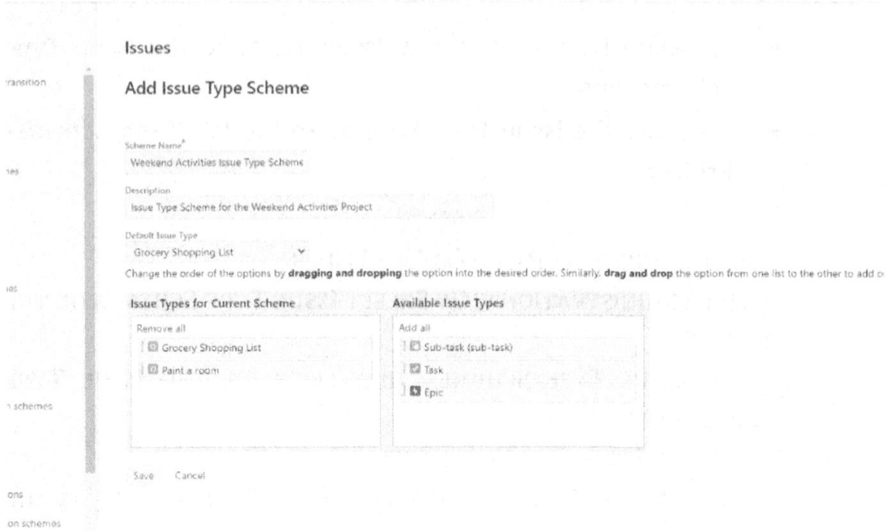

You will be brought back to the **Issue type schemes** view. DO NOT navigate away from this view.

Now you will associate the Issue Type Scheme to your *Weekend Activities* project.

6. IN THE **ISSUE TYPE SCHEMES** VIEW SCROLL DOWN TO FIND YOUR NEWLY CREATED WEEKEND ACTIVITIES ISSUE TYPE SCHEME

Notice there are **No projects** associated with this Issue Type Scheme

7. CLICK THE **ASSOCIATE** LINK IN THE ACTIONS COLUMN FOR THE WEEKEND ACTIVITIES ISSUE TYPE SCHEME
8. IN THE **ASSOCIATE ISSUE TYPE SCHEME** VIEW: GO TO THE **PROJECTS** DROP DOWN LIST AND SELECT THE *WEEKEND ACTIVITIES* PROJECT YOU WISH TO ASSOCIATE WITH THE SCHEME
9. CLICK THE **ASSOCIATE** BUTTON:

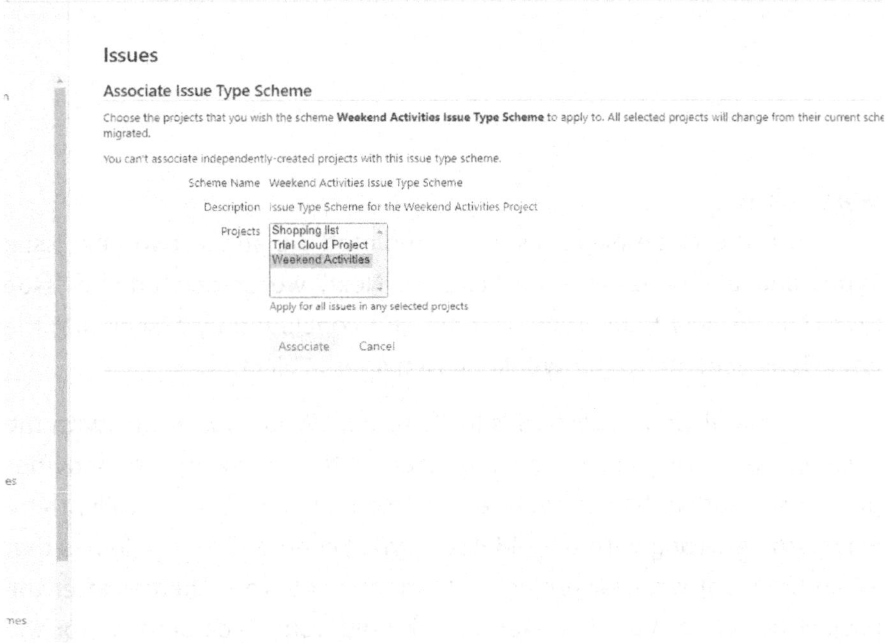

You may be asked to go through an Issue Type Migration. In that case simply follow the three or four steps to complete the Association.

10. Back on the **Issue Type schemes** view scroll down to make sure that the *Weekend Activities Issue Type Scheme* is now associated with the *Weekend Activities* project:

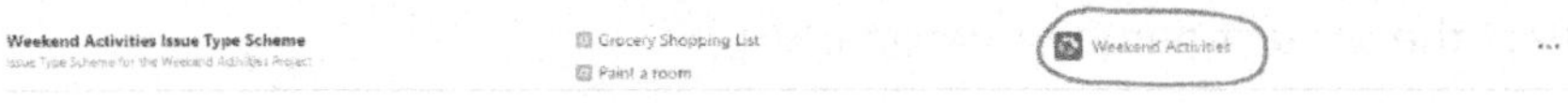

11. Select Navigation Bar > **Projects > Weekend Activities > Project settings > Issue Types**, and there you will also see the Weekend Activities List Issue Type Scheme:

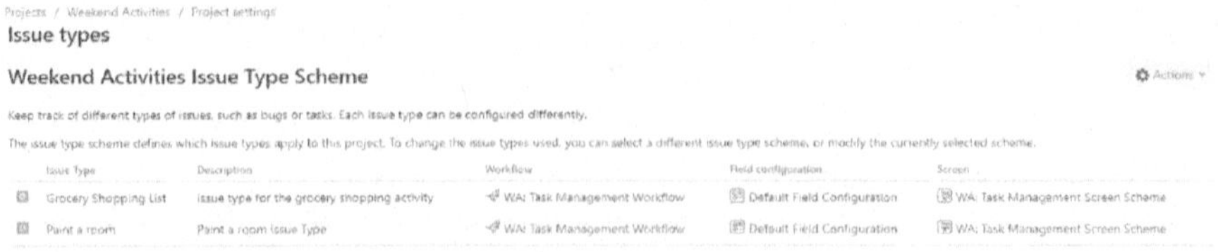

WHAT WE DID

In the three exercises just completed we added two new Issue Types and a new Issue Type Scheme. Next, we associated the Issue types to the new Issue Type Scheme and concluded by associating the Issue Type Scheme to the Weekend Activities project.

One obvious question is likely to be, "What was wrong with the existing Issue Type Scheme associated with the Weekend Activities project so that we had to replace it with a new one?" Technically, there was nothing wrong with the old Issue Type Scheme. The problem is that when Jira creates a new project, it tends to name the schemes after the project template type. For example, the old Issue Type Scheme for the Weekend Activities project was named: "WA: Task Management Issue Type Scheme". If you created 14 projects based on the Task Management project template you would end up with 14 Issue Type Schemes with basically the same name: "*XX*: Task Management Issue Type Scheme". The only difference would be the Project Key appended to the start of the Scheme name. That tends to get very confusing. That's why I like wherever possible to change the scheme names to reflect the project name more clearly.

DELETING AN ISSUE TYPE SCHEME

In the Issue Type Scheme exercise above we associated the Weekend Activities Issue Type Scheme to the Weekend Activities project. But that left us with the old scheme (WA: Task Management Issue Type Scheme) as an orphan. It is no longer is associated with a project. It is just sitting there like bad fish. Let's get rid of it before it starts to stink.

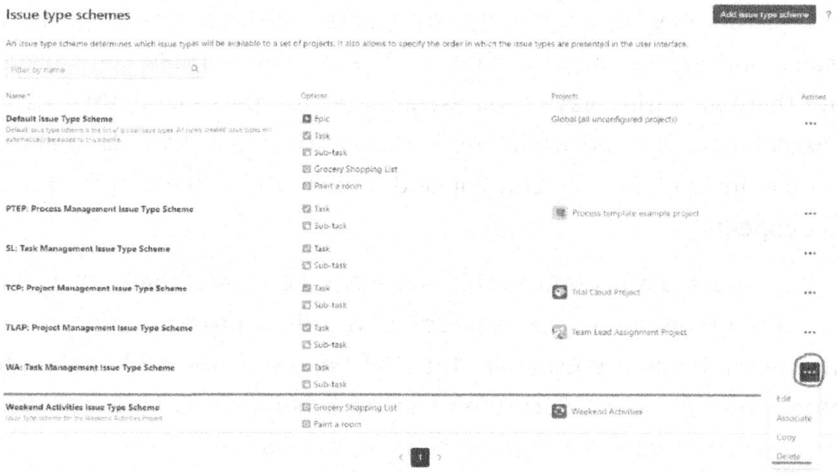

EXERCISE: DELETE AN ISSUE TYPE SCHEME

1. SELECT NAVIGATION BAR >  > **ISSUES**
2. IN THE ADMINISTRATION VIEW SELECT **ISSUE TYPE SCHEMES** ON THE SIDEBAR
3. FIND THE *WA: TASK MANAGEMENT ISSUE TYPE SCHEME*, AND CLICK ON THE **ACTIONS** (...) MENU IN THE FAR RIGHT COLUMN
4. IN THE ACTIONS MENU CLICK ON **DELETE**
5. IN THE DELETE SCREEN ENSURE YOU HAVE THE *WA: TASK MANAGEMENT ISSUE TYPE SCHEME*, AND CLICK **DELETE.**

WHAT WE DID

We deleted the WA: Task Management Issue Type Scheme. You might ask, what would have happened if there had been any Issues associated with that now deleted scheme. The answer is that there would not have been any Issues associated with the scheme. When you associated the Weekend Activities Issue Type Scheme to the Weekend Activities project, part of that action would have been to migrate any Issues from the old scheme to the new one.

Re-name a Scheme

You may be wondering why create a new scheme, migrate the Issues, and delete the old scheme? That sounds terribly complicated. Isn't there an easier way? The answer is yes, simply rename the existing scheme. That is done using the same Action menu used to delete a scheme. Instead, use the Edit link and rename the Scheme in the popup that appears.

There is a caution to this approach. Be careful that the scheme you are renaming is not shared with other projects. This is not uncommon if you are using Jira that has been with the organization for more than five years. Back then sharing schemes was fairly common, and you may have some of them hanging around.

Sub-tasks

Issue Types also allows you to create unique **Sub-task Issue Types**. If your Issue is complicated, you can sub-divide the Issue into a number of sub-tasks. These sub-tasks will be connected with the main, parent, Issue.

One of the major benefits of sub-tasks is that you can assign different default Users, workflows, screens/fields, etc. to each of the sub-tasks. This is very helpful if your work process has numerous steps and involves multiple Users.

Any Standard (i.e. not a Sub-task) Issue Type can have Sub-tasks.

Sub-tasks cannot have their own sub-tasks. But you can convert (promote) a Sub-task to an Issue. This newly promoted task can then create its own sub-tasks.

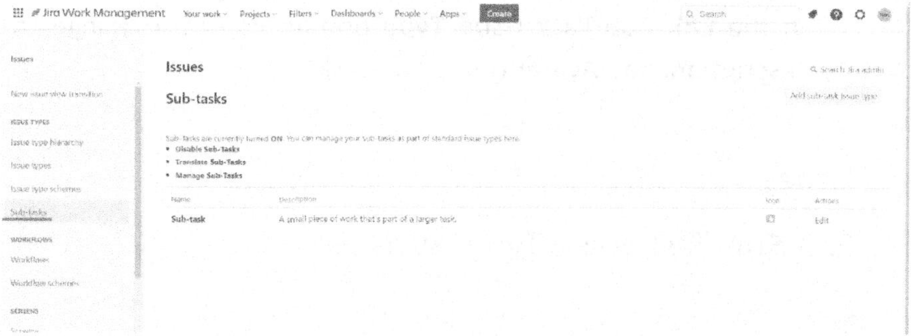

The Sub-tasks screen has four columns: **Name Description, Icon,** and **Actions**.

Name

Here is a list of your Sub-task types, listed in the order they were created.

You can add a new Sub-task by clicking the **Add sub-task issue type** button and entering a **Sub-task Name** and **Description**.

Description

As the name of this column states, here you will find the purpose of the Sub-task. I would recommend you be very specific when entering the reason for any newly created Sub-task. Often a Sub-task is created for very narrow business needs, and it is often easy to forget just why exactly it was created.

Icon

This column shows the Icon associated with the Sub-task. By now you know I am a big fan of using Icons to easily identify related elements in a project. I recommend you do the same with Sub-tasks.

Actions

In the Actions column you can Edit or Delete a Sub-task.

Edit

In the **Edit Sub-Task Issue Type** pop-up you may change the **Name, Description**, and **Avatar** of the Sub-task:

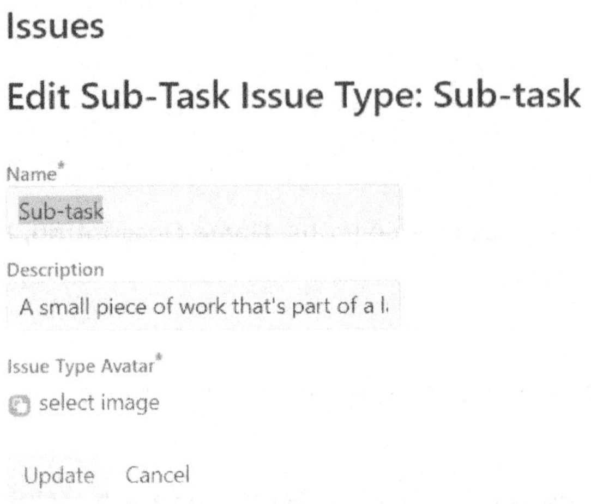

Delete

You may **Delete** any Sub-task Issue Types **not currently associated** with an Issue. If the sub-task is associated with an Issue, you must first delete the active Issue before you can delete the Sub-task Issue Type. The easiest way to do this is to open the specific Issue and delete the Issue in the **More** menu (the three dots in the upper right corner):

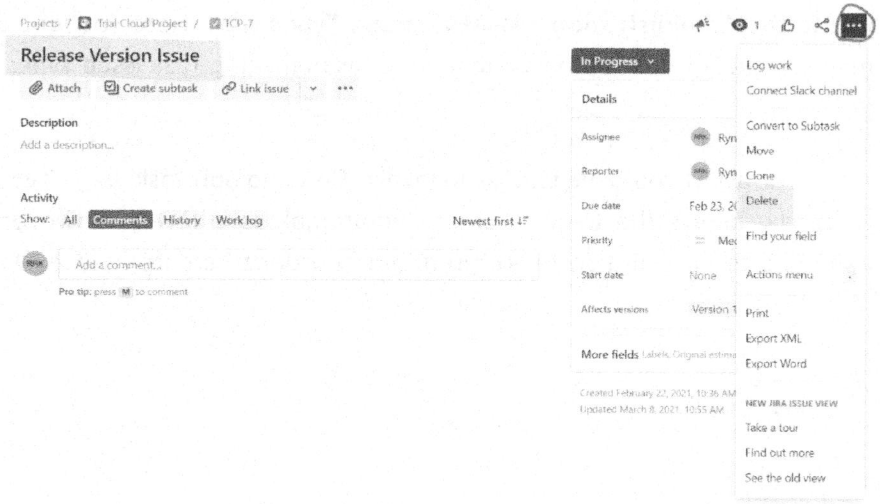

Other Sub-task functions

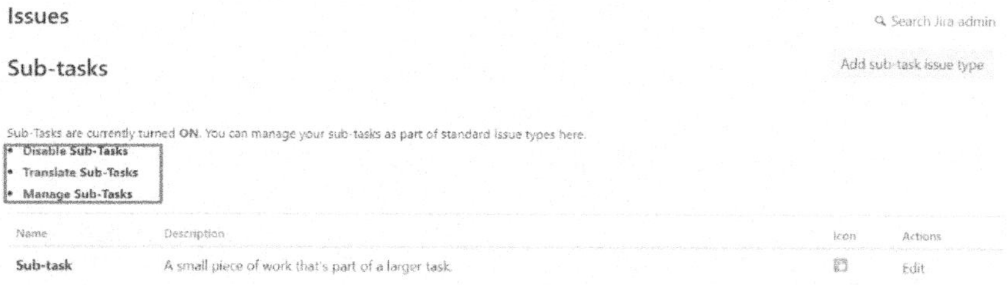

If you wish, you can also **Disable all** Sub-tasks. This function might be used to avoid confusion as it is sometimes difficult for beginners to differentiate between Tasks and Sub-tasks.

One of the great things I like about Jira is its **Translation** ability. Currently there are 24 languages/dialects supported, with more under development. We covered translation earlier; so, let's move on.

You can also **Manage Sub-tasks.** Clicking on this link will bring you to the **Administration > Issues > Issue Types** view. Here you would manage the Sub-task in the same manner as managing Task Issue Types.

ISSUE TYPE HIERARCHY

In JWM you have two Issue levels: Task and Sub-task. Issue Type Hierarchy allows the User to create additional Issue levels. However, you need to have Jira Software premium in order to create new levels.

Chapter 6 – Workflows

To avoid confusion, in this book the term "Site-admin" includes "Org-admin, Site-admin, and Jira-admin" unless specifically noted otherwise.

Chapter Objective

In this chapter you will:

- **develop a good understanding of Workflows, Workflow schemes, and their interactions with other elements**
- **create a workflow**
- **create a workflow scheme**
- **associate your workflow with an Issue Type and a workflow scheme**

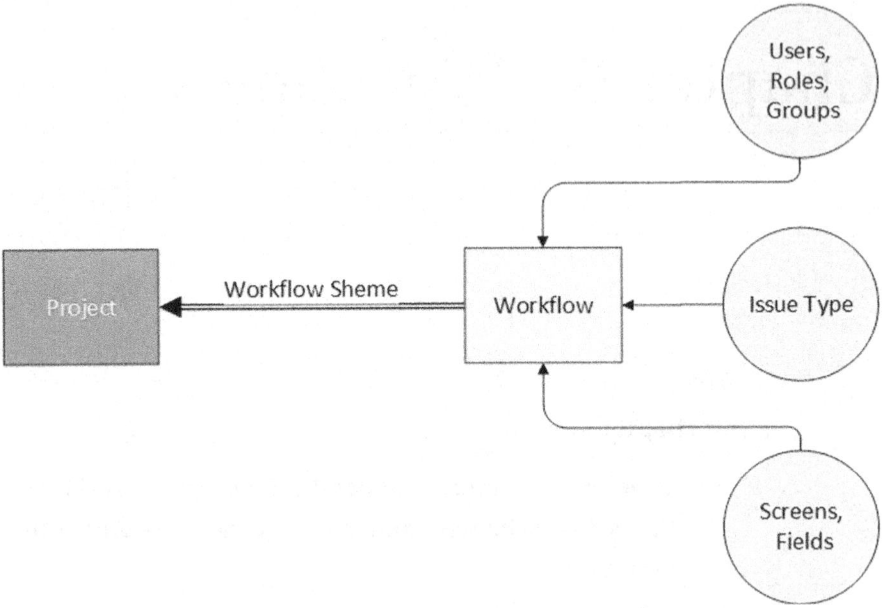

NOTE: Creating and editing workflows is NOT a basic topic. I recommend working with system provided workflows until you are comfortable with the topic. Once you have a basic understanding, I recommend you buy my book "Jira Core Workflows" (available at Amazon). This highly regarded book contains advanced level lessons about:

- creating and editing workflows
- working with and creating workflow conditions, validators, and post-functions
- automating Jira workflow functions and operations
- working with workflow events and creating notifications.

UNDERSTANDING WORKFLOWS

To me, Jira workflows are probably the best reason to purchase Jira Work Management. Quite simply, Jira workflows allow you to develop and manage work processes without involving your I.T. department. A well-trained Jira business user can easily design and implement a time saving workflow that can improve work efficiencies and collaboration.

Atlassian Documentation states that "A Jira workflow is the set of *statuses* and *transitions* that an Issue goes through during its lifecycle. *Workflows typically represent business processes.*"

At this point it is essential to understand the difference between **Process** and **Procedure**. Many people confuse the two definitions because they often overlap each other. A Process is a set of actions or steps with the purpose of accomplishing a goal. A Procedure is a step that also includes the instructions for completing that step..

Let's take the example of making a turkey dinner. We have an Issue named 'make a turkey dinner'. The workflow associated with that Issue *describes the steps involved* in making the turkey dinner: prepare the turkey, cook the turkey, carve the turkey, and plate the turkey. You can see that none of these workflow steps describes *how* to do each step. For example, it doesn't tell you what temperature to set the oven or how long it should take to preheat the oven, it doesn't tell you how long the turkey should sit in the oven, or how long it should rest afterwards.

So, please remember, **in Jira a workflow includes the steps necessary to complete an Issue, it doesn't describe *how* to do those steps**. Keeping this in mind avoids a lot of confusion later.

Status

I do like Jira's definition of a Workflow, *"Jira workflow is a set of **statuses** and **transitions** that an issue goes through during its lifecycle."* A **status** is the state, condition, or situation at a particular time in the process. A common Jira workflow has three statuses: **Open** (not yet started), **In Progress,** and **Done**.

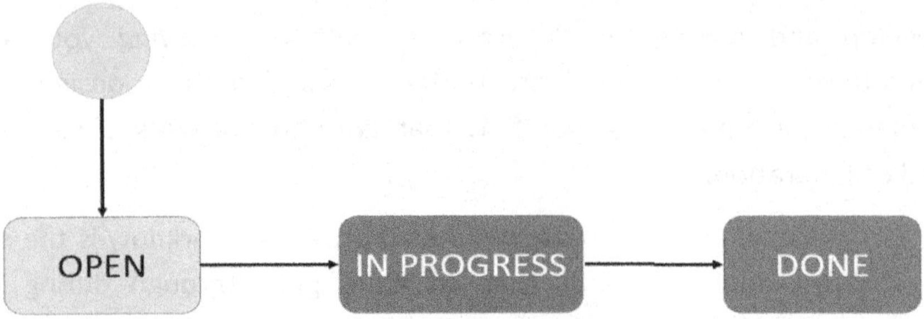

An issue **transitions** (the arrows in the diagram above) from one status to another. They appear when the Assignee clicks on the next status in the Issue's status drop down list:

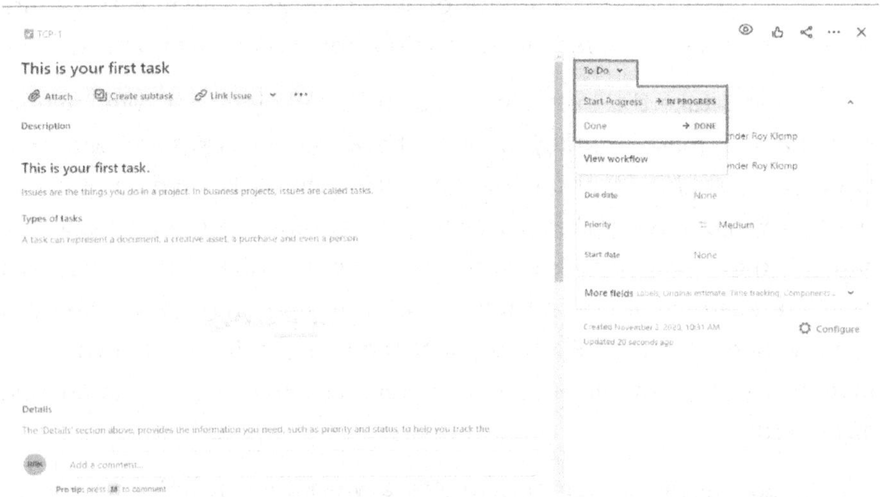

To avoid confusion between statuses and transitions, think of **a status as your current position in a workflow process, and a transition as the action that moves you to a new status.**

When an Assignee wants to transition to a new status, they do so by clicking on the status drop down menu in the Issue Details view and selecting from the available status options. What is critical to understand is that not all the statuses in a workflow may appear in the drop-down list. That is because you will only see the statuses you are allowed to transition to from your current status. For example, let's say you are working with a workflow that has four statuses in the following order: Open > In Progress > Approved > Done. If you are in the Open status and click the Status drop-down list, you are likely to see only "In Progress". That's because In Progress is the only status available to you now. You cannot go directly from Open to Approved, because there is nothing to Approve, you have not yet started work on the Issue.

Assignees typically have the permission to change a workflow status for the part of the workflow with which they are working. A business analyst may have the authority to change an Issue's status from **Open** to **In Progress** and change In **Progress** to **Resolved**. However, they may not have the authority to change **Resolved** to **Closed**, as only the Project Lead may have the authority to do so (in this example).

Remember also, the Status buttons a User sees in the Issue Details View will vary depending on the workflow associated with the Issue Type, where the User is in the workflow, and the permissions the User has.

Jira has many statuses, and these statuses are classified in one of three categories: Open (usually shown as grey in Workflow diagrams), In Progress (usually shown as blue), or Done (usually shown as green).

Below is a table showing the current statuses available in Jira including those specific to Jira Service Management (JSM) and Jira Software (JS):

Status	Status Category	Jira Application
Open	To Do	JWM
To Do	To Do	JWM
Opportunity	To Do	JWM
In Progress	In Progress	JWM

In Review	In Progress	JWM
Under Review	In Progress	JWM
Draft	In Progress	JWM
Interviewing	In Progress	JWM
Interviewing Debrief	In Progress	JWM
Screening	In Progress	JWM
Offer Discussions	In Progress	JWM
Applications	In Progress	JWM
Second Review	In Progress	JWM
Contacted	In Progress	JWM
Opportunity	In Progress	JWM
In Negotiation	In Progress	JWM
Requested	In Progress	JWM
Done	Done	JWM
Approved	Done	JWM
Cancelled	Done	JWM
Rejected	Done	JWM
Published	Done	JWM
Accepted	Done	JWM
Lost	Done	JWM
Won	Done	JWM
Purchased	Done	JWM
Resolved	Done	JWM
Reopened	Any status category	JWM
Building	In Progress	JS
Build broken	In Progress	JS
Backlog	In Progress	JS
Selected for Development	In Progress	JS
Closed	Done	JS
Waiting for Support	In Progress	JSM
Waiting for Customer	In Progress	JSM
Pending	In Progress	JSM
Escalated	In Progress	JSM
Waiting for Approval	In Progress	JSM
Awaiting CAB approval	In Progress	JSM
Planning	In Progress	JSM

Awaiting Implementation	In Progress	JSM
Implementing	In Progress	JSM
Peer review / change manager approval	In Progress	JSM
Work in Progress	In Progress	JSM
Under Investigation	In Progress	JSM
Declined	Done	JSM
Canceled	Done	JSM
Completed	Done	JSM

You may read or hear about a workflow **Step**. Very simply, a status along with **all** its **outgoing** transitions is called a **Step**. Steps were more important in earlier versions of Jira, when building a workflow could only be done using text and defining a Step name was required. With Jira's 'new', easier to use, graphical design the Step is automatically created in the background; so, you don't need to worry about it.

Transitions

While Jira Statuses are big and bold, they really don't do much. They simply tell you, and others, where you are in the Workflow process. All the power and activities in a Jira Workflow take place within the Transitions. When an Assignee selects a new status in the status drop-down list, the Assignee is really saying is "I want to go (transition) to this new status"

When a transition is activated, several things happen. First, Jira checks to see if the Assignee has the permission to execute the transition. Jira may also check to see if the transition is valid. For example, there may be a rule that a specific field must have data before transitioning to the new status. Finally, there may be post-transition functions. For example, an automatic email may be sent to a specific User stating that the Issue has transitioned to the new status and that she is now the Assignee. So, as you can see, workflow transitions are incredibly powerful.

Users usually do specific tasks during a transition. Therefore, it should be no surprise that transitions can have their own screens, called **Transition Views**. For example, if a User is required to approve an Issue, the **Approval Transition View** might contain two fields: an Approved/Not Approved checkbox field, and a Description Field meant for the User to enter details as to why the Issue was not approved. Jira has a few standard Transition Screens, but typically most are built by administrators to meet the specific requirements of the organization.

As you know by now, a new Issue can be created from a number of places in the program; and when you do so, a **Create Issue Screen** appears where you select the project name, issue type, etc. One thing not well understood or documented is that while this screen is technically an Issue Type 'Create' Screen it is also the first **Transition** in the workflow associated with your issue type. In the Jira workflow diagram notice the line (the transition) that connects the grey circle (workflow start) and Open (the first status). If you were to click on that line it would read "Create" as the name of the transition, which includes the Create Issue Screen.

WORKFLOWS

You can also create your own statuses and transitions. This is where the incredible power of Jira workflows comes into play.

I recommend that when you first start using Jira Work Management, find a default workflow that is 'good enough' to work with and practice with it until you are ready to move to a customized workflow.

> CAUTION: When practicing, make sure the first thing you do is rename the workflow to something unique such as "TEST

Workflow". I know of at least one company where an Administrator changed the workflow for his project, not fully realizing that the change affected every project in the organization using the same workflow. It was a nightmare to straighten out. I always recommend a best practice of **giving project specific workflow and scheme names to each project** to avoid these sorts of problems.

Workflows are found in the Administration Cog > Issues' sidebar:

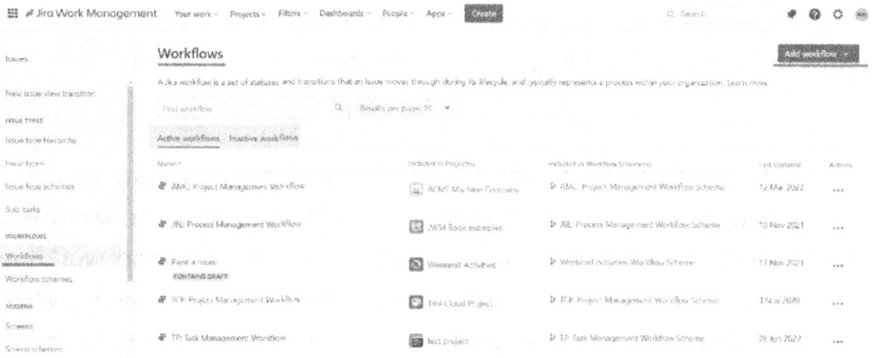

You can create a workflow by clicking the **Add workflow** link in the upper right corner. Here you can either create a new workflow or import one from the Atlassian marketplace (usually at a cost).

The workflows in the Workflow's view are sorted into two segments: Active workflows and Inactive workflows. A workflow is active if it assigned to a Jira project.

The Workflow view contains five columns: Name, Included in Project(s), Included in Workflow Scheme(s), Last Updated, and Actions.

Names

Workflow names are listed in alphabetical order. Workflow names are autogenerated when the project is created and will contain the project's key and the workflow associated with the project type (e.g. Project Management Workflow). Needless to say, this can get quite confusing. If you are going to edit the workflow, I recommend changing the workflow name to something more easily understandable.

Included in project(s)

This column lists the projects using that particular workflow. This is extremely handy if you have a workflow in more than one project (not recommended). If you do have a workflow in multiple projects, then be aware that any change you make to the workflow for one project will affect all other projects using that same workflow.

Included in Workflow Scheme(s)

A workflow can be assigned to one or more workflow schemes. A workflow must be associated with a workflow scheme to work in a project. Remember that while a project can have only one workflow scheme, you can associate multiple workflows to that scheme. Why? Because a project can have more than one Issue Types each requiring its own unique workflow.

Last Updated

This column shows the last time the workflow was edited.

Actions

In the Actions column you can View, Edit, Copy, and Delete your workflow.

View and Edit

The Workflow View and Edit screens are identical with the two exceptions shown in the highlighted areas in the image below:

Copy

When creating a new workflow, it is often easier to copy an existing workflow and rename it. Click the Copy link, and Jira will automatically name the new workflow as a copy of the original.

Delete

You can only delete a workflow if it is not associated with any workflow schemes:

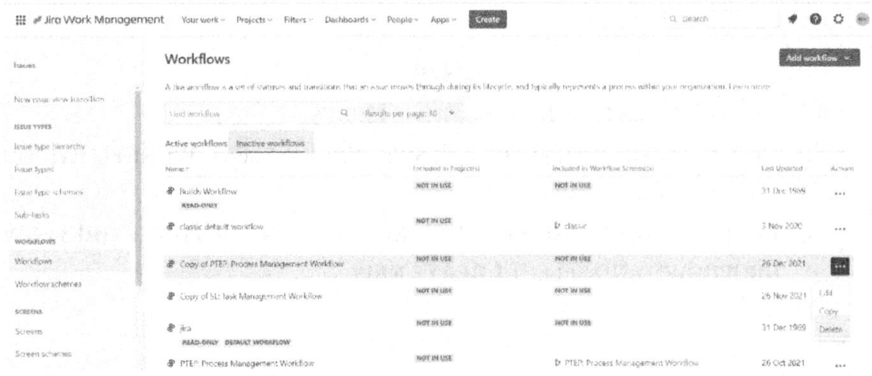

The Delete function can only be found in the Actions column in the "Inactive workflows" tab.

To make a workflow inactive you must remove the workflow from the projects and workflow schemes it is associated with. Once that is done, the workflow automatically moves from the **Active workflows** tab to the **Inactive workflows** tab. In addition, Any Issue Types using that workflow will need a replacement workflow.

You cannot delete the default system workflow.

ADD A WORKFLOW

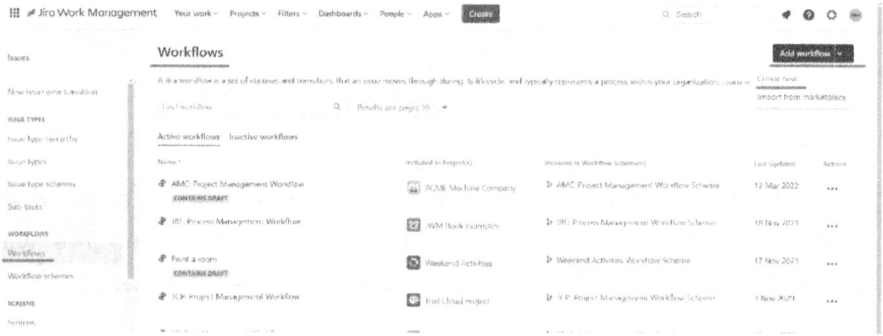

As noted earlier, you create a workflow by clicking the Add workflow link in the Issues > Workflows view. Let's create a simple workflow for our Weekend Activities project. This workflow will be used for a painting job in one of the rooms in your home.

EXERCISE: CREATE A WORKFLOW

1. GO TO NAVIGATION BAR >  > **ISSUES**
2. IN THE ADMINISTRATION > ISSUES VIEW SELECT **WORKFLOWS** ON THE SIDEBAR
3. IN THE ISSUES > WORKFLOWS VIEW CLICK ON THE **ADD WORKFLOW** DROPDOWN AND SELECT **CREATE NEW**

4. In the **Add workflow** view enter *Paint a Room* in the **Name** field, and *Workflow for painting a room* in the **Description** field
5. Click **Add**

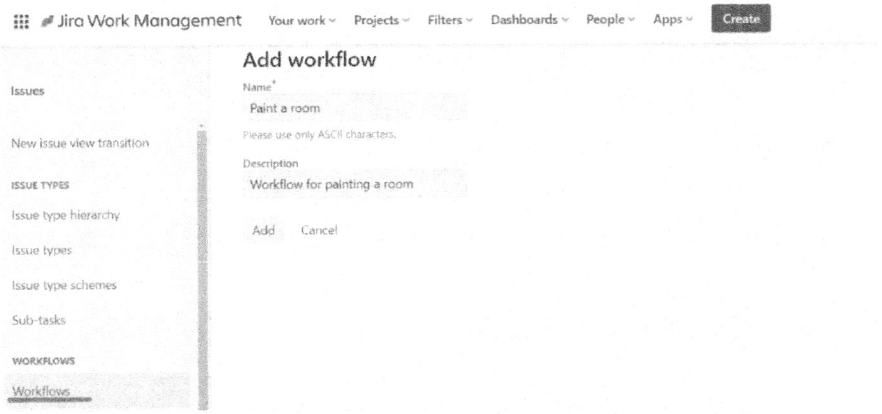

6. In the newly created Paint a room workflow designer view, make sure the **Diagram** view is selected:

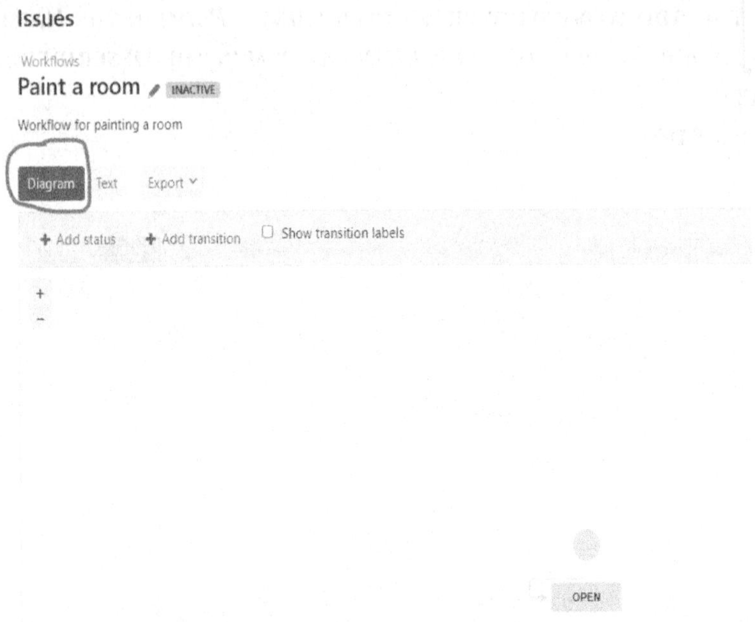

7. To give us some work space, drag the Create Issue circle and the Open status to the upper left corner.

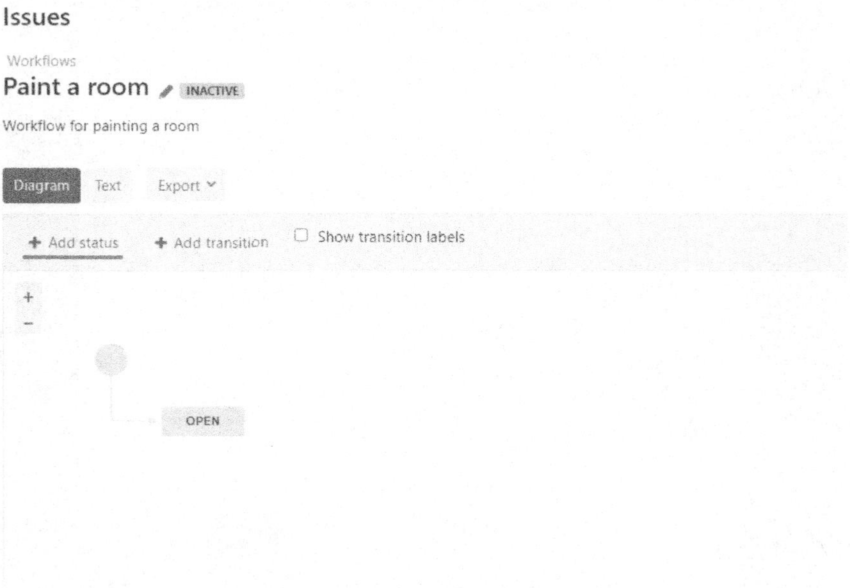

8. Click on the **+ Add status** link
9. In the **Add status** popup enter *Buy supplies* in the drop-down list, and hit **Enter**
10. Click on **Add**
11. In the **Create New Status** popup ensure *Buy paint supplies* is in the **Name** box
12. Skip over the Description box
13. Select **In Progress** in the Category drop-down list
14. Leave the "Allow all statuses to transition to this...." unchecked
15. Click **Create**:

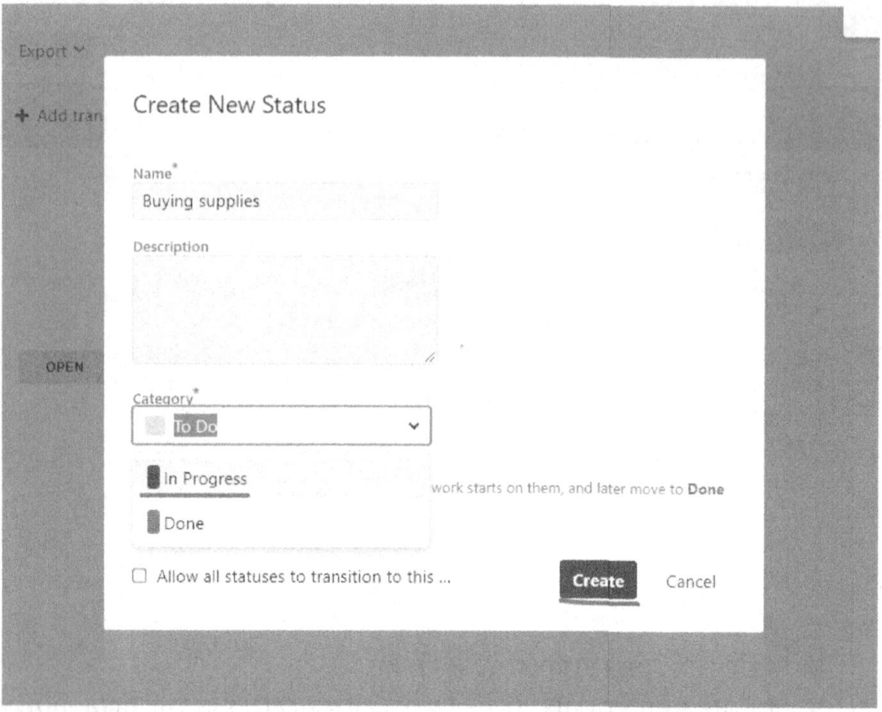

16. Back in the Paint a room workflow design view you should see your newly created status:

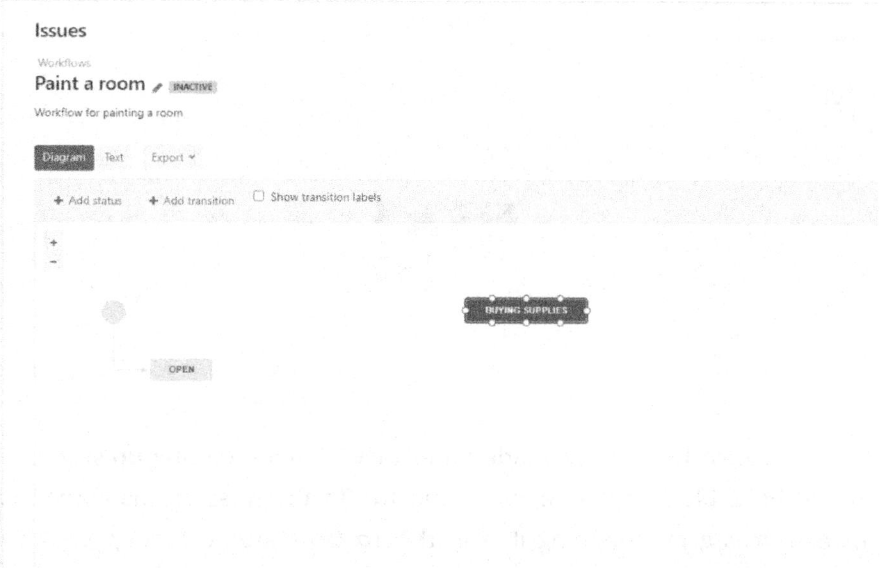

17. Repeat steps 8-15 for the following new statuses:
    i. Prepping room
    ii. Painting room
    iii. Cleaning up

You should see something like the image below. Probably the new statuses will be overlapping. Simply drag them into a logical order: Buying supplies, Prepping room, Painting room, and Cleaning up.

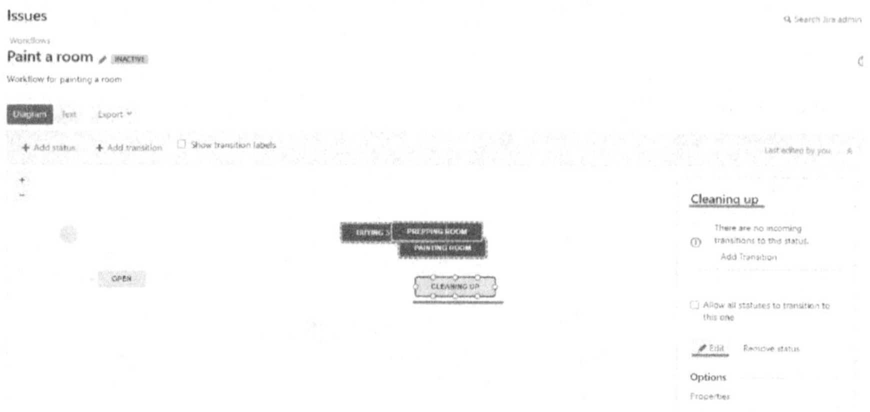

Notice that I have made an error with my **Cleaning up** status. It should be a blue colour representing the **In Progress** status category. Instead, it is grey, meaning it is in the **To Do** status category. Let's fix that.

18. CLICK ON THE **CLEANING UP** STATUS
19. THE CLEAN UP **STATUS PROPERTIES BOX** WILL APPEAR ON THE RIGHT-HAND PART OF THE SCREEN. ENSURE IT SAYS "CLEANING UP" AT THE TOP AND THEN CLICK THE **EDIT** BUTTON
20. IN THE EDIT STATUS POPUP SELECT IN PROGRESS IN THE **CATEGORY** DROPDOWN:

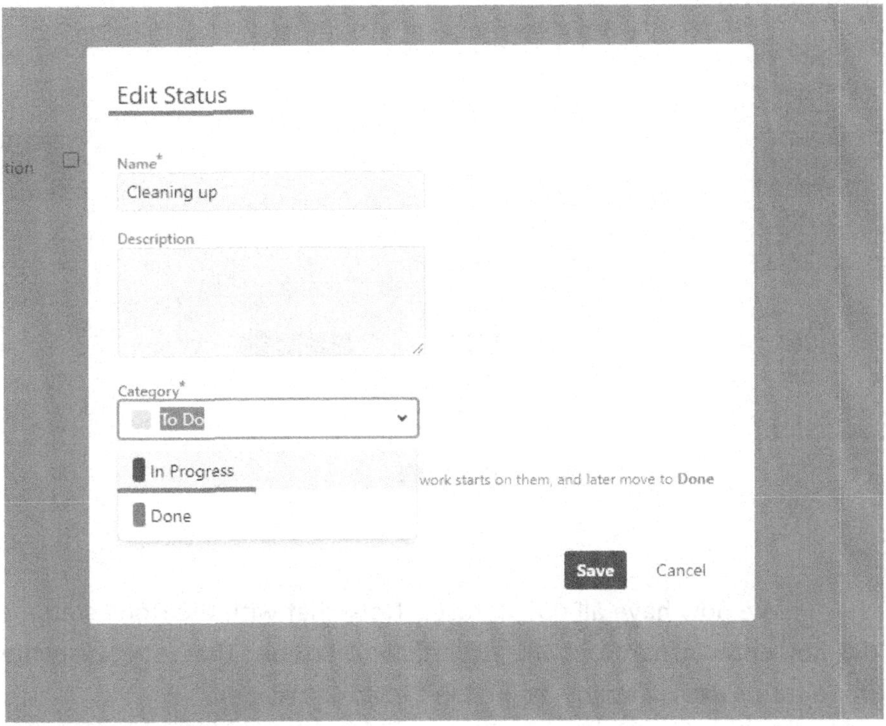

21. CLICK **SAVE**
22. BACK IN THE PAINT A ROOM WORKFLOW DESIGNER VIEW CLICK ON **+ ADD STATUS**
23. IN THE DROP-DOWN LIST SELECT DONE AND CLICK ADD:

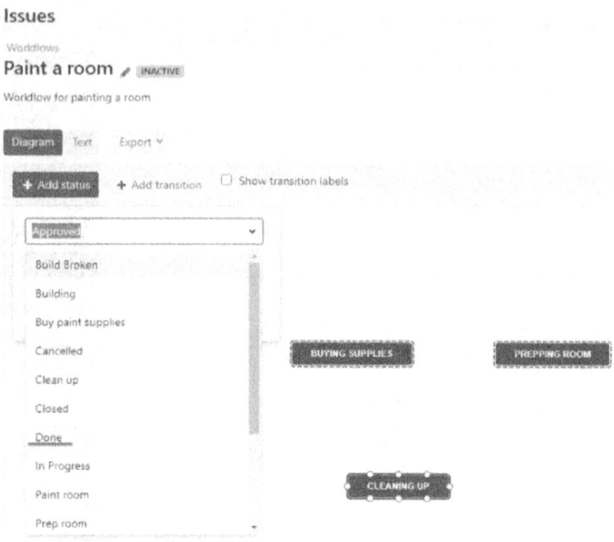

We now have all our statuses. Note that with the Done status, I did not enter a name in the drop-down list box. That's because the Done status exists already, and I don't need to create it.

While our statuses are all in the designer view, and dragged into order, they need to be connected by transition lines. That's our next step in this exercise.

24. In the "Paint a room" Workflow designer view click on **+ Add transition**
25. In the Add transition popup ensure that the **New Transition** tab is selected
26. In the **From status** drop box select *Open*
27. In the **To status** drop box select *Buying supplies*
28. In the Name text box enter Buy supplies
29. Click on **Add**

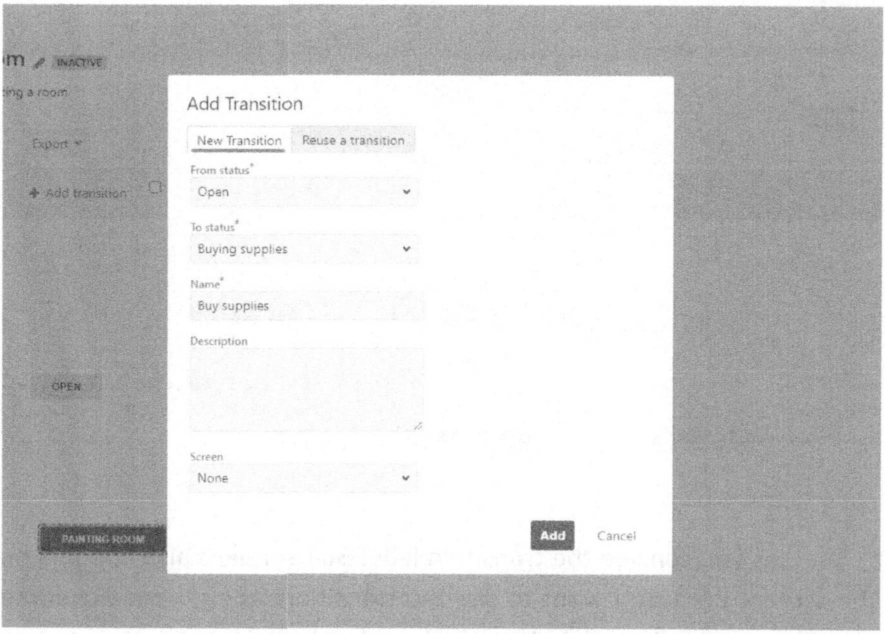

While it is difficult to see, there is now a line connecting the **Open** and **Buying supplies** statuses. In addition, there is an arrow pointing into Buying supplies which indicates the direction of the transition (**from** “Open” **to** “Buying supplies”):

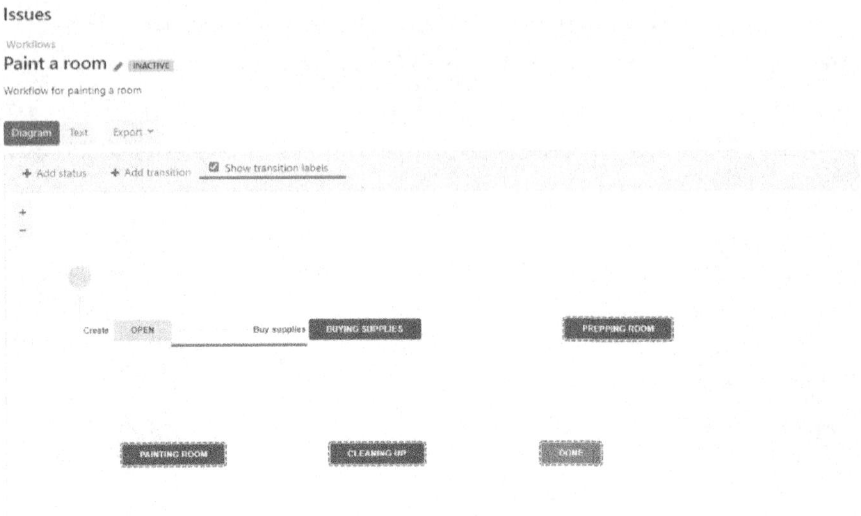

As you can see the transition label **Buy supplies** also appears on the screen. Because I want to see the transition labels, I have checked the **Show transition labels** checkbox located next to the **+ Add transition** link.

30. USING THE TABLE BELOW, CREATE THE ADDITIONAL TRANSITIONS:

From status	To status	Transition name
Buying supplies	Prepping room	Prep room
Prepping room	Painting room	Paint room
Painting room	Cleaning up	Clean up
Cleaning up	Done	Close Issue

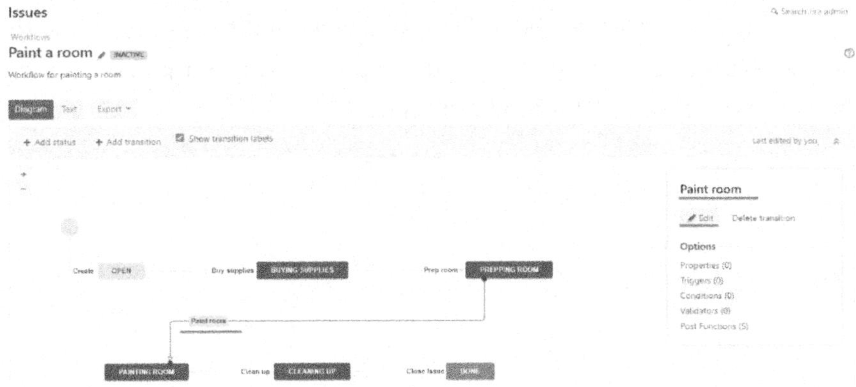

The image above shows the completed workflow containing our statuses and transitions. If you make an error with a transition, simply click on the transition name. The Transition properties panel will appear on the right part of the screen. Confirm that you have the correct transition, click Edit, and make your corrections in the popup that appears.

Naming conventions

When adding new statuses and transitions you should make sure to be consistent with your naming format. You probably noticed that I use verbs in both the status and transition names. However, I use "situational" verbs in statuses: buying, prepping, painting, cleaning. And I use "command" verbs in the transitions: buy, prep, paint, clean. That way I am consistent in my naming, and it makes it easier for my Users to understand. You do not have to use my naming convention, but you need to use a naming standard that is consistent.

WORKFLOW SCHEMES

After you create a Workflow, you will need to associate it with a specific Project and a specific Issue Type for the workflow to work. That's the purpose of Workflow Schemes.

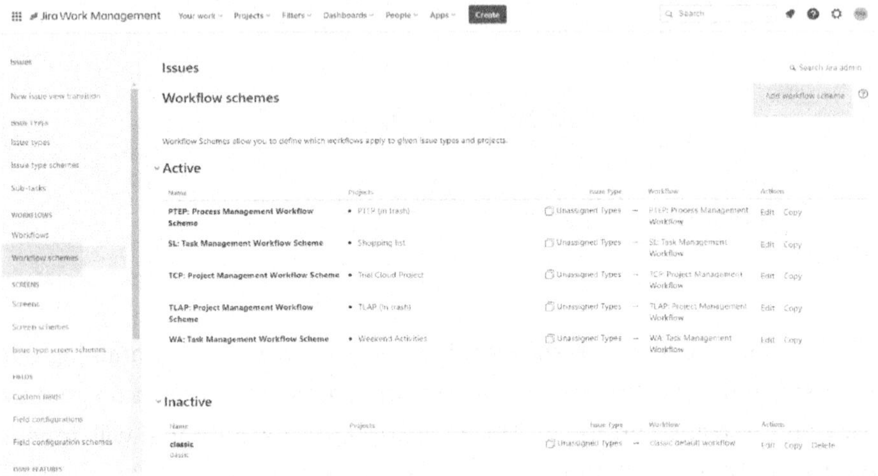

Adding a workflow scheme is as simple as clicking on the **Add Workflow Scheme** button at the top right corner of the Workflow Schemes view and then entering a Workflow Scheme **Name** and **Description**.

The **Workflow schemes** view contains five columns: **Name, Projects, Issue Type, Workflow,** and **Actions.**

NAME

Here is a list of your Workflow Schemes. They are sorted into two categories: **Active** and **Inactive**. A Workflow Scheme is Active if it is associated with a Project. Workflow Scheme names are listed alphabetically within each category.

When you open the Workflow Schemes' view you first see Active workflow schemes:

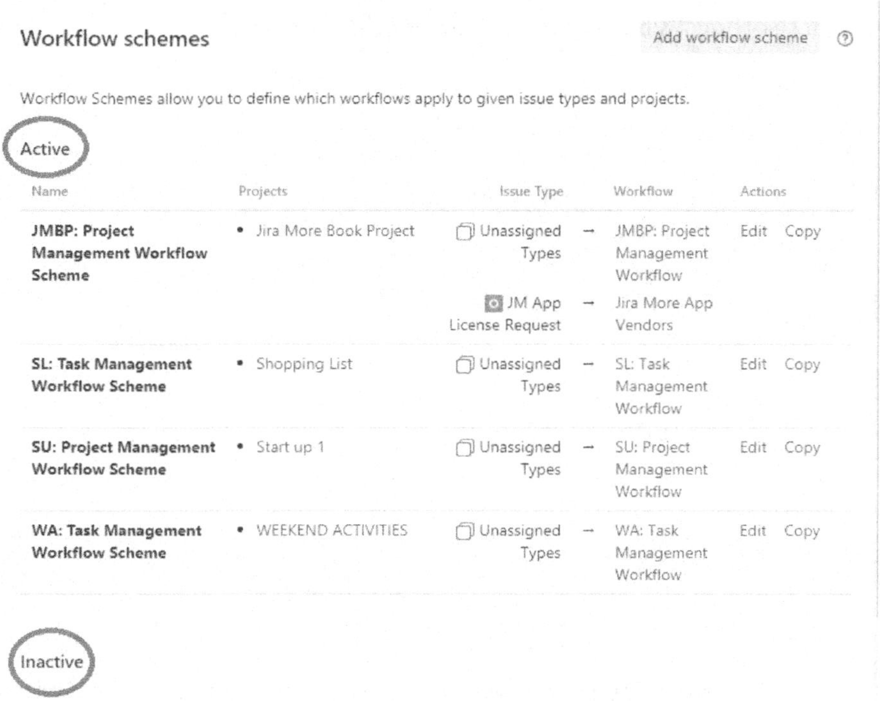

PROJECTS

In this column the projects associated with your Workflow schemes are displayed. You can have only one Workflow Scheme associated with a Project. However, the reverse is not true: you can have multiple projects associated with a workflow scheme. This allows you to reuse existing schemes; so, you don't need to recreate them in new projects. Just remember, if you have two or more projects sharing a workflow scheme, then any time you make a change to the shared scheme in one project you will affect all the other projects sharing that scheme.

NOTE: To switch a Project's Workflow scheme, click on the **Back to Project** button on the upper right corner, or go to the **Project Settings view** (Navigation bar > Projects (select your project) > Project settings (at the bottom of the Project's sidebar)), find the **Summary** link in the Project Settings' sidebar and find the workflow scheme:

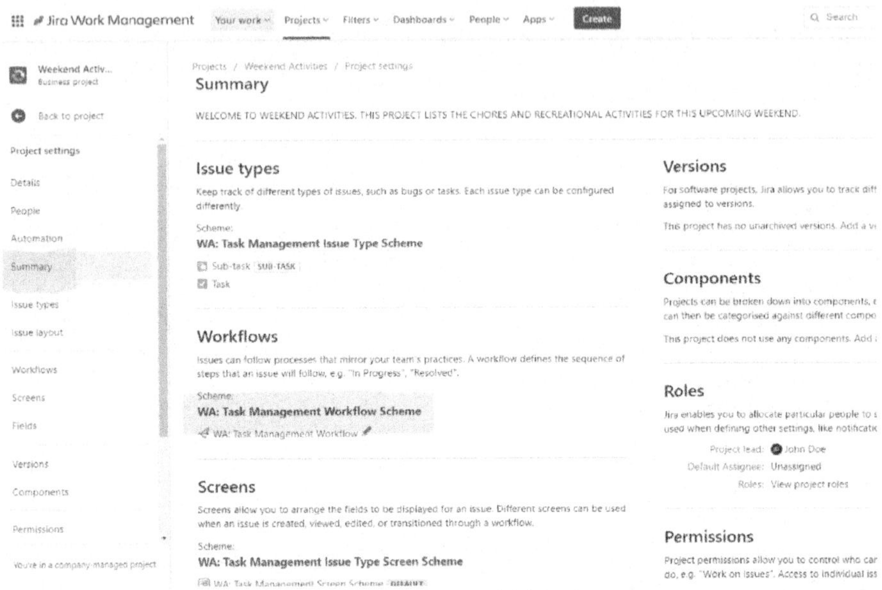

The **Workflows** view will open, where you will find the **Switch Scheme** button:

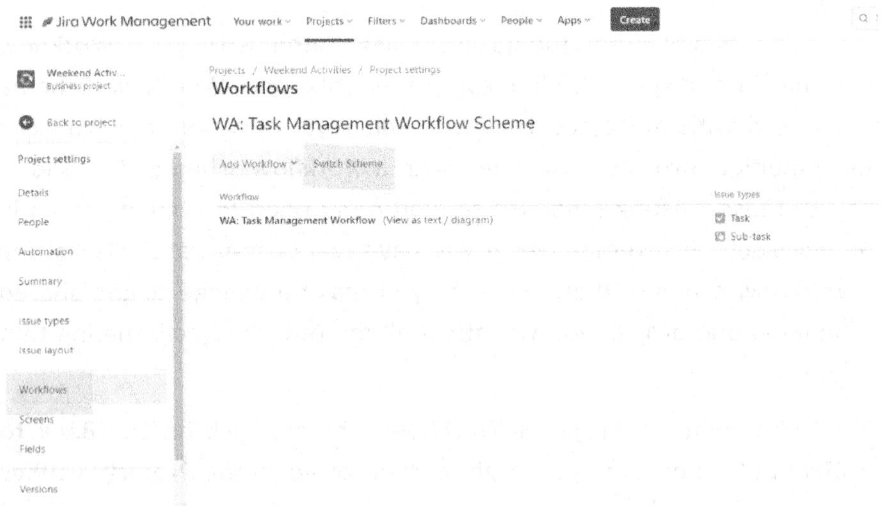

In the opened **Associate Workflow Scheme to Project** wizard select the **Workflow** scheme you want from the drop-down list and follow the wizard steps to associate the new scheme with your project.

ISSUE TYPE

Back in the Navigation bar >  > Issues > **Workflows scheme** view we next see the Issue Type column:

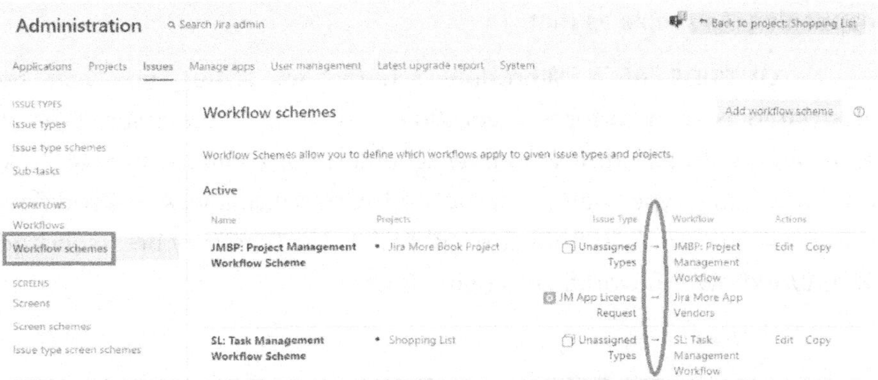

This column lists the Issue Types associated with the Workflow Scheme. As we have just seen, while you may have more than one Issue Type in a Workflow Scheme, and you can more than one Workflow in a Workflow scheme. But the catch is that each Issue Type can only be associated with a single Workflow within the Scheme. That's why you see **the arrow**. Each arrow is pointing at the only workflow it will work with in the Workflow Scheme/Project combination.

If someone in your organization did not manually associate an Issue Type with a specific workflow, then the system will regard that Issue Type as "unassigned" and will automatically associate it with the standard workflow that came with your project template.

Workflow

The Workflow column shows you the Workflow(s) associated with the Issue Type(s) in your Workflow Scheme. Please note that an **Issue Type can be associated with only one Workflow in a particular Workflow Scheme**. However, the reverse is not true. **A workflow can be associated with more than one Issue Type within a Workflow scheme.** Sounds confusing? Here is the bottom line: if an Issue Type were to be associated with more than one workflow within a project, the software wouldn't know which one to use, causing the program to have a nervous breakdown. So, Jira put in a rule preventing this from happening. As simple as that.

OUTSIDE of a Workflow scheme an Issue Type can be associated with a different workflow, but only if the Issue Type is associated with different workflow schemes. For example, in Project A, the Task Issue Type may be associated with Workflow X in Workflow scheme Alpha, while in Project B the Task Issue Type may be associated with Workflow Z in workflow scheme Beta:

Allowed:

Issue Type	Workflow	Workflow Scheme	Project
Task	Workflow X	Alpha	Project A
Sub-task	Workflow Y	Alpha	Project A
Task	Workflow Z	Beta	Project B

Not Allowed:

Issue Type	Workflow	Workflow Scheme	Project
Task	Workflow X	Alpha	Project A
Task	Workflow Z	Alpha	Project A

Actions

In our final, **Actions,** column you can **Edit, Copy,** or **Delete** a workflow.

Edit

The **Edit** link will take you to the **Workflow Scheme** view where you:

- may see the workflows associated with the scheme in more detail
- can add a new workflow to the scheme
- associate new Issue Types to a Workflow by clicking the **Assign** link.

CAUTION: It is highly recommended you NOT experiment with **Workflow Schemes** until you have a good understanding of the program.

Copy

It is often easier to copy an existing Workflow scheme and use it as a starting base for a new scheme than it is to build one from scratch. Just be aware that, unlike most of the other copy functions in Jira, a pop-up will NOT appear asking you to rename the Workflow Scheme when you click the copy link. Instead, a new copy is immediately created and placed in your list of Inactive Workflow Schemes.

Delete

You can only delete Inactive Workflow schemes. First, you must disassociate any projects from your screen, which is done through the Switch Schemes operation we discussed in the Project section earlier in this chapter.

Exercise: Rename existing Workflow scheme

In this exercise you will:

- rename the existing workflow scheme in the Weekend Activities project to a more user-friendly name

1. Go to Navigation Bar >  > **Issues**
2. In the Administration > Issues view select **workflow schemes** on the sidebar

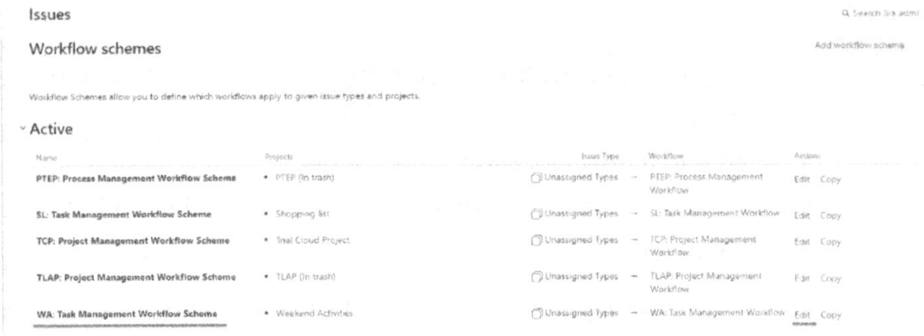

3. Find the *WA: Task Management Workflow Scheme* and click on the **Edit** link in the Actions column
4. In the Workflow scheme view click on the *WA: Task Management Workflow scheme* name:

5. In the greyed name field enter "Weekend Activities Workflow Scheme"
6. Click the **checkmark** at the right side of the name box:

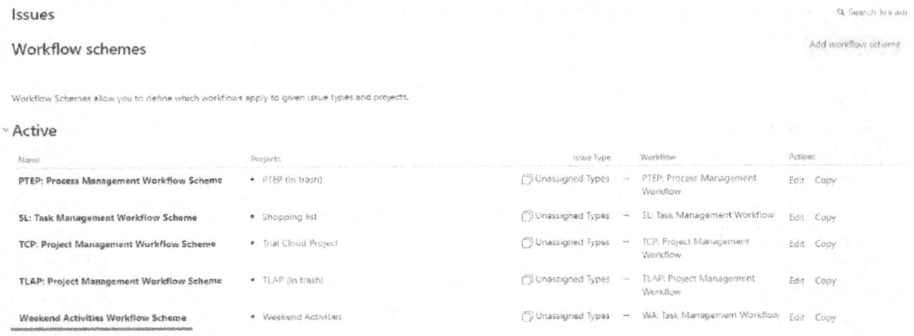

Exercise: Associate an Issue Type and Workflow to the Workflow Scheme

Next you are going to associate the "Paint a room" Issue Type you created in the previous chapter, and the "Paint a room" Workflow you created earlier in this chapter to the newly renamed Weekend Activities Workflow Scheme.

1. Go to Navigation Bar > Projects > Weekend Activities and click on **Project Settings** in the sidebar
2. In the Project Settings view click on **Workflows** in the sidebar
3. In the Workflows view click on the **Add Workflow** drop down and select **Add existing**
4. In the Add Existing Workflow popup select *Paint a room*, and then click **Next**:

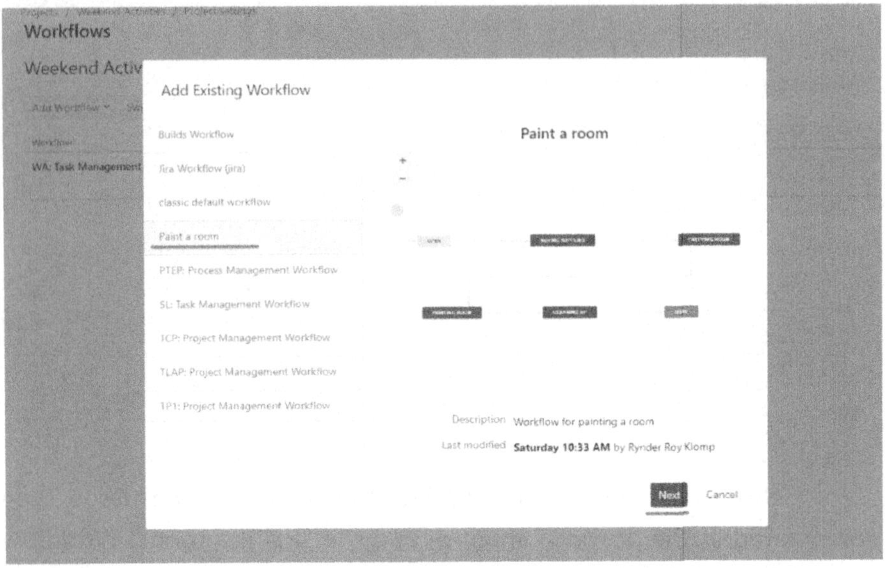

5. IN THE ASSIGN ISSUE TYPES TO "PAINT A ROOM" SELECT THE **PAINT A ROOM CHECKBOX** AND CLICK **FINISH**

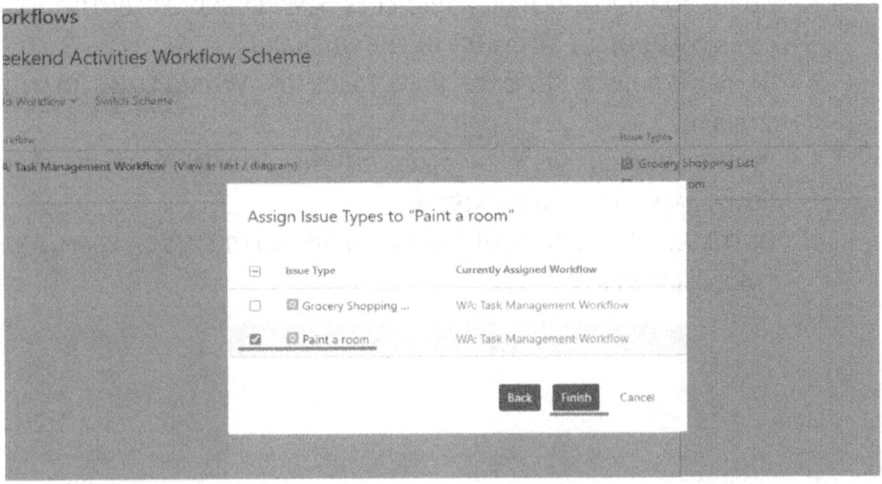

6. BACK IN THE WEEKEND ACTIVITIES WORKFLOW SCHEME VIEW CLICK ON **PUBLISH** NEAR THE TOP OF THE SCREEN:

WHAT WE DID

In this last exercise you associated the "Paint a room" Issue Type and "Paint a room" Workflow with the Weekend Activities Workflow Scheme. Since the Weekend Activities Workflow Scheme is already associated with the Weekend Activities project you can now create a "Paint a room" Issue and it will use the "Paint a room" workflow. Try it and see.

ISSUE RESOLUTION

So, you have completed your Issue and then clicked a transition button that changes your status to Done. You would logically assume that your Issue is Closed. And you would be very, very, wrong!

Clicking a transition button to change your status to Done, Cancelled, Rejected, Published, Accepted, Lost, Won, Purchased, or any other "Done" type status does nothing more than indicate to you, and others interested in your Issue, that you have completed the Issue. But, and this is a big 'but', it means nothing to Jira. The software still thinks your Issue is 'open', and it will continue to think your Issue is open until you specifically tell Jira that it is closed, and that is called "Resolving" an Issue.

When you resolve an Issue, you do two things: you formally close the Issue in the software, and you state the reason for resolving the Issue. Jira has several default resolution reasons:

- Done
- Won't Do
- Duplicate
- Cannot Reproduce
- Known Error
- Hardware failure
- Software failure

There are two ways of Resolving an Issue: Automatically or Manually.

AUTOMATICALLY

Automatic resolutions are used when you want to use only one resolution reason.

With an Automatic resolution, you can program a transition to automatically resolve the issue when the User clicks that transition. For example, you may have a Status transition called "Done". When you click "done", your workflow status changes to Done (or whatever you are using for the final status), and the Resolution field also changes from Unresolved to Done, or whatever you have selected to indicate that your Issue is formally resolved (Done is an example of a resolution option):

In the image above, when I clicked the Done status another field (highlighted) appears that contains the word "Done" with a checkmark beside it. That is the resolution field. The checkmark indicates the Issue is Resolved with a resolution of "Done".

Automatic resolutions are built using a workflow transition **post-function**.

MANUALLY

With a Manual resolution, when you click that Status transition button a pop-up appears (called a "workflow transition screen") containing a resolution field. This resolution field will contain a list of resolution options (Done, Won't Do, etc.):

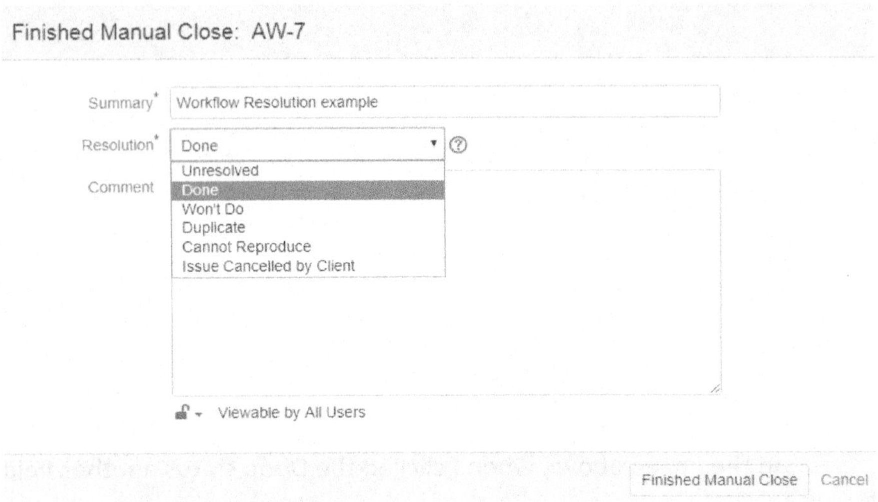

The user selects one of the options and exits the pop up. The status has now changed to Done (or whatever you are using as the final status), and the resolution field will show the option you selected from the resolution field drop down list. Manual resolutions are also set up using a workflow transition post-function.

Automatic works fine if you have only one resolution option to choose from: you will need the manual option if you want to have your User select from multiple resolution options.

Once you have resolved an Issue, Jira will formally close it out in its database. In other words, it will no longer show in your Open Issues list.

Jira Admins can add new resolutions by clicking on the Resolutions link in the sidebar of the Navigation Bar > COG > Issues view.

Chapter 7 - Screens

To avoid confusion, in this book the term "Site-admin" includes "Org-admin, Site-admin, and Jira-admin" unless specifically noted otherwise.

Chapter Objectives

In this Chapter you will:

- **gain a working knowledge of Jira Work Management Issue Screens and Workflow Transition Screens**
- **learn of Screen Schemes, Issue Type Screen Schemes, and the differences between the two**
- **create a custom screen for your project along with a related Screen Scheme and Issue Type Screen Scheme**

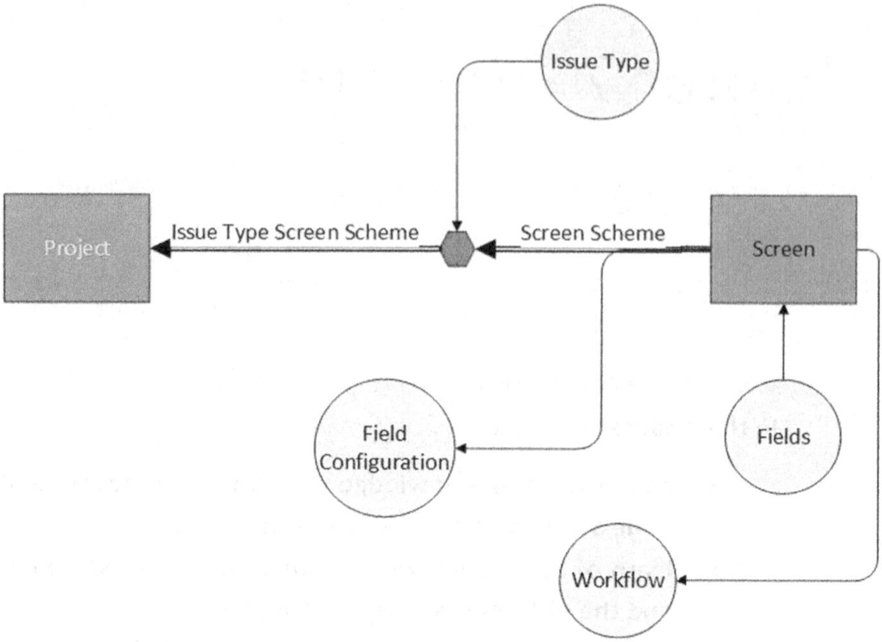

Screens and Schemes

Screens

A **Screen** is a unique User view, containing fields for a specific purpose.

A Screen can:

- provide information
- enable an action (clicking a button for example)
- collect information (filling in a field, or selecting an item from a list of options, etc.)

Screens are typically designed to support the type of work associated with an Issue. For example, if you need to "Order a New Railroad Car" you don't need to see a "Bake a Cake" Screen. You want to see a **Screen** showing the fields, and only those fields, necessary for the "Order a New Railroad Car" process.

What Users will be able to see on a screen is based on their project **User Role**, type of **Permissions** (security) they have, and the type of work needing to be done at that moment.

When adding new fields, you can add them to an existing standard Jira Issue Screen, to a Workflow Transition Screen (View), or to a custom-made Screen.

Jira uses its screens in two distinct ways: for Issue Operations, and for Workflow Transitions.

Issue Operations Screens

When working with an Issue the User is typically doing one of three things:

- creating the issue
- adding, deleting, or changing the data in the fields of the Issue
- looking at the information in the issue.

Jira calls each of these activities an **'Issue Operation'**. These Issue Operations are called **Create Issue Operation,** and the **Edit / View Issue Operation**. Why "Edit / View"? That's because earlier versions of Jira saw Edit and View as separate screens which performed differently. Quite frankly, it was very clumsy to work with, so Atlassian has simply combined the two.

Each of these Operations **must** have their own screen: a Create Issue Operation screen, and an Edit / View Issue Operation screen. Many times, you will want the two screens to be the same; so, if you wish, you can reuse the same screen in each operation. However, there are also instances where - for a particular Issue Type - you may want the two screens to be a little, or a lot, different. Having the two Issue Operation types allows you to have these distinct screens. We will discuss Issue Operations in more detail later in the chapter.

Workflow Transition Screens (Views)

This segment needs to start off with a bit of context; but stay with me because it: a) explains workflow transition screens; and b) will help you avoid errors.

Once upon a time, Jira started with only Issue Operation screens (Create, Edit, View). Then someone suggested adding screens to transitions. In other words, when you clicked a transition button, a screen made specifically for that transition would open. This sounded like great (I know I thought it a fantastic idea) because this would allow Users to enter data in a transition screen that related directly to that step in the workflow. Unfortunately, there were two problems with this approach. First, if you needed to open that transition screen later (to add or change data, for example), you needed to navigate back to a point in the workflow prior to that transition and then click the transition to re-open the screen. This meant building transitions whose sole purpose was to get you back to a transition screen. So, instead of a nice clean workflow, you ended up with a complicated workflow with transitions going everywhere and anywhere. Think of how confusing that would be to the average User. The second problem was that once the transition screen closed, you couldn't see the data anymore unless you made a duplicate of that field in the Issue Operation Edit / View screen. So, Site-admins started, rightfully, asking, "What's the point of designing a workflow transition screen, if the field is also available in the Issue Operation screen?" Bottom line, Workflow Transition screens are great in theory and almost completely useless in real life.

However, there are three specific areas where workflow transition screens are useful or necessary.

Traditional Transition Screen

There may indeed be cases where a transition screen is of value. For example, despite how Atlassian classifies it, the Create Issue screen works like a transition screen. When you clicked the Create Issue button it opened a screen, where you entered data. Once you entered the data in the Create Issue screen and clicked Create, it transitioned to the Open or To Do screen. You also see the data from the Create Issue screen, because it is duplicated in the Edit / View screen.

RESOLVE ISSUE SCREEN

As you know, when you click the Done Status transition in an Issue having a standard workflow, the Issue resolution field in the Issue indicates that the Issue is resolved with a "Done" resolution. However, there are likely circumstances where you want the User to choose from several resolution options. "Done", "Won't do", "Duplicate", "Cannot Reproduce", and "Known Error" are default Jira resolutions. You can also create your own custom resolutions (e.g. "Arrested Suspect", "Released Suspect", "Assigned to Cold Case Squad", etc.).

This is how it works. First, you need to start with "To Do" type, or "In Progress" type status button that you want to transition to a "Done" type status. You will then connect a transition to any "Done" type status (e.g. "Done", "Closed", "Resolved", etc.) When you add the transition, select the "Resolve Issue Screen" in the Screen dropdown.

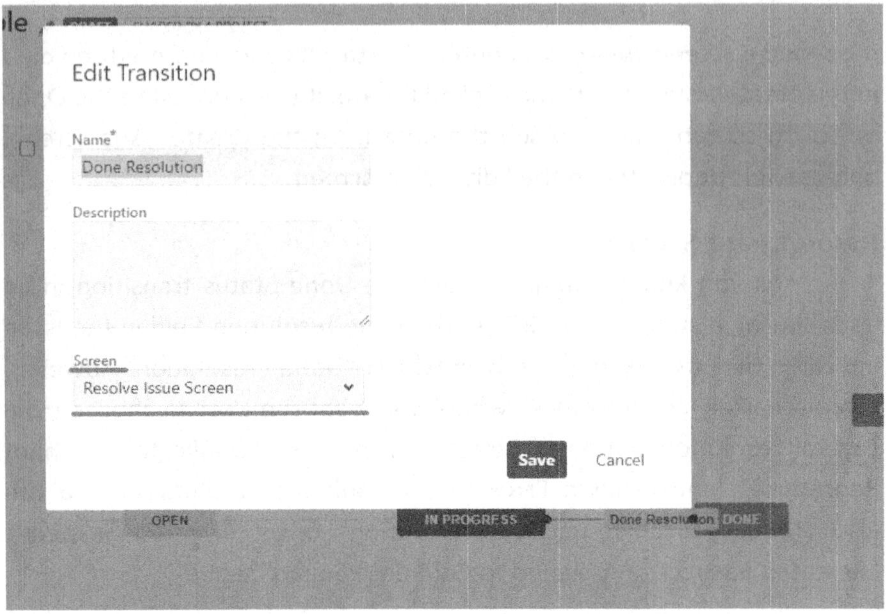

And that's how you add the transition screen. When working with the Issue, once you click the appropriate Status transition, a transition screen will open where you can choose from a list of resolutions.

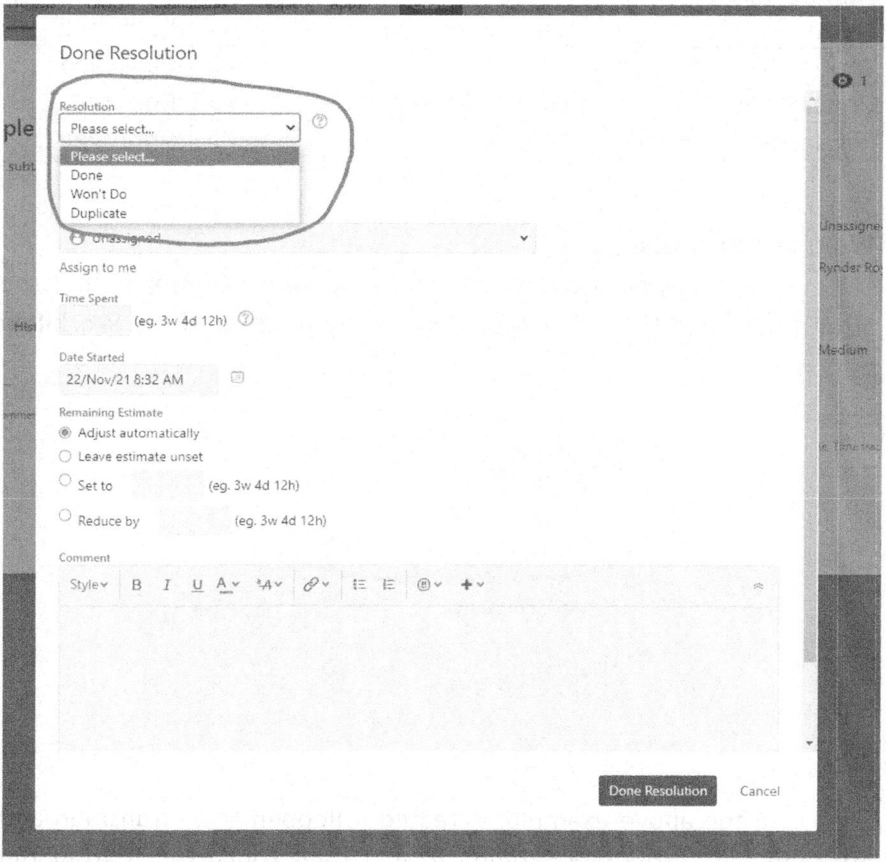

Choose one, click the transition button at the bottom of the screen, and then a) the Issue is formally closed; and b) the resolution choice shows on the Issue View screen.

Below are some examples of acceptable Resolution transitions to help describe what I mean:

"Open" or "In Progress" type status	>	Resolution transition	>	"Done" type status
Open	>	Create a transition and use the "Resolve Issue Screen"	>	Done
Open	>		>	Closed
In Progress	>		>	Accepted

Painting Room	>		>	Resolved
To Do	>		>	Published
Waiting for Customer	>		>	Cancelled
Under Review	>		>	Rejected
Requested	>		>	Approved

WORKFLOW SCREEN

There will be occasions when you will need to reopen an Issue after it has been formally closed. That is the purpose of the **Workflow** screen.

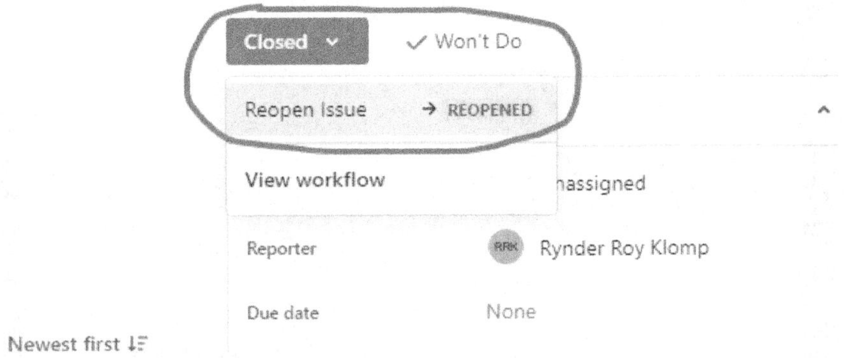

In the above example, I created a Reopen Issue transition and attached the "Workflow Screen" to it. I then connected it from the Closed status to the Reopened status. When I clicked that status transition, this Workflow screen opened:

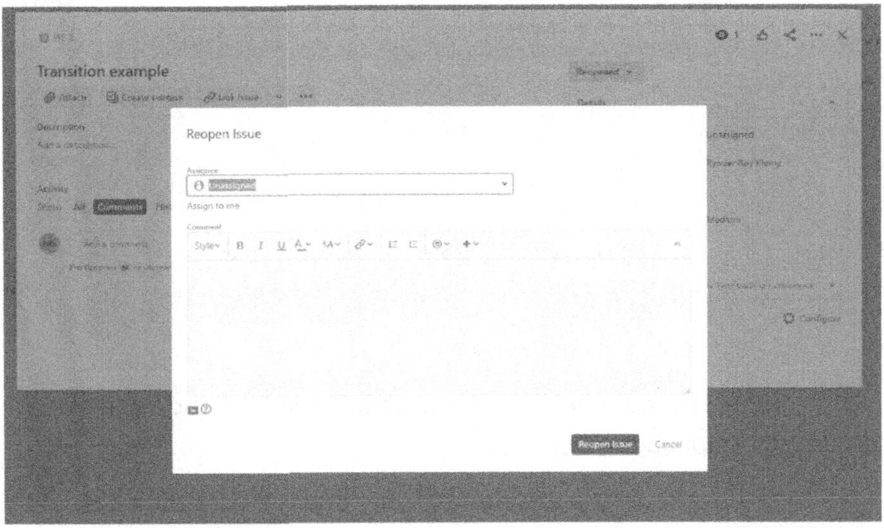

As you can see this is a very simple screen and that asks the User to Assign the Issue to someone, and to add a comment if necessary (for example, the reason for the Issue being reopened).

And again, the two fields (Assignee and Comment) are both fields that exist and are visible in the Issue Edit/View screen.

Clearly, there are -rare- occasions when a transition screen is of value. But if you are considering building one, weigh the pros and cons carefully.

Let's move on and look at how Jira manages screens.

View Screens Page

1. Navigate to  > Issues > **Screens**

The View Screens page has four main columns: **Name, Screen Schemes, Workflows,** and **Actions.**

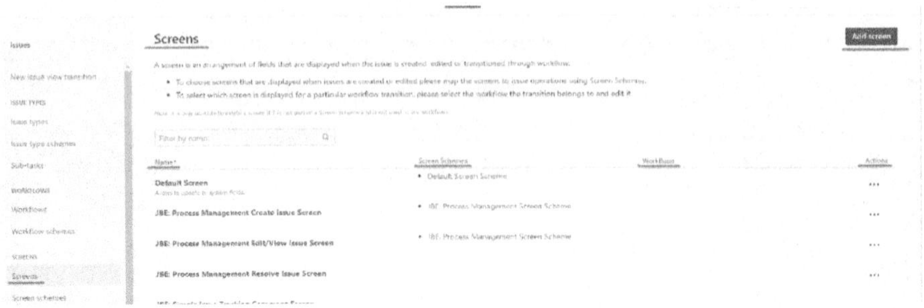

NAME

Here, to no one's surprise, the names of the **Screens** are displayed in alphabetical order.

> CAUTION: As always, do NOT mess with the **Default Screen**. If you want to make changes, copy the default, rename the copy, and make the changes in the new version.

SCREEN SCHEMES

One of the more confusing and technically challenging things about Jira is its Screens Schemes and how they work.

A **Screen Scheme**, like Issue Type Scheme and Workflow Scheme, serves as a connection. It connects a Screen with a specific **Issue Operation**: **Create** an Issue or **Edit / View** an Issue. These are discussed in more detail later in the Screen Schemes section.

The Screen Schemes column in the **View Screens** page indicates which **Screen Schemes** are associated with the Screen listed in the Name column.

WORKFLOWS

A **Workflow Screen** (technically called a **Workflow Transition View**) is the screen a User may see at a particular step in the Issue lifecycle.

The Workflow column shows what Transition Views are associated with the Screen listed in the Name column.

Actions

The Actions column allows you to **Configure**, **Edit**, **Copy**, or **Delete** your Screen.

Configure

On the Configure Screen page you design or edit your Screen layout.

You can do a remarkable number of things with the Configure Screen page. You can:

- Remove unnecessary fields by hovering your mouse over the field and clicking the **Remove** button that appears on the right side of the screen.
- Add standard Jira fields, or Custom Fields you have already created, to the Screen by using the **Select field ...** drop-down list at the bottom of the page.
- Reorder the field layout by hovering your mouse over the hatch field (see image below) to the left of the field name. When your mouse arrow turns into a four-direction arrow, drag the field up or down to its desired position:

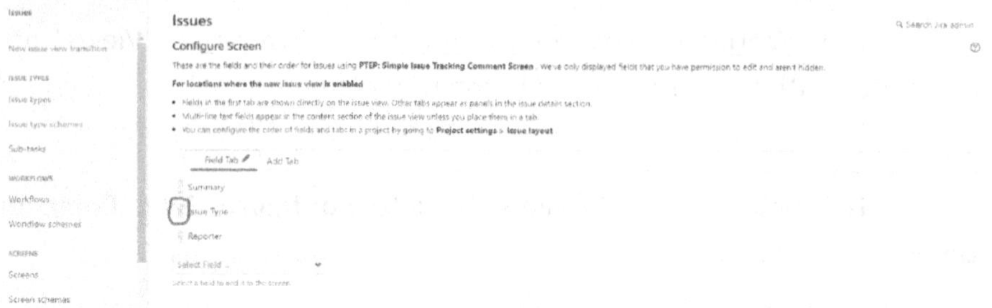

- Name the tab by editing the **Field Tab** at the top of the list of Fields. When working with the screen, the user will see that tab name. The User will NOT see the tab title if you don't change the Field Tab name AND there is only one tab in the Screen.
- Add new 'tabs' on the Screen and include additional fields by clicking on **Add Tab** at the top of the list of fields. Tabs are a helpful in two ways. First, it is great for squeezing a lot of information in a small space, and it is recommended if you believe your Screen will commonly be seen on a mobile device. Second, it is excellent for organizing your data fields into logical groupings. If you believe the screen will be edited often during a workflow process, you may consider sorting the fields into logical work groups with each tab representing a distinct function or step in the process.

EDIT

The Edit function allows you to change the **Name** of the Screen and to change its **Description**.

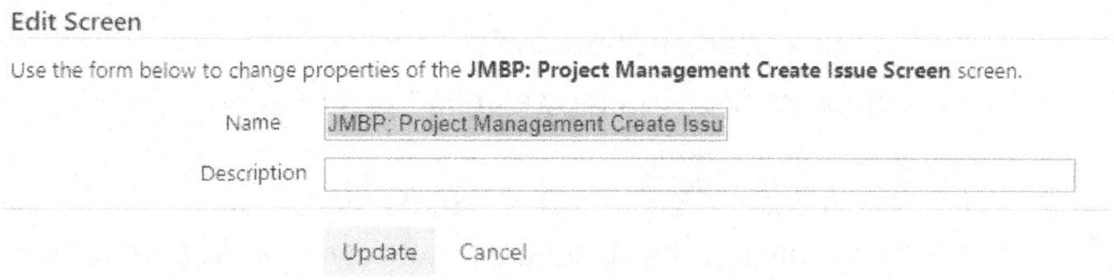

Copy

Copy does just that, it allows you to copy an existing Screen and rename it. This is helpful if you have an existing Screen you want to use in a new project and need a unique name for project management purposes. It is also helpful if an existing Screen has almost, but not everything, you want for a new Screen. You can make a copy and use that as the starting point for building your new Screen.

Delete

You can delete a Screen if there are no **Screen Schemes** and no **Workflows** associated with it. If there *are* existing **Screen Schemes** or **Workflows**, you must delete those first before you can delete the Screen.

Add Screen

You create a new Screen by clicking the **Add Screen** button on the upper right corner of the **Screens** page. A pop-up appears asking for the Name and Description of the new Screen and that's it. A new Screen is created.

Of course, you need then to configure it using the configure link in the Actions column.

Exercise: Create and Add Screen to Project

We will now add a Screen to our *Weekend Activities* project. This Screen will, later, be used for custom "Grocery shopping list" fields to be associated with the Grocery Shopping list Issue type.

In this exercise we will:

- Create a Grocery Shopping List Screen
- Configure the Screen by eliminating unnecessary fields

1. NAVIGATE TO  > ISSUES > **SCREENS**
2. IN THE OPENED **VIEW SCREENS** PAGE CLICK ON **ADD SCREEN**
3. IN THE **ADD SCREEN** POP-UP ENTER *"GROCERY SHOPPING LIST SCREEN"* IN THE **NAME** FIELD
4. ENTER *"SCREEN FOR GROCERY SHOPPING LIST"* IN THE **DESCRIPTION** FIELD
5. CLICK **ADD**
6. BACK IN THE SCREEN PAGE, FIND YOUR NEWLY CREATED **GROCERY SHOPPING LIST** SCREEN AND CLICK ON **CONFIGURE** IN THE **ACTIONS** COLUMN

In this page you will add the fields for creating a shopping list to the newly created Shopping List Screen.

7. IN THE **CONFIGURE SCREEN** PAGE, SELECT THE FOLLOWING FROM THE **SELECT FIELD** DROP-DOWN LIST:
    i. SUMMARY (AND CLICK **ADD** BUTTON)
    ii. ASSIGNEE (AND CLICK **ADD** BUTTON)
    iii. DUE DATE (AND CLICK **ADD** BUTTON)
    iv. PRIORITY (AND CLICK **ADD** BUTTON)
8. CLICK ON **SCREENS** ON THE SIDEBAR TO GET BACK TO THE **SCREENS** PAGE

You have now set up a basic Shopping List Screen.

In many cases, Jira provides enough standard fields for you to complete your Issue. However, in this instance, we still need some additional fields (a list of products, for example), which we will create a little later in the Custom Fields section.

Since you only have one tab, you don't need to edit its name.

TIP: If you want to add or delete fields later, simply go to the **Screens** page, find your Screen, and click on the Configure link in the Actions column. After that it is straight forward: you can add, remove, and move fields up or down.

Screen Schemes

In my opinion, the Screen Scheme is probably the most complex and confusing of the puzzle pieces because to build it correctly you must do three things:

1. Associate a **Screen to a Screen Scheme**
2. Associate the **Screen Scheme to an Issue Operation**
3. Link a **Screen to an Issue Type by associating** the **Screen Scheme to an Issue Type Screen Scheme**

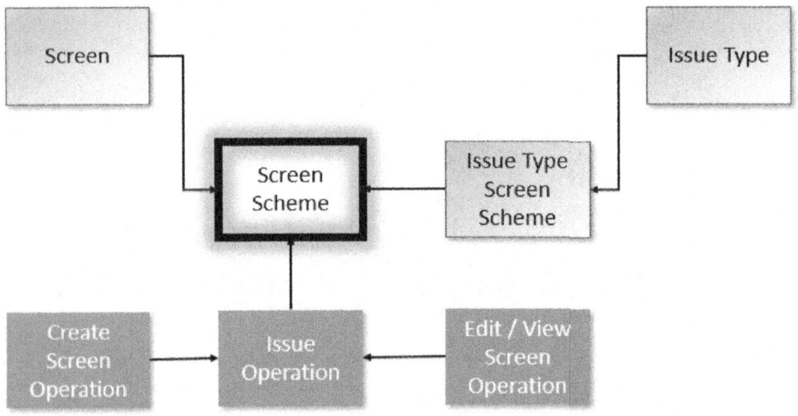

A Screen Scheme does two things. First, it ties a Screen to an Issue Operation. Second, it enables the creation of an Issue Type Screen Scheme. Issue Type Screen Schemes will be discussed soon in this chapter. But for now, let's look at Issue Operation in more details.

Issue Operations

Screen Schemes dictate what a User can do with a Screen during an **Issue Operation**.

There are two Issue Operations:

Create Issue = Screen shown when issue is **being created**

Edit / View Issue = Screen shown when the issue is being **edited or viewed**

Why do we need different Issue Operations?

Almost every beginner, including myself, has no idea what an Issue Operation is; and what Create, Edit, and View an Issue means in this context. But the answer is simple.

CREATE ISSUE OPERATION

As you remember, when you create an Issue, a screen pops up where you enter data and then click Create. This is, unsurprisingly, the **Create Screen** and it is also the **Create an Issue Operation**. A Create Issue Operation occurs only once for each issue you create.

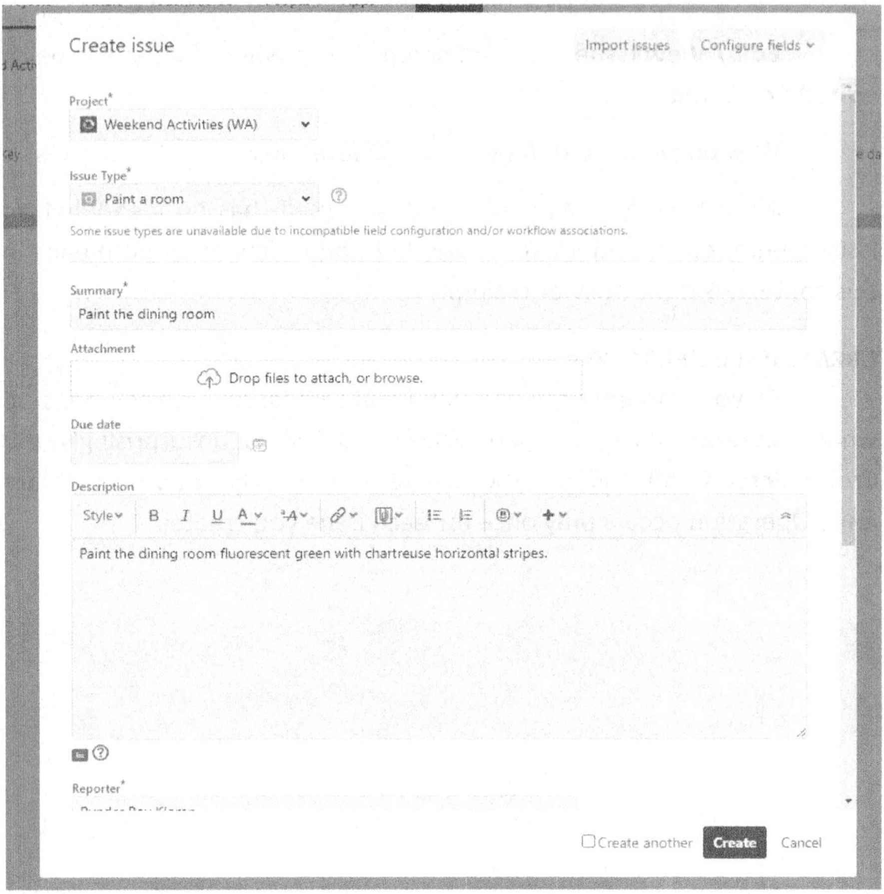

EDIT / VIEW ISSUE OPERATION

When you want to Edit the data in an Issue, you simply open the Issue and click on the field you want to edit. For example, for some reason my wife did not like my paint choice of "fluorescent green with chartreuse horizontal stripes" and has changed the color to "sage green".

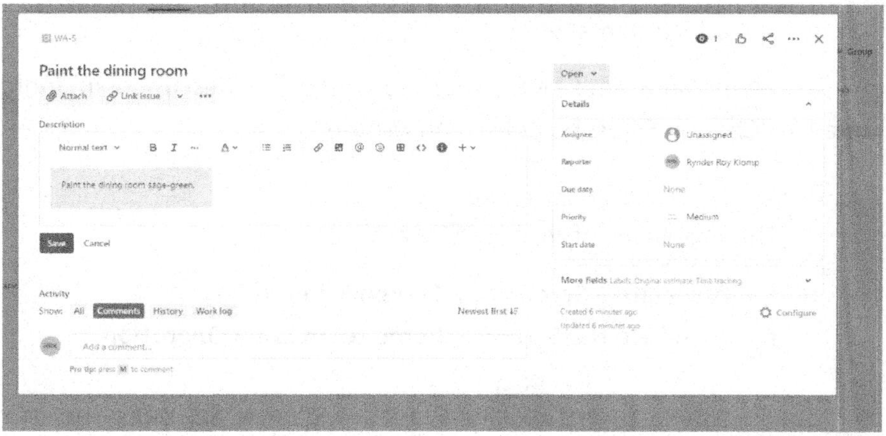

Finally, you can view the Issue's data in the same **Edit / View Issue screen**. These two collectively are called – unsurprisingly - the **Edit / View Operations.**

WHAT'S THE DIFFERENCE BETWEEN EDIT AND VIEW?

At its most basic, you can either Edit fields in a screen (Add, Change, or Delete data), or you can simply look at the contents of the screen.

Of course, the question quickly becomes, "*Who* can edit and who can view the Issue?" Do you want everyone and anyone to edit or view your Issues? Jira has done a great job with security by setting up permissions so that you can:

- edit the fields in an Issue. Of course, that means you can also view the Issue, because it is rather difficult to edit a field that you cannot see
- view, but not edit, an Issue. This is just as it sounds. You can see the contents of an Issue, but cannot edit (add, change, delete) any of the information
- view, and edit some of the fields in an Issue. Typically, this means you can see the contents of an Issue but can only

change a few fields (Comment field, Watcher, Votes, attachments, etc.)

Permissions and permission schemes are described in more detail in "Chapter 9: Users, Roles, and Groups".

Exercise: Associate Screen Schemes and Issue Operations

The objectives of this exercise are

- Associate a **Screen to a Screen Scheme**
- Associate the **Screen Scheme to an Issue Operation**

1. Navigate to > Issues > **Screen Schemes** (on the sidebar)
2. In the Screen Schemes page click on **Add Screen Scheme** button
3. In the Add Screen Scheme pop-up enter "*Grocery Shopping List Screen Scheme*" in the **Name** field
4. Enter "*Screen Scheme for the Grocery Shopping List Screen*" in the **Description** field
5. Select *Grocery Shopping List* in the **Default Screen** Field
6. Click **Add**
7. Back in the **Screen Schemes** page, find your newly created **Shopping List Screen Scheme**, and click on **Configure** in the **Actions** column
8. In the Configure Screen Scheme page click on **Associate an Issue Operation with a Screen** button

9. In the Associate an Issue Operation with a screen pop-up select *Create Issue* from the Issue Operation list
10. Select *Grocery Shopping List* from the **Screen** list
11. Click **Add**

You have now associated a Create Issue Operation with a Screen. When you next create an issue with this project, the Shopping List Screen will appear. Unfortunately, your Edit / View screen will show nothing. So, we need to associate this same screen with the Edit / View Operation.

12. In the Configure Screen Scheme page click on **Associate an Issue Operation with a Screen** button
13. In the Associate an Issue Operation with a screen pop-up select *Edit Issue* from the Issue Operation list
14. Select *Grocery Shopping List* from the **Screen** list
15. Click **ADD**
16. In the Configure Screen Scheme page click on **Associate an Issue Operation with a Screen** button
17. In the Associate an Issue Operation with a screen pop-up select *View Issue* from the Issue Operation list
18. Select *Grocery Shopping List* from the **Screen** list and click **ADD**

Issue Operation	Screen	Actions
Default Used for all unmapped operations.	Grocery Shopping List	Edit
Create issue	Grocery Shopping List	Edit Delete
Edit issue	Grocery Shopping List	Edit Delete
View issue	Grocery Shopping List	Edit Delete

Issue Type Screen Schemes

So, you have built a **screen** and associated the screen with various **Issue Operations** using a **Screen Scheme**. But you still need to associate your screen and screen scheme with an **Issue Type**; otherwise, the Issue Type and the Project will never know which screen to use. That is done using an **Issue Type Screen Scheme**.

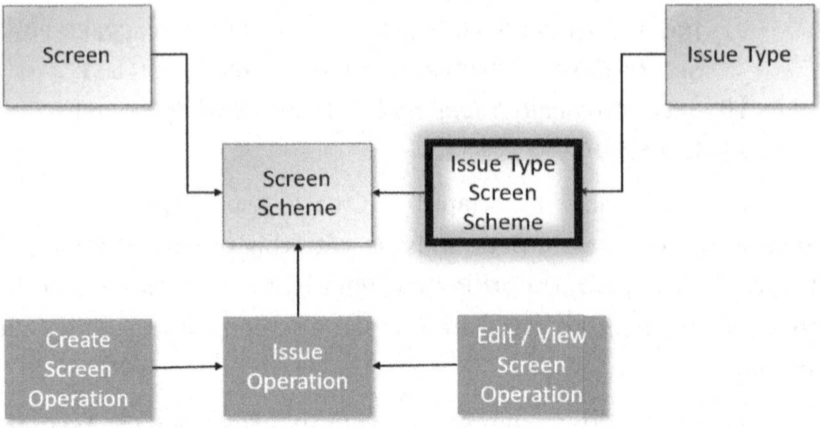

The **Issue Type Screen Scheme** link is located below the Screen Schemes link in the Administration > Issues > Sidebar. Clicking that link opens the Issue Type Screen Scheme page. The Issue Type Screen Scheme page has three columns: **Name, Projects,** and **Actions.**

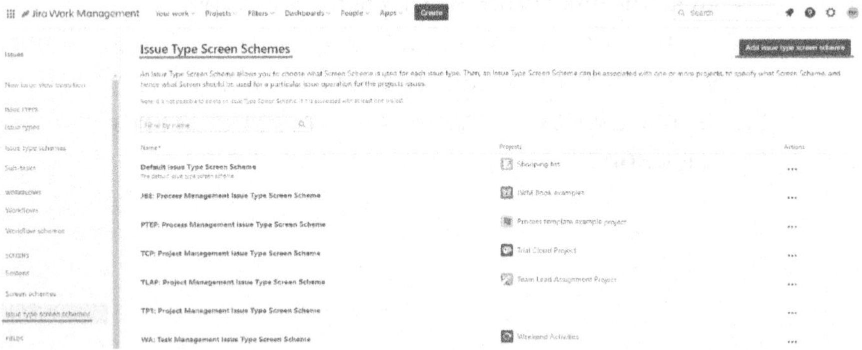

NAME

This column contains the names of the Issue Type Screen Scheme. Issue Type Screen Schemes are listed in alphabetical order.

Projects

This column lists the projects associated with the Issue Type Screen Scheme. While you can have only one Issue Type Screen Scheme per project the reverse is not true, multiple projects can be associated with an Issue Type Screen Scheme.

I believe it is easier to create a new Issue Type Screen Scheme for each project. That way, if you have to make a change to a particular project's Issue Type Screen Scheme you won't affect any other project. The good news is that Jira takes care of this for you; it automatically creates a unique scheme for your project when it is created.

> CAUTION: You cannot associate an Issue Type Screen Scheme with a project in this page; instead, you need do it through the **Project's Settings** view.

Actions

The Actions column allows you to **Configure, Edit, Copy,** and **Delete** the Issue Type Screen Scheme.

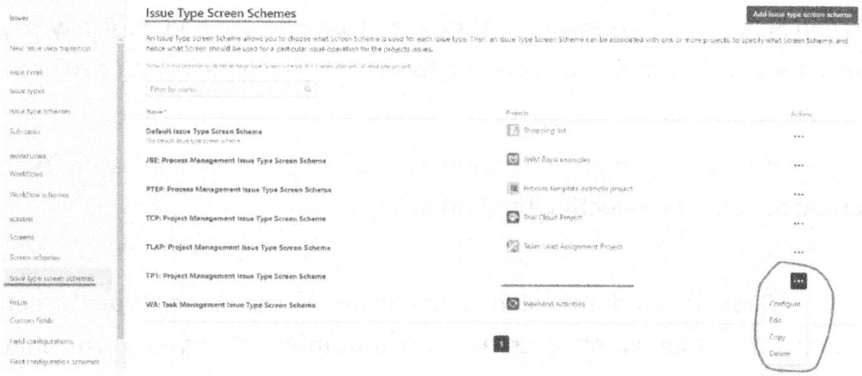

Configure

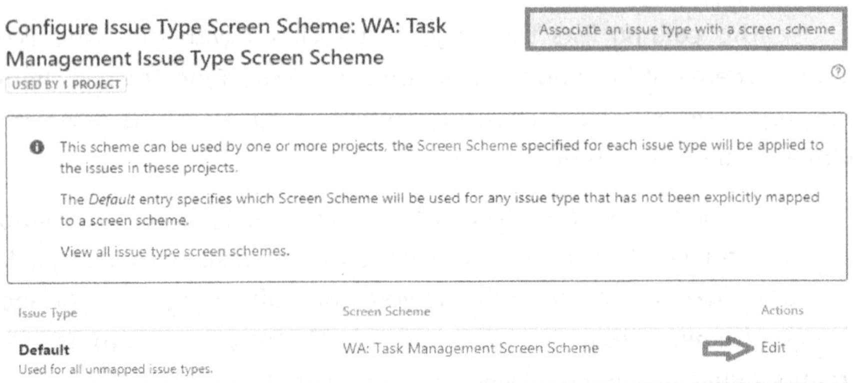

You can do two things in the **Configure Issue Type Screen Scheme** page. First, you can change the Screen Scheme associated with the Issue Type Screen Scheme by clicking **Edit** link and selecting another Screen Scheme in the pop-up.

Second, on this page you associate another **Issue Type** with a different **Screen Scheme** by clicking **Associate an Issue Type with a Screen Scheme**. You can associate as many different Issue Types with Screen Schemes as you want, if they are all unique. Indeed, typically you will have a different Screen Scheme for each Issue Type in your project.

Edit

You can change the name and description of the Issue Type Screen Scheme by selecting the **Edit** link.

Copy

Copy is used to make a duplicate of the Issue Type Screen Scheme. You may want to do this for a number of reasons. You may want to test a new Issue Type Screen Scheme without the risk of damaging your existing Issue Type Screen Scheme. You may want to reuse it in another project and believe, as I do, that it is a good practice to have "a one Issue Type Screen Scheme to one Project" relationship.

Or you may want to use the Issue Type Screen Scheme as a starting point for a slightly different Issue Type Screen Scheme version.

Delete

You can delete your Issue Type Screen Scheme if it is not associated with any project.

Add a New Issue Type Screen Scheme

You can create a new Issue Type Screen Scheme by clicking on the **Add Issue Type Screen Scheme** button located at the upper right corner of the page.

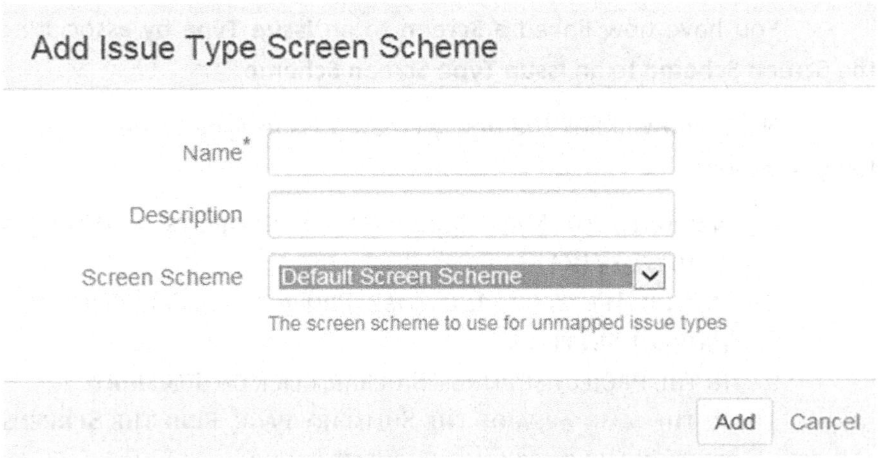

The pop-up will ask you for the **Name, Description** AND, most importantly, the **Screen Scheme** you want associated with this new Issue Type Screen Scheme.

Exercise: Link Screen to Issue Type and Project

We will now:

- Link a **Screen to an Issue Type** by associating the Screen Scheme to an Issue Type Screen Scheme
- Associate the **Issue Type Screen Scheme to a Project**

1. NAVIGATE TO > ISSUES > **ISSUE TYPE SCREEN SCHEMES** (IN THE SIDEBAR)
2. IN THE OPENED ISSUE TYPE SCREEN SCHEMES, CLICK ON **ADD ISSUE TYPE SCREEN SCHEME** BUTTON
3. IN THE **ADD ISSUE TYPE SCREEN SCHEME** POP-UP TYPE IN "*WEEKEND ACTIVITIES ITSS*" IN THE **NAME** FIELD
4. ENTER "*ISSUE TYPE SCREEN SCHEME FOR THE WEEKEND ACTIVITIES PROJECT*" IN THE **DESCRIPTION** FIELD
5. SELECT *GROCERY SHOPPING LIST SCREEN SCHEME* FROM THE **SCREEN SCHEME** LIST
6. CLICK **ADD**

You have now linked a **Screen** to an **Issue Type** by associating the **Screen Scheme** to an **Issue Type Screen Scheme.**

Next, you will link the newly created Issue Type Screen Scheme to your project.

7. NAVIGATE TO MAIN MENU BAR > **PROJECTS** > *WEEKEND ACTIVITIES (WA)*
8. IN THE *WEEKEND ACTIVITIES* PROJECT SIDEBAR CLICK THE **PROJECT SETTINGS**
9. IN THE PROJECT SETTINGS' SIDEBAR, CLICK ON **SUMMARY**
10. IN THE MAIN AREA OF THE SUMMARY PAGE, FIND THE **SCREENS** SECTION AND CLICK ON THE SCHEME SHOWN:

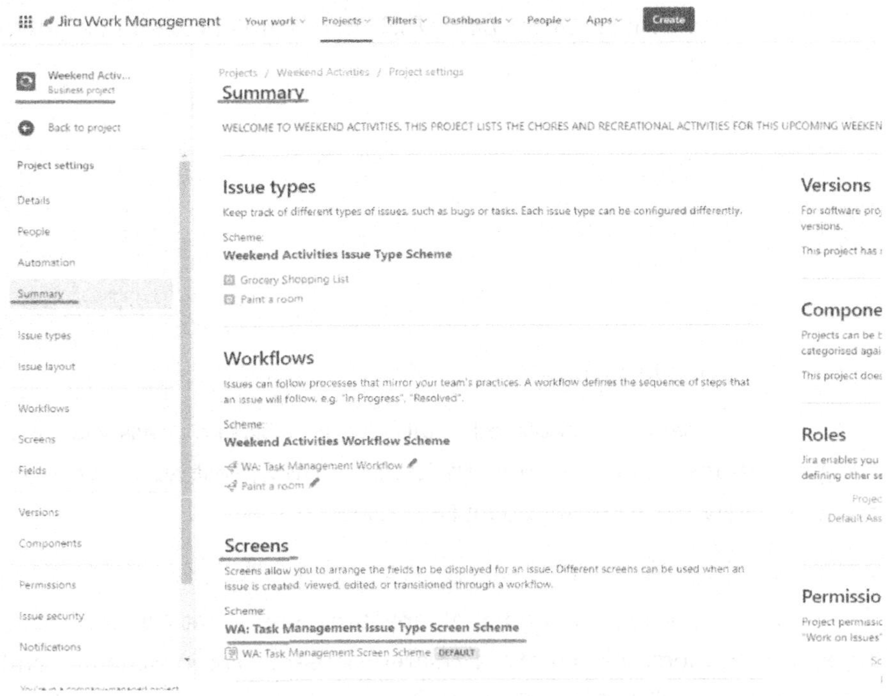

11. In the opened **Screens** view click on **Actions** button in the upper right corner
12. Select *Use a different scheme* from the **Actions** drop down list:

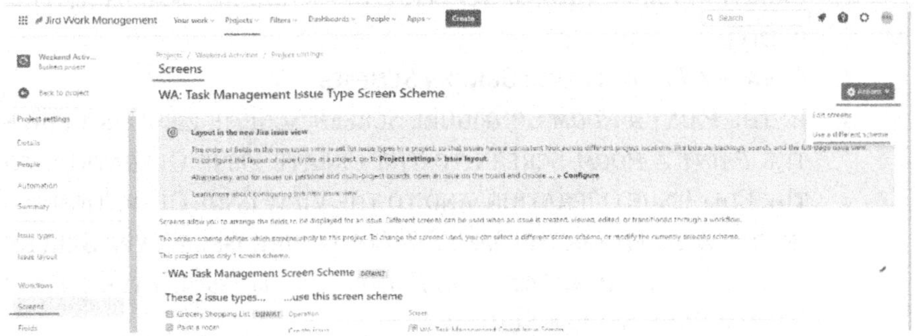

13. IN THE **ISSUE TYPE SCREEN SCHEME ASSOCIATION** VIEW SELECT *GROCERY SHOPPING LIST ITSS* FROM THE **SCHEME** DROP DOWN LIST:

14. CLICK ASSOCIATE

You have completed all your Screen associations! Congratulations, that was not an easy journey. Test your work by creating a new "Grocery Shopping List" Issue.

EXERCISE: PAINT A ROOM SCREENS AND SCHEMES

I strongly recommend that any time you create a new Issue Type, you immediately create a related Screen, Screen Scheme, and associate them with Issue Operations and your project's Issue Type Screen Scheme. So, let's go back and do that for an Issue Type we created in a previous chapter.

In this exercise you will repeat the previous exercises for the Paint a Room Issue Type. In the Administration > Issues area you will:

1. CREATE A *PAINT A ROOM* **SCREEN** (DON'T ADD ANY FIELDS AT THIS POINT)
2. CREATE A *PAINT A ROOM* **SCREEN SCHEME**
3. IN THE *PAINT A ROOM* CONFIGURE SCREEN SCHEME VIEW, ASSOCIATE THE *PAINT A ROOM* SCREEN TO THE CREATE ISSUE OPERATION, TO THE EDIT ISSUE OPERATION, AND TO THE VIEW ISSUE OPERATION
4. IN THE *WEEKEND ACTIVITIES ITSS* **CONFIGURE ISSUE TYPE SCREEN SCHEME** PAGE, **ASSOCIATE** THE *PAINT A ROOM* **ISSUE TYPE** TO THE *PAINT A ROOM* **SCREEN SCHEME**

WHAT YOU DID

In this last exercise you created and associated all the elements necessary to work with the Paint a room Issue Type.

Chapter 8 – Fields

To avoid confusion, in this book the term "Site-admin" includes "Org-admin, Site-admin, and Jira-admin" unless specifically noted otherwise.

Chapter Objectives

In the Fields chapter you will gain a deeper understanding of:

- **Fields**
- **Custom Fields**
- **Field Types**
- **Field Configurations**
- **Field Configuration Schemes.**

You will also be given a brief overview of the remainder of the Administration > Issues Page's Sidebar items: Issue Features, Issue Attributes, and Notifications.

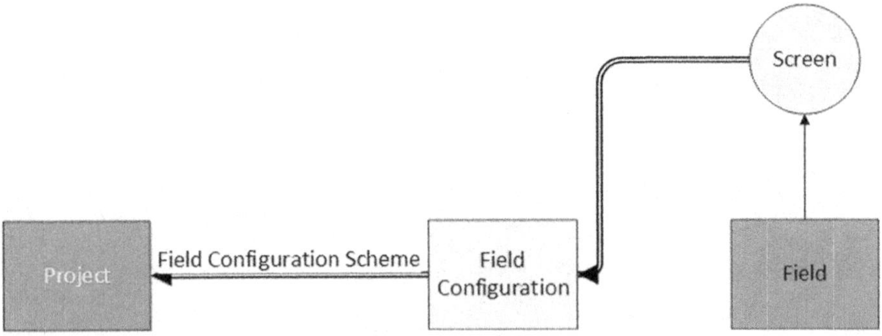

Fields

Fields are the boxes on a screen where you enter, select, change, or view information. Jira has several different types of fields, such as:

- **Single line or multi line text** boxes where you enter details (your name, for example)
- **Number** fields
- **Calendar** fields where you select a date or a date and time combination
- **Multiple choice, single choice,** and **Cascading** Select lists
- **Radio Button** lists
- **Labels, URL,** and **User Picker**

Jira Work Management already comes with a great many standard fields (called 'System' fields), which you can use when building screens. Some examples are:

- Summary (text field)
- Type (single select list)
- Due (calendar)
- Labels (labels)
- Description (multi line text field)
- Assignee (User picker)

Custom Fields

Jira Work Management also allows you to create **Custom Fields**. For example, you may want to create a list of sports activity options for you and your buddies to choose from. In this case, you could create a custom 'drop down list' field with activities such as: *Golf, Tennis, Hunting, Fishing, Poker, Tiddlywinks, Needlepoint*, etc.

Atlassian has also helped by supplying you with numerous pre-built custom fields. Be aware that some will only work with Jira Service Management or Jira Software applications.

You can reach the Custom Fields page by

Navigating to ⚙ *> Issues >* ***Custom Fields*** *in the sidebar:*

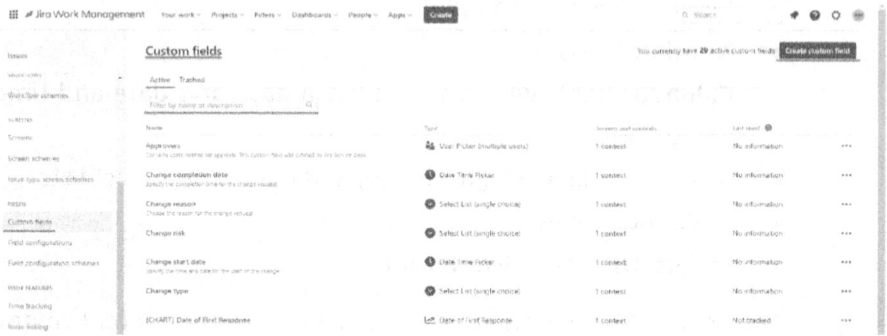

In the **Custom Fields** page you have a Search box and order filters such as Project, Screen, and Last used. The Search box will only look at Name or Description fields.

Below the Search/Filters row there are five columns: **Name, Type, Screens and Contexts, Last used,** and **Actions**.

Name

The **Name** column includes Jira's system fields and those custom fields already built by you or your organization. They are listed in alphabetical order.

You may also see a number of 'LOCKED' fields. These are custom fields supplied by Atlassian for Jira Work Management, Jira Service Desk, or Jira Software *and* you cannot change (configure) them.

You can change the order of the field by clicking the up or down arrows next to the column title.

Type

This column indicates the **type** of field used, such as Text, Number, Date, Checkbox, Radio buttons, Select list (single choice), etc. At the time of this writing there are over 36 different types of custom fields shown with your licensed version of Jira Work Management. Just remember that some may require the purchase of Jira Service Management or Jira Software licenses.

Screens and Contexts

This column shows the screens which contain the field.

In addition, it shows the context(s) associated with the field. Context is a combination of two things: the **Issue Type** with which the Custom Field is associated, and the **Projects** associated with the Custom Field. If a Custom Field is not associated with a specific Issue Type, it is available to all Issue Types (i.e. **Global (all issues)**). Contexts are extremely handy and are described in more detail in the Actions > "Context and default value" section on the next page.

You can change the order of this field by clicking the up or down arrows next to the column title.

Last used

This column shows the last time the field was edited in any Issue.

You can change the order of this field by clicking the up or down arrows next to the column title.

Actions

In the Actions column (with fields that are not Locked), when you click the **COG** down arrow five options will be listed: **Edit details, Contexts and default value, Translation options, Associate to Screens,** and **Move to trash.**

Edit details

The details you edit will depend on the type of field selected (for example a text field will not allow you to use a "Date Time Range picker"), but the two most common changes allowed are to the Field name and the Description.

Context and Default Value

Sometimes you may have a custom field you want to reuse in another project, but you need to change some of the data options in order for those options to be relevant in that new project. For example, you may have a Jira project that you use in Eastern USA which contains a list of employees who can be assigned to inspect factory equipment. You want to duplicate this project for Western USA but use a different list of employees for that region. That's where a Context comes into play.

Add New Context is fundamentally **a copy function**. It lets you add a new context to the Custom Field by adding a new Configuration Scheme **Label and Description**. You can associate different **Issue Types and Projects** to the new **Context.**

The **Edit Default Value** function allows you to set Custom Field Defaults by selecting the value from your existing list of options. Let's say you have a list of three addresses, but your users most often select address number three. Jira allows you to select one value to place first in a Select List (dropdown list). This will become the **first value**, the **Default Value**, the user sees when selecting from the list.

You can only have one custom field context per project.

Translation Options

Here you have the option to enter a Custom Field name and description in a different language, as long as it is one of the twenty-four in the drop-down list.

Associate to Screens

This link takes you to the **Associate field to screens** view. Here you can add the Custom Field to more screens or change the current Custom Field/Screen association. When you are done, do not forget click on **Update** at the bottom of the view.

Move to trash

And of course, you can always **Move to trash** a Custom field if you no longer need it. The Move to trash link takes the Custom field to the trash area where it is kept for 60 days. After 60 days it is deleted permanently.

Create Custom Field

To create a custom field, you start by clicking on the **Create custom field** button in the upper right corner of the Custom Fields view. When you do so, the **Select a Field Type** pop-up opens. This is where you start creating a Custom Field:

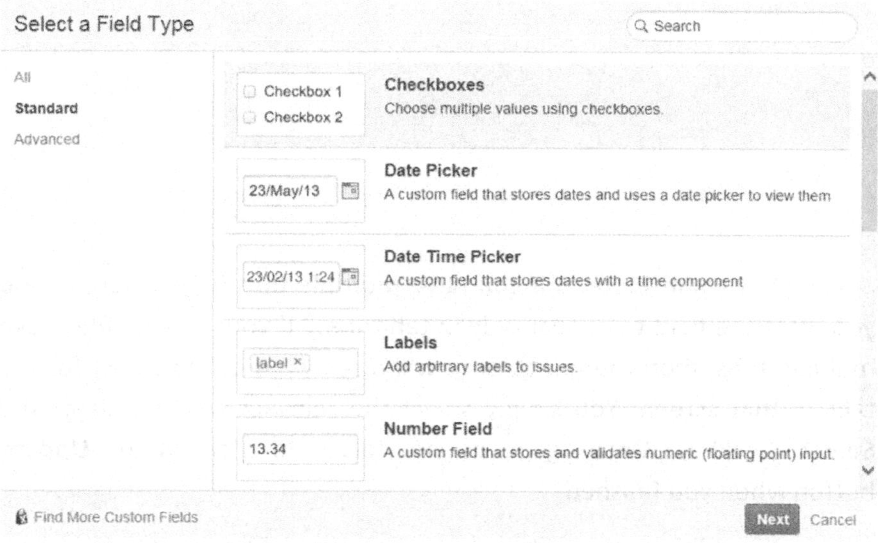

When creating a Custom Field, you go through three steps:

1. Select the type of Custom Field
2. Configure the Custom Field
3. Associate the Custom Field to a Screen

The image above is Step 1 of the Create a Custom Field process. After selecting the Custom Field, you click **Next**, and in the opened

Configure pop-up add a **Name** and **Description** (Step 2). Clicking on **Create** brings you to the view below, where you associate the newly created Custom Field to your desired Screen(s) (Step 3) by checking the relevant check box in the **Select** column:

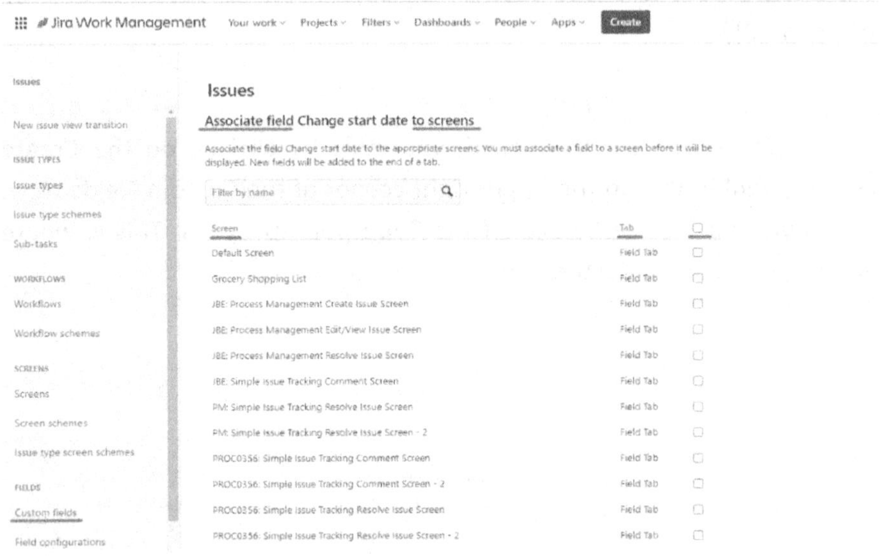

But what happens if you have **multiple tabs** in your screen and you want the field to appear only in tab three? If your screen *does* have multiple tabs, then the tab column will display a drop-down list for the tabs in that screen. You simply select the relevant tab and check the **Select** checkbox. Once again, do not forget to click on the **Update** button when you finished.

In addition, remember that when you add a custom field to a screen with this method, the field will be added to the bottom of that screen. If you want the field to be somewhere else in the screen you need to, first, open View Screens page (COG Jira Administration > Issues > Screens on the sidebar). Second, find your screen in the Name column and then click on the Configure link in the Actions column.

Exercise: Create Custom Fields

In this exercise we will:

- Create two custom Fields
- Associate the new Custom Fields to Screens

We will start by making a check list of commonly purchased grocery items. Please feel free to alter the list to meet your real-life needs.

1. Navigate to >  >**Issues**
2. In the **Administration Issue** view Select **Custom Fields** from the sidebar
3. In the Custom Field view click on **Add Custom Field**
4. In the **Select A Field Type** pop-up, click on **Checkboxes** and select **Next**
5. In the **Configure 'Checkboxes' Field** pop-up, Enter *Commonly Shopped Grocery Items* in the **Name** Field
6. Enter the purpose of the list in the **Description** field
7. In the **Options** field, Enter the Following, Click **Add** after each entry:
    - Northern Himalayan Organic Yak Milk
    - Island of Elba Goat Butter
    - 27 Grain Bread
    - Siberian Free Range Quail Eggs
    - Escargot
    - Brussels Sprouts from Brussels
    - Caviar
    - Kobe Beef
    - Champagne
    - Cognac
8. Click **Create**

9. IN THE **ASSOCIATE FIELD <NAME OF YOUR NEW FIELD> TO SCREENS** VIEW, FIND THE *GROCERY SHOPPING LIST* SCREEN IN THE **SCREEN** COLUMN AND CHECK ITS **SELECT** BOX
10. CLICK **UPDATE** AT THE BOTTOM OF THE VIEW

You have just added the new field to your *Grocery Shopping List* Screen. There are three ways to confirm this:

First,

1. NAVIGATE TO >  > **ISSUES**
2. IN THE **ADMINISTRATION ISSUE** VIEW, SELECT **SCREENS** FROM THE SIDEBAR
3. LOCATE THE *GROCERY SHOPPING LIST* SCREEN, AND CLICK ON THE **CONFIGURE** LINK IN THE **ACTIONS** COLUMN

You should see your newly created field in the list of fields for that screen:

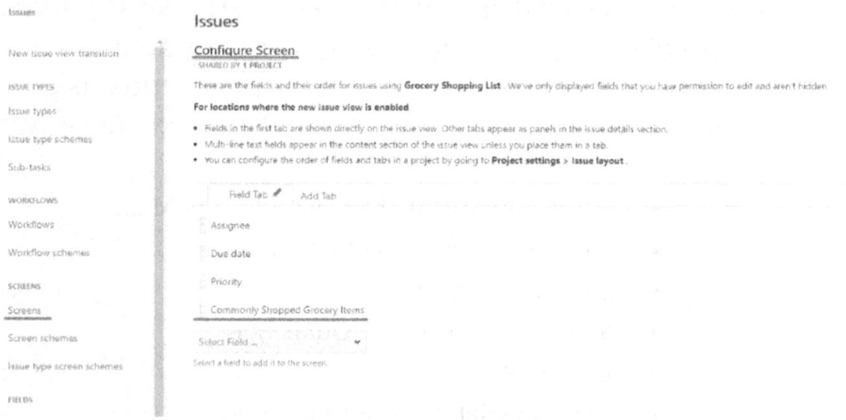

Second,

1. NAVIGATE TO > **PROJECTS** > *WEEKEND ACTIVITIES*
2. IN THE *WEEKEND ACTIVITIES* **PROJECT** CLICK **PROJECT SETTINGS** IN THE SIDEBAR
3. IN THE PROJECT SETTINGS SIDEBAR, CLICK ON **ISSUE LAYOUT**

4. IN THE ISSUE LAYOUT PAGE, FIND *GROCERY SHOPPING LIST*, AND CLICK ON **EDIT ISSUE LAYOUT**
5. IN THE GROCERY SHOPPING LIST PAGE, LOCATE THE COMMONLY SHOPPED GROCERY ITEMS FIELD:

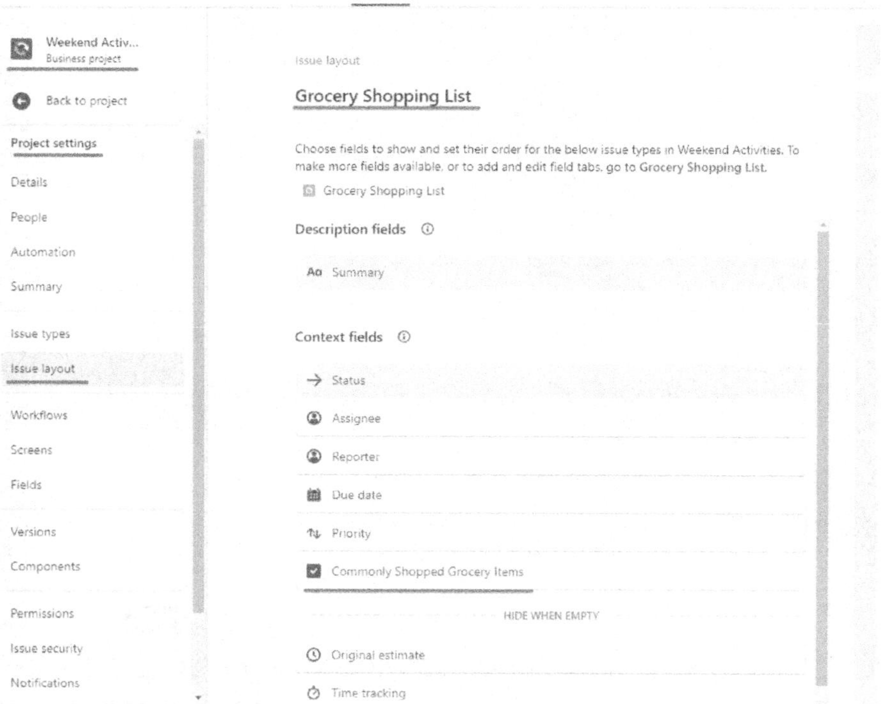

Third, now that I have made you jump through complicated hoops, the easiest way to check is to simply **Create** a *Grocery Shopping List* Issue. Your field should be on the Create screen.

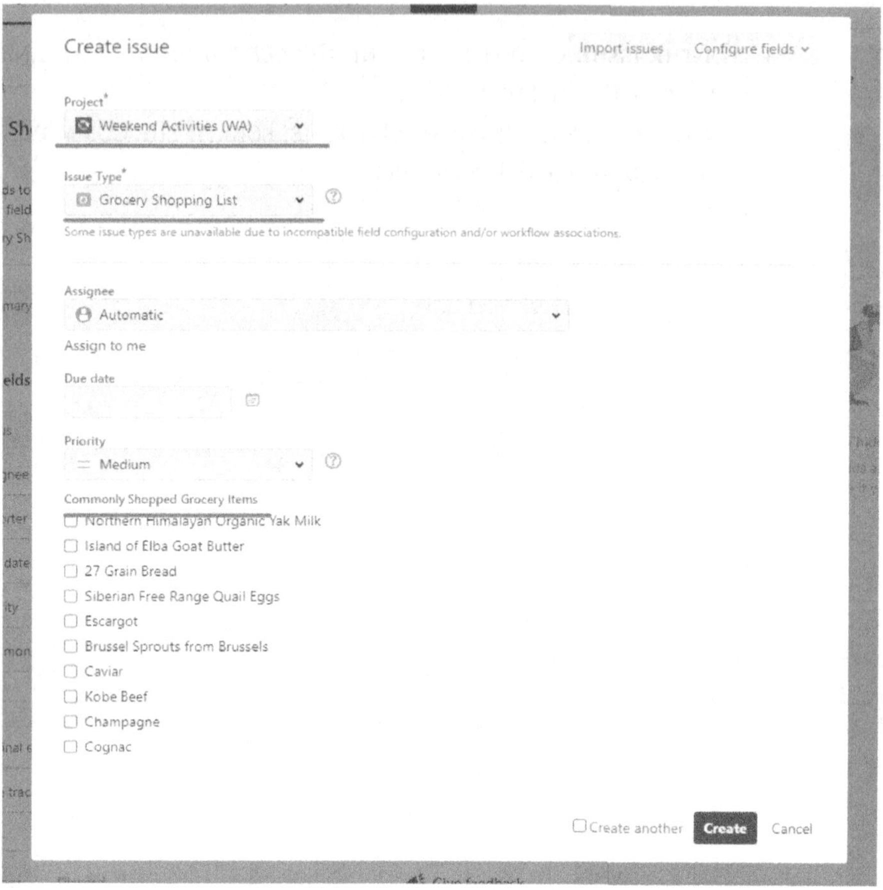

EXERCISE: CREATE MULTI-LINE TEXT BOX

It is convenient to have a list of commonly purchased grocery items; however, you probably purchase other items when you run out of stock. So, now you will create a multi-line text box where you can enter additional items for a specific shopping trip.

1. NAVIGATE TO >  >**ISSUES**
2. IN THE **ADMINISTRATION ISSUE** VIEW, SELECT **CUSTOM FIELDS** FROM THE SIDEBAR
3. IN THE CUSTOM FIELD VIEW CLICK ON **CREATE CUSTOM FIELD** BUTTON

4. IN THE **SELECT A FIELD TYPE** POP-UP, SCROLL DOWN TO **PARAGRAPH (SUPPORTS RICH TEXT).** CLICK ON IT, AND SELECT **NEXT**
5. IN THE **CONFIGURE 'PARAGRAPH (SUPPORTS RICH TEXT)' FIELD** POP-UP, ENTER *"ADDITIONAL GROCERY ITEMS"* IN THE **NAME** FIELD
6. ENTER *"ADDITIONAL ITEMS TO BE PURCHASED AT THE GROCERY STORE"* IN THE **DESCRIPTION** FIELD
7. CLICK **CREATE**
8. IN THE **ASSOCIATE FIELD <NAME OF NEW FIELD> TO SCREENS** VIEW, LOCATE *GROCERY SHOPPING LIST* IN THE **SCREEN** COLUMN AND CHECK THE **SELECT** BOX
9. CLICK **UPDATE** AT THE BOTTOM OF THE SCREEN

You have now created two new custom fields for your *Shopping List Screen*: a **checkbox field** with commonly shopped grocery items, and a **text box field** where you can enter additional food items for your shopping. Congratulations!

FIELD CONFIGURATION

Field Configuration allows you to modify fields. Here you decide if a field will be visible or hidden, optional or required, and where the field will be positioned on the Screen.

FIELD CONFIGURATION SCHEMES

Field Configuration Schemes link **Field Configurations** to specific **Issue Types** and from there to specific **Projects**. Field configurations allows you to:

1. Create custom descriptions that will appear below, or next to, a field (this is a great way to add data entry instructions for a specific field)

2. Show or hide a field
3. Make a field "required" or "optional"
4. Determine which renderer - "plain text" or "rich (HTML) text"- to use for text fields

ISSUE FEATURES

TIME TRACKING

Time tracking is an extremely powerful tool in Jira.

If you happen to click on the **COG Administration > Issues > Time Tracking** link in the sidebar (under Issue Features), you will be taken to the Time Tracking page:

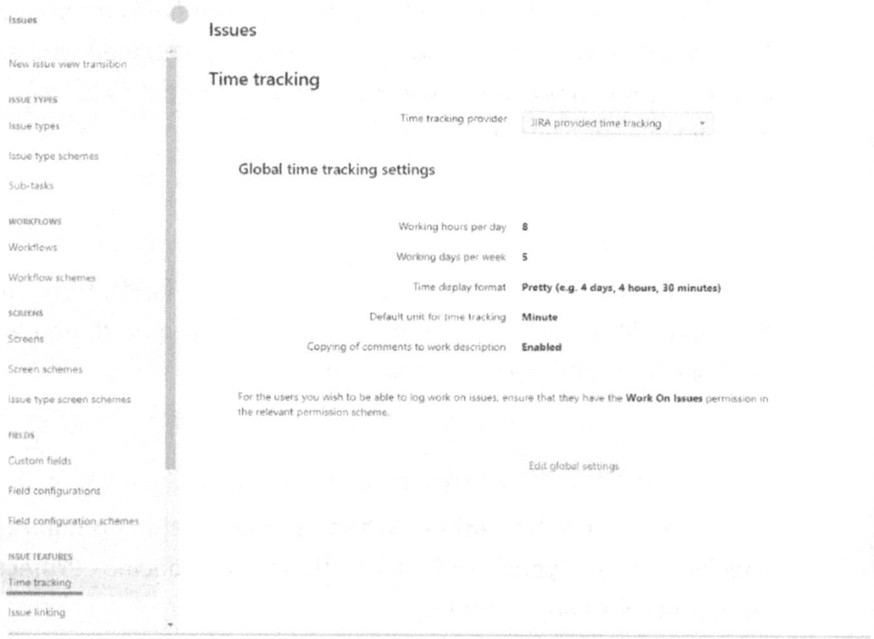

The screen will tell you who is providing the Time tracking: by Jira or an Atlassian Marketplace app.

By default, time tracking is always on in Jira.

This view will also tell you the default working hours per day, working days per week, and some other key metrics.

You can change these metrics by clicking on the **Edit global settings** button at the bottom of the view. In the Time Tracking settings pop-up you can change:

- Number of working hours per day
- Number of working days per week
- Time format
- Default time unit (e.g. minutes, hours, days, etc.)
- Copying of comments

"**Chapter 10 - Managing Time**" dives much deeper into time tracking and other Jira time management features.

Issue Linking

Issue linking allows you to associate one issue to another. For example, it lets you know if you need to complete Issue X before starting work on Issue Y. The good news is that the program informs you about this in the Issue Detail View. The bad news is that if you haven't completed Issue X, it won't stop you from starting Issue Y. In other words, Issue Linking is simply a notification method.

The User will need the **Link Issues** permission in order to perform this function.

Issue Attributes

Statuses

Most workflow design is done in the workflow section, so I am not quite sure why Statuses is included here. I would avoid it altogether to keep things simpler. However, if you need to translate a status this is the place to do so.

Resolutions

In Jira, resolution tells the software – and others - you are formally finished with the issue, and it will now be closed out in the system. A resolution is NOT a status. Jira has three default resolutions. You can add your own Resolutions at the bottom of the View Resolutions page. For example, I have added a resolution in my Jira called "Issue Canceled". I use it to let me close out an Issue from any status in the workflow.

Priorities

You may, when creating an **Issue,** want to associate a **Priority** to that Issue. It's quite easy: when creating an Issue simply click on the **Priority field** and select the priority you want. The Priority Field is included in the standard Task Issue Type, and you can also add it to any custom screen you build. In addition, you can change a priority in the **Issues Detail View** after an issue has been created.

If you don't like the default priority format, you can change it.

Exercise: View Priorities

1. Select Navigation Bar >  > **Issues**
2. In the **Issues** View, select **Priorities** in the sidebar:

The **Priorities** view shows you all current **Priorities**. In this view you can edit, delete, translate priority, change its color and icon, etc.

If your organization or team uses a different priority structure, then you can add new priorities at the bottom of the screen. This is helpful if you have a specific **Priority** structure in your organization (as many do). Just remember that if you do add new priorities, those new priorities will be visible to every User in the organization. So, if it is critical for you to have two different priority schemes, and you don't want to have them both in the same project, you will need to set up a new site, install a new instance of JWM and create a new priority hierarchy and delete the default. Needless to say, that's a little frustrating, so let's hope Atlassian comes up with a change that allows you to create multiple priority schemes for a project.

CAUTION: You can only assign a priority to the entire issue, not to a specific field in an issue.

Issue Security Schemes

Issue Security Schemes are described in more detail in the next chapter.

Notifications and Notification Schemes

One of the great strengths of Jira is its ability to create automated email notifications to specific people based on events that happen during the lifecycle of an issue. For example, you can have an automated email go to the next person in the process once you click a specific status transition in an Issue. Or you can set it up so that an automated email will be sent to the project manager or Issue Owner's boss indicating the issue is late and should be checked into.

There are a few defaults set up in the program. The most obvious is that you will get an email as soon as you are assigned to a project issue. However, you can also bespoke notifications based on almost any condition or event that might occur in your project.

Notifications need Notification schemes to be associated with a project. Notifications is not a beginner topic.

Permissions and Schemes

You probably don't want anyone and everyone to see all the details of your project and make any change they want. Imagine if someone from sales started making changes to the manufacturing process, or vice versa. The Permissions (and Security) areas are where you assign people to Groups and Roles, and where you decide the Screens they can see, or not, and the things they can edit, or not.

Why not just assign those things directly to individuals? That's because individuals often leave the organization or change jobs. You could spend a whole bunch of time giving an individual specific permissions and security clearances, only to see that person win the lottery. You would have to redo all that work for the person who replaces her. Better to create a **Role**, assign all the permissions to the role and simply link the individual to the Role.

Of course, Permissions need Permission schemes to work with a Project.

We look at permissions and schemes in more detail in the next chapter.

Chapter 9 - Users, Roles, and Groups

To avoid confusion, in this book the term "Site-admin" includes "Org-admin, Site-admin, and Jira-admin" unless specifically noted otherwise.

CHAPTER OBJECTIVES

By the end of this Chapter, you will have a working understanding of:

- **Users, Roles, and Groups**
- **Permissions and Permission schemes**
- **Issue Security Schemes**

You will be able to:

- **invite a User**
- **assign Users to a Role**
- **create a Group and assign a User to the Group**
- **assign a Global Permission to a Group**
- **Create a Project Permission Scheme**
- **Create a Project Admin Role**

NOTE: You must have a paid version license of Jira Work Management to work with Roles and Permissions (i.e. you are not able to work with Jira Roles and advanced Permissions with the Free Basic version of Jira Work Management).

Users, Roles, and Groups

Overview

While Jira Work Management is fantastic at automating a great many tasks and operations, a project still involves people, and there needs to be a way of managing people within Jira and within specific projects.

Jira manages people using two - connected - methods: with Permissions, and with Groups/Roles.

A permission is an authorization, or approval, to do something. In Jira you need permission to do anything. Literally. Want to create an Issue? You need permission. Want to edit an Issue? You need permission. Want to comment, view, see other Users? Permission. Permission. Permission. You cannot breathe in Jira without a permission.

At the time of writing this book, there are over 34 different permission/security settings and 18 global permissions available in Jira Work Management, though some require licenses for Jira Service Management or Jira Software.

How does it work?

Jira allows you to be directly assigned to projects or issues. But this means every time you are assigned to a new project or issue, someone needs to manually go through that long and tedious permission checklist and determine what you can and cannot do in that project or issue.

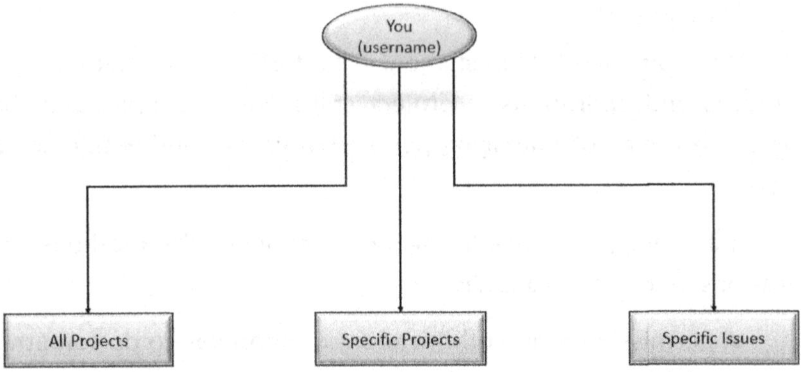

It might be manageable if you have only five or six people in your organization, but you can imagine the headaches if you have 1,000 employees. And what happens when you win the lottery, and the supervisor must go through that same permission checklist for your replacement. Things get ugly real fast using this method. That's why Jira implemented **Groups and Roles**.

Groups and Roles are ways of easily managing permissions and Users. Groups deal with **all** Jira Projects and Issues. Roles are restricted to specific Projects and Issues.

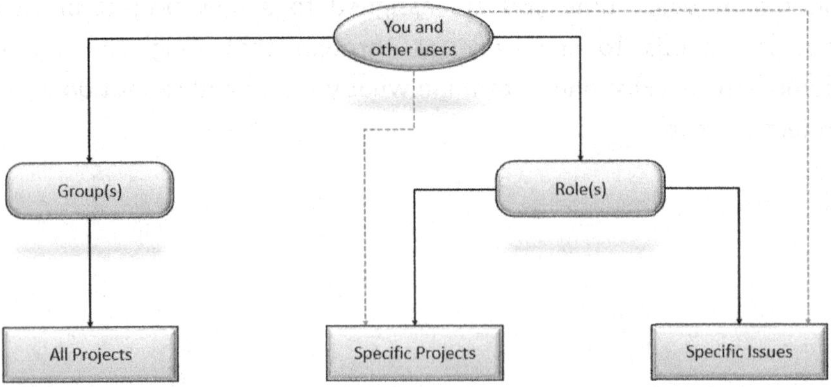

When working with Groups and Roles, you go through three steps:

1. A Group or Role is created
2. Permissions are associated with the Group or Role
3. Users are then assigned to the Group or Role

The advantage to this approach is that when people change jobs or leave the organization you simply remove – from the group or role - the username of the person who left and replace it with the new username. You don't need to go through that long permission checklist again.

GROUPS VS. ROLES

But what's the **difference between a Group and a Role in Jira**? Great question.

Groups have what are called 'global' permissions. This means they work with all projects, no exceptions. You cannot say, "I want this Group to work with all my organization's projects except this one project over here". It is all or nothing.

By default, any User who is licensed is assigned to the Jira-workmanagement-users Group AND is given Application Access (a permission). That means they can view and work with any Issue in any project. That's not a bad idea if you have a small company and everybody does everything. You don't need to go through all the bother of creating Roles, permission schemes, and then assigning people to those Roles and projects. But as you grow, you are likely to find it necessary to restrict what your team members can see and do. Do you really want Sam in Distribution to have access to the Finance project?

A **Role** is not global. Roles are meant for a specific project or projects. For example, you might create a Role called 'Denver Sales

Representative' and associate it with the Denver project. Or you may design a Human Resources role that can be used in several projects.

Personally, I would think of the difference between Roles and Groups this way: Groups have permission and security rules that are applicable regardless of Role. A Role has job specific rules. For example, you may create two Roles, one a Supply Chain Analyst and one a Quality Control Analyst. Just by the titles you can see each will have different requirements and need unique restrictions. The most obvious Role specific requirements and restrictions may be that the Supply Chain Analyst will have access to Supply Chain projects and no other, while the QC Analyst can work only with QC projects.

One common misconception about Groups and Roles is that they are distinct. You can belong to a Group but not a Role (or vice versa). This is not true. Groups and Roles are designed to work together. Let's look at the most obvious. Everyone who has a Jira Work Management license belongs to the "Jira-workmanagement-users" group. You can also belong to – for example - the "Supply Chain Management" Role within a specific project or projects. Each Role will have specific permissions ("Create Issues" or "Edit Issues" for example). Group permissions are completely different from Role permissions and there will be no conflict between the two.

Now that we have a good idea of the differentiation between Users, Roles, and Groups let's look at each in more detail.

Jira Work Management Default Groups

August of 2021 saw Atlassian implementing major changes to Administration groups and permissions. This change was necessary to cleanup and streamline things after the move from Server to Cloud versions of Jira. If your organization implemented Jira before August 2021, you will have one set of Administration groups; and those who implemented Jira during or after August 2021 will have another.

We will use the default groups for Jira Work Management instances created after August 2021.

After August 2021 there are three default groups for Jira Work Management: Site-admins, Jira-admins, and Jira-workmanagement-users.

The table below details the group permissions associated with each of these default groups.

Group Permission Comparisons (post Aug 2021)

Permission	Site admin	Jira Admin	Jira User
Access to billing	Y	N	N
Access to all org. level settings	Y	N	N
Access to all site level settings	Y	N	N
Access to all products in the site	Y	N	N
Create new User	Y	N	N
Assign Users to Groups	Y	N	N
Grant product access	Y	Y	N
Create and admin projects	Y	Y	N
Create global Issue types	Y	Y	N
Create global fields	Y	Y	N
Create global workflows	Y	Y	N
Create global schemes	Y	Y	N
Browse Users and groups	Y	Y	N
Share dashboards and filters	Y	Y	N
Manage group filter subscriptions	Y	Y	N
Create team-managed projects	Y	Y	Y
Make Bulk changes	Y	Y	Y
Log in to JWM	-	-	Y

Jira Work Management Basics

Groups

Logging in to JWM

The Jira-workmanagement-users group has two fundamental purposes. First, everyone who is licensed to work with Jira Work Management is automatically assigned to the Jira-workmanagement-users group. Everyone. Once you are a member of the Jira-workmanagement-users group, you can then be assigned to additional groups (e.g. Jira-Admin) as needed. Second, being a Jira-workmanagement-user means you have a license to use JWM. And of course, it is used to count how many licenses your organization currently has. Atlassian uses this to calculate your license billing charges.

While there are some exceptions, being a User allows the individual to:

- view all the Issues in the Project
- Create Issues within that Project

Make bulk Changes

If, for example, you want to delete numerous Issues at one time, you do so using the bulk change feature. Users have this permission by default. However, this permission can be turned off for specific project roles (this is done in the Project Role permission scheme).

Create team-managed projects

Any licensed JWM User can create team-managed projects. Remember that a team-managed project is a very basic stripped-down project with no flexibility. It is useful for small teams performing very local simple tasks. If you want the full features of a Jira project, that needs to be built by a Jira-admin or site-admin.

About Admins

One of the most common questions I get about Jira has to do with "Admins". There seems to be more admin groups in Jira than the sudden appearance of long-lost relatives and acquaintances showing up at the door of a lottery winner. Some of this has to do with the revisions Atlassian made in August of 2021, but that still leaves us with a gaggle of admin groups. To be familiar with these various admin groups let's start by understanding the Atlassian/Jira cloud environment.

As you know, Atlassian is now a cloud environment. In this environment Atlassian has a group called "System-admin". These are Atlassian employees, and their role is to ensure the Atlassian cloud environment works correctly. They can log into your applications to provide you technical support, and they also provide regular system maintenance tasks (e.g. product updates).

When you first sign up for an Atlassian product (JWM, Confluence, JSM, etc.), you are given an "Organization". Your work is done within the Organization.

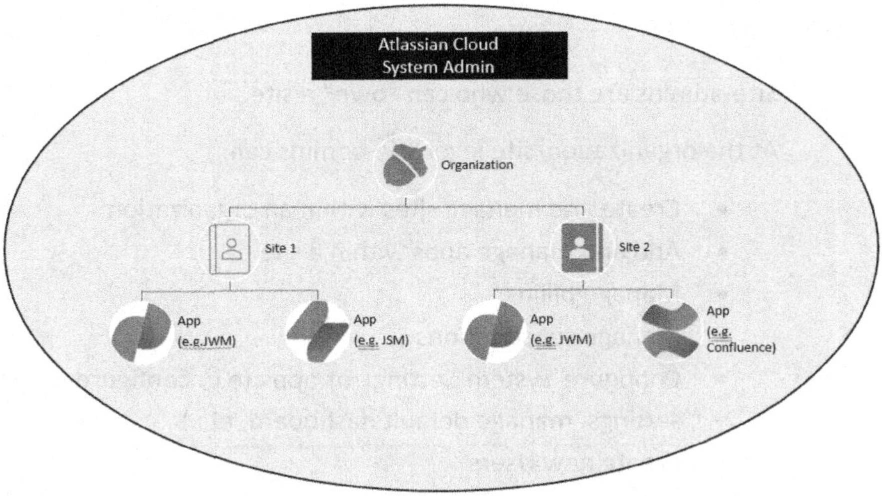

Jira Work Management Basics

After your organization has been set up, you can create one or more Sites within the organization. A site can contain multiple Atlassian apps (e.g. Jira Work Management, Confluence, Jira Software, Opsgenie, Jira Service Management, etc.). But you can only have one instance of an app inside the site. For example, in a Site you cannot have two instances of Jira Work Management. If you need two instances of Jira Work Management, you need to create two sites within the Organization and add a JWM instance to each of them.

So, to recap, within your Atlassian environment there are three levels: Organization, Site, and Apps. How does that structure affect Admins? In other words, who does what?

Org-admins

The Org-admin is the "highest level" administrator. Having said that, while the Org-admin can do most of the stuff the Site-admin and Jira-admin can do, they tend to focus their attention on two areas:

- Licensing, Billing, password policies, etc.
- System Admin "Lite" activities", such as connecting to Google Workspace and other external actors, APIs, etc.

For the purposes of this book, we can ignore the Org-admin.

Site-admins

Site-admins are those who can "own" a site.

At the organization/site level Site-admins can:

- Create and manage sites within an organization
- Add and manage apps within a site
- Manage billing
- Manage subscriptions
- Configure System Settings of apps (e.g. configure email settings, manage default dashboard, etc.)
- Create new Users

- Allow product access
- Assign Users to groups
- Have access to all apps on a site
- Perform Jira-administrator level activities

Jira-Administrators

Jira-administrators work at the app level within a specific site. They are assigned to a site and to specific apps within that site by Site-admins.

At the app level Jira-administrators can:

- Create and manage projects within the site
- Configure projects with the site
- Create schemes, workflows, custom fields, etc. within the app
- Make a User into a Project-admin for a specific project(s)
- Perform Project-admin functions

Jira Project Admin

A Jira Project Admin is technically a Jira User who has been given permission to manage a project or projects. Despite being called an "Administrator" they have very few administrator permissions and are extremely limited in what they can do. Do not think of them as an "Admin" like a Site-admin or Jira-administrator. They are more like a team-lead or a project manager.

Within their assigned project, Jira Project Admins can:

- Customize the appearance of the project
- Add and remove existing Jira Users
- Do some minor configuration tasks
- Have visibility to their project's schemes (but cannot make changes to them)

- Assign and manage Issues
- Ensure the data within the project is correct
- Request changes or additional functionality for their project (e.g. ask a Site-admin or Jira-administrator to create a new custom field or workflow step)

USERS

EXERCISE: VIEW USER MANAGEMENT

1. NAVIGATE TO> ⚙ > **USER MANAGEMENT**
2. THE **USERS** VIEW WILL OPEN:

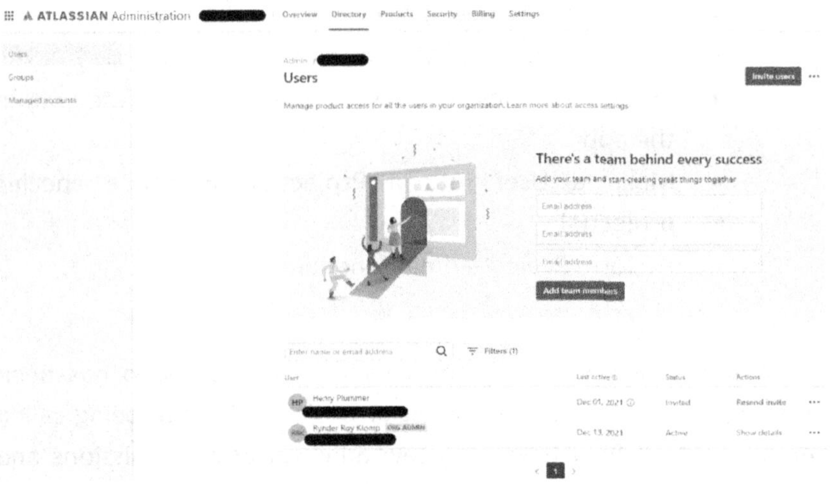

In the Users view you can:

- invite new Users to join Jira
- invite existing Jira Users to join a team
- find Users
- see details about the Users

Invite Users

Exercise: Invite User

1. On the Navigation bar, click on the **Administration COG**, and select **User Management**
2. In the Administration > User Management view, click on the **Invite User** button in the upper right corner of the view:

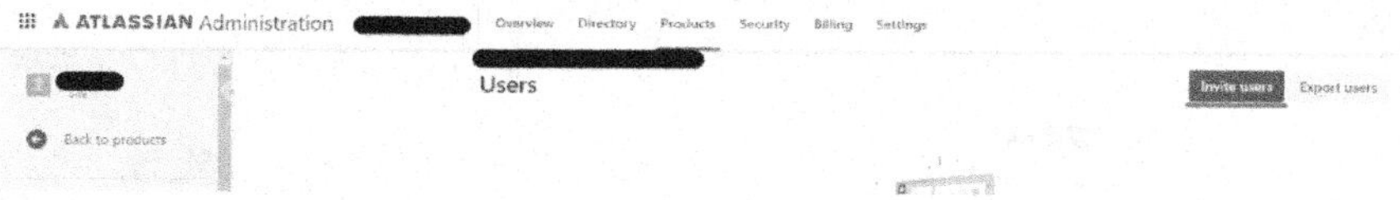

This brings you to the Invite Users pop-up:

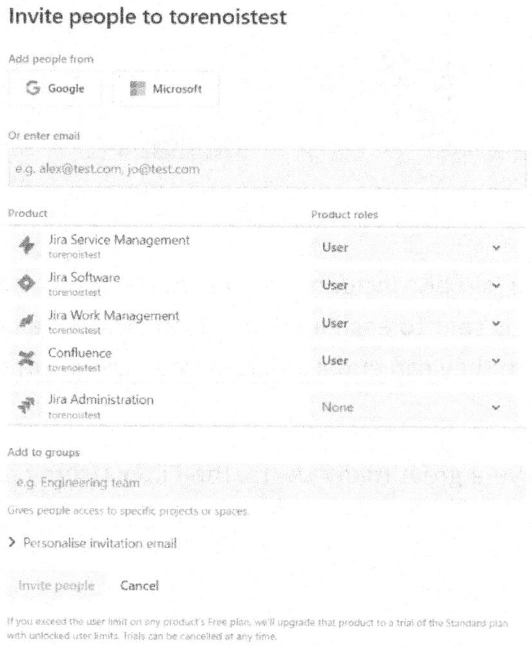

3. Start inviting a User by entering their **email address**
4. Click on the **product** you want the User to join, and select the **User Role**

5. CLICK **UNSELECT ALL** IN THE PRODUCT ROLES DROPDOWNS FOR ALL OTHER PRODUCTS
6. SKIP OVER ADD TO GROUPS
7. ADD A PERSONAL INVITATION EMAIL IF YOU WISH
8. CLICK ON INVITE PEOPLE

INVITE USERS – QUICK VERSION

Another way of inviting Users is to use the form in the Users view:

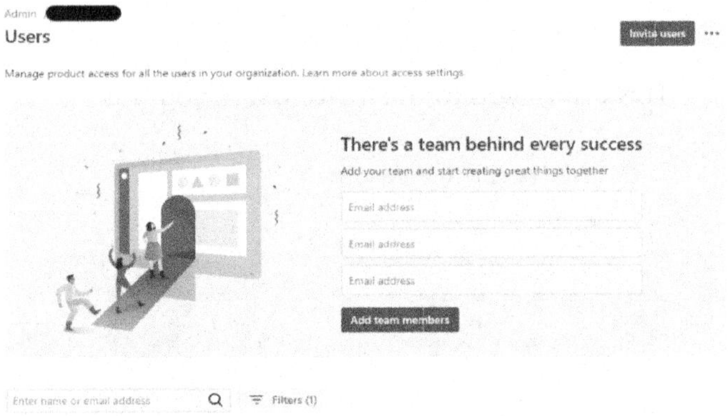

Here you simply include one or more email addresses. An automated email is sent to each invitee, which includes a link to the Jira signup view where they can enter a User-name, password, etc.

FILTER USERS

If you have a great many Users, the **Filter Users** feature is quite handy.

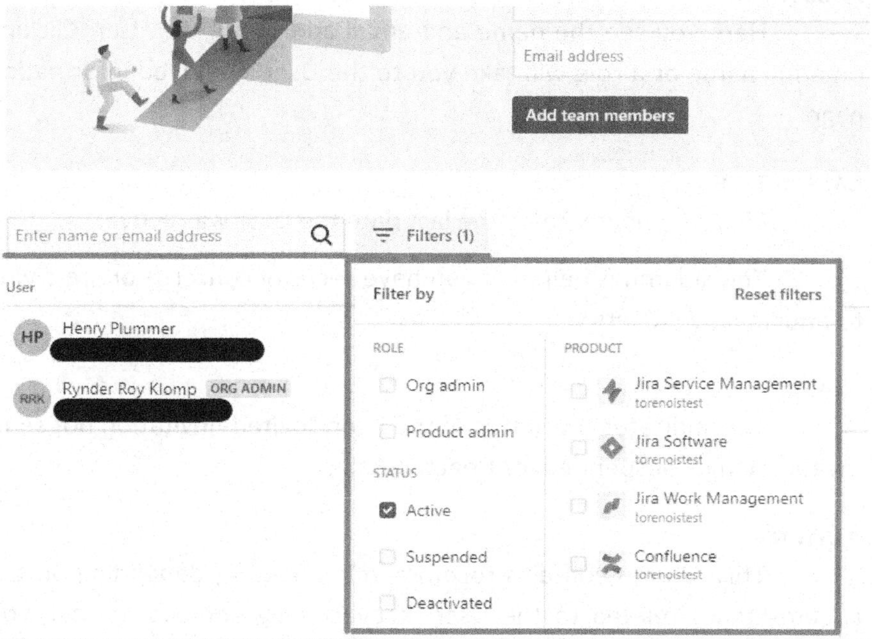

The easiest method is to enter the name or email address of the User you want to find.

If that doesn't work, then click on the **Filters** link and a drop down will appear with a number of **Filter by** options. Here you can filter **by Jira Role**, Atlassian **Product**, of by the **Status** of the User.

Clicking the **Reset filters** link clears all the fields.

The User's Columns

The **Users** view has five columns: **User** name**, Last active, Status, Actions**, and **More**.

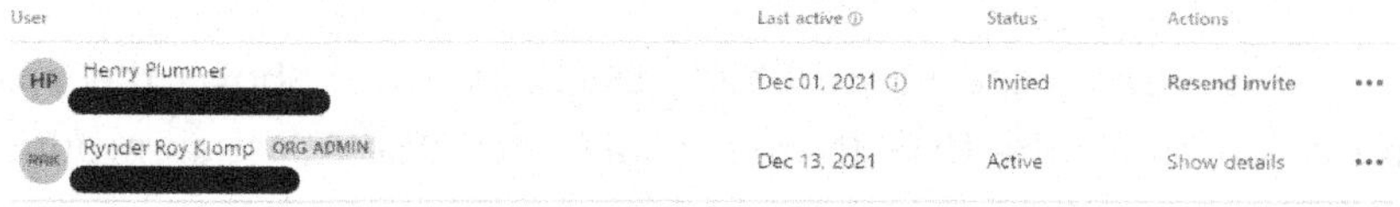

FULL NAME

Here you see the name and email address of the User. Clicking on a full name or a role will take you to the User's detailed information page.

LAST ACTIVE

This column indicates the last date the User was active.

The column is helpful if you have security concerns or are trying to find 'inactive' Users.

STATUS

This indicates the status of the User: Invited- Invitation not sent, Invited, Active, Suspended, or Deactivated.

ACTIONS

This column contains recommended actions, depending on the circumstances related to the User. If everything appears normal, you will probably see "Show details", which will take you to the User's details view. However, if there appears to be something abnormal, you may see a recommended action. For example, if you invited someone to become a User and they have not responded within 7 days, you may see "Resend invite" in the column.

MORE

The **More (...)** column will, depending on the User's status, allow you to open the User's details view (**Show details**), **Add User to group**, or **Suspend Access** to Jira. Let's take a deeper dive into the "Show details" view.

Show details

The next image is the User's Details view. It shows the basic information about the User (Name, email, etc.), the Atlassian products the User is licensed to use, and the Groups to which the User belongs.

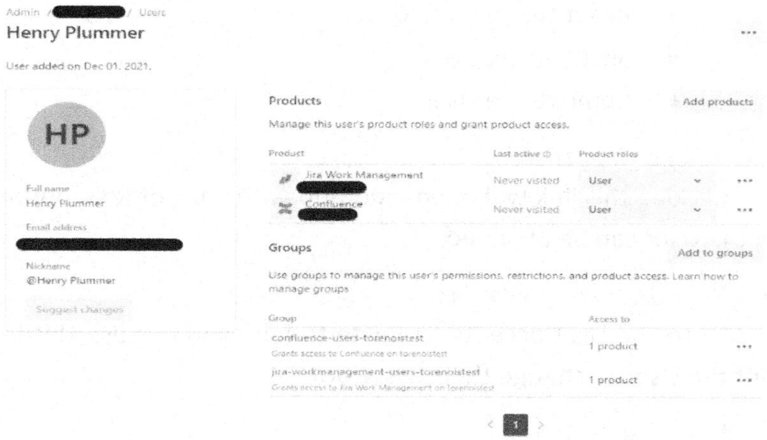

Add products

Clicking on the **Add products** link opens a pop-up where you can grant the User access to an Atlassian product and assign them to a Role within that product.

Add to groups

Clicking on the **Add to groups** link will open a pop-up where you can add the User to a group or groups. Simply click on the "Group name" field and a drop-down list appears with groups available for the User to join.

When clicking on the More (...) link, in the User's detail's view, a further sub-menu appears:

Here you can:

- Assign the User to a Role
- Reset the password
- Suspend access
- Remove the User

Assign User to a Role

Clicking this link will open a pop-up with a list of Role options to which the User can be assigned.

Prompt reset password

Once the User accepts an Invite to join, you can use this link to prompt the User to change their password.

Suspend access

The "Suspend access" link is very helpful if you don't want to delete the User, for example a User who has gone on sabbatical or pregnancy leave. A **Suspended** User cannot access Jira and will not receive any further email notifications. Possibly most important, an **Inactive User no longer counts as a Licensed User**, which is quite beneficial if you are near or at your License limit.

Remove User

Finally, you can delete a User by clicking the **Remove User** link. As the warning will tell you, Deleting a User cannot be undone.

Working with Groups

A **Group** is a collection of individuals in Jira who have the same global permissions, *regardless* of their **Project Role**. For example, the most common group in Jira Work Management is the **Jira-workmanagement-users** Group. Anyone with a JWM license is assigned to this group; and being a member of the User Group allows the individual to use JWM.

Groups can work together with:

- Global permissions

- Project roles
- Workflows
- Permission Schemes
- Email Notification Schemes
- Issue Security Schemes
- Issue Filters
- Dashboards

GROUP PERMISSIONS

There are six global permissions available:

Global Permission	Comments
Administer Jira	Primary permission allows the Administrator to create and administer all aspects of projects. Note: a Jira Administrator cannot manage Users, import/export data, or edit system email settings by default. Those permissions must be granted by the Site-Admin in the User Management area.
Browse Users and Groups	A permission to view and select all Jira User names and group names. Also, to share Issues.
Share Dashboards and Filters	A permission to share a filter or dashboard globally or with specific groups. Many organizations have people who specialize in creating all the filters and dashboards for the

	organization.
Manage Group Filter Subscriptions	A permission to create and delete group filter subscriptions.
Bulk Change	A permission for the bulk operations: -Bulk Edit -Bulk Move -Bulk Workflow Transition -Bulk Delete
Create team-managed projects	Allows the User to create stand-alone projects (i.e. the projects cannot associate with any other Jira project).

Often large organizations will create specific groups for: **Browse Users and Groups, Share Dashboards and Filters, Manage Group Filter Subscriptions**, and **Make Bulk Changes**. They then assign specialists to each of these groups. This tends to limit the potential for chaos that may occur if everyone is given the ability to Make Bulk Changes (for example).

GROUP VIEW

EXERCISE: VIEW GROUP

1. NAVIGATE TO>  >**USER MANAGEMENT**
2. IN THE ADMINISTRATION > USER MANAGEMENT'S SIDEBAR CLICK ON **GROUPS**

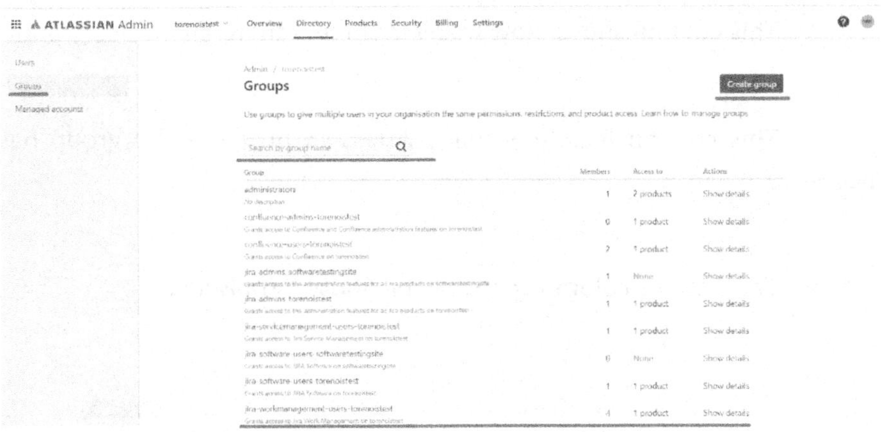

I like this view as it has all the 'Group stuff' in one place. Here you can: Create a group, use a Filter to narrow your group search, and see a listing of all your Groups.

CREATE GROUP

In the **Create Group** text box simply type in the name of the new Group, fill in the Group's Description, and click the Create Group button. That's it. Your new Group appears instantly in the Groups page.

FILTER GROUP

Type in the name, or partial name, of a **Group** in the **Filter Group** text box and click the **magnifying glass** button to narrow your range of Group Names.

THE GROUPS COLUMNS

The **Groups** view contains four columns: **Group, Members, Access to,** and **Actions.**

GROUP

This listing contains the names of your **Groups**, shown in alphabetical order. You cannot have duplicate group names.

Members

This column shows how many members there are in this group.

Access to product

This column lists how many Atlassian products the group has access to.

Actions

The Actions column contains the **Show details** link.

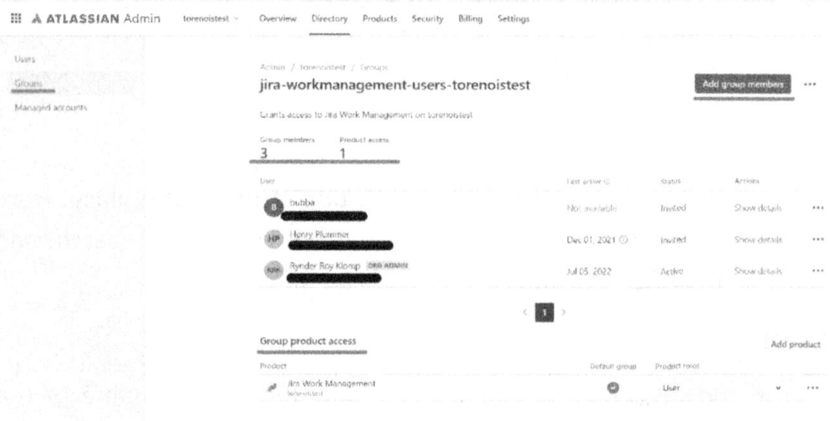

The **Groups' Show details** view, well, shows you the members who belong to the group and the products to which the groups have access.

You can also add members to the group with the **Add group members** button in the upper right corner. Or you can associate the group to other products by using the **Add product** button.

When you click the More (...) drop-down menu, you can either Edit the description of the group or delete custom groups.

More (...)

Back in the Groups view, the last column (...) allows you to remove the member from the group. This column appears after you have added at least one group member.

Exercise: Create Group

In the exercises below you will:

- Create a Group
- Add a User to a Group
- Give the Group a Global Permission

1. Navigate to>  >**User management**
2. In the Administration User Management's Sidebar click on **Groups**
3. In the Groups view, click on the blue **Create group** button
4. In the Create group pop-up, enter "*Test Group*" in the **Group name** text box
5. Enter "*Temporary test group for JWM lessons*" in the **Description field**
6. Do not click the *Add members in next step* check box
7. Click the **Create Group** button

You have created the Group.

Next, you will add a User to the Group.

Exercise: Add User to Group

1. In the **Test Group** page, click on **Add Members** link
2. In the **Add members to group** pop-up, enter your name in the text box, or select your name from the list that appears.

NOTE: The list will appear for a limited time. If no action is taken, it will disappear. Don't worry, because once you start typing in the text box the list will reappear

3. Click the **Add** button

You have just added your name to the newly created Test Group.

The next thing we need to do is ensure your newly created group will be able to work with JWM.

EXERCISE: GRANT GROUP ACCESS TO JWM

1. IN THE **TEST GROUP'S** VIEW, CLICK THE **ADD PRODUCT** LINK IN THE GROUP PRODUCT ACCESS AREA
2. IN THE **ADD PRODUCTS TO GROUP** POPUP, CLICK ON THE **PRODUCT ROLES** DROP-DOWN FOR JIRA WORK MANAGEMENT AND SELECT **USER**
3. MAKE SURE ALL OTHER PRODUCTS IN THE POPUP READ NONE IN THEIR DROP-DOWNS
4. CLICK **ADD**

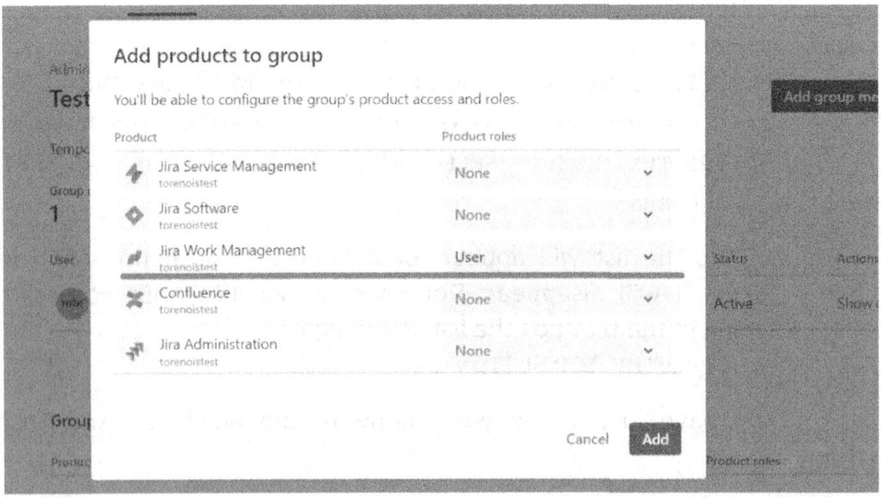

So far you have created a Group, added a member to that Group, and activated that Group to work with JWM. Next, we will give the Group a Global Permission.

Exercise: Grant Group Global Permission

1. Navigate to>  > **System**
2. In the Administration System's sidebar click on **Global Permissions** in the Security section
3. Scroll to the Bottom of the **Global Permissions** page to the **Grant Permission** area
4. Select *Create team-managed projects* in the **Permission** drop down list
5. Select *Test Group* in the **Group** drop down list
6. Click the **Add** button

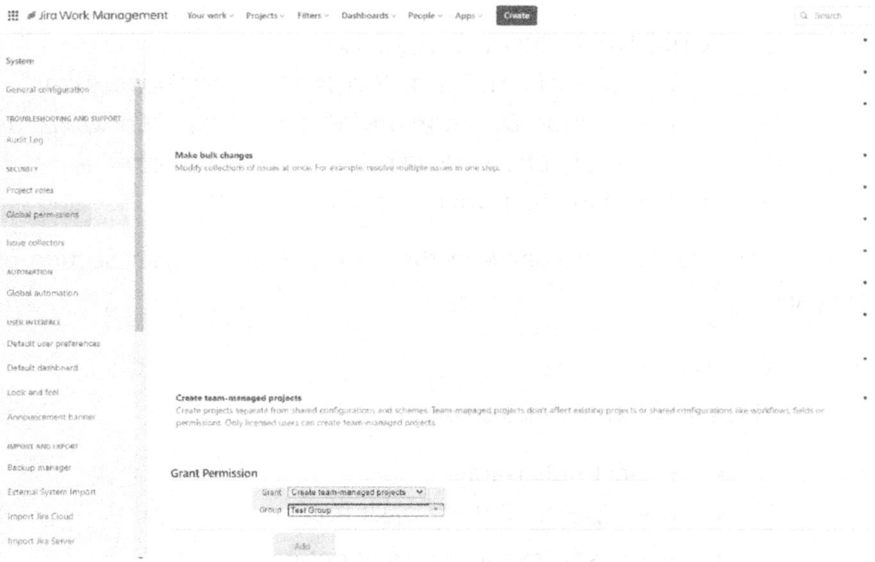

You have associated your newly created group to a Global Permission.

Working with Roles

Think of a Role as a "Job". A User is assigned to a job (a Role) that has specific responsibilities (permissions) for a specific project or projects.

Exercise: Create a User Role

1. Navigate to>  >**System**
2. In the System view sidebar, select **Project roles**

3. In the **Add Project Role** section:
   i. In the **Name** field, enter "*Activity Coordinator*"
   ii. In the **Description** field, enter "*Coordinator Role for the Weekend Activities Project*"
4. Click Add Project Role

The new role will show in the Project Role Browser section of the page.

Project Role Browser

This section contains 3 columns:

- Project Role Name
- Description (of the Project Role)
- Actions (with four possible options)

Project Role Name

This column shows all available project roles, listed in alphabetical order. I advise you consider applying a standard format for Project Role Names, so you can easily identify them later.

I recommend, whenever possible, creating Project Role names by duplicating existing Job Titles within your organization. For example, in your organization you may have a Marketing Analyst job title with five employees as well as a Marketing Analyst Manager with one employee. Each job title, if done correctly in your organization, should have a very clear job description associated with it. I suggest you follow the same practice. After all, the work of defining a Role and determining what the User does within the Role has already been done for you by the organization. Additionally, why would you create Roles that are different from existing job titles? Doing so will: a) just confuse people, and b) make employees very suspicious if they see themselves attached to a different job title (Role). *"Does this mean my job is changing?" "Will I have to learn new tasks?" "Will I have new responsibilities?"* Why would you want to risk trouble by making up new Role names?

Of course, speaking out of the other side of my mouth, part of the reason for implementing Jira Work Management may be because you want to change work processes **and** Roles, or create new ones. In this case, I recommend you create a dramatically different Project Role names. Do you want to send a clear message that this is a different job? Just don't forget to coordinate with your HR department and implement your **Change Management** strategy before you do.

The second thing to consider when creating Project Role names is the name of your Project. If the role is meant for only one project, then you should include the role name *and* abbreviation of the **project name**, as the first part of the Project Role name; for example, ACME Project Supply Chain Analyst.

Description

The Description of a Project Role should include both an expanded explanation of the Project Role Name and more details around the role itself. If the Project Role is going to be integrated into a workflow, it is recommended you add a warning line informing that, for example, deleting the role or editing its name will cause the workflow to fail.

Actions

The Actions column contains four possible functions: View Usage, Manage Default Members, Edit, and Delete.

View Usage

This view shows which projects, workflows, and various schemes (notification, permission, and issue security) are using the Role. A nice thing about this view is that it also shows which projects are using which schemes.

Manage Default Members

In many organizations there is typically a single person or team of people assigned to a particular role. The **Manage Default Members** link allows you to assign a User, or number of Users, as the default individual(s) for the Project Role. In this approach you don't need to search through your entire database of Users to assign someone to the project role every time you create a new project.

As you can see, assigning a **Default User** to a Project Role is straight forward. You can also change the **Default Group** associated with a Project Role.

A good thing to keep in mind is that any changes you make to the Default User will not affect existing projects, it only takes effect with newly created projects. It is important to note that adding a Default User will only affect projects created after adding the default User. Any existing projects using the same role will continue with the existing User assigned to that role.

EDIT

In this view you can edit the name or description of the role.

CAUTION: Be very careful when making a Role Name change, especially if the existing Name is deeply integrated with **workflows.** If you change the Role name, it is highly likely the workflow will fail because it will try to access the old name.

DELETE

This view allows you to delete the role from all projects and schemes with which it is associated.

CAUTION: Remember that when you delete a project role, you are not just deleting it from the current project, you will also delete it from **all projects** and **all schemes** with which the project role is associated.

EXERCISE: ASSIGN A USER TO A ROLE AND A ROLE TO A PROJECT

In the previous exercise we created a Project Role. In this exercise you will assign a User to that Role. At the same time, we will add the Role to the project. We do that through the project itself.

1. ON THE NAVIGATION BAR, OPEN THE **PROJECTS** MENU AND SELECT *WEEKEND ACTIVITIES*

2. In the **Weekend Activities** project's sidebar, select **Project Settings**
3. In the Project settings view sidebar, select **People**

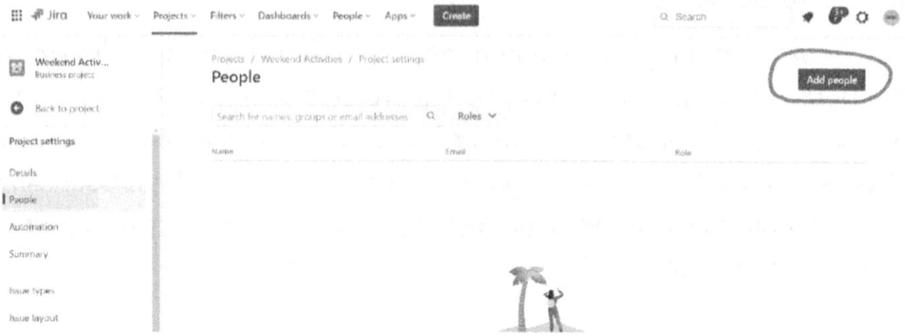

4. In the People view, click on the **Add people** button
5. In the Add people pop-up, enter your name in the **User name** field
6. In the **Role** field select *Activity Coordinator*

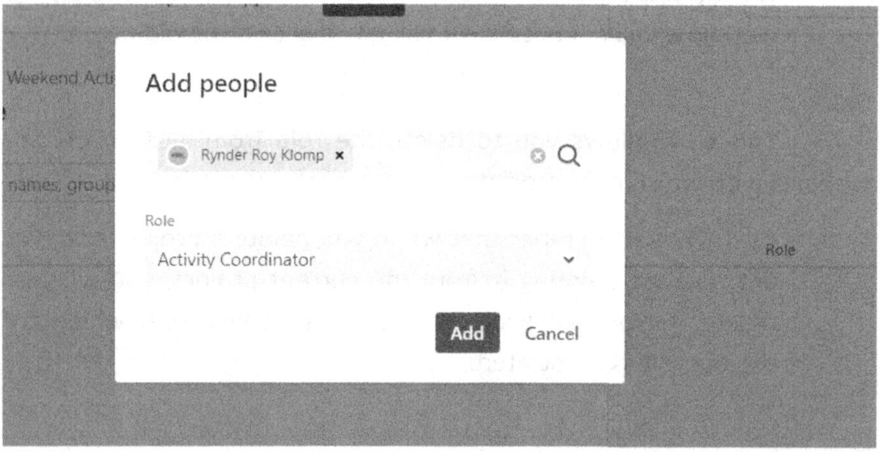

7. Click **Add**

You are now assigned to the Weekend Activity project in the Role of Activity Coordinator.

Permissions

Earlier in this chapter we explained how to create Users, assign them to Roles and then assign them to Projects. All of that work is a complete waste of time unless we also address project permissions.

Here is a scenario that happens frequently when new Site-admins start working with Roles. First, you create a new "Top-Secret" project. Then you create a "Top-Secret Scientist" Role. Then you assign George to the Role. You finish by associating the Role with the Project. All is good, now only George can work on the Top-Secret project. But a little while later you find, by accident, that everyone can see and work with the Top-Secret project and its Issues. What's going on?

The problem is with the original sign-up process. Remember, when a User is created, s/he is associated with the **jira-workmanagement-users** Group and is given "Application Access". This is typically where the difficulty lies. Let's take a look.

Exercise: View Default Permission Scheme

1. Go to Navigation Bar >  > **Issues**
2. In the Issues Sidebar, click on **Permission Schemes** (should be the last option in the Sidebar)
3. In the Permission Schemes' view, locate the **Default Permission Scheme**, and click on **Permissions** link in the **Actions** column
4. In the Default Permission Scheme view, find the second Project Permission: **Browse Projects**

You will notice that the Browse Projects permission is granted to "Any logged in User". That means that any Jira User can see any Jira Project and Issues that uses the Default Permission scheme.

To ensure that only George can view your Top-Secret Project, you need to create a project-specific permission scheme and then make two changes to the Browse Projects permission. You first need to remove "Any logged in User" from that permission. Next, you need to give the "Top-Secret Scientist" role the Browse Projects permission in that Top Secret project's permission scheme. This will do a couple of things:

- It ensures only George and those assigned to the "Top-Secret Scientist" role have visibility and access to the Top Secret Project and its Issues
- It blocks Jira's Default Permission Scheme from the Top Secret project. A Default Scheme only works with projects that do not have a Project Permission Scheme.

Let's create a Project Permission Scheme and see how it works.

NOTE: Remember that you must have a paid version of Jira Work Management to work with Roles, Permissions and Permission schemes. The free version will not allow you to access to these areas.

Exercise: Create a Project Permission Scheme

1. Go to Navigation Bar >  > **Issues**
2. In the Issues Sidebar, click on **Permission Schemes** (should be the last option in the Sidebar)
3. In the Permission Schemes view, click on **Add Permission Scheme** button (in the upper right corner)
4. In the Add permission scheme page, enter "*Weekend Activity Permission Scheme*" in the **Name** field
5. Click **Add**
6. Back in the **Permission Schemes** view, find our newly created *Weekend Activity Permission Scheme* and click on **Permissions** link in the **Actions** column
7. In the opened Weekend Activity Permission Scheme page, click **Update** link in the **Administer Projects** row
8. In the **Grant Permission** pop up, click on **Single User**, then enter your name in the field that appears below:

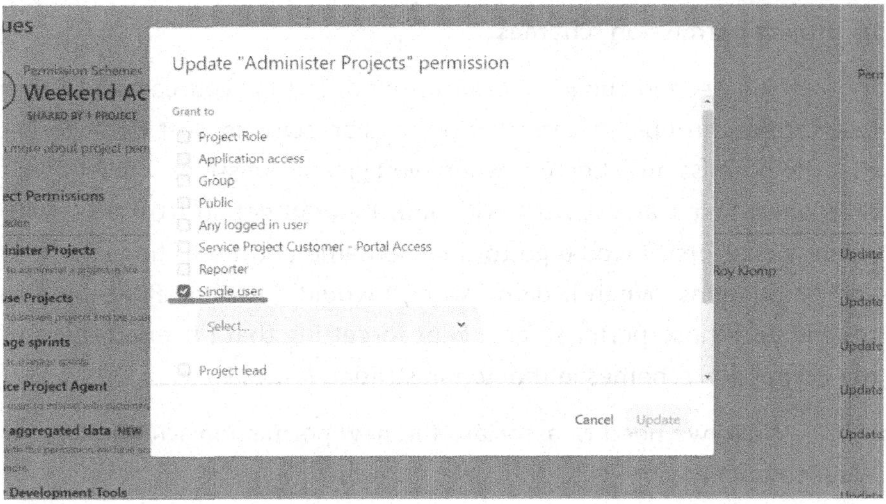

9. CLICK **UPDATE**
10. BACK IN THE WEEKEND ACTIVITY PERMISSION SCHEME PAGE NOTE THAT YOU NOW HAVE THE PERMISSION TO ADMINISTER THE PROJECT:

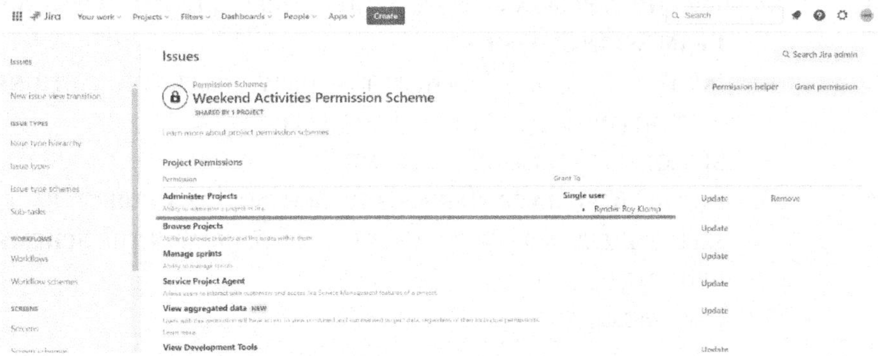

You have just created your first Project Permission Scheme, and, by the way, we have also made you a project administrator for this project. But a couple of things to be aware. First, this is a duplicate permission, because – as a Site-admin – you still have access to the project. Second, any other Site-admin also has access to the project.

Remember, **Site-admins have global permissions that are not affected by project permission schemes.**

The second thing to keep in mind, is that you can add other Users, roles, groups, etc. to your permission scheme. Just don't forget that the permission scheme is where you give permissions. I must admit that when first starting work with Jira, I would get so frustrated with permissions. First, I would go to the username and try to find where to add permissions. When it didn't work, I would go to the Roles area to try and add those permissions. I kept forgetting that I needed to go to the Permission schemes in the Administration Issues view.

Next, we need to associate the new permission scheme to your Weekend Activity project.

EXERCISE: ASSOCIATE THE PERMISSION SCHEME WITH THE PROJECT

1. OPEN YOUR *WEEKEND ACTIVITIES* PROJECT
2. OPEN THE **PROJECT SETTINGS** FOUND IN THE PROJECT SIDEBAR
3. IN THE **PROJECT SETTINGS** PAGE, SCROLL DOWN THE SIDEBAR TO THE **PERMISSIONS** AREA, AND CLICK ON THE **DEFAULT PERMISSION SCHEME** LINK
4. IN THE **PROJECT PERMISSIONS** VIEW, CLICK ON **ACTIONS** BUTTON (IN THE UPPER RIGHT CORNER)
5. SELECT USE A DIFFERENT SCHEME
6. IN THE **ASSOCIATE PERMISSION SCHEME TO PROJECT** PAGE, SELECT *WEEKEND ACTIVITY PERMISSION SCHEME* IN THE **SCHEME** DROP-DOWN LIST
7. CLICK ASSOCIATE

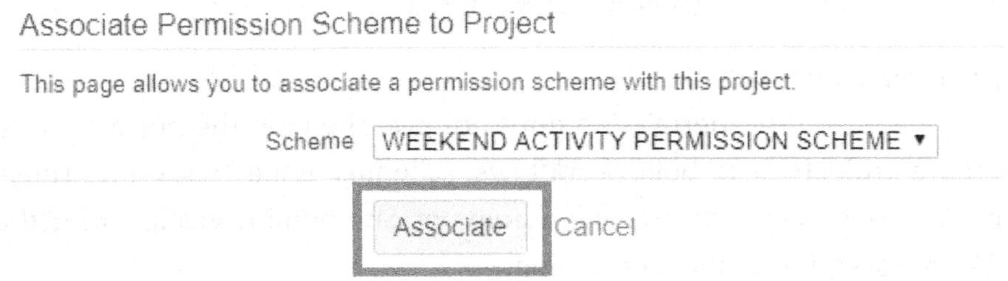

And that's all. You have now created your first Permission scheme and associated it with your project.

Project Permissions Overview

Let's finish this segment by looking at all the Project Permissions. Remember that these permissions/permission schemes are for company-managed projects.

There are 35 Jira Work Management Company-managed Project Permissions divided into six areas.

- Project permissions
- Issue permissions
- Voters and Watchers permissions
- Comments permissions
- Attachments permissions
- Time tracking permissions

Project Permissions

There are seven project permissions:

- Administer projects
- Browse projects
- Manage sprints
- Service Project Agent
- View aggregated data

- View development tools
- View (read-only) workflow

ADMINISTER PROJECTS

NOTE: This permission does not give the User the permission to Create projects or to build workflows, schemes, Issue Types, etc. Those permissions belong to the Jira-admins or Site-admins groups with the "Administer Jira" global permission.

The Administer projects permission is granted to a licensed User to manage a project in Jira Work Management by allowing them access to the project's settings. The individual can edit the project role membership, components, versions, and some of the high-level project details such as Project Name, Project Lead, Project Description, URL.

Users with this permission cannot create projects. A Jira-admin or Site-admin must create the project and then assign the Administer Projects permission to a Project Manager.

This permission is great if you have 'traditional' Project Managers or Department Managers and you want them to be able *to manage* the project, but don't want them to have the ability *to create* projects, fields, schemes, screens, workflows, etc.

BROWSE PROJECTS

By default, this permission can be given to anyone logged into the Jira site.

This permission is more important than it sounds. Yes, it gives the User the permission to view all projects and issues (unless there is an Issue Security block) in the organization site. It also allows the User access to the Issue Navigator.

In addition, the User must have this permission for other types of permissions (Transition Issues, for example) to work.

If you don't give the "Browse Issue" permission, then the User will be restricted to viewing only the issues to which they are specifically assigned.

MANAGE SPRINTS

This permission is used with Jira Software.

SERVICE PROJECT AGENT

This permission is used with Jira Service Management.

VIEW AGGREGATED DATA

This permission can be given to anyone logged into the Jira site.

NOTE: this permission allows views of project and issue level information. If you have sensitive projects or issues, it is recommended you think carefully before granting this permission.

"Aggregate data" means to collect separate sets of data and present it together or in a summary form.

VIEW DEVELOPMENT TOOLS

This is only available to Jira Software Users (i.e. not Jira Work Management Users).

ISSUE PERMISSIONS

There are 13 Issue permissions:

- Assign issues
- Assignable User
- Close issues
- Create issues
- Delete issues
- Edit issues
- Link issues
- Modify reporter

- Move issues
- Resolve issues
- Schedule issues
- Set issue security
- Transition issues

NOTE: Issue permissions only work if you can view the project. That means you need to first give the Role, Group, or User the **Browse Projects** permission.

Issue permissions give the User the ability to edit (and view) issues for his or her projects. If a User has the **Administer Jira** global permissions, then the Issue permissions are global. If the User is assigned to specific projects, rather than *all* projects, then the permissions apply only to those projects to which the User is assigned.

ASSIGN ISSUES

This allows the User to assign the project's Issues to other Users. It does not allow a User to be assigned to an Issue (that is the Assignable User permission). Fundamentally, this permission allows one team member to hand over tasks to another User when changing a step of work in an Issue.

ASSIGNABLE USER

This means the User is available to be assigned to Issues. It does not give the User the ability to Assign Users. You might toggle this permission in circumstances where workers are unavailable for long periods because they are working on other projects, for example. Once finished that other Issue, they can be brought back into the work queue by making them Assignable.

CLOSE ISSUES

NOTE: The **Transition issues** and **Resolve issues** permissions are required for this permission to work.

The Close issues permission allows the User to formally close Issues by setting the **Resolution field** to a closed value.

You may want to restrict the ability to close Issues to specific Roles. For example, you may want only Supervisors, or Quality Control, to have the ability to close an Issue.

CREATE ISSUES

This permission gives the User the ability to create Issues within the project or projects.

This permission is very helpful if you have projects that allow anyone who logs in to create an Issue. This is often the case if you want Customers or Employees to make requests or communicate problems.

A Create Issue permission also gives the User permission to create sub-tasks if they are enabled on the site.

DELETE ISSUES

The ability to give Users the permission to Delete issues is very risky. Make sure that you don't hand out this permission like candy at Halloween. It should be limited to designated individuals in a supervisory role. It seems reasonable to give people the ability to delete issues and therefore keep projects 'clean'. Unfortunately, what happens too often is that a User may delete issues by accident; or even worse they try to hide their mistakes by deleting the offending Issue.

EDIT ISSUES

If you can Create an Issue, you probably have been given the permission to Edit the issue. This is logical. But there may be instances where you want to give an individual the right to Create but not Edit an Issue. Imagine if you have a project where a customer can create an Issue for product defects, but then keeps changing the cause of the problem. So, don't just automatically give your Users the permission to Edit, think about the possible consequences.

Having the Edit issues permission does not allow you to Assign issues, Schedule issues, or Modify reporters in an Issue. Those need separate permissions.

This permission also gives the User the ability to convert sub-tasks to tasks, and tasks to sub-tasks, if sub-tasks are enabled on the site.

You cannot delete Issues with this permission.

If you are concerned about an 'audit trail', remember that any time an Issue is edited, a notation of that edit is recorded in the History tab in the Activity area of the Issue Details View.

LINK ISSUES

Issue linking allows you to establish a relationship between Issues. You need to have Issue Linking enabled (Go to Navigation **Bar >** **> Issues > Issue Features** area (on the sidebar) **> Issue Linking**) for this permission to work.

Typically issue links are used to identify Issues that need to be completed before, after, or in conjunction with another Issue or Issues. For example, the "Investigate Problem" Issue needs to be completed before the "Repair Product" Issue is started.

For Link Issues to work both the originating Project and the target Project or Service Management need to have the same permission.

It must be remembered that the Link Issue function does nothing other than informing the User that there is a link between two or more Issues. For example, let's say Issue A "blocks" Issue B (i.e. Issue A must be completed before Issue B can start). Both Issue A and Issue B will have a notice informing the User of the link, but it doesn't actually block the User from starting Issue B whenever the User wishes.

Modify Reporter

In Jira, the Reporter is the individual who creates an Issue. If that sounds confusing, remember Jira was first built to identify and help manage the fixing of software bugs. The Reporter was someone who "reported" a bug.

The **Modify reporter** permission allows User A to create issues on behalf of User B. Jira Work Management recommends that this permission be granted only to administrators. While I understand their caution, I don't quite agree with it. For example, most Administrative Assistants/Secretaries have delegated authority over their boss's email, calendar, and schedule and are trusted with those sensitive areas. It is probably safe to assume that most Users can be trusted with the Modify Reporter permission. Just use common sense when delegating.

Move Issues

NOTE: the User must have the Create Issue permission in addition to the Move Issues permission.

This permission allows the User to move an Issue from either project to project, or from one issue type to another issue type within the same project.

Resolve Issues

NOTE: the User must also have the Transition issues permission for the Resolve Issue permission to work.

With this permission, the User can resolve *and* can reopen Issues. It does not give the User the permission to Close issues (that requires the Close issues permission).

Schedule Issues

This permission lets the User edit the Due Date of an Issue.

I have never liked giving this permission to the Current Assignee for the obvious reasons. I always recommend that this permission be restricted to a Supervisory role.

SET ISSUE SECURITY

The Set Issue Security permission allows the User to set the security level on an Issue. Recommended for Administrators or someone in a supervisory position.

TRANSITION ISSUES

This allows the User to change the status of a workflow. Depending on the type of work you may want to give this permission to a team member or restrict it to a supervisory role.

The permission does not allow the User to close or resolve the Issue (those need the **Close issues** or **Resolve issues** permissions).

VOTERS & WATCHERS PERMISSIONS

There are two Voters & Watchers permissions:

- Manage watcher list
- View voters and watchers

NOTE: These permissions also need the **Browse Projects** permission to work.

MANAGE WATCHER LIST

When a User is on a Watch List, they will receive updates whenever something changes with the issue they are watching.

With the Manage Watcher List the User can see who is watching an issue; and, can add Users to, or remove from, the watcher list of an issue.

VIEW VOTERS AND WATCHERS

This allows the User to see who is on the Voter List and Watcher List of an Issue. This doesn't give them permission to edit either list.

Comments Permissions

There are five Comments permissions:

- Add comments
- Delete all comments
- Delete own comments
- Edit all comments
- Edit own comments

The comments permissions require the Browse Projects permission.

Add Comments

This gives the User the ability to add comments but does not give them the permission to edit or delete comments.

Delete All Comments

This gives permission to delete all comments in an Issue, regardless of who wrote the comment. Be very careful with this permission. Are you going to want an audit trail? Comments are very helpful in an after-project review. Ask yourself why you need to give someone the ability to delete all comments? What is the business reason?

Delete Own Comments

This permission restricts the ability to delete comments to the User's own comments. Again, do you want an audit trail? What is the business reason for allowing a User to delete his or her own comments? Because a User regrets creating a 'flame mail' type of comment, doesn't necessarily mean the individual should have the ability to delete any of their own comments.

Edit All Comments

Another permission to approach with caution. Do you really want to give a User the ability to edit any comment in an Issue, regardless of who made the comment?

When a comment is edited, a notation will appear in the comment field that the comment was indeed edited, but it will not show *what* was edited.

Edit Own Comments

This allows the User to Edit his or her own comments. Again, is this something you want?

When a comment is edited, a notation will appear in the comment field that the comment was indeed edited, but it will not show *what* was edited.

Attachments Permissions

There are three Attachments permissions:

- Create attachments
- Delete all attachments
- Delete own attachments

The attachments permissions require the Browse Projects permission.

Create Attachments

With this permission the User can attach files to an issue. Of course, you will need to have attachments enabled (Go to Navigation **Bar >** [gear icon] **> System > Advanced** area (on the sidebar) **> Attachments**).

Delete All Attachments

This gives the User the ability to delete any and all Attachments.

Delete Own Attachments

This limits the User to being able to delete only the attachments s/he attached.

Time Tracking Permissions

There are five Time tracking permissions:

- Work on issues
- Delete all worklogs
- Delete own worklogs
- Edit all worklogs
- Edit own worklogs

NOTE: all Time Tracking Permissions will only work if **Time Tracking** is enabled, and Users have the **Browse Projects** permission.

Work on Issues

At first glance this Issue looks like it should belong in the Issue permissions area. But what it really does is allow the User to work with the time tracking field in the User's Issues. It permits them to create a work log entry, to enter time spent and time remaining, and a description of work accomplished.

Delete All Worklogs

This gives the User the ability to delete any and all worklogs by any User working on the Issue. I don't need to remind you to be cautious with who gets this permission, especially if you use worklogs for audit, budget, or billing purposes.

Delete Own Worklogs

Again, do you want to give a User the ability to delete his or her own worklogs? I would suggest that if a User has entered incorrect worklog data, then they request a supervisor (who has the Edit or Delete all Worklogs permission) to make the correction.

Edit All Worklogs

You can also give a User the ability to Edit all worklogs, regardless of who created them. Needless to say, be careful with this permission.

Edit Own Worklogs

If need be, you can give a User the permission to edit his or her own worklogs. To be annoyingly repetitive, is this something you really want to allow?

Issue Security Schemes and Levels

NOTE: Editing or configuring issue-level security is not available with the Free plan for JWM, Jira Software, or Jira Service Management.

Sometimes, you have Issues and Issue Types that are quite sensitive, and you want to restrict who can see those Issues within the project. That's where Issue Security Schemes and Levels come into play.

Issue Security Schemes and Levels are complex to set up and manage. And, if done incorrectly, they can cause havoc in your project. I strongly recommend that if you really need to set up a security level, you do so in the company of an experienced Jira-admin or Site-admin.

I am not a big fan of Issue Security Schemes and Levels for a few reasons. First, they are not easy to set up. They are not easy to set up because: a) plain and simple they are complicated to set up; and b) they are set up so very rarely that the Site-admin typically has to go to the JWM documentation to set the Scheme up. This means it is easy to make mistakes when creating them. Which kind of defeats the whole purpose of a secure scheme. Second, you need someone to constantly monitor them, and this individual is likely to get constant calls by frustrated Users being blocked from some or all of the Issues in the project. Third, those people blocked from the Issue tend to develop an "attitude" when realizing they are blocked while others on the team are not.

In my mind a much better solution is to create a special project, create a unique permission scheme for that project, and assign only those Users to the project who have the permission to see and work with the "restricted" Issues.

And if security is really, really important, then take advantage of the Atlassian cloud set up. Remember that when you create an Atlassian account you are setting up an "organization". That organization can have multiple Jira sites. So, simply set up a Jira Work Management Top Secret site and place all your security sensitive projects in that site.

Chapter 10: Managing Time

"Oh! Do not attack me with your watch. A watch is always too fast or too slow. I cannot be dictated to by a watch."
Jane Austen (1775 – 1817)

To avoid confusion, in this book the term "Site-admin" includes "Org-admin, Site-admin, and Jira-admin" unless specifically noted otherwise.

Chapter Objectives

In this chapter you will develop expertise with:

- **Setting Jira Work Management work hours**
- **Permissions needed for Time Tracking**
- **Logging Work**
- **Tracking time**
- **Creating an Original Time Estimate**
- **Tracking time with Issues and Sub-tasks**
- **Creating a project time tracking report**
- **Creating a User Workload report**

Many companies require employees to track how much time they work on tasks in one of two ways.

First, in many instances the User is simply required to track how much time it takes to complete a task. This is often the case, where customers are billed by the hour.

Second, the User may be required to provide an estimate of how long the task will take. This is quite often the case with repairs. That estimate must then be approved, either by management or by the customer. After that, the User must track time against the estimate.

Jira is very good at managing both types of time tracking.

VIEW TIME TRACKING

By default, Time tracking is on, but let's make sure we are using the Jira provided time tracking function.

EXERCISE: CONFIRM TIME TRACKING IS 'JIRA PROVIDED TIME TRACKING'

1. GO TO NAVIGATION BAR >  >**ISSUES**
2. IN THE ADMINISTRATION ISSUES VIEW, SELECT **TIME TRACKING** IN THE SIDEBAR IN THE ISSUE FEATURES SECTION
3. IF THE VALUE IN THE **TIME TRACKING PROVIDER** READS, "*JIRA PROVIDED TIME TRACKING.*", ALL IS GOOD. IF NOT, SELECT "JIRA PROVIDED TIME TRACKING" FROM THE DROPDOWN LIST.

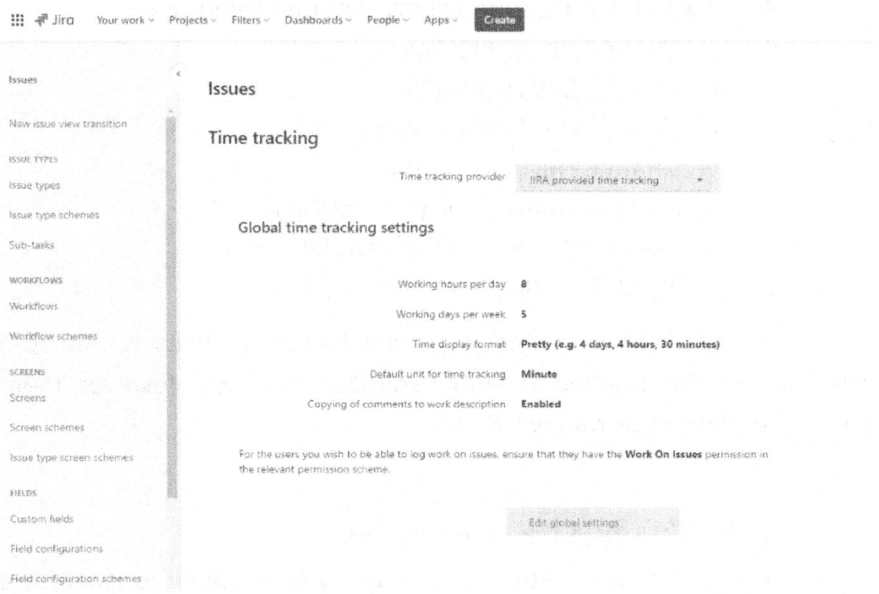

Changing Default Time Tracking settings

While we are in the Time Tracking page, notice that we can also change the default Time Tracking settings.

> NOTE: If you change the current Time Tracking settings, you will affect every Jira Work Management project on that site. So, if there are multiple Jira Admins in your organization, make sure you have consensus before making any changes.

Exercise: View Change Time Tracking Settings

1. Go to Navigation Bar >  > **Issues**
2. In the Issue Features area of the Administration Issues view sidebar, select **Time Tracking**
3. In the Time Tracking view, Click the **Edit global settings** link
4. In the **Time Tracking settings** pop-up you can:
    i. Change Hours per day
    ii. Change Days per week
    iii. Choose the Time format
    iv. Change the default unit
    v. Select legacy mode (ignore this)
    vi. Copy Comment to Work Description
5. Click the **Save** button when done

Jira Work Management does not have the ability to set up a calendar, nor can it define non-work statutory holidays. However, there are marketplace apps that will do so.

Time Tracking Permissions

In order to work with Time tracking you will need to make sure the proper permissions are set. There are five Time Tracking Permissions:

- Work on Issues: This allows the user to log work (required)
- Edit own worklogs: Allows the user to edit own worklog (optional)
- Delete own worklogs: Allows the user to delete own worklogs (optional)
- Edit all worklogs: Allows the user to edit ALL worklogs; it doesn't matter who logged the work (optional)
- Delete all worklogs: Allows the user to delete ALL worklogs; it doesn't matter who logged the work (optional)

Only the "Work on Issues" permission is required to work with Time tracking. The other four allow you to further refine what the User can or cannot do with Time Tracking.

How to Log Work

Some Jira Work Management projects or Issue Types simply require the user to record the amount of time worked on an Issue. There are no special fields or screens to set up, this time tracking ability is built right into the program and available in the **More** drop-down list in an Issue Details View. In other words, you don't have to do anything to configure Log.

Before we go much farther, let's create a new project for our Time exercises.

In the exercises in this chapter, we will:

- Create a Project for our Time tracking exercises
- Create a standard Task Issue
- Demonstrate Time tracking
- Create a Time estimate for the Issue

Exercise: Create Project and Issue

NOTE: In step 6 below, it is critical to select "Company-managed" in the **Project type** field. Company-managed will give you access to all the Time Tracking features. "Team-managed" projects provide only the basic time-tracking functions.

1. Go to Navigation Bar > Projects > **Create Project**
2. In the Project templates sidebar, select *Work Management*
3. In the Work Management view, select **Project Management**
4. In the project management view, click on **Use template**
5. In the **Create project** view, Enter *ACME Machine Company* in the **Name** Field
6. In the **Project type** field, Select *Company-managed*, and click **Create Project**
7. With the *ACME Machine Company* project open, click the Blue Issue **Create** Button on the Main Menu Bar
8. Ensure *ACME Machine Company* is selected in the **Project** Field
9. Ensure **Task** is selected in the **Issue Type** field
10. Enter *Log Time Demo* in the **Summary** Field
11. Ensure you are the **Assignee**
12. Click **Create**

Now that the Project and related Issue have been created, we want to start logging time.

Exercise: Log Time

NOTE: if you do not see the Time Tracking fields highlighted in the image above, click the "More fields" drop down to have them appear. If you do not see the "Original Estimate" field, you probably selected "Team-managed" in the Project type field in step 6 of the previous exercise. If so, you need to delete the project (Admin Cog > Projects > Manage Projects > More (the three dots) > Move to trash) and start over.

1. Open the newly created *Log Time Demo* issue
2. In the *Log Time Demo* **Issue Details' View**, click on the **Time tracking** field (where it should read "No time logged")
3. In the **Time Tracking** pop-up, enter *3.5d* in the **Time spent** field

NOTE: Jira Work Management will always assume you mean minutes in the **Time spent** field unless you specify w (Weeks), d (Days), or h (Hours) after the time entered (e.g. 12h).

4. Enter *4d* in the **Time remaining** field
5. In the **Date started** field, select the current date

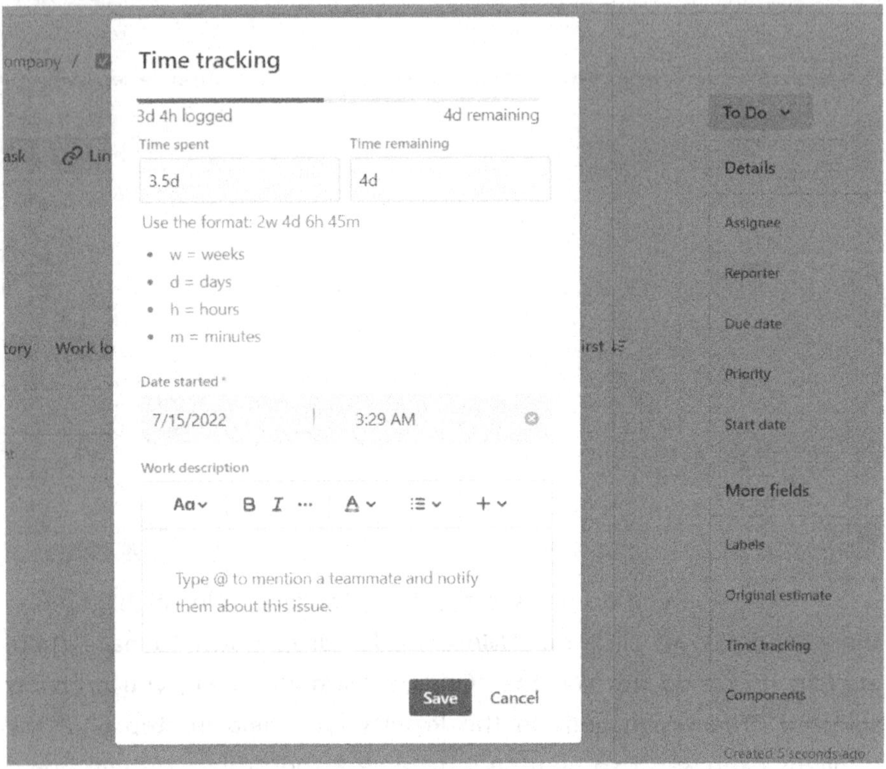

6. IN THE **WORK DESCRIPTION** FIELD, ENTER *DID STUFF*
7. CLICK THE **SAVE** BUTTON

Back in the *Log Time Demo* Issue Details View notice that the Time Tracking section now contains the information added in the Time Tracking popup:

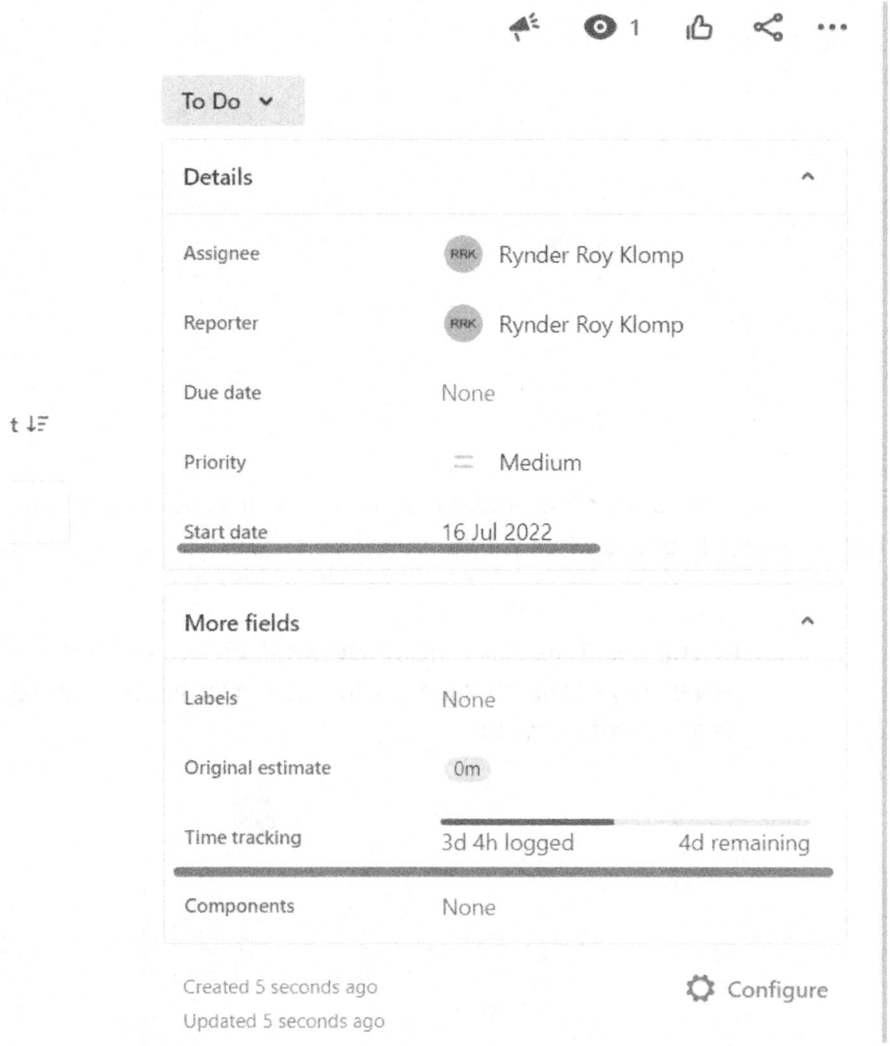

The Time Tracking section now shows two fields **Logged** and **Remaining**. The **Start date** field is also populated.

But where is the Work Description you entered when you Logged work? This is found in the **Work Log tab** of the **Activity** area. If you click on this tab, you will find all the work log details recorded:

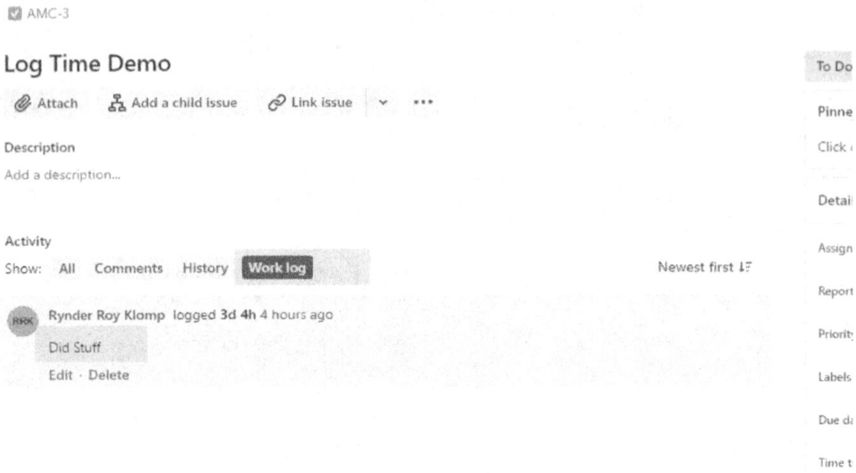

Any time a user logs additional work, it will be recorded here. Let's see what happens when we do.

EXERCISE: LOG ADDITIONAL WORK

1. IN THE *LOG TIME DEMO* **ISSUE DETAILS' VIEW**, CLICK ON THE **MORE** MENU (THE THREE DOTS IN THE UPPER RIGHT CORNER) AND SELECT **LOG WORK**

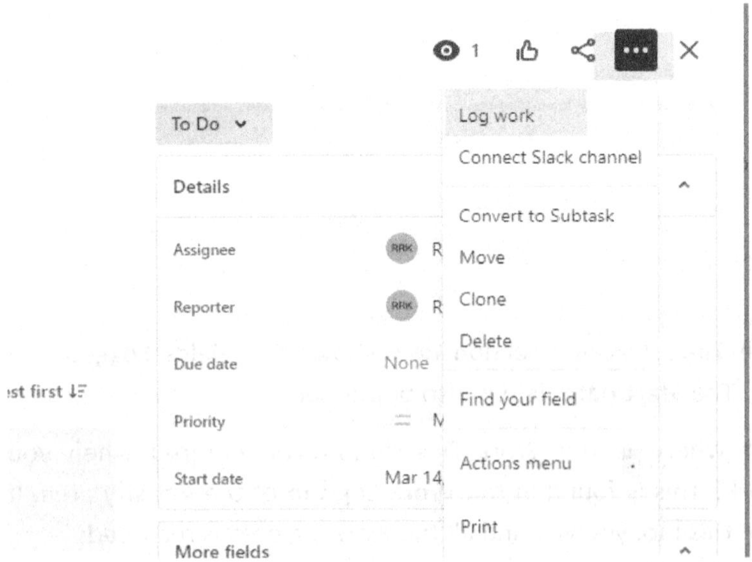

2. IN THE **TIME TRACKING** POP UP, ENTER *12M* IN THE **TIME SPENT** FIELD
3. IN THE **WORK DESCRIPTION** FIELD, ENTER *DID MORE STUFF*
4. CLICK THE **SAVE** BUTTON

In the **Time Tracking** area notice that the time logged has now changed to read 3d 4h 12m, which reflects the additional 12 minutes you just logged. The "4d" time remaining amount will also be reduced by 12 minutes.

In the **Work Log** Tab of the **Activity** area see that you logged 12 minutes of work and the log includes a date and time stamp.

Jira Work Management will time stamp your log **with the date and time when the Log button is clicked.**

You will also see the "Did more stuff" comment from your latest work description.

Only those users who have the Work On Issues permission for a particular project are able to log work on the issue. However, those who have Browse Project permissions are able to see how much time has been logged. If you don't want everyone to have the ability to log work or edit the log, you will need to set that up with the appropriate Permission Scheme.

At its very basic, this is all the user needs to do to log work.

TIME ESTIMATING

Of course, you can do much more than just logging work. In many instances it is mandatory to submit an estimate of the time required to complete work (tasks) before the work is approved to begin. When building a project plan, for example, we need to provide an estimate of how much time it will take to complete a specific task or set of tasks. This is done to set a budget for the project. Many businesses will also set estimates for certain types of tasks. Dentists have industry standards for the estimate times of common procedures. Similarly, many auto repair shops will charge a flat rate of 2.5 hours for a brake job (for example) based on an industry standard estimate for the make and model of car. If the actual time to complete the job comes in more than the estimate, the shop loses money. On the other hand, if it took less time to complete (than the estimate) the shop makes additional profit. In cases like this it is essential to record the estimate first and then to track time against that estimate.

ORIGINAL ESTIMATE FIELD

If you ever worked with the Server edition of Jira, you know how incredibly complicated (and frustrating) it was to work with Time Estimating. You will be pleasantly surprised at how easy it is in the paid Cloud version. First, you don't have to jump through 137 steps to set it up. There is a default field in the "Task" issue type. Second, it is extremely easy to use. You simply enter the Estimate. That's it. It's all set up and ready to go.

Let's create a new Issue and work with the **Original estimate** field.

EXERCISE: USING THE ORIGINAL ESTIMATE FIELD

1. IN THE *ACME MACHINE COMPANY* PROJECT, **CREATE A NEW "TASK" ISSUE**
2. IN THE **SUMMARY** FIELD ENTER, "*ORIGINAL ESTIMATE TEST 1*"
3. MAKE SURE YOU ARE THE **ASSIGNEE**
4. CLICK **CREATE**
5. IN THE *ACME MACHINE COMPANY* **LIST** VIEW, CLICK AND OPEN THE NEWLY CREATED ISSUE
6. OPEN THE "**MORE FIELDS**" DROP DOWN IF IT IS NOT ALREADY OPEN
7. IN THE **ORIGINAL ESTIMATE** FIELD ENTER *4H*

8. Click on the **Time tracking** field (where it reads *"No time logged*"
9. In the **Time tracking** pop-up, enter *2h* in the **Time spent** field and click **Save**

Once you click save you are back in the Issue details field, and you will see three things:

- The **Original estimate** field reads *4h*
- The **Time tracking** section reads *2h logged*
- The **Time remaining** section reads *2h remaining*

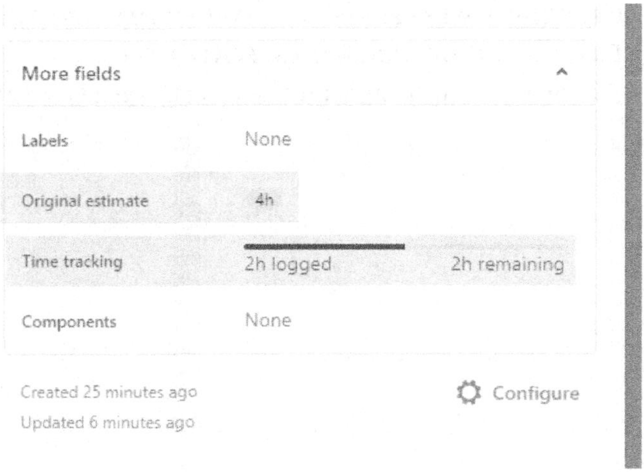

And that's all there is to use the Original estimate field. Any time you log time, it subtracts that amount from the Original estimate field and shows you, based on the estimate, how much time is needed to complete the task.

Now let's take a look at a few options. What happens when:

- the logged work time exceeds the Original estimate while still working on the task
- You log time with sub-tasks

- You are ready to close the task and:
  - the logged work time equals the Original estimate
  - the logged work time is greater than the Original estimate
  - the logged work time is less than the Original estimate

EXERCISE: LOGGED TIME EXCEEDS ORIGINAL ESTIMATE

1. IN THE *ACME MACHINE COMPANY* PROJECT, **CREATE A NEW ISSUE** AND CALL IT *ORIGINAL ESTIMATE TEST 2*. MAKE SURE YOU ARE THE **ASSIGNEE**
2. OPEN THE NEWLY CREATED *ORIGINAL ESTIMATE TEST 2* ISSUE
3. ENTER *6H* IN THE **ORIGINAL ESTIMATE** FIELD
4. ENTER *9H* IN THE **TIME TRACKING** FIELD, AND CLICK **SAVE**

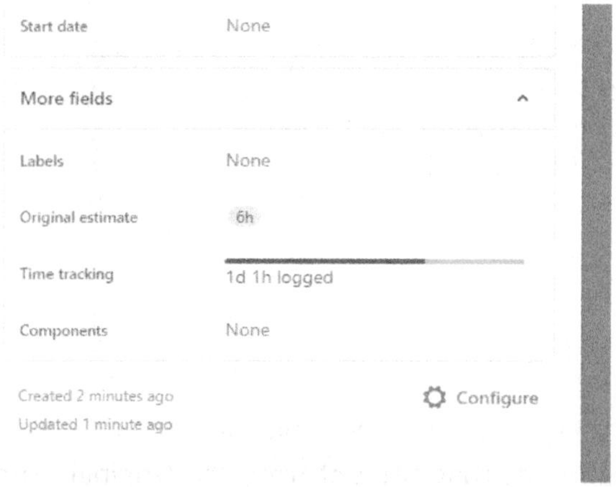

Notice that the time tracking field indicates 1 day 1 hour logged (8 hours = 1 day). And there is now a blue and gold line in the **Time tracking** field. The blue line represents the Original estimate and the gold line represents the logged time that exceeds the Original estimate.

And that's about it. You will not get any sort of warning message or other flags indicating your **Logged work** amount exceeds the **Original estimate**. And to be fair, you should not need anything more.

Original estimate with Issues and Sub-tasks

I often get calls from Users who complain that the Time Tracking fields seem to show inflated numbers. The first thing I do is ask them to check that they are not 'double counting', as this is the most common reason for the problem. Let's say you think it will take five hours for a machine repair: one hour for the estimate, three hours for the repair, and one hour for billing. So, when you create the issue, you enter five hours in the Original Estimate field. In the Issue Details View you see that the Original Estimate field does indeed show 5h. You assign the Estimate to Charles. Charles creates an estimate sub-task (in that repair Issue) and figures it will take him one hour to complete the estimate. He enters 1h in his Estimate sub-task Original Estimate field and clicks Create. Unfortunately, when you check the Parent Issue's Details View, you see that the Time Tracking Estimate field now records 6 hours remaining to complete the Issue. That's because the software has added the Sub-task's original estimate amount to the Parent Issue's Original Estimate. This is a remarkably common problem.

I recommend that if you are going to have Sub-tasks, then either use Original Estimate in the parent Issue Create screen, or in the Sub-tasks' Create screen(s), but not both. The way to make sure is to look at the "Include subtasks" check box. If it is checked, then your issue will sum the Original estimate fields in the Parent's Issue and all Sub-task Issues.

ORIGINAL ESTIMATE AND CLOSING AN ISSUE

How does closing an Issue affect an Original Estimate and Logged time? It doesn't. When you close an Issue, JWM doesn't care if the amount of work logged is equal to, less than, or greater than the Original estimate. It simply accepts the results.

You can also log work when you are closing or resolving an issue. Remember that there is no recording of the status of an issue when you log work. Consequently, if it is important for you to track the time related to closing or resolving an Issue separately, you should either create a separate sub-task, or include a note in the Log Work description field that you are closing the task.

BEST PRACTICES FOR THE ORIGINAL ESTIMATE FIELD

EDITING THE ORIGINAL ESTIMATE FIELD

One of the major challenges with the Original estimate field - in the Jira Cloud version - is the ability to edit it. As stated earlier, the Original Estimate is often used for Budget and Approval purposes. Having the ability to change the field after the fact makes it tempting to 'low ball' the original estimate and raise it after the budget has been approved or approval given.

Unfortunately, at the time of writing Atlassian has not implemented any method to prevent the Original estimate field from being edited.

If it is critical for your organization to restrict changes to the Original estimate field, I recommend you look at building a custom field as described by Sanooj Kumar on October 20, 2021 in the Atlassian community site. I copy it here for your reference (thanks Sanooj):

"A work around would be to add a custom field and populate it with the original estimate when it is entered for the first time. The

custom field can be a non editable field which can be populated thru automation. This will help you capture if the estimation was modified or not and still have the original estimate recorded."

Don't need an Estimate?

If you don't need an estimate for a job, then simply log work with the Time Spent field. Don't bother with the Remaining Estimate area if it serves no essential business need, if it isn't important to the customer (and that's the ultimate measure), and if it isn't used for budget or approval purposes. So, what would be the point of using it if it does not meet those criteria? The only thing I tend to hear is that managers want it to benchmark their employees.

Need an Estimate?

If you do need an Original Estimate, I recommend two basic steps. First, the Original Estimate field should be completed by the individual who knows the subject matter best. Second, the User, who is doing the work, fills in the Time Spent field (s/he may be the Subject Matter Expert as well as another individual). If the Original Estimate turns out to be inaccurate and **must** be revised, then I recommend the project manager or administrator field make the change after receiving approval, and that the change be noted in the **work description** field so it is captured in the work log.

Time Tracking Reporting

Time Tracking isn't of much use without the ability to report it. Jira Work Management has several reporting methods, including exporting to a spreadsheet, that you will find quite useful.

Exercise: Create an Issue Time Tracking Spreadsheet report

If you need a simple Time Tracking report for a specific Issue:

1. Open the **Issue**, and click **"..."** (**More**) in the upper right corner of the Issue Details view
2. Select the report format you want: **Export XML**, **Export Word** (a Word document), or **Print** (printed copy)

Go ahead and click on any, or all, option(s) to see what the formats look like. In all cases you will see the Original Estimate, Remaining Estimate, and Time Spent results. You will not see a detailed breakdown of the Work Log.

One must admit that while there is certainly a lot of information in these reports, they are not very user friendly. Especially if you want to perform analysis against them.

Work Log Report

I must admit that Jira Work Management's reporting functions for the Work Log are quite weak. Several companies have built reporting add-ons which include Work Log reporting capability; so, you might want to check them out.

Create a Work Log Report

If you do want a very basic means of creating a Work Log report for a specific issue, proceed with the exercise below.

Exercise: Workarounds for Work Log Report

1. Open the **Issue**, and click on the **Work Log tab** in the **Activity** area of the Issue's Details view
2. With the **Work Log tab** open, and work log details showing, use your web Browser's Print method to print the page (or use a snipping tool to cut and save an image)

You can print the details of the Issue Details View as well as the Work Log details. It's not a perfect solution, but it does give you the work log details that you can keep as a record.

Project Time Tracking Report

The final report we want to look at in this chapter is the Jira Work Management Time Tracking Report for a Project, which is located in the Project report area.

Exercise: Create a Project Time Tracking Report

1. Open the Project for which you want a report
2. In the Project's sidebar, select **Reports**
3. In the All Reports view, scroll down and click on **Time Tracking Report** link in the **Forecast and Management** area
4. In the **Configure – Time Tracking Report** view select the following options:
5. *No Fix Version* in the **Fix Version** drop-down

This typically refers to software versions, so you can probably ignore this field and select No Fix version (if not selected).

ii. *LEAST COMPLETED ISSUE* FIRST, IN THE **SORTING** DROP-DOWN

This sorts your uncompleted tasks from top to bottom based on the amount of Estimated Time Remaining. When selecting Least Completed, Issues with the greatest amount of Estimated Time Remaining will be shown first. If you select Most Completed, Issues with the least amount of Estimated Time Remaining will be shown first.

iii. *ALL* IN THE **ISSUE** DROP-DOWN

When you select All, you will see all incomplete and completed Issues and Sub-tasks (assuming you selected No Fix Version and are including all Sub-tasks).

If you choose Incomplete Issues only, then Issues where the Estimate Time Remaining field is zero, or Issues that do not have an Original Estimate will be excluded. In this report "Incomplete" has nothing to do with the Status of the Issue.

iv. *INCLUDING ALL SUB-TASKS* IN THE **SUB-TASK INCLUSION** DROP-DOWN

Two out of the three options are related to Version control; so, you are probably safe simply selecting Include all Sub-tasks.

6. CLICK **NEXT**

The Time Tracking Report for a particular project starts off with Description of the report. More importantly, it contains a link allowing you to create an Excel version of the report (more about that later).

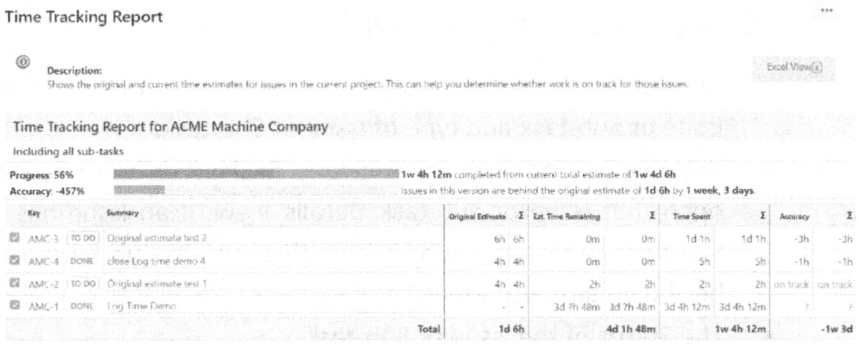

Time Tracking Report

Description:
Shows the original and current time estimates for issues in the current project. This can help you determine whether work is on track for those issues.

Excel View

Time Tracking Report for ACME Machine Company

Including all sub-tasks

Progress: 56% — **1w 4h 12m** completed from current total estimate of **1w 4d 6h**

Accuracy: -457% — Issues in this version are behind the original estimate of **1d 6h** by **1 week, 3 days**.

Key		Summary	Original Estimate	Σ	Est. Time Remaining	Σ	Time Spent	Σ	Accuracy	Σ
AMC-3	TO DO	Original estimate test 2	6h	6h	0m	0m	1d 1h	1d 1h	-3h	-3h
AMC-4	DONE	close Log time demo 4	4h	4h	0m	0m	5h	5h	-1h	-1h
AMC-2	TO DO	Original estimate test 1	4h	4h	2h	2h	2h	2h	on track	on track
AMC-1	DONE	Log Time Demo	-	-	3d 7h 48m	3d 7h 48m	3d 4h 12m	3d 4h 12m	?	?
		Total		1d 6h		4d 1h 48m		1w 4h 12m		-1w 3d

Next are two bars. The top bar shows your project's progress by comparing the percentage of completed issues against incomplete issues. It does not consider *what portion* of an incomplete issue is actually completed; if the whole issue is incomplete, it gets zero percent.

The second bar measures the overall accuracy of all the original estimates versus all of the current estimates. The current estimate amount is calculated by adding the Time Spent and Estimated Time Remaining fields.

This two-bars area will also show you your actual work versus your estimates:

- If the two bars are of equal length, then your actual work is meeting your estimate.
- If the bottom bar is shorter than the top bar, then you are slower than your estimate.
- If the top bar is shorter than the bottom bar, then you are faster than your estimate.
- The text area to the right of the bars provides you how much (in weeks, days, and hours) you are ahead or behind the estimate(s).

Now we are moving to the details area, which includes a few columns. Let's look at them from left to right:

- An Issue type icon indicating whether the row relates to an Issue or Sub-task and type of Issue or Sub-task.
- The Key for the Issue of Sub-task. Clicking on the key will open that Issue or Sub-task Details View. If an Issue has a Sub-task, the Issue will be shown first, and its Sub-tasks will be shown directly below it.
- The Status of the Issue or Sub-task.
- The Summary of the Issue or Sub-task. Clicking on the summary will bring you to the same Issue or Sub-task Details View as clicking on its key.
- Original Estimate. The left column will show the Original Estimates for any Issues and Sub-tasks. The right column in the Parent Issue line will show the sum of the Sub-tasks' Original Estimates for that Issue.
- Estimated Time Remaining. The left column will show the Estimated Time Remaining for any Issues and Sub-tasks. The right column in the Parent Issue line will show the sum of the Sub-tasks' Estimated Time Remaining for that Issue.
- Time Spent. The left column will show the Time Spent for any Issues and Sub-tasks. The right column in the Parent Issue Line will show the sum of the Sub-tasks' Time Spent for that Issue.
- Accuracy. The Accuracy column compares the Original estimate against the sum of the Time Spent and Remaining Estimate amounts. It then indicates whether the Sub-task or Issue is On-track or not. The left column will show the Accuracy for any Issues and Sub-tasks. The right column in the Parent Issue line will show the sum of the Sub-tasks' Accuracy for that Issue.

NOTE: when we configured this report, we chose to include Sub-tasks in the report. If you choose to ignore Sub-tasks, then you will only see one column in Original Estimate, Estimated Time Remaining, Time Spent, and Accuracy. You will not see a Sum column (because there are no sub-tasks to sum, of course).

Exporting the Time Tracking Report

At the top of the report we saw that the user can export the report to an Excel spreadsheet (I find it also works fine with the LibreOffice spreadsheets). Simply click on the link and (assuming you have Excel) a downloadable spreadsheet will be created for you. Be aware that depending on your version of Excel you may get a caution pop up. If that occurs, click yes (Legal Warning: I accept no responsibility for any adverse effect).

User Workload Reporting

You may want to see how many workload hours a User is assigned. Let's create such a report.

Exercise: Create an User Workload Report

1. Open the **Project** for which you want a report
2. In the Project's sidebar, select **Reports**
3. In the Reports sideview, scroll down and click on the **User Workload Report** link in the **Forecast and Management** area
4. In the Configure – User Workload Report:
5. Enter your name in the **User** field
6. In the **Sub-task inclusion** dropdown, select "Only including sub-tasks assigned to the selected user"
7. Click **Next**

And you will see something like this:

User Workload Report

Workload report for user Rynder Roy Klomp (choose another)

Projects	Assigned Issues	Workload
Trial Cloud Project	1	4 days
JWM Book examples	1	7 hours
ACME Machine Company	2	2 hours
Total	**4**	**1 week, 1 hour**

The report shows all the projects assigned to the User, how many assigned Issues, and how much time allocated for the User to complete the work. While it doesn't show the duration of time for that work, it is a handy reference tool.

Chapter 11 – Dashboards

To avoid confusion, in this book the term "Site-admin" includes "Org-admin, Site-admin, and Jira-admin" unless specifically noted otherwise.

Chapter Objectives

In this chapter you will:

- **Explore the Jira Work Management Dashboards and common Gadgets**
- **Create a custom dashboard**
- **Customize dashboard gadgets**
- **Learn how to share a dashboard**

What is a Jira Work Management Dashboard?

A Jira dashboard is the User's "central control" view providing a high-level picture of his or her Jira Work Management settings, individual project activities, or issues. It often contains quick links to more commonly used Jira elements. I like Matillion Business Intelligence's definition of a dashboard as "a tool that provides a simplified overview of the key performance indicators" (in their article "How to Create Compelling Business Dashboards").

Types of Jira Work Management Dashboards

There are two types of Jira Work Management dashboards: System and Bespoke. Whereas a default dashboard tends to be used as the global default dashboard for the organization or project team, a 'bespoke' dashboard is meant to be customized for individuals, specific projects, or roles.

Jira Work Management Basics

When you log on to Jira Work Management, you may open to a Default dashboard:

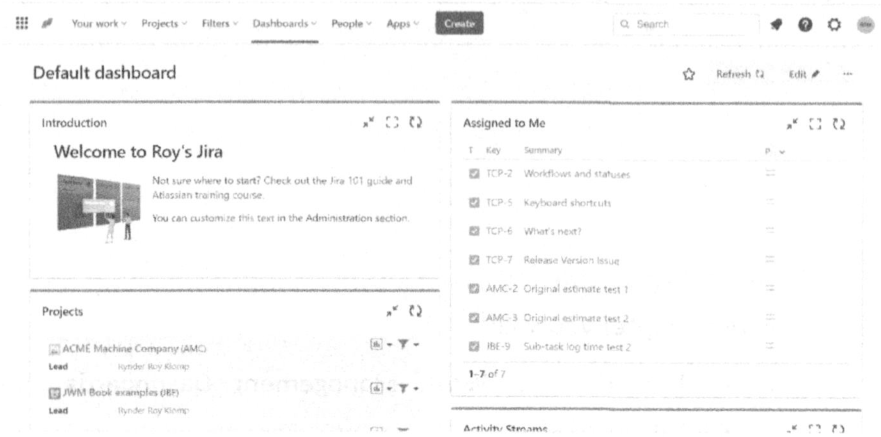

A **Default dashboard** is typically used:

- As the default dashboard for all members of an organization, and for those who have not added any customized dashboards
- To provide instruction or training material for the User
- To display Issues assigned to the User
- To display company activity
- To display quick links to other areas of Jira
- To limit views of gadgets based on permission schemes. For example, non-administrators will not see any administration gadgets

A **Bespoke** dashboard can:

- Be customizable to individual Users, projects, roles or groups
- Be created and managed by Users

- Display project status details
- Display a list of Issues
- Provide quick links to other areas within the project

While there is only one default dashboard, any number of Bespoke Dashboards can be created for either an individual User or sets of Users (usually for individuals performing a similar job or task, or working on the same project).

Gadgets

A dashboard is made up of one or more 'Jira gadgets'. A gadget is a small application focused on a specific topic. For example, the Default dashboard shows four gadgets: Introduction, Assigned to Me, Projects, and Activity Stream.

There is a large library of standard Jira gadgets available, and more can be found in the Atlassian Marketplace.

A Tour of the Default dashboard

Let's take a tour of the Default dashboard, though I must admit this is going to be a rather short tour as there really isn't that much to show. I should also caution, that your organization may have changed the default dashboard a little, or a lot, depending on requirements.

Navigation Bar

The Jira Work Management Navigation Bar includes **Dashboards** as one of the menu headings. Opening this Dashboard's menu will show a list of recent dashboards you have opened and will also contain links to **View all dashboards** and to **Create dashboard**.

1. Click on Default Dashboard in the Dashboard Menu.

Default Dashboard

The main part of the system Default Dashboard view includes three elements: the title "Default Dashboard", the gadgets, and the

Tools menu buttons (see the image at the beginning of the chapter). The title needs no further explanation, but let's look at the other two areas in more detail.

The Gadgets area

As stated earlier, a dashboard Gadget is essentially a mini-app that performs a specific function.

When a User opens the Default Dashboard s/he will see at least four Gadgets: **Introduction, Assigned to Me, Projects,** and **Activity Stream.** The **Introduction** gadget can include any message you might want to place there. If you are a Jira Administrator, you will also be shown the **Administrator Guide** gadget, which includes documentation to help you manage or customize Jira, and the **Atlassian Training Course** link.

The gadgets area typically contains operational applications, mostly reports related to your organization's or Users' projects.

There are many gadgets available for you to mix and match in order to create your own dashboard. Categories of gadgets include Charts, Jira, and Wallboard gadgets though, truth to tell, many of them are quite similar in function.

Tools

In the upper right corner of the Default dashboard view, you will see a number of dashboard tools. These include a star, the refresh link, the edit link and the Tools More menu (the three dots).

Star

If the star is simply a star outline, then clicking the star will make it a "favorite" dashboard. Conversely if the star is filled, then clicking it will remove it from the favorite list.

Refresh

This link simply refreshes the page.

Edit

This link allows you to add gadgets and to change the layout of the Dashboard.

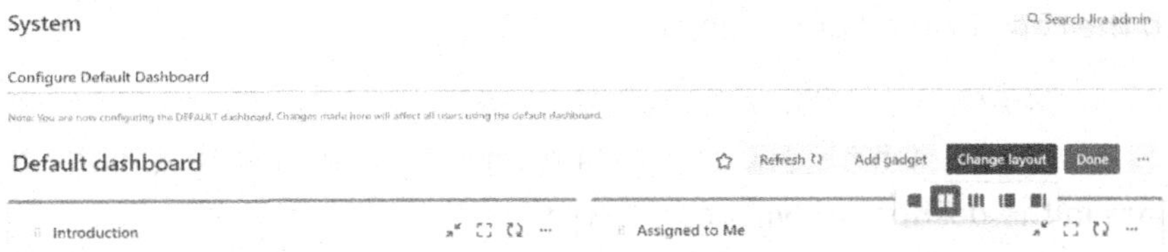

Be cautious, as any changes you make to the Default dashboard will affect everyone in the organization.

More (...)

NOTE: You are limited in the options available with the Default Dashboard. To avoid repetition, this list will include all options available for the Default and Custom dashboards.

This list of **More** options allows you to:

- Rename and Share (not available in the Default Dashboard)
- Copy Dashboard
- Configure automatic refresh
- View as Wallboard
- Move to trash (not available in the Default Dashboard)
- View wallboard slideshow
- Configure Wallboard slide show
- Create Dashboard
- View all dashboards

Rename and Share

The Rename and Share function is not available in the Default Dashboard. However, in all other custom dashboards this link allows you to Rename the Dashboard, or to change who the Dashboard is shared with.

Copy

The copy dashboard option allows you to copy the dashboard and rename it. This is handy if you have a dashboard that contains most of what you want in the new dashboard. You simply make your changes to the copy instead of starting over.

Configure automatic refresh

This is where you can define (in minutes) how frequently the data in the dashboard will be updated.

View as Wallboard

A wallboard is just as it sounds. A large board hung on a wall. Typically, it is used to show the status of individual tasks in a project. In the ancient days of twenty years ago, a classic wallboard using Agile Project Management methodology would have the physical board sorted into four columns: Not Yet Started, In Progress, In Testing, and Complete. In these columns would be a number of Post-It notes, with each note representing a task. As the task progressed, the Post-It note would be moved from column to column until it was complete. The Jira wallboard performs that same function. Or you can use it to show status reports that are better suited to a larger view environment. It's very flexible.

Move to trash

This function will move the dashboard to the trash area. After 60 days the dashboard will be permanently deleted.

View wallboard slide show

Once you have configured a wallboard slide show, you can click this link to start or stop it.

Configure wallboards slide show

A Wallboard Slideshow is simply a number of dashboards that display as a slideshow. You can customize the slideshow to display the wallboards in random order, and to have any one of 10 transition effects. You can also set the cycle period (how long each wallboard will be shown before it transitions to the next).

Additionally, after you set up a Wallboard slide show (two or more dashboards that will automatically rotate their views on a set schedule), you will activate another menu option: "View Wallboard Slideshow".

Create a dashboard

Use this option when you want to build a dashboard without applying the copy function.

View all dashboards

This link will take you to the Dashboards view. This view is covered in more detail at the end of this chapter.

Customizing the Default dashboard

You can customize the Default dashboard as little or as much as you desire. However, as it is a Default dashboard, you will need Site-admin rights to modify it (in other words, a Project Admin does not have permission to change the Default dashboard).

NOTE: If there is more than one Site-admin in your organization, make sure to talk with them before changing the Default dashboard. There should be agreement amongst all Site-admins as to any changes. Better yet, there should be only one "owner" of the Default dashboard.

How to Modify the Default dashboard

Exercise: View Configure Default dashboard

1. Go to Navigation Bar> Dashboards > Default dashboard
2. In the default dashboard view, click on **Edit** in the upper right corner

CAUTION: Notice the warning below the view header, "You are now configuring the DEFAULT dashboard. Changes made here will affect all users using the default dashboard." If you want to make a change affecting all users, then continue. However, if you want to make a change affecting only yourself or a specific group of users, then exit this view as soon as possible and make a custom dashboard described in the Local Dashboard section of this chapter.

CONFIGURE GADGET APPEARANCE

In the Configure Default dashboard view you will see your current gadgets. Each gadget's title bar has four icons: a two-direction arrow, maximize square, refresh, and the More icon (three dots):

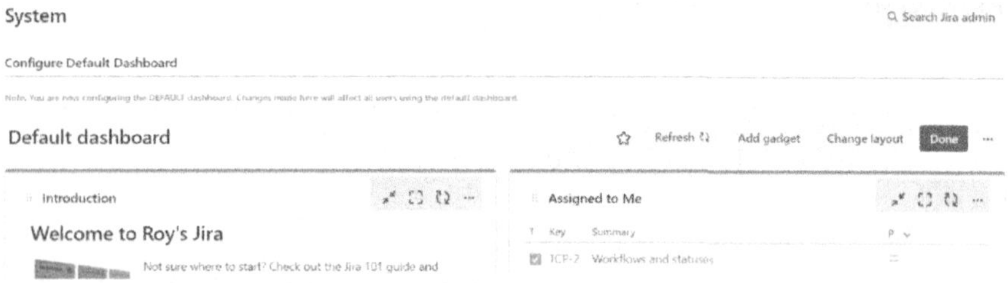

But first, if you transition your mouse down over the top border of a gadget you will notice the mouse changes to a hand. This hand is used to change the location of your gadget. When you hold the mouse button down you can use the hand to drag-and-drop the gadget around the page.

The two-headed arrow is used to minimize the gadget, so that only the gadget's header appears. This is helpful if you have a lot of gadgets and don't want to spend hours and days scrolling down the page to find the gadget you need.

The next icon, the square, is a maximize icon that allows you to maximize the gadget by hiding all other gadgets.

Next is the refresh link. Clicking this will refresh the data in the gadget.

The More icon allows you to choose the color of the gadget's title bar, to rename the gadget or to delete it.

Configure Default Dashboard

Near the top of the Configure Default dashboard view, there are numerous functions where you can make changes to the default dashboard: **Star, Refresh, Add Gadget**, **Change Layout**, **Done**, and **Tools**:

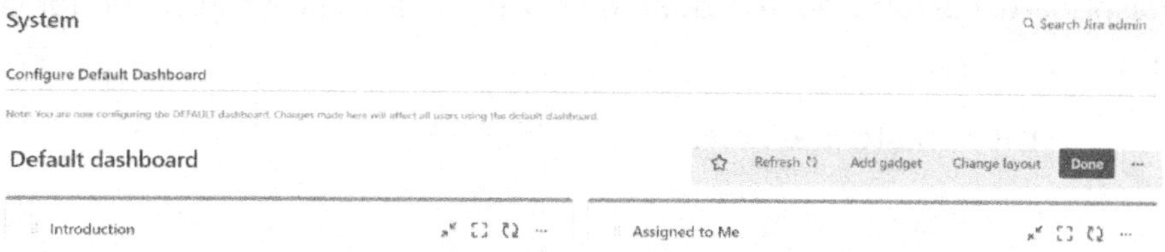

We have already looked at the Star, Refresh, and More functions earlier in this chapter, so let's skip over them and look at the new functions.

Add Gadget

The **Add Gadget** button brings you to the **Add a gadget** view. At the time of writing there are over 30 gadgets listed in categories such as: Jira, Charts, and Wallboard. You will find most of the gadgets are focused on reporting about specific projects or User activity.

If you click on a gadget, it will be included in the Configure Default dashboard view when you exit the **Add Gadget** pop-up. You can then drag it to a location you think best suited to your needs.

One thing to note is that in the default settings you are limited to 20 gadgets per dashboard page.

Change Layout

The Change Layout button is a 'one trick pony'. Here you select the number of columns you want for your Default dashboard, and in some cases, the width of some of the columns.

DONE

When finished with your changes, make sure to click the Done button to activate the new configuration.

CUSTOM DASHBOARD

In addition to the default dashboard many users want to see a dashboard customized for their own use, a specific project, or for a group of users.

Let's create one now.

EXERCISE: CREATE NEW DASHBOARD

1. GO TO NAVIGATION BAR> DASHBOARDS > **CREATE DASHBOARD**

2. IN THE **CREATE DASHBOARD** POPUP, TYPE THE NAME OF THE NEW DASHBOARD SUCH AS "*TEST DASHBOARD*" IN THE **NAME** FIELD
3. IN THE **DESCRIPTION** FIELD ENTER, "*TEST DASHBOARD FOR <ENTER YOUR NAME>* "
4. IN THE **VIEWERS** DROPDOWN SELECT *PRIVATE*
5. IN THE **EDITORS** DROPDOWN SELECT *PRIVATE*
6. CLICK **SAVE**

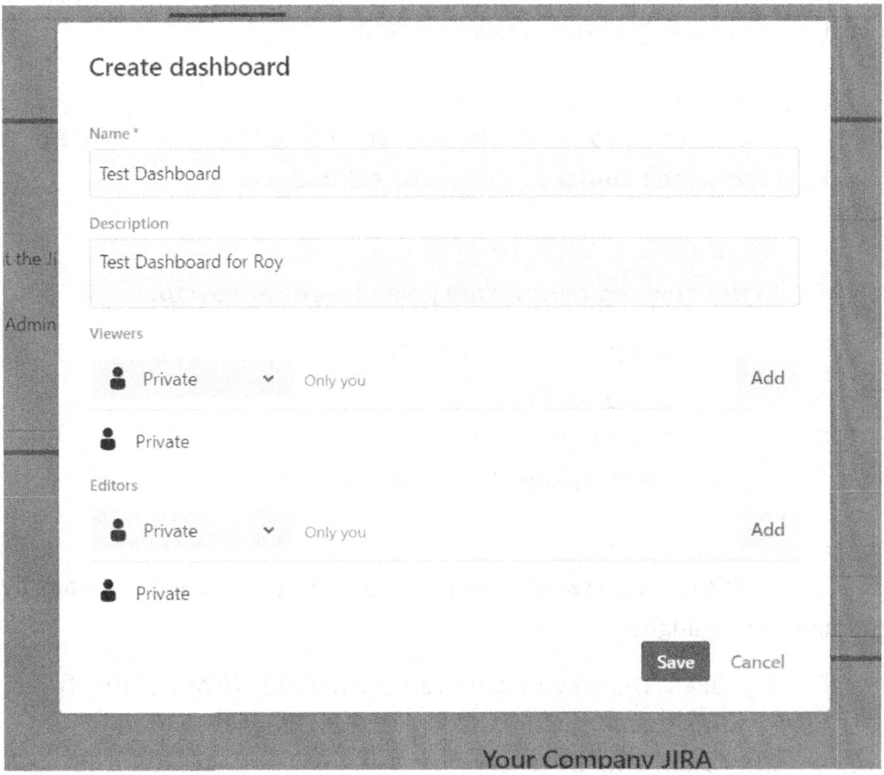

The Name and Description fields need no further explanation, but let's look at Viewers and Editors in a little more detail.

VIEWERS

As it appears, Viewers defines those who can view the dashboard (but may not be able to Edit it). The **Viewers** field informs you if you are sharing your dashboard (or not) and with whom. By default, when you create a dashboard, it is not shared with anyone, it is Private. There are four possible Viewer settings: **Private**, **Project**, **Group**, **and My Organization**. When you select any of the latter three options, you may see additional dropdowns appearing to further refine your selection. For example, if you select Group, another dropdown appears with a list of available groups to select from.

EDITORS

The Editors dropdown defines who can edit your Dashboard. It works in the same manner as the Viewers dropdown.

WORKING WITH GADGETS

In this next segment we are going to look at how to:

- add gadgets to a dashboard
- configure the gadgets
- edit an existing gadget
- use the gadget's navigation features

EXERCISE: ADDING GADGETS

In this exercise we are going to bespoke your new dashboard by adding some gadgets.

1. OPEN THE NEWLY CREATED DASHBOARD (NAVIGATION BAR > DASHBOARDS, AND CLICK ON *TEST DASHBOARD*)
2. CLICK THE **EDIT** LINK IN THE UPPER RIGHT OF THE *TEST DASHBOARD*
3. IN THE EDIT VIEW, CLICK ON THE **CHANGE LAYOUT** BUTTON

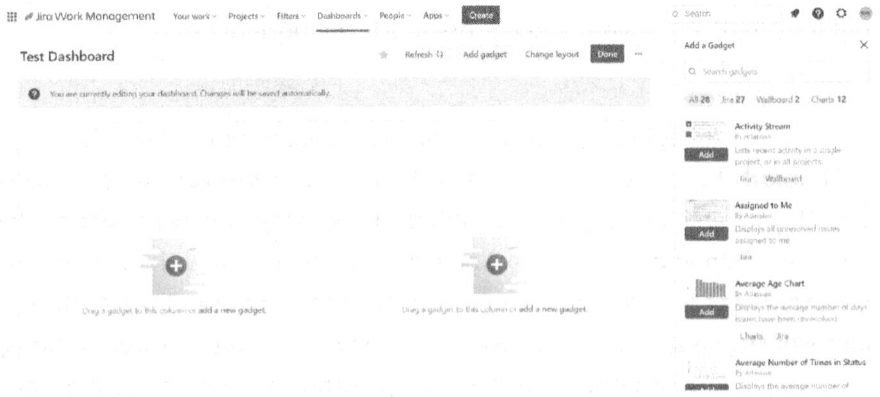

4. SELECT THE SINGLE COLUMN LAYOUT:

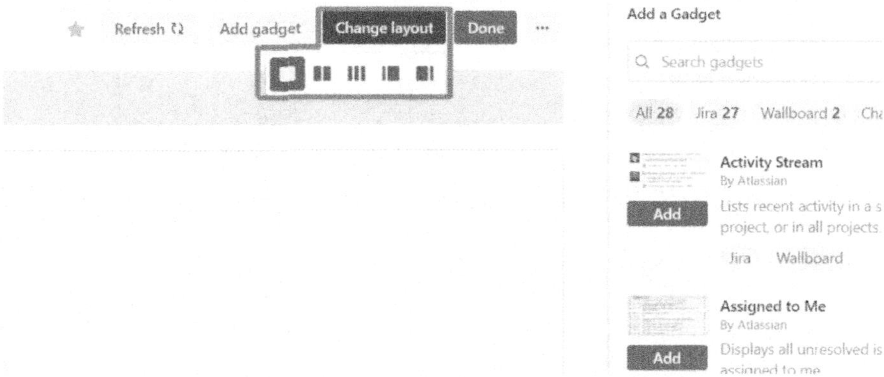

Next, let's add some Gadgets to our Dashboard.

5. IF THE ADD GADGET SIDEBAR IS NOT ALREADY OPEN, CLICK THE **ADD GADGET** BUTTON IN THE UPPER RIGHT OF THE VIEW:

The top of of the **Add a Gadget** sidebar categorizes the various gadgets: All, Jira, Wallboard, Charts. When you open the **Add a gadget** view by default, you will see all of the gadgets available in alphabetical order). Let's add three to our dashboard.

6. FIND **ISSUE STATISTICS** AND CLICK ON ITS **ADD** BUTTON
7. DO THE SAME FOR ASSIGNED TO ME AND CREATED VS. RESOLVED
8. CLICK THE **X (CLOSE)** ON THE TOP RIGHT OF THE ADD A GADGET POP-UP

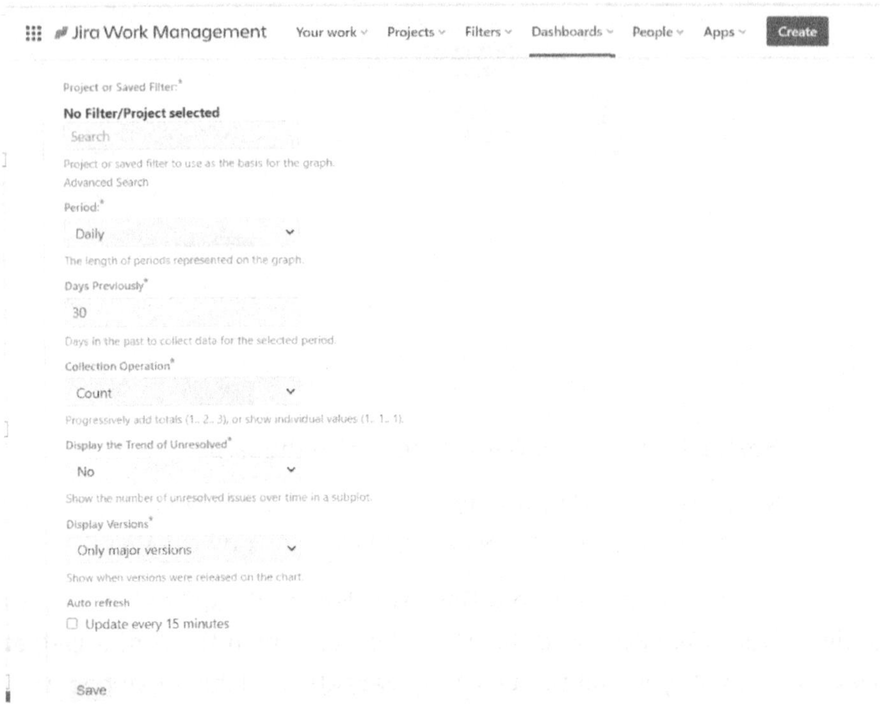

As you can see, there is still some work required to set up the gadgets for this particular dashboard. Let's start with the Statistics (Issue Statistic).

EXERCISE: CONFIGURE ISSUE STATISTICS GADGET

1. IN THE **PROJECT OR SAVED FILTER** SEARCH BOX TYPE IN THE NAME OF AN EXISTING PROJECT (OR SAVED FILTER). CLICK **ENTER** WHEN DONE

NOTE: Suggestions will be provided in the Search box as you type:

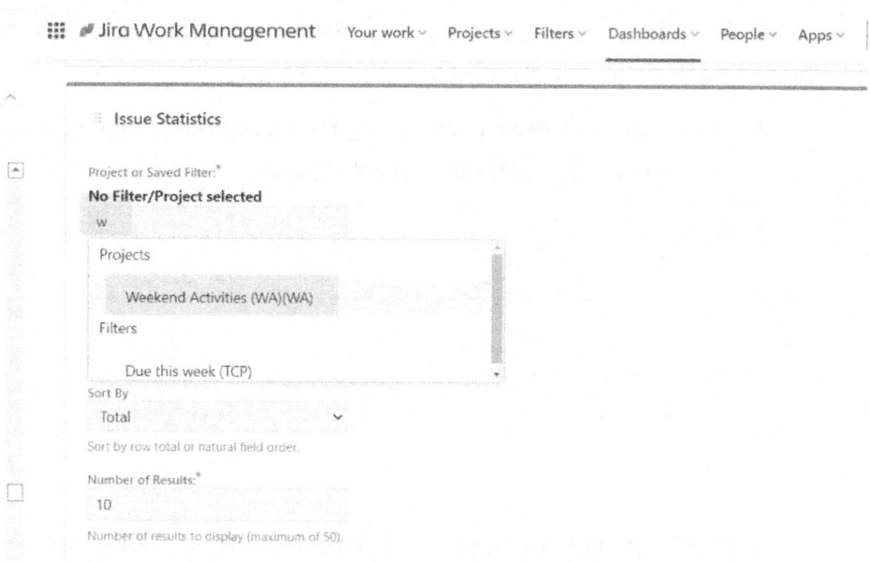

2. IN THE **STATISTIC TYPE** DROP-DOWN LIST SELECT *STATUS*

NOTE: You can select from almost every custom and standard field available to you. Just remember the fields available to you are also based on your Jira Work Management permissions.

3. IN THE **SORT BY** DROP-DOWN LIST SELECT *NATURAL*
4. IN THE **SORT DIRECTION** DROP DOWN LIST SELECT *ASCENDING*
5. IN THE SHOW RESOLVED ISSUE STATISTICS SELECT *YES*
6. CHECK THE **AUTO REFRESH** BOX SO THAT THE GADGET UPDATES *EVERY 15 MINUTES*
7. CLICK **SAVE**

Take a look at your results:

Exercise: Configure the Assigned to Me Gadget

This gadget, like the Issue Statistics gadget, needs to be configured before it shows anything. Let's do it now.

1. Click on the **Edit** link in the Dashboard header bar, and then expand the gadget if necessary:

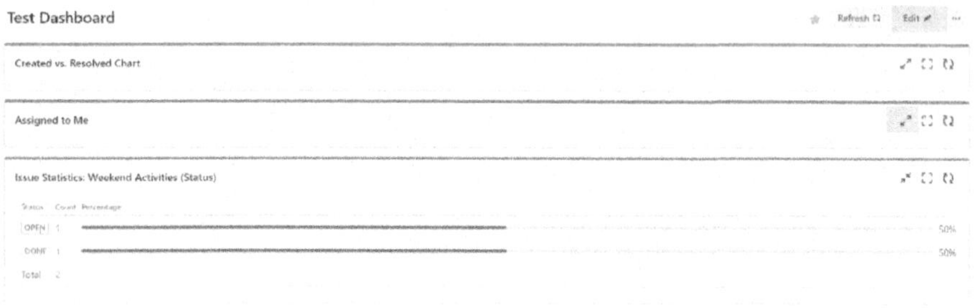

2. Expand the gadget, if necessary, by clicking on the double arrows:

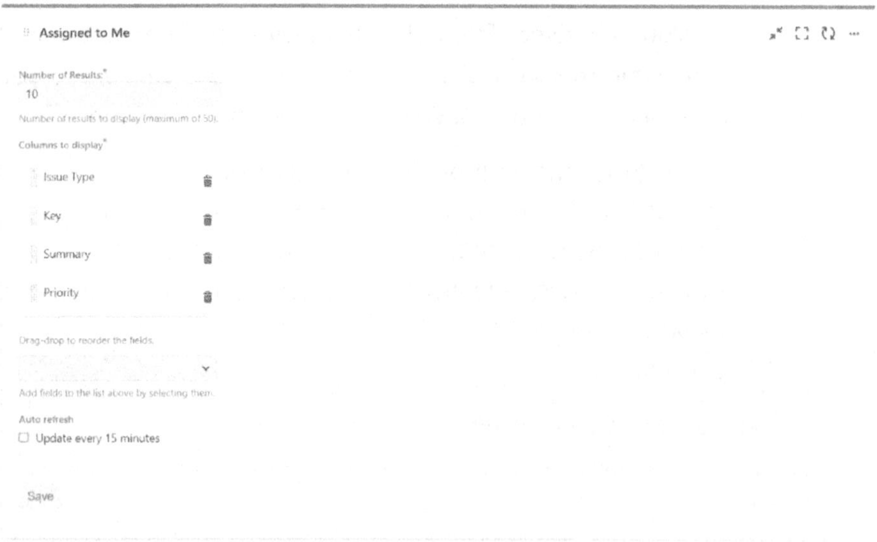

3. Leave Number of Results at 10
4. Delete *Key* from the **Columns to display** list (by clicking on the trash can icon)

5. Select and click on *Created* in the **Add fields** drop-down list
6. Select and click on *Due Date* in the **Add fields** drop-down list
7. Check the **Auto Refresh** check box
8. Click **Save**
9. Click **Done** in the Test Dashboard header Bar

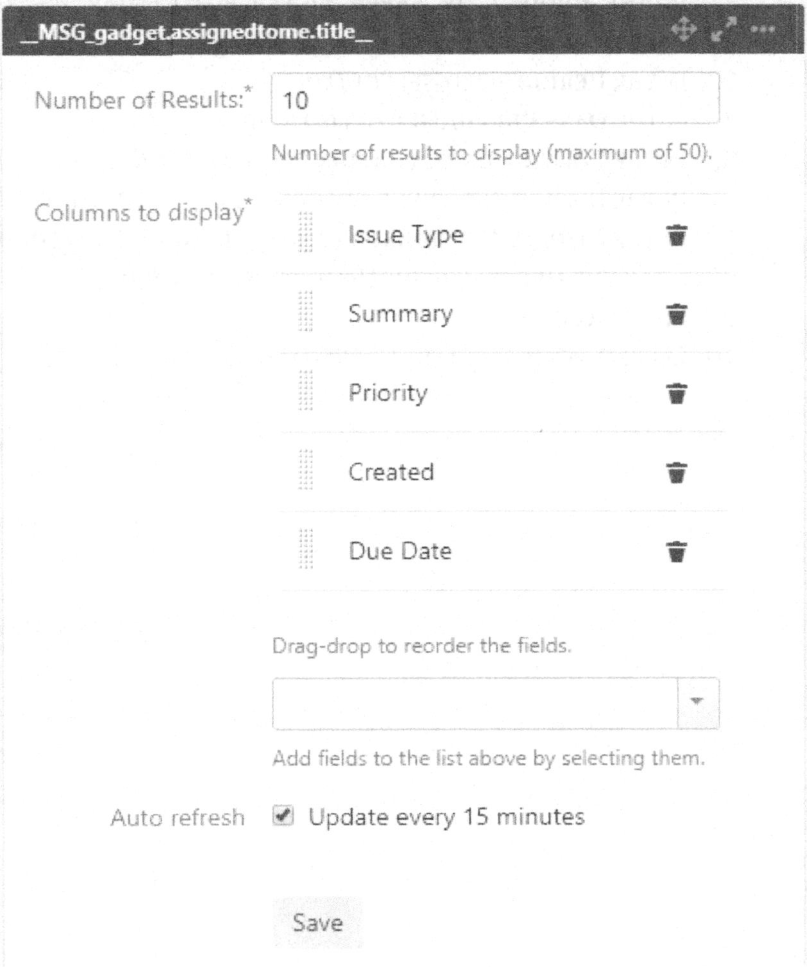

Great! This shows all of my issues along with the summary and priority, when they were created (i.e. how old they are), and when they are due.

Next, let's configure our last gadget.

EXERCISE: CONFIGURE THE CREATED VS. RESOLVED CHART GADGET

1. CLICK ON THE **EDIT** LINK IN THE DASHBOARD HEADER BAR, AND THEN EXPAND THE GADGET IF NECESSARY
2. IN THE **PROJECT OR SAVED FILTER** FIELD ENTER *WEEKEND ACTIVITIES*
3. IN THE **PERIOD** FIELD, SELECT *DAILY*
4. IN THE **DAYS PREVIOUSLY** FIELD, ENTER *30*
5. IN THE **COLLECTION OPERATION** FIELD, SELECT *COUNT*
6. IN THE DISPLAY THE TREND OF UNRESOLVED FIELD, SELECT *NO*
7. IN THE **DISPLAY VERSIONS** FIELD, SELECT *ONLY MAJOR VERSIONS*
8. CLICK THE **UPDATE EVERY** 15 MINUTES CHECK BOX
9. CLICK **SAVE**
10. CLICK **DONE** IN THE TEST DASHBOARD HEADER BAR

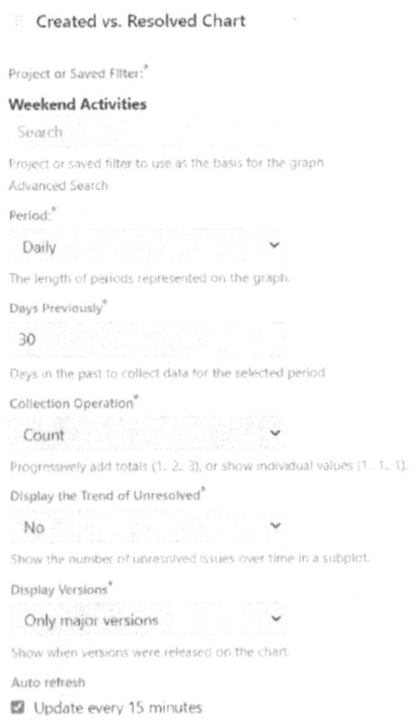

But I just realized that I have one field missing. Let's go back and edit the gadget.

EXERCISE: EDIT A GADGET

1. CLICK ON THE **EDIT** LINK IN THE **TEST DASHBOARD** HEADER BAR
2. IN THE **ASSIGNED TO ME** GADGET, CLICK ON THE MORE (**...**) MENU, THEN CLICK **CONFIGURE**

3. SELECT AND CLICK ON *PROJECT* IN THE **ADD FIELDS** DROP-DOWN LIST
4. IN THE **COLUMNS TO DISPLAY** LIST, DRAG PROJECT SO THAT IT IS BETWEEN SUMMARY AND PRIORITY
5. CLICK **SAVE**

OK, that's better. Since I am working on multiple projects, having this additional column, showing the project associated with the Issue, helps me keep track of things a little easier.

By now you should be comfortable with adding and configuring gadgets; so, go ahead and experiment on your custom, not the Default, dashboard.

The Gadget header bar

We have already touched on a couple of the Gadget's header bar items, but let's go through them all anyway.

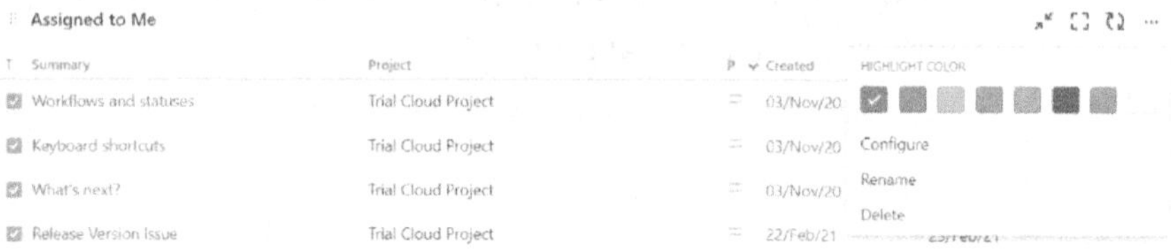

Expand/Collapse

The first item is the two arrows icon. Click on this to expand or collapse the Gadget.

Maximize

The Box shaped icon will allow you to expand the gadget so it takes up the full screen.

Refresh

Clicking the circular arrows will refresh the data in the gadget.

More ...

The More (...) menu will let you change the Highlight (border) colour of the gadget. This is helpful if you want to organize your gadgets around themes (e.g. projects or Users).

The Configure link allows you to edit or reconfigure the gadget.

As you can guess the Rename and Delete links allow you to rename or delete the gadget. Deleting a gadget does not delete it from the system, it simply removes it from your dashboard.

Agile gadgets

You may notice a good many Agile gadgets available and most of them look interesting. The reason I did not include them in the example has to do with the fact that they tend to require a 'sprint' due date. A sprint is a designated period within an Agile project. In a sprint there are a number of tasks to be accomplished. So, when using an Agile gadget, you typically need to a) create an Agile project, b) create a sprint, and c) create a finish date for the sprint.

Having said that, if you have purchased the Jira Software package and have set up a sprint, please feel free to experiment with the Agile gadgets.

Sharing Dashboards

In the previous section we showed how to share a bespoke dashboard when we are in the process of building one. But how do we make share changes *after* we have created a dashboard?

Exercise: Share a Dashboard

1. Open the **Test Dashboard**, and click on the **More** (...) menu in the Dashboard header bar
2. In the **More** menu click on **Rename and Share**
3. In the **Rename and share dashboard** popup, select *Project* in the **Viewers** dropdown menu
4. In the **Projects** dropdown that appears, select *Weekend Activities*
5. Click **Add** (Ignore the **roles** dropdown)
6. click **Save**

In this "Share a Dashboard" exercise there are a few things to note. First, though the name of the function is "Rename and Share", it is not necessary to rename the dashboard. Rename is simply one of the functions you can do in this popup. Second, as you saw, when you selected an option in the Viewers dropdown, another dropdown appeared to further refine your selection. Finally, we did not select a Role in the Rolls dropdown for the simple reason that there were no project roles associated with the Weekend Activities project.

VIEW ALL DASHBOARDS

The last item we want to look at on the dashboard More menu is **View all Dashboards**.

In the Dashboards view you can:

- create a new dashboard (upper right corner)
- filter the dashboards
- view all of your dashboards
- perform a number of actions with the dashboard(s)

CREATE DASHBOARD

This is another link to the Create dashboard popup. We covered this in more detail in the **Create new Dashboard** exercise earlier in this chapter.

FILTER THE DASHBOARDS

Directly below the Dashboards title is a row of fields. There are many organizations that have dozens or even hundreds of dashboards. These sets of fields help you quickly find a particular dashboard or dashboards. The first field is the standard search field. As you start entering the name of the dashboard, Jira will automatically start narrowing the list. The next three fields are filter dropdowns. You can filter by Owner, Project, Group, or any combination of the three.

VIEW ALL YOUR DASHBOARDS

This is the main area of the Dashboards view. This area lists all the Dashboards you have permission to see. This list contains seven columns.

STAR

By clicking on an "empty" star you then make that dashboard a favorite. Dashboards that are favorites will appear in the Navigation Dashboard menu. Conversely, clicking on a "solid" star will remove that dashboard from your favorites list.

NAME

The name column lists all the dashboards you have permission to view.

This column is sortable (up and down arrows next to the column title).

OWNER

This column lists who is the "owner" of the dashboard. Typically, this is the User who created the dashboard.

This column is sortable (up and down arrows next to the column title).

VIEWERS

This column lists all those who have permission to see the dashboards. This topic was covered in more detail earlier in the chapter.

Editors

The Editors column lists all those who have permission to edit the dashboard. This topic was covered in more detail earlier in the chapter.

Starred by

This column indicates how many Users have made this dashboard a favorite. This is helpful when determining if a dashboard should be deleted or not.

This column is sortable (up and down arrows next to the column title).

More...

The More column has four actions: **Copy dashboard, Rename and share dashboard, Change owner,** and **Move to trash**. We have covered **Copy dashboard**, **Rename and share**, and **Move to trash** earlier in the chapter so there is no need to revisit them here.

Clicking the **Change owner** link opens the Change owner popup. Just be aware that if you do transfer ownership of the dashboard to another User, that action may prevent you from viewing the dashboard.

PROJECT SUMMARY: STATISTICS VIEW VS DASHBOARD VIEW

As you know each project has its own Summary Statistic's overview.

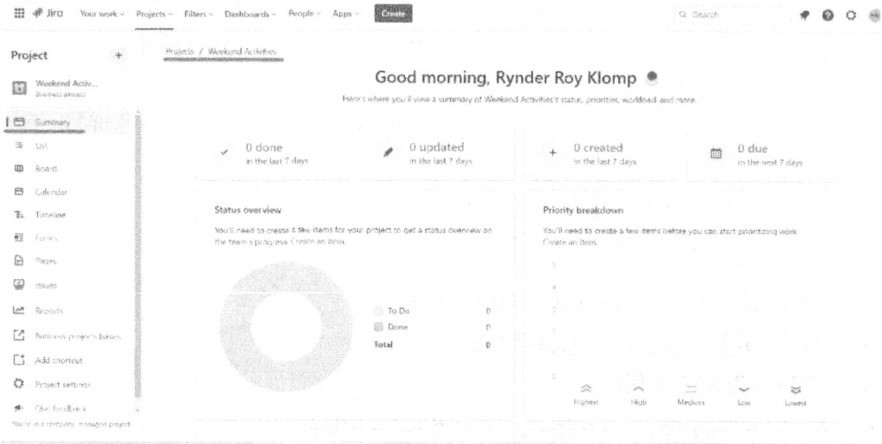

Many users confuse this view with a Dashboard view and spend a good deal of time and frustration trying to add gadgets and configure it. A project Summary Statistic's view cannot be changed.

Chapter 12 – Filters and Reports

To avoid confusion, in this book the term "Site-admin" includes "Org-admin, Site-admin, and Jira-admin" unless specifically noted otherwise.

CHAPTER OBJECTIVES

In this chapter you will:

- **Understand Filters in greater detail**
- **Build and save a custom filter**
- **Subscribe to a filter**
- **Build a Dashboard gadget based on a Filter**
- **Build a filter report**
- **Export a filter**

I must admit that when first learning Jira, I didn't spend much time focusing on Filters and Reports. I was too busy trying to figure out how the program worked. Only later, as I gained experience with Jira, did I realize its flexibility and power.

Filters and Reports are two sides of one coin. Reports cannot exist without filters. The reports, charts, and report gadgets included with Jira Work Management when you purchase the software are based on filters.

Filters fundamentally do three things. They let you:

- Search for something in Jira Work Management
- Customize lists of issues
- Create Jira Work Management reports

Let's start with searching for something in Jira Work Management.

SEARCH AND FILTER

NOTE: The results of a search or filter will depend on your Jira permissions. If you do not have permission to view a project or Issue, then you will not see those in your search results. For example, let's say you want to see all the Issues John Doe is working on in his 10 projects. One of those projects is a top-secret project that you do not have permission to view. In this case you will see the all the Issues John is working on in 9 of those projects and you will not see anything from the top-secret project.

When opening Jira Work Management and looking for an issue, most beginners typically select a project from the **Projects** menu in the **Navigation Bar** and then click on **List** in the sidebar:

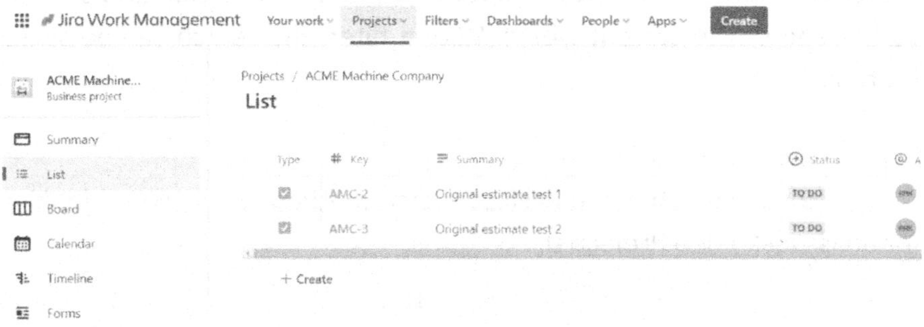

Alternatively, a User might click on **Your work** in the **Navigation Bar,** and if that issue, hopefully, is listed in the **Assigned to me** or **Recent Issues** section, they would click on it. If not so lucky, they head back to the Projects button described in the previous paragraph and scrounge around until they find the Issue. Bottom line, it usually takes a good number of mouse clicks to get to your specific issue.

Jira Work Management Basics

So, it is probably a good time to make your life easier by reintroducing the Issue Search functions. As you recall, there are several types of Search and Filter functions in Jira Work Management:

- Quick Search (Search)
- Search for People (Search)
- Basic Search (Filter)
- Advanced Issue Search (Filter)

Difference between a Search and Filter

In the list above I noted that the first two items are "Searches" and the last two are "Filters". But what is the difference between the two?

A search looks for an Issue, Project, or Person. It contains only one criterion (the name of the Issue, or Project, or Person). A search cannot be saved.

A filter is a search that can contain one or more criteria (e.g. Search the ACME project for all Issues assigned to John Doe and are due by the end of the current week). With a filter, the search can be saved for reuse.

Quick Search

Quick Search is the easiest search method to use when looking for an Issues(s) or a Project(s).

Clicking on Quick Search will open a drop-down list of recent issues, projects, or filters. It also has number of **Go to all** links redirecting you to Issues, Projects, Issues, Filters, and People views.

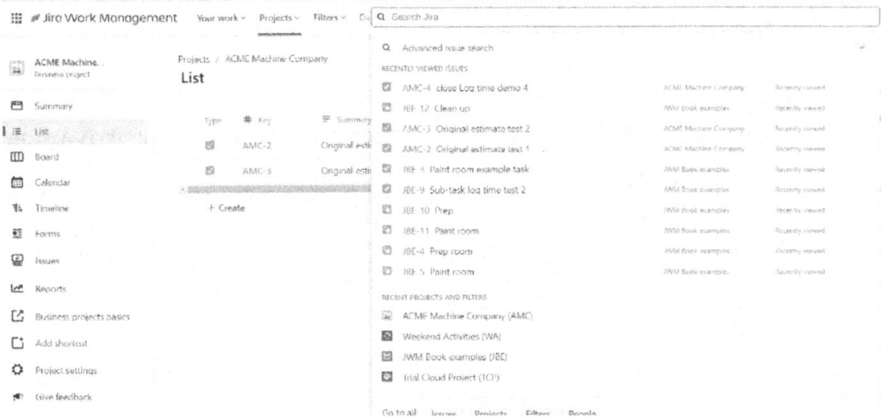

SEARCH FOR PEOPLE

Often, you may want to search for Users instead of Issues or Projects. In this case simply click on the **People** menu in the Navigation bar and select **Search for people and teams**.

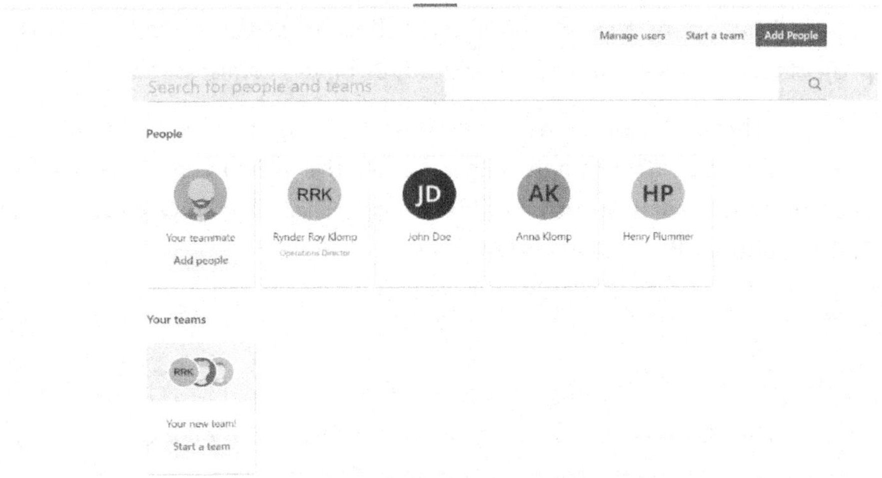

Then, enter the name or Username of the individual in the search field.

BASIC SEARCH

The Basic Search is a filter.

EXERCISE: VIEW "BASIC SEARCH"

1. GO TO NAVIGATION BAR >**FILTERS**, AND SELECT **ADVANCED ISSUE SEARCH**

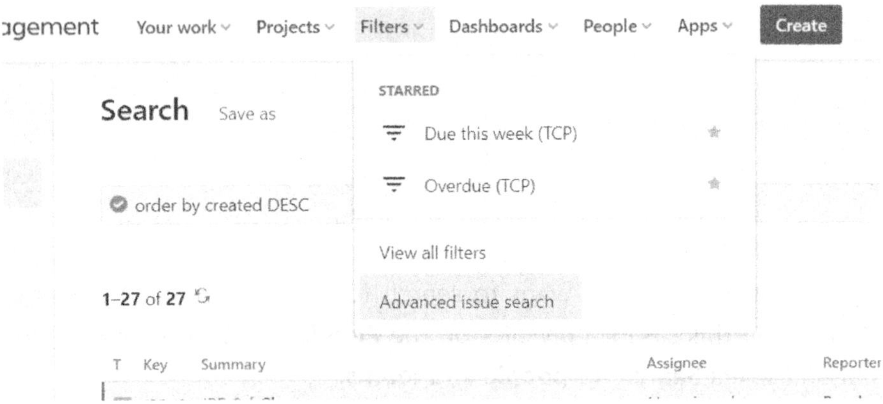

This opens the **Search View**, listing all of the issues for **all the projects** with which you are associated, or have permission to view.

When you open the Search view, you may see one of two search methods. The image below shows the **Advanced issue search**. We will come to that later in this chapter, but for now click on the **Switch to basic** link at the end of the search field:

The Basic search view comprises a row mostly containing drop-down lists. Collectively, they are the **Basic Search**.

These drop-down lists make up the filter, allowing you to narrow your search as little or as much as you wish.

In the image above, you see that there are five drop-down filters and one text box. It is important to remember that these filters are subsets of other, previous, filters. For example, let's say you select "To Do" in the Status filter and then want to select John Doe in the Assignee filter. You don't select anything in the Project and Type drop downs. The query is going to perform the following:

1. It will look in all Projects the User who created the query is authorized to view

AND THEN

2. It will search all Issue Types (e.g. Task or sub-task) in those projects

AND THEN

3. It will only look at those Issues where the status of the Issue is **To Do** in those Issues and projects

AND THEN

4. It will look for John Doe as the assignee in those projects and **To Do** Issues

Jira Work Management builds searches in the order that the filters were selected. Therefore, when building a multi-filter search, remember to organize the search in the proper filter order.

Let's take a closer look at the filters.

Project

This filter will allow you to filter your issues by project. The drop-down list will contain all the projects you have permission to see. The filter is multi-select, which means you can select more than one project if you wish.

If, after initially setting your project filter, you realize you need to include additional projects, then simply go back to the drop down and select those projects you now want to include. There is no need to clear your filter and start over.

If you are currently viewing issues associated with one project and want to see *all* your issues across all projects, then uncheck the project. When there are no projects checked, Jira Work Management will automatically select ALL projects.

You can also filter a project by entering its name or key in the Find Projects search field.

TYPE

This filter allows you to narrow your search based on Issue Types or Sub-Task Issue Types. Simply check the Issue Type(s) you want to see, or type in the name of the Issue Type in your Find Issue Types search field.

You need to remember that if you have selected a particular project or projects to view, you will only see the Issue Types associated with that project or projects.

If there are no Issue Types selected, you will see ALL issues, depending on your Project filter setting.

STATUS

This filter allows you to narrow your search based on Status type.

Once again, the number of statuses available in this search will be limited if you have already narrowed your search with the Project and Type filters.

If you do not select any status, you will see ALL issues depending on your Project and Type filter settings.

Assignee

This filter allows you to narrow your search based on Assignee.

The number of Assignees available in this search will be limited if you have already narrowed your search with other filters.

More

The More filter is quite powerful. It contains all the other standard and custom fields available to you. Well, almost all. It will only show you the fields in your Projects or Issue Types. For example, if you do not have any Epic projects, you won't see any Epic fields.

Since these fields are going to be used in a Filter argument, Jira Work Management calls these fields 'criteria'.

When you select any of these criteria, another pop-up will show up to narrow the search even further. For example, if you select the Due Date field, a pop-up will appear with several criteria options you can use to narrow the filter results even further:

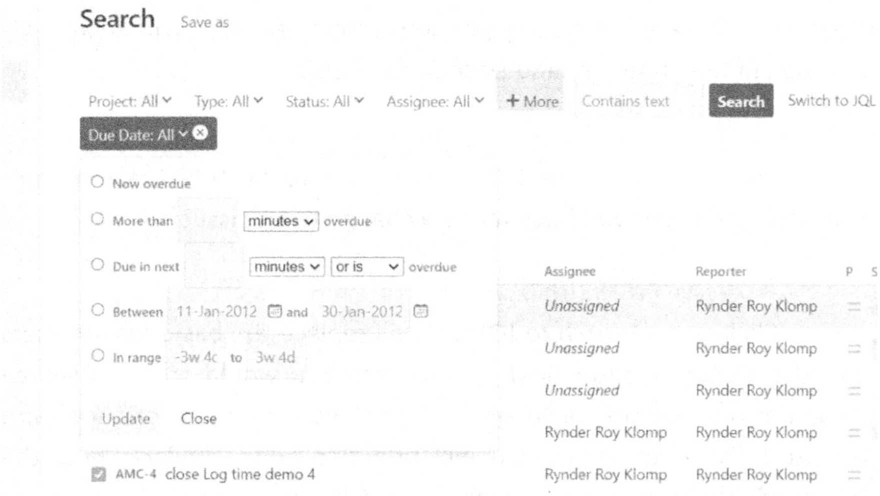

If you have built a Custom Field that contains a list of options, you can also use those options as criteria for your More filter. In the image below, I am using a Custom field called Approved, which has two options. I can select either Yes or No to further narrow my filter:

You can also repeat the More search as many times as you want if you remember that each More filter is a subset to previous filters.

If you want to delete a More filter, you will need to unclick the selected field name.

Contains text (Search Field)

Any criteria (must be text) or key words typed in this search field will be dependent on any previous filters selected. This search will only look in the Summary and Description fields

Search button

The purpose of the Search button is to execute the search or refresh the search if you have made a change to any issue.

Advanced Issue Search

Clicking on **Switch to JQL** link will replace the basic search filters with the advanced filter field. In this field you would create a search using the Jira Query Language (JQL). If you have experience with Microsoft Excel functions, you will find this quite similar. Using the Advanced function involves creating a JQL command followed by a criterion or criteria. Let's try one. But before we do, look at the format table below we will use in the JQL exercises:

Font	Purpose	Example
Regular	Instruction	Enter
Bold	Specific text to be Entered	**Project**
Regular italic	A value you should enter (such as a project or field name in your Jira program); or should select from the drop-down list	*My first project*
[]	Instruction to enter a space	Project[]=[]*My first project*
= + - > < !	Argument operator	Project =

Exercise: View Advanced Field

1. In the JQL field, enter (or select from the drop-down list that appears as you start to type):

    i. **Project**[]=[]select the name of a project that appears in the list[]**Order By**[]**Issuekey**

After you enter Project and a space, you will see a drop-down list of project names, select one of them. Make sure to leave a space after the project name. Next, enter (or select) Order By, make a space and enter (or select) Issuekey. After you have entered a few of the Issuekey letters, a list of words related to Issue will appear. You can select Issuekey from that list or continue to manually enter the word:

Project instructs Jira Work Management to look for a project name. ORDER BY is a command, and Issuekey is the criteria. In this case your issues will be sorted by the issue key, with the lowest number Issue key at the top of the list. I like this search as I prefer to see my list of issues **in the order they were created**, rather than the Jira default that lists issues based on create time (most recent issue listed first).

Notice how, when you are entering the argument, Jira offers options for you to choose from. This makes the building of the argument much easier.

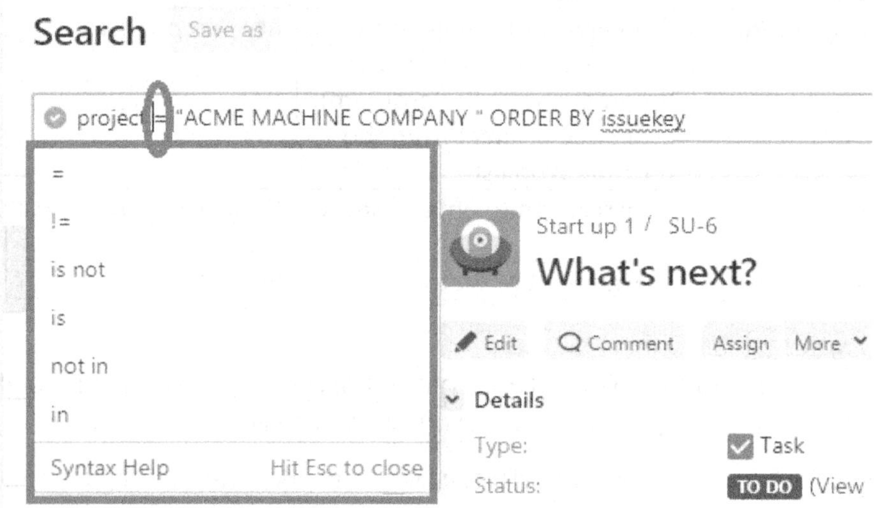

We won't go any further in this book about searches and JQL. However, if you are interested in following up, please purchase my book Jira JQL Basics and Reference guide. Available at Amazon:

Jira JQL Basics and Reference Guide: Everything you wanted to know about Jira Query Language but were afraid to ask!: Klomp, Rynder Roy: 9781988018195: Amazon.com: Books

Change View

The last item in the Search row (at the far right) is an icon allowing you to change your issue view:

One is a list view of your issues. The other is a combined view with a list of your issues on the left, and a detailed view of the issue selected.

Save Search

Of course, when most people go to the effort of building a search, they usually plan on viewing that search a number of times. Saving the search means the user doesn't need to reenter the search criteria every time s/he wants to view it.

Exercise: Save Search As

1. Click on the **Save As** button
2. Type in a Filter Name in the Save Filter Pop Up and click **SAVE**.

Once you click the save button your Search (really a filter) will be saved in the **Filters** sidebar.

Build a Custom Filter

Technically, any Saved search is defined as a Custom Filter. We are going to create one using the More filter.

In this specific filter we want to see those Issues that will be due in two days or less, but not those that are already overdue. Later in this chapter we will create an issue subscription so that you will receive system generated emails containing all your tasks that are due in two days or less (hopefully you are so organized that the list will be quite small or non-existent).

EXERCISE: BUILD A CUSTOM FILTER

1. GO TO NAVIGATION BAR > FILTERS >**ADVANCED ISSUE SEARCH**
2. IN THE SEARCH VIEW, MAKE SURE YOU ARE IN THE BASIC SEARCH, IF NOT CLICK THE **SWITCH TO BASIC** LINK

3. IN THE BASIC SEARCH VIEW, CLICK ON THE **PROJECT** DROP-DOWN LIST AND MAKE SURE THE PROJECTS, TYPE, STATUS, AND ASSIGNEE DROPDOWN FIELDS ARE SET AT THE VALUE "**ALL**"
4. IN THE FILTER MENU BAR, CLICK ON THE **MORE** DROP-DOWN LIST AND SELECT (OR START TO TYPE IN THE SEARCH TEXT BOX) *DUE DATE*
5. IN THE DUE DATE POP UP GO TO THE **DUE IN NEXT** OPTION AND CLICK THE RADIO BUTTON:

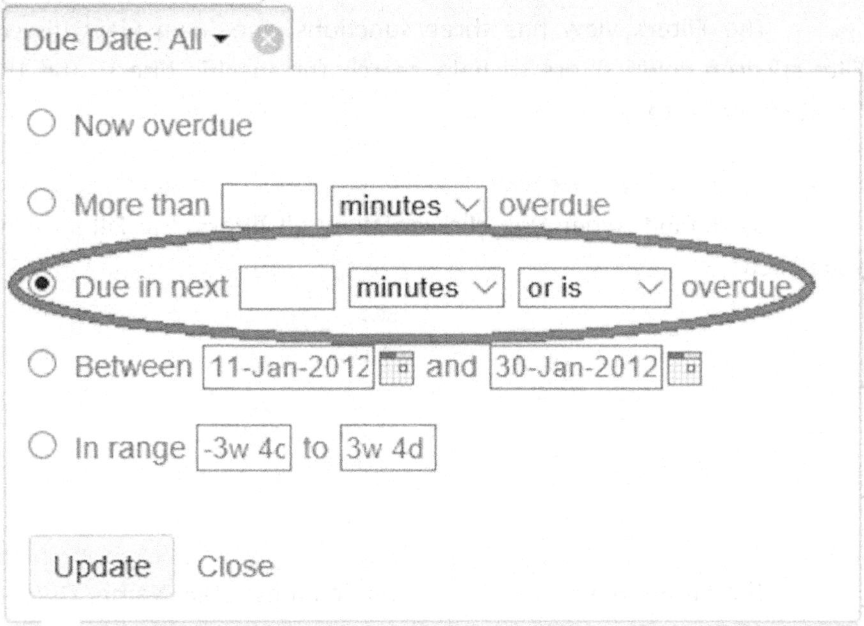

6. In the first entry field in the **Due in next** option, enter the number *2*
7. In the drop-down list next to the **Due in next** entry field select *Days*
8. In the next drop-down list select *and not* as the option for **Overdue**
9. Click the **Update** button
10. Click the **Save as** button
11. In the **Save Filter** pop up text field, type "*Issues due in 2 days or less*"
12. Click **Submit**

The saved filter should appear in the Filters sidebar. Now any time you want to see those Issues due in 2 days or less, simply click this filter to find the results.

Manage Filters

The Filters view has three functions: the Main view (list of Filters), drop-down filters to help search for specific filters, and the Create filter button.

Filters Main View

By default, when you click on **View all filters**, the Filters view will appear:

The **Filters main** view has seven columns: **Star**, **Name, Owner, Viewers**, **Editors, Starred by** and the ubiquitous More **(...).**

Star

The star column is simply a way of identifying your favorite or most important filters. A solid star indicates the filter is a "starred" or favorite filter. Simply click on the star to make it a starred filter or to un-star it.

A starred filter will appear in your Filters menu for ease of access.

Name

This column lists all your filters in alphabetical order. Clicking on the filter will cause the filter to run.

Owner

This column lists the name of the owner of the filter. Typically, this is the individual who built it. It is handy in the event you want to modify the filter but are not the owner. This means it is a shared filter, and you will need to contact the owner who will (possibly) make the modifications. It is typically easier in this case to copy the filter, rename it, and make your own modifications.

VIEWERS

When the Filter was created, a creator either made it a private filter, or can be viewed by others. This column indicates who can view the filter. In the next (Editors) segment there will be an exercise showing how to add or change viewers and editors.

EDITORS

The Editors column will show who can edit the filter.

Let's look at how to add or change Filter viewers or editors. We will do so using the newly created "Issues due in 2 days or less" filter.

EXERCISE: ADD OR CHANGE FILTER VIEWERS OR EDITORS

1. GO TO NAVIGATION BAR > FILTERS, AND SELECT VIEW ALL FILTERS
2. IN THE **FILTERS** VIEW, CLICK ON "*ISSUES DUE IN 2 DAYS OR LESS*"
3. IN THE *ISSUES DUE IN 2 DAYS OR LESS* VIEW, CLICK ON **DETAILS**

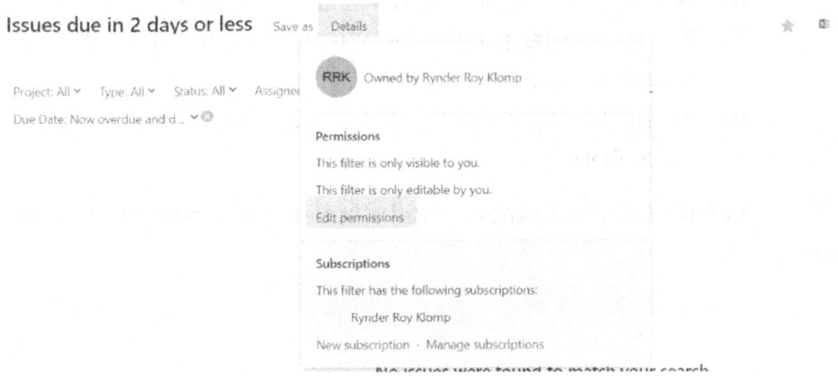

4. IN THE FILTER DETAILS POP-UP, CLICK ON **EDIT PERMISSIONS** IN THE PERMISSIONS SECTION

5. In the **Edit filter** pop-up, confirm *Issues due in 2 days or less* is in the name field

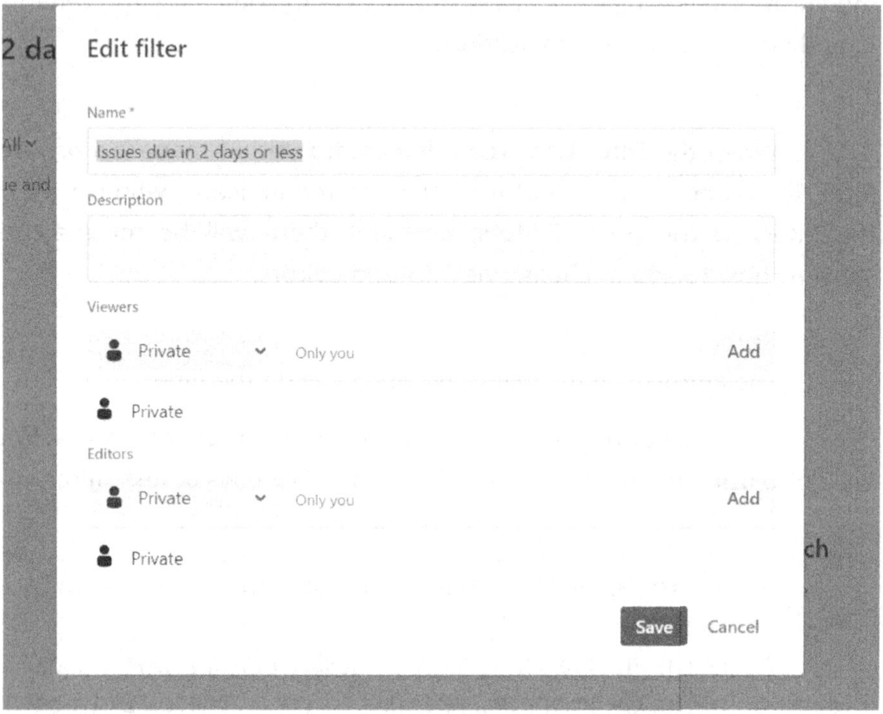

6. In the Viewers drop down select **Project**
7. In the **project** drop down that appears select *ACME Machine Company project*
8. In the **roles** drop down select *All roles*
9. Click **Add**

ACME Machine Company and all roles will appear in the Viewers list.

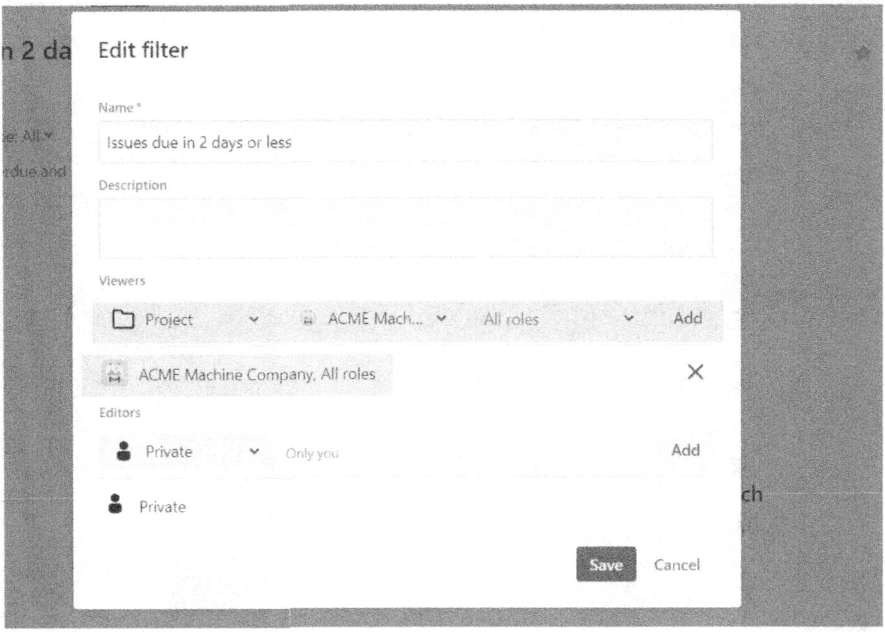

10. In the **Editors** drop down select *Group*
11. In the **Group drop down** that appears, select *site-admins*
12. Click **Add**

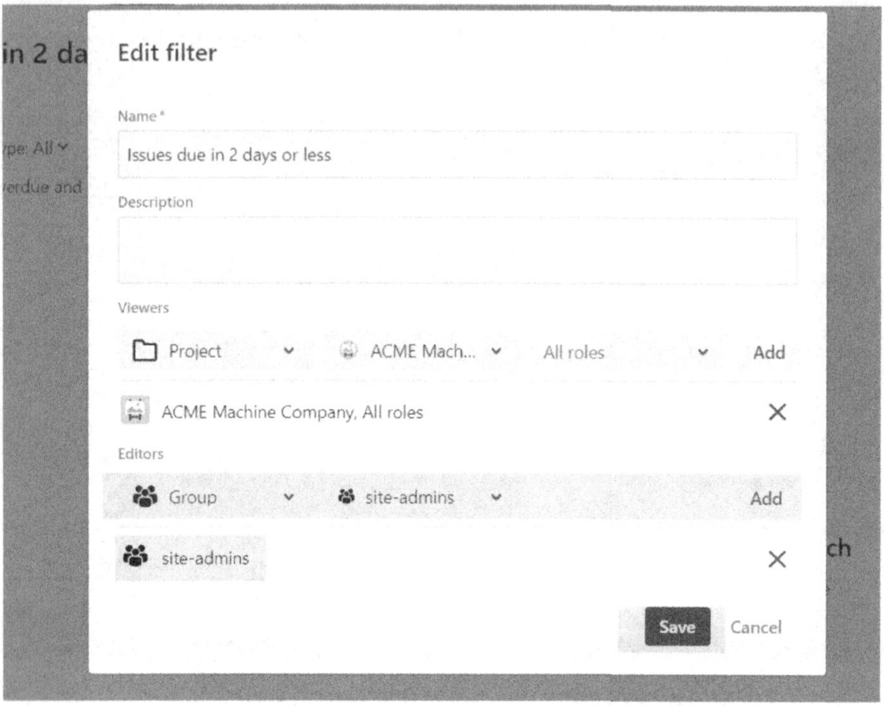

13. CLICK **SAVE**
14. GO TO NAVIGATION BAR > FILTERS, SELECT **VIEW ALL FILTERS**

As you see, the Viewers and Editors fields now show the changes we made.

STARRED BY

This column shows you how many Users have starred this filter. It is a good indication of the filter's popularity.

More (...)

The More column provides five options:

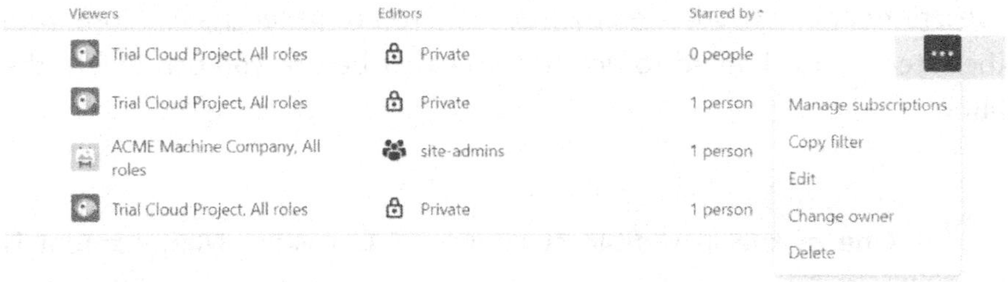

Manage Subscriptions

As we saw in a previous exercise, this is where you can add, edit, delete Filter subscriptions.

Copy Filter

The copy filter link is a great tool if you find an existing filter that is close, but not exactly what you want. Simply copy and rename the filter. You can then proceed to open the filter and change it to meet your needs.

Edit Filter

The edit filter allows you to change the name, description, viewers and editors of the filter (if you have the proper permissions, of course). It does not allow you to edit the contents of the filter. In order to edit the contents, you need to click on the filter name. That opens the filter, where you can make your changes.

Change Owner

This option allows you to change the owner of the Filter. This happens quite often when the original owner leaves the project, the position, or the company.

DELETE

As the name indicates, this is where you delete the filter. You will get a simple Delete pop-up, if there are no associations (e.g. Filter subscriptions) with other elements. If there are other associations with the filter, you will need to delete those first before you can delete the filter.

SUBSCRIBE TO A FILTER

One of the incredible strengths of Jira Work Management is the ability to be notified, by email, of any Issue or Issue condition. This is done by subscribing to a filter. Building a custom filter and then subscribing to it is one of the most amazing productivity and risk management tools I have run across. And subscribing is incredibly easy to do.

EXERCISE: SUBSCRIBE TO A FILTER

1. GO TO NAVIGATION BAR > FILTERS >**VIEW ALL FILTERS** (LOCATED NEAR THE BOTTOM OF THE OPENED FILTERS MENU)IN THE FILTERS VIEW, FIND THE *ISSUES DUE IN 2 DAYS OR LESS* FILTER IN THE **NAME** COLUMN, THEN CLICK ON THE **MANAGE SUBSCRIPTIONS** LINK IN THE **MORE (...)** COLUMN:

2. IN THE **Subscriptions** View for the Issues due in 2 days of less, click on the **Add subscription** BUTTON:

3. Ensure *Personal Subscriptions* is selected in the **Recipients** drop-down list
4. Check *Daily* in the **Schedule** options
5. In the **Interval** area select *Once per Day* and at *1:00 AM* in the following drop-down lists (or select some other time if you wish)
6. Leave the "Email this filter, even if there are no issues found" unchecked
7. Click Subscribe

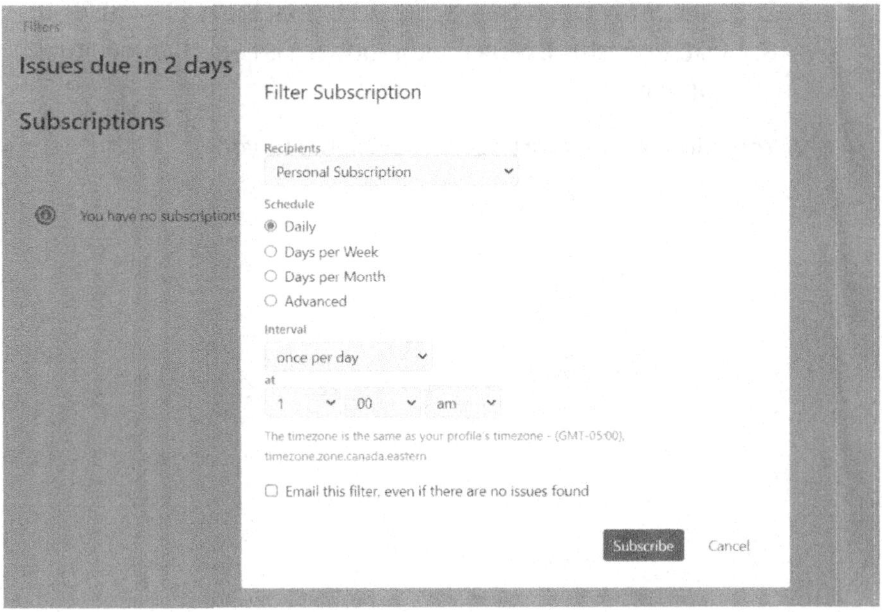

CREATE FILTER

The Create filter button will bring you to the search page where you can create a new filter. As we discussed how to create a filter earlier in the chapter, there is no need to repeat that exercise here.

EXPORT A FILTER'S REPORT

There may be occasions when you need to export the results of a filter as a report. This happens when you need to send the contents to someone who isn't licensed for Jira Work Management. Or you may want to save the Filter results as a snapshot in time, to be reviewed at a later date. One of the many great things about Jira is that you can easily export Filter contents in many different ways.

EXERCISE: EXPORT A REPORT

1. GO TO NAVIGATION BAR > **ISSUES**
2. SELECT **MY OPEN ISSUES**, OR ANY OTHER **FILTER** IF YOU WISH
3. CLICK ON THE **EXPORT** DROP-DOWN LIST IN THE UPPER RIGHT CORNER

You will see 11 export options available to you:

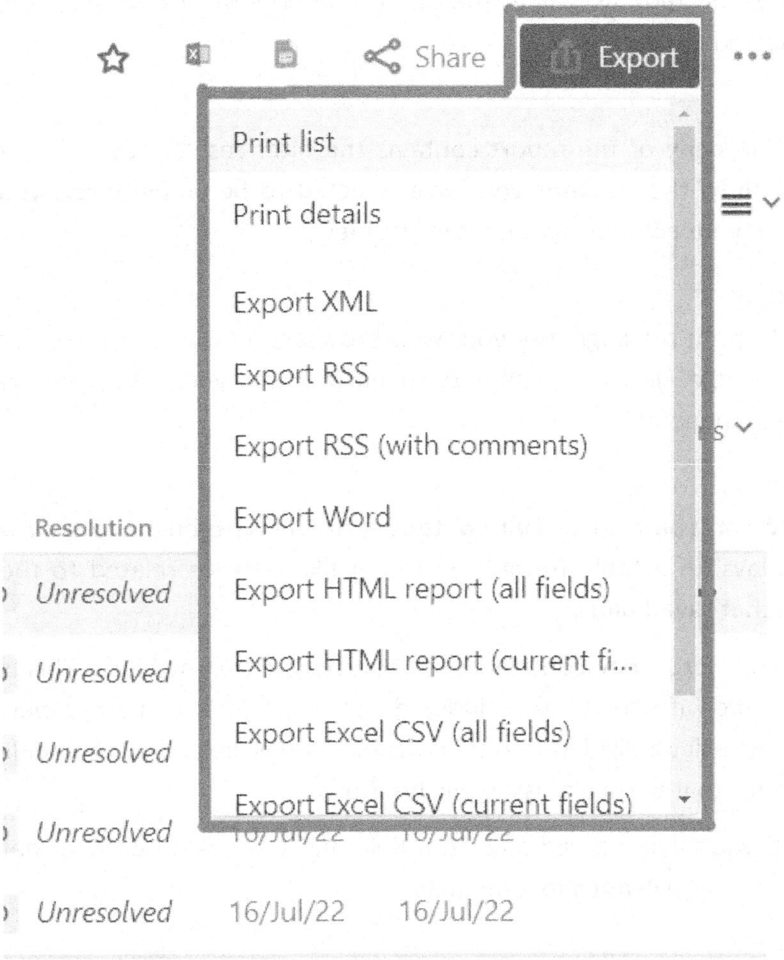

PRINT LIST

Printable option is designed to view your filter's issues in printable format. It has two parts: Header and Body.

HEADER

The header contains the name of the Organization or Jira Work Management (i.e. the Title name of your Jira Work Management program found in the Navigation Bar), the project or projects (if previously selected), as well as the other filter criteria such as assignee, status, sorted by, etc.

Body

The body of the report contains the filter results. Note that it will only show the columns you have selected to be visible when you configured your column layout in the List View.

Printing

To print the page, use your web-browsers print method (e.g. for Microsoft Edge click the right mouse button and select Print in the menu that appears).

Print Details

When you choose **Full Content,** you will be brought to a view that displays, in a table format, all the available fields related to the issues in that saved filter.

Your filter may contain issues that have different fields. This is quite common if your filter includes different projects or issue types. Your report will be divided into sections for each issue and all the fields available for that particular issue will be shown.

If you have created a custom field and there is no data in that field, the report will not show the field.

Printing

To print the page, use your web-browsers print method (e.g. for Microsoft Edge click the right mouse button and select Print in the menu that appears).

Export XML

Selecting Export XML will open a page containing the HTML code of your Saved Filter. Since this book is written for business users and not I.T. professionals, we will not dive any deeper into this export option.

Export RSS and Export RSS with comments

RSS means Really Simple Syndication and it can provide constant updates of information (such as Issue Status Updates, etc.). However, you need to set up a place (webpage) to host the RSS feed. And since that is pure I.T. stuff, we will move on to our next Export item.

Word

You can export your Saved Filter report to Microsoft Word. When you do so, the format will look very similar to the Full Content format.

One convenient feature is that Word will insert a page break after each issue. This means each issue will start on a new page. This is quite useful if you want to print out specific issues.

It should go without saying that you must have a copy of MS Word (or program compatible to Word) on your computer for this option to work.

Export HTML report (All fields)

When selecting this option, a new page will open in your browser (e.g. Google, Firefox, Microsoft Edge, etc.) and display every *common* Issue field.

What does "common" mean? Well, your HTML page will only display a field if every issue in that filter has that field. For example, let's say your filter contains 10 Issues and 9 of those Issues contains the field Due Date, but the 10th does not. In this case the Due Date field will not appear.

When you select the All fields option, be aware that every field you have permission to see will be exported to the spreadsheet report, even those unrelated to the issues in your saved filter.

Additionally, despite Jira saying it will export All Fields, it does not export the comments related to the issues.

Jira Work Management limits the number of issues you can export to 1,000.

Export HTML report (Current Fields)

When selecting this option, a new page will open in your browser (e.g. Google, Firefox, IE Explorer, etc.) and display the fields shown in your list view.

Additionally, despite Jira saying it will export All Fields, it does not export the comments related to the issues.

Jira Work Management limits the number of issues you can export to 1,000.

Export Excel CSV (All fields)

You can export your Saved Filter report as a CSV (comma separated value) format to a spreadsheet format such as Microsoft Excel. This is great if you want to rearrange or do something with the data. Needless to say, you must have a copy of MS Excel (or another compatible spreadsheet program) on your computer.

When you select the All fields option, be aware that every field you have permission to see will be exported to the spreadsheet report, even those unrelated to the issues in your saved filter.

Additionally, despite Jira saying it will export All Fields, it does not export the comments related to the issues.

Jira Work Management limits the number of issues you can export to 1,000.

You may also get a pop-up warning in Excel that the file is corrupted, or something like that. This is because Jira inserts two ‘header’ rows at the beginning of the spreadsheet, and that tends to confuse Excel. Don’t worry about it, import the sheet anyway.

Export Excel CSV (Current fields)

When selecting the Current Fields option, you will receive an CSV report that only contains the columns you have visible in the Jira Saved Filter.

As with the ALL Fields option, Jira Work Management limits the number of issues you can export to 1,000.

Create dashboard gadgets

This format allows you to export a Saved Filter as a gadget to any Jira Work Management Dashboard you have permission to edit.

When you click **Create dashboard gadgets** you are presented with a number of Gadget options to choose from. Depending on the type of Saved Filter you may not be able to choose all Chart types shown; if that happens, keep experimenting until you find one you like and that works for your Saved Filter.

Once you have selected the Chart you want, click the **Save to Dashboard** button. That will open another view where you will select the Dashboard you want to host your chart. In addition, you can enter the name of the Filter and that title will appear in the header bar of the chart.

After you have selected the Dashboard, click **Save**. The Dashboard you selected will open, and your chart will be inserted as the first (top of page) gadget in the Dashboard. From there you can reposition it if you wish.

CUSTOMIZING YOUR ISSUE LIST VIEW

One of the really great things you can do in Jira Work Management is tailor any of the filters' views by adding or deleting columns in the Issue List view. This allows you to modify your Issue List view so that only the critical fields are shown, and the need to go to each Issue's Detail View is eliminated. For example, I have added my custom 'Follow Up Date' field to the Issue List view; so, I can immediately see those issues that will soon require this action.

You can customize your Issue List view using the **Columns** drop-down. Clicking on Columns will open a drop-down list with two tabs: My Defaults and System:

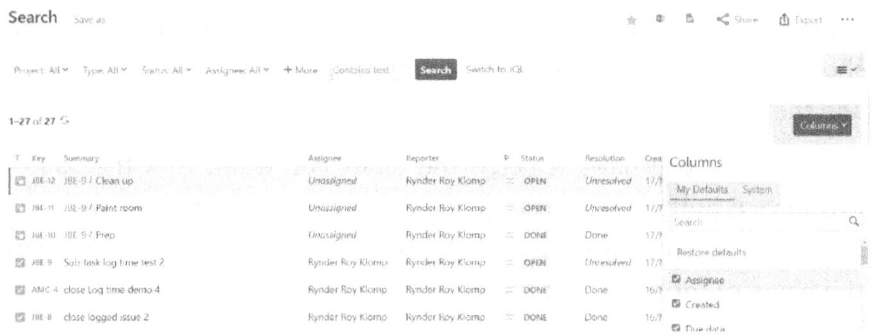

My Defaults allows you to create your own customized list view. It is applicable only to your views.

In the **System** tab the Jira Work Management Administrator can define the columns for *all* users who have not created their own default views. Having said that, making changes in the System area may over-write the custom views of some users; so, be careful when you use this configuration. To confirm my words, click on the system tab and see the warning note.

Changing the Issue List View

After you click either the **My Defaults** or **System** tabs in the Columns dropdown you will see a number of fields accompanied by check marks. Clearing a check box will eliminate that field from the Issue List view.

If you want to add a field to that configuration, simply continue to scroll down to find an option you need and select one or more to include them in your view; or, type that option in the Search box right below the My Defaults tab.

Make sure to click **Done** when you are finished.

Just one note of caution. When making your My Defaults configuration, remember you are in the general Search Issues view. Otherwise, you may end up accidentally making a configuration to a Saved Filter.

If you are unhappy for some reasons with your result and want to restore your defaults, click on **Restore Defaults** link under Search box in the Column pop up.

Sorting

You can also reconfigure your list view by clicking on any of the column headings. Doing so will give you an option as to how to sort the column. For example, clicking on the Key column will change the sorting from smallest to largest or largest to smallest Key number.

Re-arranging Columns

You can also move Issue columns (in the List View), by clicking on the column title and then drag-and-drop to the new location.

PROJECT REPORTS

In a previous chapter, we learned how to build Dashboards and add Gadgets to them. Most of the time a Gadget is a type of report, though there are exceptions.

You can also build project specific reports, and that's what we will do now.

EXERCISE: BUILD A PROJECT REPORT

1. GO TO NAVIGATION BAR> **PROJECTS**
2. SELECT ANY PROJECT
3. NAVIGATE TO THE SIDEBAR OF THE PROJECT, CLICK ON **REPORTS** (THE ICON WITH THE GRAPH)

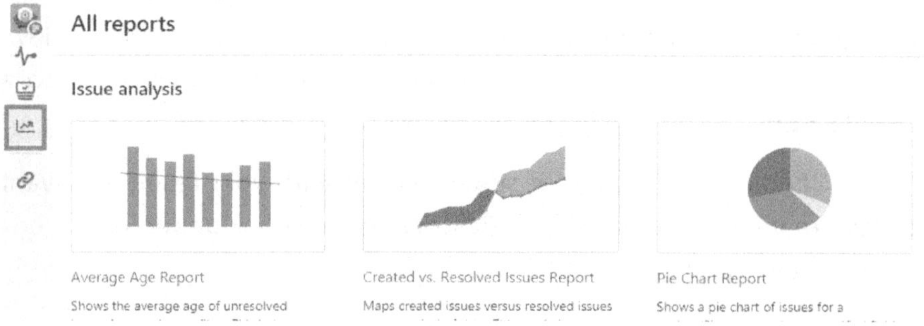

The opened view is full of different report types. However, sometimes there may be only one specific report shown. If that is the case, go to the top of the view and where it says **Reports**, click the down arrow next to it, then click **All Reports** on the menu.

4. CLICK ON ANY REPORT

Clicking on a report will open its configuration view. Here you will answer a number of questions specific to that report. Since they are all different, we won't try to explain them all here. I recommend you click on a report that seems appropriate for your type of project and then configure it in a number of different ways (e.g. try different reporting periods) to determine what works best for you.

Once you configure a report click the **Next** button to see the results.

After the report is created you can revise the report by clicking on the **Configure** button in the top right of the Report view.

Dashboard Filter Reports

In a previous chapter we created the Test Dashboard using Jira's Core Gadgets. Many of those gadgets are based on Jira Work Management built-in filters. In this chapter I want to introduce you to Filters gadgets.

Remember that a Project Report will appear only in a Project and will only display information about that project. A Dashboard Filter Report can cover multiple projects and will appear only in a Dashboard.

Exercise: Add a Report Gadget to a Dashboard

1. Go to Navigation Bar > **Dashboards**
2. Select any **Dashboard** (except for the System Dashboard)
3. Click on **Add Gadget** button in the upper right corner of the Dashboard
4. Scroll down until you see **Filter Results** and **Starred Filters,** click **Add** for each

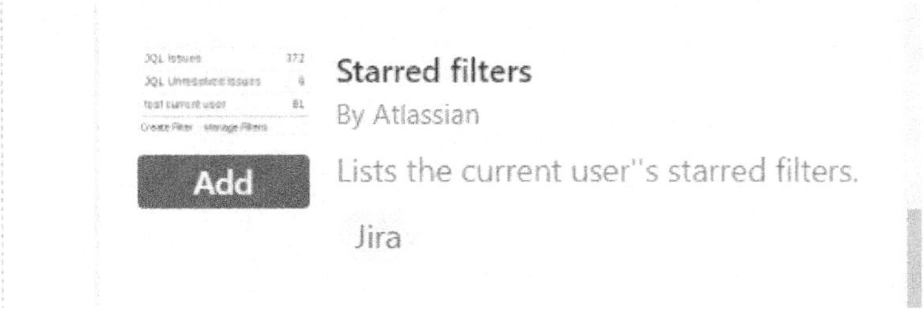

Filter Results

This gadget will place a Filter Results configure view on the Dashboard. Select the Saved Filter you want to see, answer the other questions, save the results, and those results will now be shown in the dashboard.

Starred Filters

Selecting this gadget will place a list of your favorite filters on the dashboard. Clicking any filter will bring up that specific filter report.

Chapter 13 – System Settings

To avoid confusion, in this book the term "Site-admin" includes "Org-admin, Site-admin, and Jira-admin" unless specifically noted otherwise.

Chapter Objectives

In this chapter you will:

- Understand what you can and cannot do with Jira Work Management System Settings
- Develop an understanding of the JWM System Settings
- Practice with exercises to configure some basic JWM settings

What you can / cannot do with System Settings

Many applications require the involvement of a "System Administrator". This is the individual(s) who understands the infrastructure, the plumbing, of a program. Their job is to install, configure, and maintain, the application so it works within their organization. For example, they are the people who install upgrades to the software, or who make sure your organizations email system integrates with the application.

The good news is that with Jira Work Management's Cloud environment Atlassian takes over this role. They manage the upgrades, they make sure you can email, and they fix any bugs or problems.

While it is a challenge to clearly define what is the responsibility differences between a Atlassian's System Admin and your Site-admin, you can generally state it this way: the Atlassian System Admin's role is to make sure the application works, while the Site-admin's role is to manage Users, and to create/customize Projects, Issues, and their elements. For example, the System Admin makes sure the applications email system operates properly in the application. S/he makes sure that other applications integrate properly with JWM. The Site-admin customizes the appearance (colors, column layout, Site name, etc.) of the site. S/he designs, builds, and maintains custom workflows.

Bottom line. You cannot perform the traditional System Admin hardware operations in JWM. You can, however, configure settings in JWM to alter the appearance of, or to determine how Users will work with, the application.

A TOUR OF SYSTEM SETTINGS

1. GO TO NAVIGATION BAR > COG > AND CLICK ON **SYSTEM**

The System's page contains a sidebar and main view. Let's take a tour.

SYSTEM'S PAGE SIDEBAR

The system's page sidebar is comprised of ten segments:

- General configuration
- Troubleshooting and support
- Security

- Automation
- User interface
- Import and export
- Mail
- Admin Helper
- Shared items
- Advanced

There is so much here, I could probably write another book just on the System area.

Some areas are out of your control (managed by the Atlassian System Admin only), and other's require special licenses. Consequently, we are going to touch on the most critical areas for you. As you gain expertise with JWM, you will find yourself going back to this area to deal with more complicated configuration elements.

General configuration

General configuration or "system settings" is where you customize the basic settings for this particular site (remember, you can have more than one JWM site in your Atlassian Organization). The main view has three key areas: the **System Settings main** view itself, **Advanced Settings** link, and the **Edit Settings** link.

System Settings Main View

The main view shows the details of your current configuration. It is divided into three areas: General Settings, Internationalization, and Options.

General Settings

The General Settings area contains the **Application title** of your particular site, **Email from**, and **Introduction**.

The Application title is the name of this particular site. Typically, this is the name of the organization, or if you have multiple Atlassian sites within your organization, it would be the name most relevant for this site. For example, some organizations keep one site for company business and keep another site for extremely confidential Issues such as new product development or company strategy.

"Email from" is the email address from which system generated notification emails will be sent. Leave this alone unless you have a really good reason to change it.

"Introduction" is an area where you can add a short message that will show on the default dashboard. Usually it explains the purpose of the site (e.g. "Welcome to Roy's Jira, this site is used to .....").

Internationalization

This area does three things. It defines the **Indexing language**, the **default language**, and the **default user region and time zone**.

The Indexing language is the language used to conduct searches in your JWM. The default is "English – aggressive stemming." What does that mean? Consider the word "looking". The root of the word "looking" is "look". Looking is an extension (a stem) of that root word "look". With aggressive stemming, the application will first identify the root of "looking" and then find all extensions of "look" when doing a search (e.g. look, looking, looked, looker, etc.).

Default language sets the language the application will use and display. However, if your profile says that you want to use US English, and the application's default language is set to Chinese, you (your Username) will still see US English. At the time of writing, JWM has 27 languages or dialects available.

Default user time zone should indicate the location where most of the Users of this site would recognize as appropriate. For example, if most of the Users live and work in Toronto, it probably doesn't make much sense to set the default time zone for Seattle Washington.

OPTIONS

The final area in the System Settings Main view defines the options for the JWM site. Most of these are straight forward and don't need any explanation. If you don't understand one or more at this time, that's probably a good indication not to change them. Leave that for a more experienced Admin.

EDIT SETTINGS

The Edit Settings area is where you edit the items seen on the System Settings Main view.

1. CLICK ON THE **EDIT SETTINGS** LINK IN THE UPPER RIGHT CORNER OF THE SYSTEM SETTINGS MAIN VIEW

I really like the way Atlassian set up the editing for the System Settings page. It is incredibly easy and intuitive to use. Atlassian also does a great job of explaining each field. Just remember to click the Update button at the bottom of the page after you make your changes.

Advanced Settings

1. In the System Settings main view, click on **Advanced Settings**

Notice the first caution sentence, "The following are advanced options. Do not change them unless you know exactly what you are doing." We now have a circular argument. If you know what you are doing, you don't need me to explain anything. If you don't know what you are doing, I should not be explaining the page to you. So, let's exit this page and move on to another topic.

2. Click on the **General Settings** button located in the upper right corner of the System **Advanced Settings** view.

Trouble shooting and Support

The **Audit Log** contains all the changes made by the Users on this site. Clicking the "Time" link allows you to narrow your search.

The Actions drop down in the upper right corner allows you to change some basic settings and also has a link to the Atlassian's Audit Log documentation page.

You can also export the Log in a CSV file format (e.g. MS Excel).

Security

The Security area comprises three links: **Project roles**, **Global permissions**, and **Issue collectors**.

Project roles and Global permissions

Here is where you add and manage project roles. It is also where you grant global permissions. We covered these topics in Chapter 9 - Users, Roles, and Groups; so, there is no need to repeat it again.

Issue collectors

Issue collectors are a great tool developed by Atlassian. It allows you to collect Issues on any website you manage, even if they are not websites devoted to Atlassian products. For example, you may have developed your own company website for the purpose of selling your products online. Once you complete the Issue Collector form in JWM, you will be issued an embed code. You can then insert that embed code into your company website. Visitors to that site (they don't need to be a licensed Jira User) can then access this embedded form and use it to create Issues in your project.

Exercise: Create an Issue Collector

1. Open a project where you want to manage the Issues submitted by the website users. You must have the Create Issue permission
2. In the Project's sidebar, click on **Project settings**
3. In the Project settings' sidebar, scroll down and click on **Issue collectors**

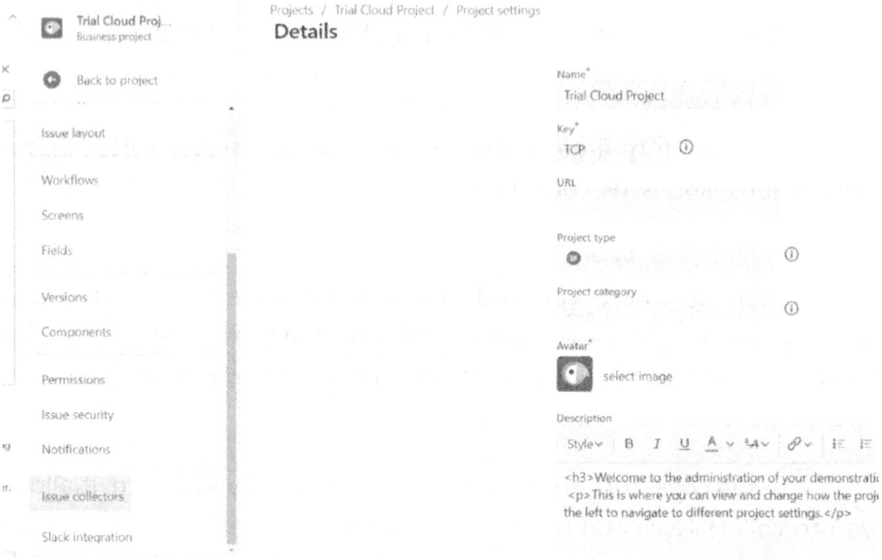

4. IN THE ISSUE COLLECTORS VIEW, CLICK ON **+ADD ISSUE COLLECTOR** IN THE UPPER RIGHT CORNER:

5. IN THE ADD ISSUE COLLECTOR VIEW **FILL OUT THE FORM.** NOTE THAT SOME OF THE OPTIONS PROVIDE PREVIEWS SO FEEL FREE TO EXPLORE THE VARIOUS OPTIONS
6. CLICK **SUBMIT** WHEN FINISHED.

After you click submit you will be taken to the **Embedding the issue collector** view:

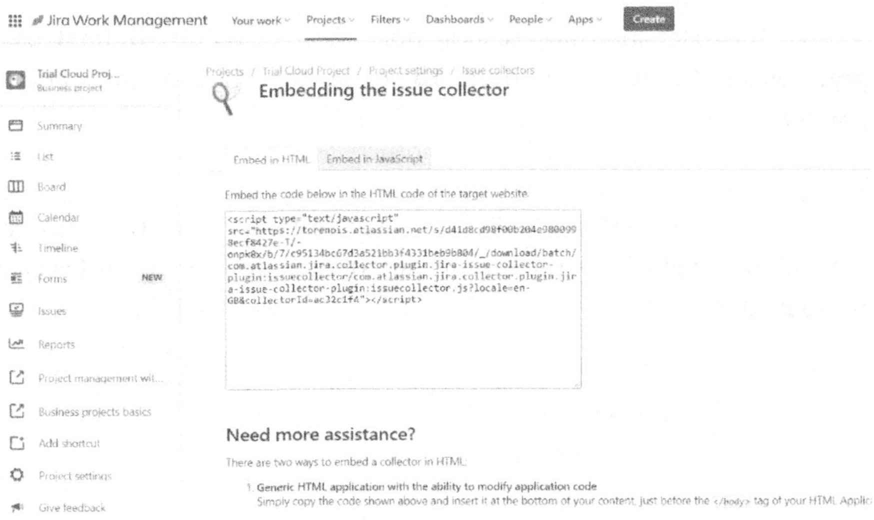

The embed code is created in both HTML and JavaScript format. Copy the code most appropriate for your website and embed it in your website.

Caution: if you are not an experienced coder, or are not authorized to edit the website, do not do anything with the embed code until approved by the website owner. The author of this book assumes no responsibility if something goes wrong.

Automation

One of the tremendous benefits of JWM is the ability to create automation rules. These are operations that work automatically when something "triggers" the rule to start. For example, you can create a rule that sends an automated email to a specific email address when an assignee is changed in an Issue.

You can use one of the Automation rules in the Jira library, or you can create your own. Jira has an excellent tutorial to get you started, so I highly recommend you use it before creating your first Automation rule.

USER INTERFACE

The User interface section holds four elements: **Default user preferences, Default dashboard, Look and feel**, and **Announcement banner**.

DEFAULT USER PREFERENCES

Below is a list of the Default User settings. If the User has not set their own options (in their profile area), then the default settings will be applied.

You can edit the settings using the **Edit default values** button in the upper right corner.

Below is a table listing the settings and your options:

Setting	Options
Default outgoing email format	Text or html
Number of Issues per page	Enter a number, technically unlimited
Default sharing for filters and dashboards	Private or Public
Notify users of their own changes	Yes or No (checkbox)
Autowatch own issues	Yes or No (checkbox)

DEFAULT DASHBOARD

This where you can edit your sites default dashboard. This was covered in Chapter 11 – Dashboards.

Look and Feel

The look and feel view is where you change your site's Logo and Title.

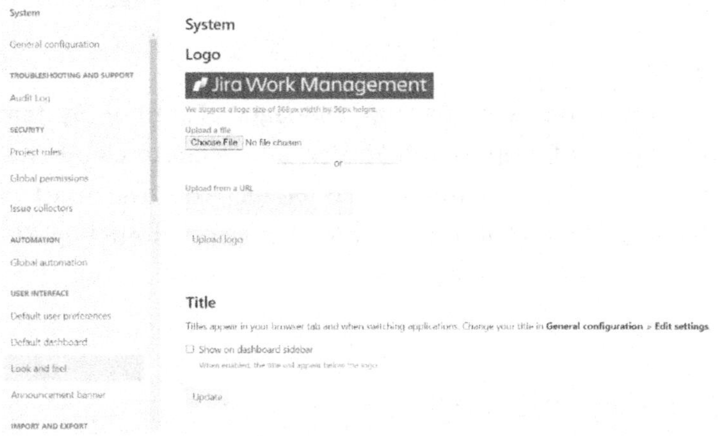

If you are going to change your logo, make sure to abide by the logo size requirements (368 px width and 56px height), otherwise you will be very disappointed with the results. Also, in many large organizations there are strict rules about logo dimensions and aspects. If you don't obey those rules, the logo police will make your life very uncomfortable.

Announcement Banner

The announcement banner is, I feel, a tool that is too often overlooked.

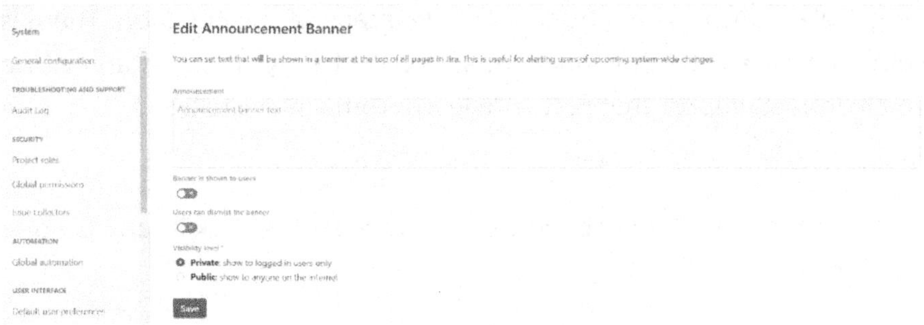

It is a tremendous tool for communicating to your team or anyone viewing your site. The announcement banner will show on top of all your Jira pages. If you have an emergency, use the announcement banner. If you have a major announcement, use the announcement banner. It is a wonder tool for communicating easily to your team.

IMPORT AND EXPORT

This section comprises: **Backup manager**, **External System Import**, **Import Jira Cloud**, **Import Jira Server**, and **Migrate cloud site**. Almost all require specialized IT training, so we will skip over most of this section. The only area I want to touch on is External System Import.

EXTERNAL SYSTEM IMPORT

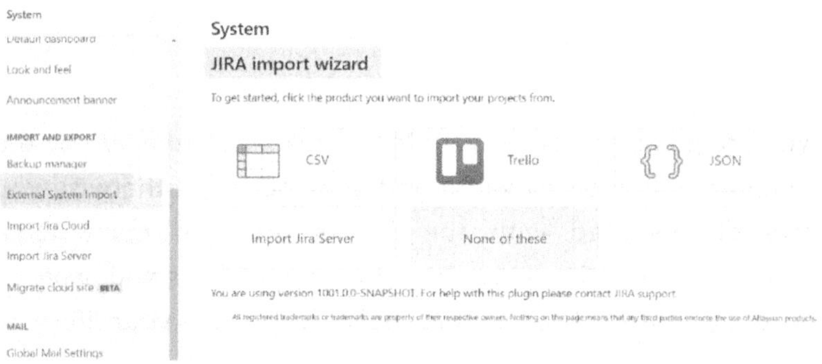

You may have your project or projects housed in another application, for example Microsoft Project or Excel. The Jira import wizard allows you to import those projects into Jira and convert them to Issues. If you are comfortable working with CSV or JSON formats, or with Trello, I encourage you to take advantage of this function. There is some learning with this function, so I would suggest you start with a small project, import that first, and learn from any mistakes.

MAIL

Mail is another section that requires strong IT skills and is not a basic topic.

ADMIN HELPER

Admin helper is made up of Permission helper...

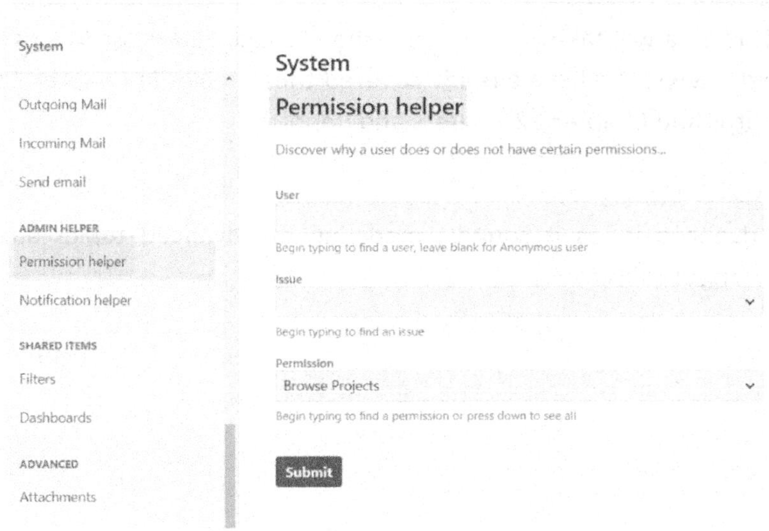

...and Notification helper.

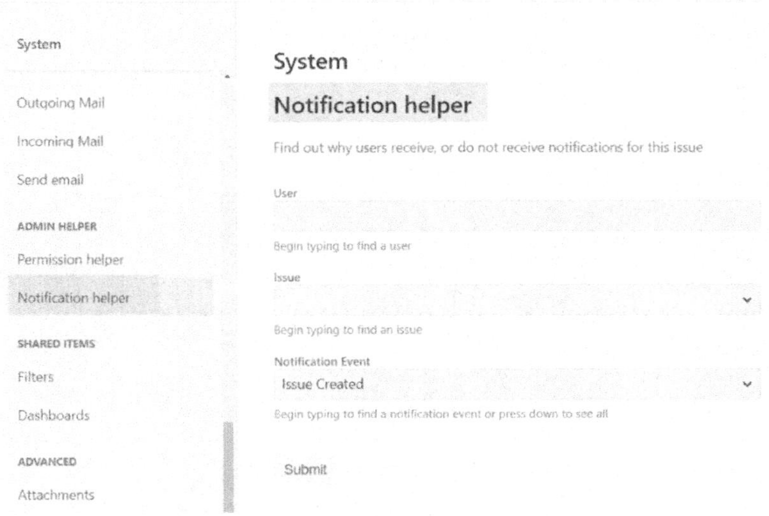

These are tremendous tools to help you determine why a User does not have permission to do something or why a User is not receiving notifications for a specific Issue. Simply fill in the templates, click **Submit**, and you will receive an answer.

Shared Items

This area will take you to either the Manage Filters, or Manage Dashboards views. We have already covered these topics in Chapter 11 – Dashboards and Chapter 12 – Filters and Reports.

Advanced

Advanced is, as it sounds, made up of advanced topics and require strong IT skills.

Chapter 14 – How To...

Chapter Objective

In this chapter you will find:

- **instructions to setup JWM Cloud and configure the site**
- **'scripts' to create or edit the most common Jira Work Management elements, such as Projects, Issues, Schemes, etc.**

PART 1: How to Install JWM Cloud and JWM

Introduction

Installing JWM Cloud is incredibly easy. But before we start we need to understand the differences between an Organization, Site, and Product as it relates to Atlassian.

Jira Work Management Basics

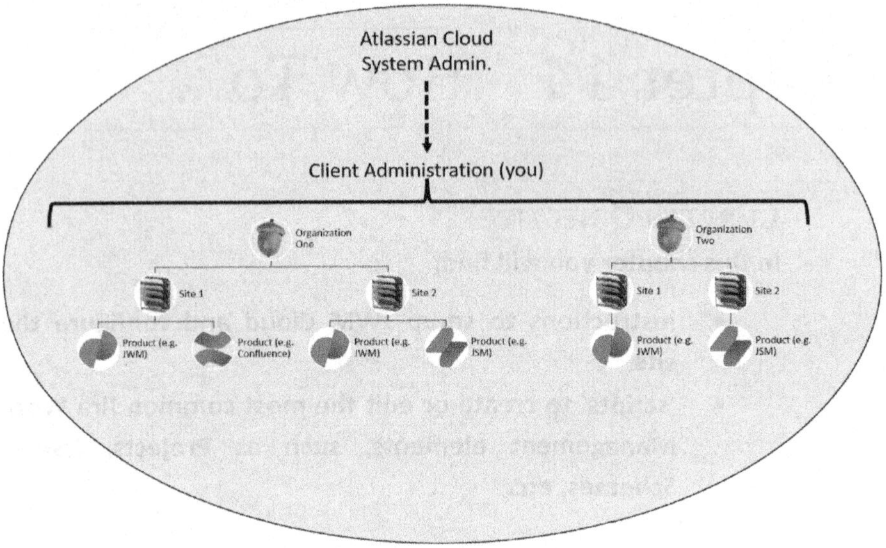

The first time you sign up for an Atlassian product like JWM, four things happen for you:

- An Administration area is set up
- An Organization is set up
- A Site is set up
- The Product is activated

Administration

The Administration area contains all your billing, licensing, and User information for all of your Organizations (you can have multiple Organizations within your Administration).

Organization

An Organization is situated within the Administration. You can have more than one Organization within an Administration. An Organization contains one or more Sites.

Site

An Atlassian site is contained within an Organization. A site holds one or more Atlassian products (e.g. JWM, Jira Service Management, Confluence, etc.)

An Organization can have multiple sites. With the Standard and Premium plans you can have up to 10,000 Users per site for Jira Work Management.

If you assign a User to multiple sites, each site will regard that User as a separate license. For example, if John Smith is assigned to three sites within the same Organization, then that will count as three licenses being used. The exception is if you have an Enterprise license. In that case you can place a User in as many sites as you want, and it only counts as one User.

Even though licenses and Users are managed at the Organization level, billing for licenses occurs at the Site level. Let's say you have three sites, you will receive three bills each month, one for each site. The exception is the Enterprise plan. Billing there takes place at the Organization level.

Why multiple Organizations or sites?

Why do you need multiple Organizations or sites? Well, there are a lot of reasons.

Cost Centers/ Billing

If it is important for you to track the expenses associated with a specific department, customer, project, etc. you may find it easier to set up a distinct Organization for each of those items. As your company is billed separately for each Organization/site, that will make the tracking of expenses easier.

TEST SITES

In addition to having a production (regular business) site you may also need a "sandbox" or test site. The sandbox site is where you build all your new workflows, screens, automation rules, etc., and then test them before implementing the new features into your regular production site.

SECURITY

You may want to have multiple Organizations or sites for security reasons. You many have your production Organization/site, and then a "top secret" Organization/site where you manage the development of a new product, or business strategy.

LEGAL

You may need to maintain separate Organizations or sites for legal reasons. For examples, in many countries banks are required to keep their consumer banking and investing banking businesses separate. Similarly, if you have offices in multiple countries there may be different legal requirements about the security of data.

LANGUAGES

You may have offices in different countries with different languages, or the same country can have multiple languages. You may want to set up different Organizations or sites to accommodate your English speakers or French speakers for example.

REGIONS

Let's say you have offices in New Zealand and Europe. You may find it more convenient to set up an Organization or site for each region. Why? Legal, currency, language, time zones, etc. are all possible reasons.

CLIENTS' NEEDS

You may have two clients who are direct competitors. They may not be comfortable with sharing the same Organization or site in case information about their company is inadvertently disclosed to the other.

In this case having separate Organizations or sites goes a long way to alleviate their concerns.

EFFICIENCIES

It may simply be more efficient to create different sites based on the type of work being done. For example, you may have Site 1 for your software developers which contains an instance of JWM and Jira Software. You may have another site for your service desk which contains an instance of JWM and Jira Service Management. Finally, you may have a third site that contains an instance of JWM and Confluence for your documentation team.

BRANDS, COMPANIES

Your Organization may be made up of different brands (quite common in the food, clothing, automotive industries, for example). It may be more effective to set up a separate Organization or site for each Brand.

PRODUCTS

An Atlassian application (e.g. JWM, Jira Service Desk, Jira Software, Confluence, Trello, etc.) is regarded as a "product". You can have multiple instances of a product within an Organization. But you can have only one instance of a product within a site. The table below demonstrates what is allowed within an Organization:

Site	Products
Site 1	JWM Jira Service Management
Site 2	JWM Jira Service Desk Confluence
Site 3	JWM Jira Software Jira Service Management Confluence

This next table demonstrates what is not allowed within an Organization:

Site	Products
Site 1	JWM #1 JWM #2 Jira Service Management
Site 2	JWM Jira Service Management #1 Jira Service Management #2 Confluence
Site 3	JWM #1 JWM #2 Jira Software Jira Service Management Confluence

How to install Jira Work Management

IMPORTANT: When installing Jira Work Management, you will also – at the same time - be creating an Organization and Site. The critical thing to remember is that your email address is the element that ties everything together. Later on, when you want to add more products or add more sites to your Organization you will need to use the same email address. If you don't it is likely you will inadvertently create another Administration or Organization. You can fix that error, but it is not an easy task. So, make sure you remember the email address you use when creating your first Organization.

NOTE: Be aware that Atlassian changes the layouts and structure of their website more often than most people brush their teeth. Consequently, the images below and the instructions may not be what you see when you sign up. However, the process is essentially the same and they do a good job of onboarding you easily

1. GO TO WWW.ATLASSIAN.COM
2. AT THE ATLASSIAN SITE, CLICK ON THE **PRODUCTS** MENU AND SELECT **JIRA WORK MANAGEMENT**

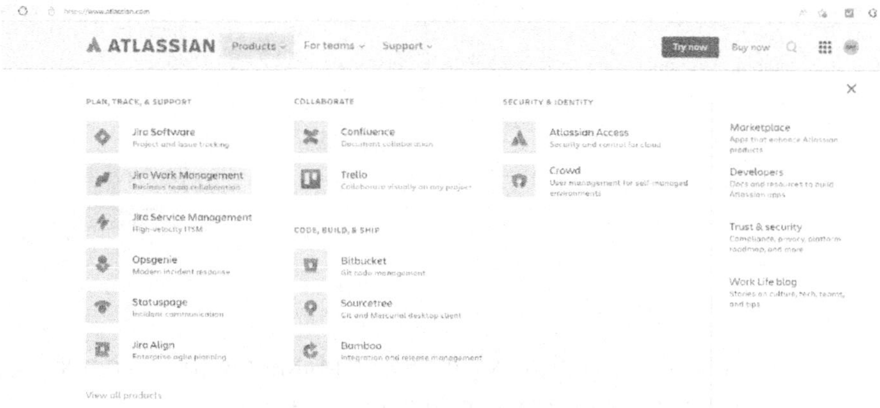

3. IN THE JIRA WORK MANAGEMENT VIEW, CLICK ON **GET IT FREE TODAY**

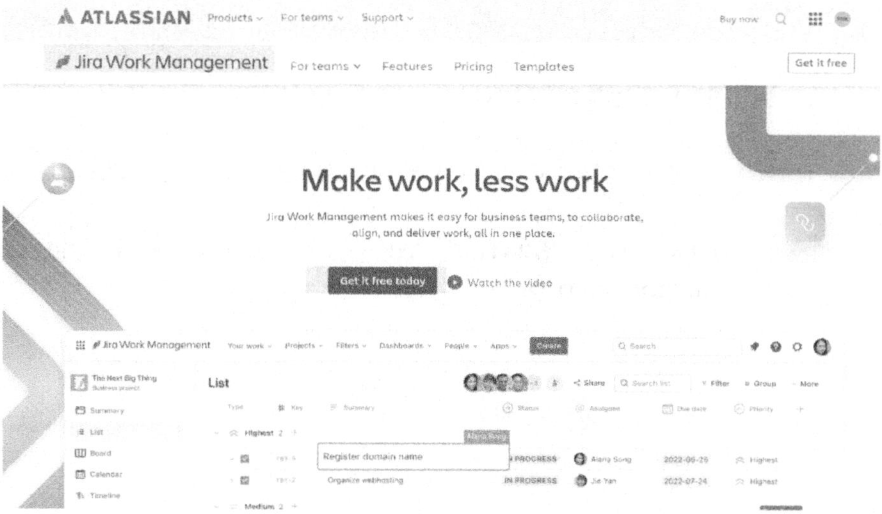

4. IN THE "YOU SELECTED" VIEW, EITHER SELECT A SECOND PRODUCT (OPTIONAL) OR CLICK NEXT

5. ON THE NEXT SCREEN (JIRA WORK MANAGEMENT – CLOUD FREE) YOU WILL BE ASKED FOR YOUR EMAIL ADDRESS.
6. YOU WILL NEXT GO THROUGH THE STEPS OF CREATING A NEW ACCOUNT (ORGANIZATION). WHILE ATLASSIAN IS CREATING THE ORGANIZATION, IT WILL AUTOMATICALLY CREATE A SITE, AND INSTALL THE PRODUCT(S) YOU SELECTED INTO THAT SITE.

WORKING WITH ORGANIZATIONS

ADD A NEW ORGANIZATION TO AN EXISTING ACCOUNT

1. OPEN THE **SWITCH TO**  MENU AND SELECT **ADMINISTRATION**

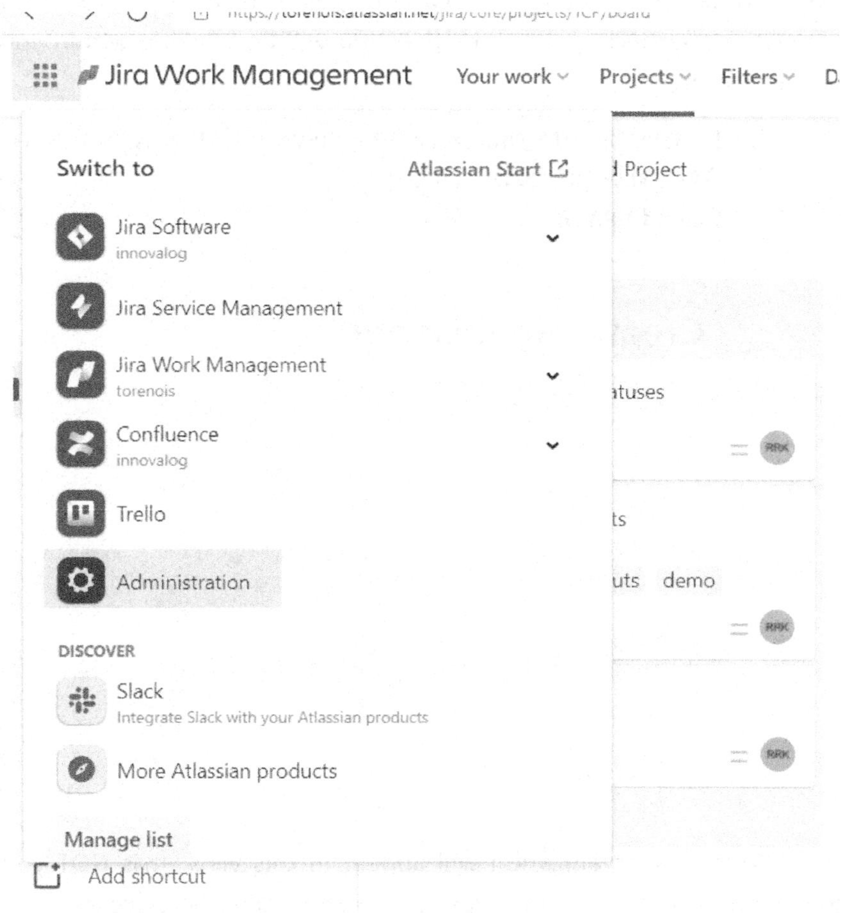

2. In the Atlassian Admin view, change the URL from HTTPS://ADMIN.ATLASSIAN.COM to HTTPS://ADMIN.ATLASSIAN.COM/O/CREATE

NOTE: You can probably do this without going through step one, but this tw-step approach guarantees that you will be working within your existing account.

3. In the Create organization view, enter a Name in the **Organization name** field
4. Click **Create**

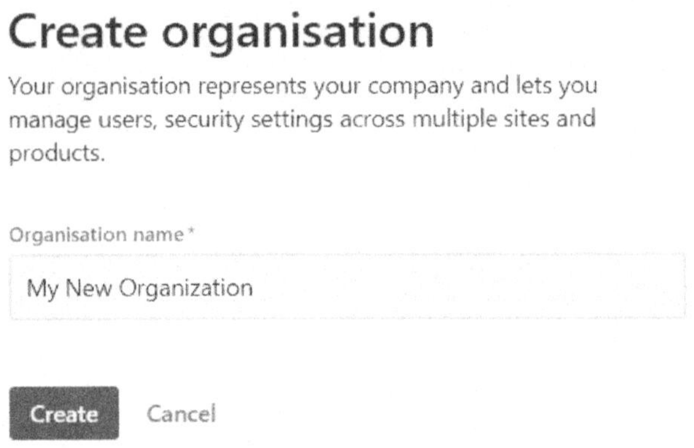

Your new organization will appear in this view. It is NOT your Administration site, it is a link page to sign up to Atlassian Access.

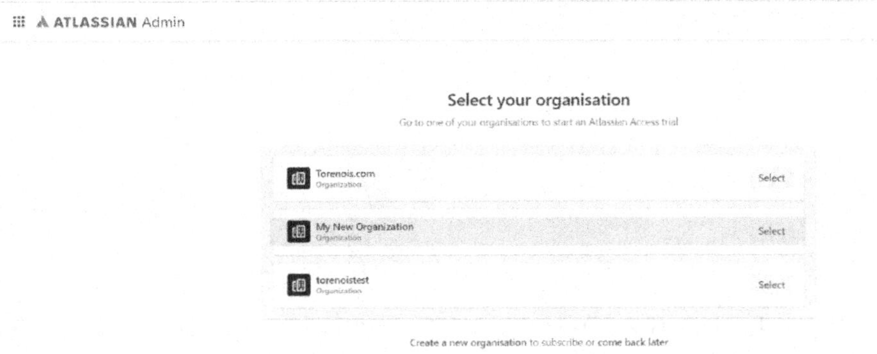

5. To get to your proper view, click on the **Switch to** menu and select **Administration**

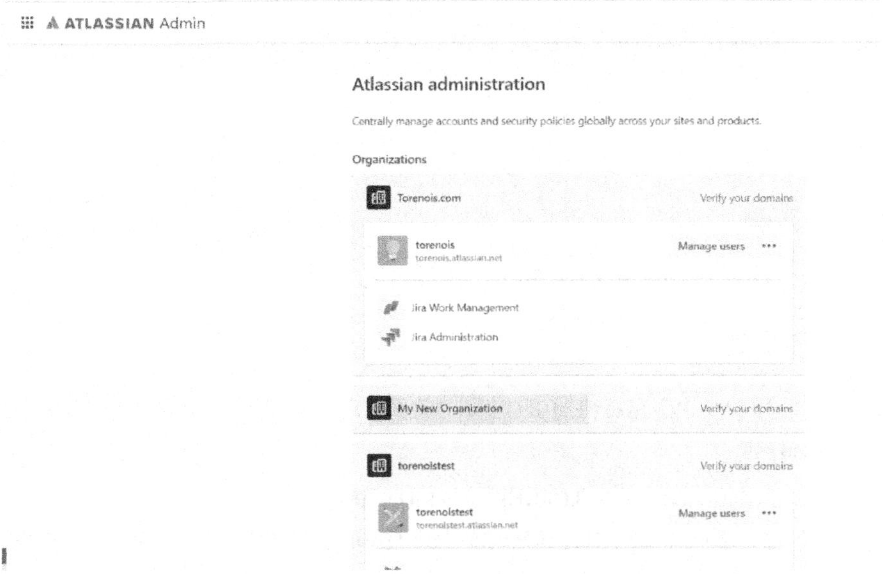

How to edit an Organization's settings

1. Go to your **Administration** area
2. Click on the name of the Organization you want to edit
3. In the Admin area for that particular organization, click on the **Settings** menu

4. IN THE DETAILS VIEW YOU CAN EITHER CHANGE THE ORGANIZATION NAME, OR YOU CAN TRANSFER ALL THE PRODUCTS TO ANOTHER ORGANIZATION THAT YOU ADMINISTER

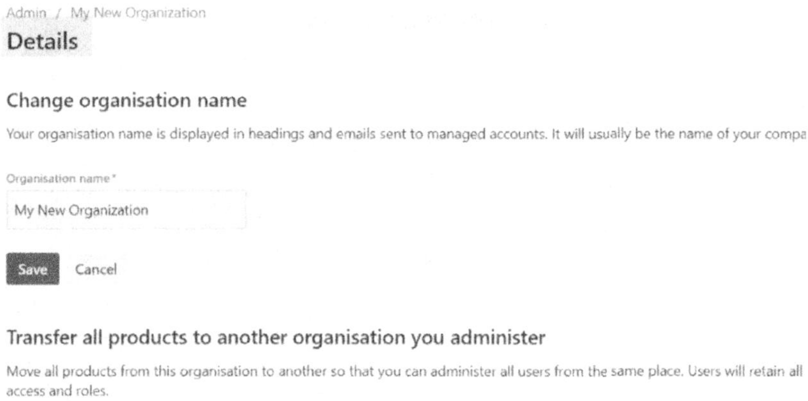

HOW TO MOVE PRODUCTS FROM ONE ORGANIZATION TO ANOTHER

1. GO TO YOUR **ADMINISTRATION** AREA
2. CLICK ON THE NAME OF THE ORGANIZATION YOU WANT TO MOVE THE PRODUCTS **FROM**
3. IN THE ADMIN AREA FOR THAT PARTICULAR ORGANIZATION, CLICK ON THE **SETTINGS** MENU
4. FOLLOW THE INSTRUCTIONS FOR "HOW TO EDIT AN ORGANIZATION'S SETTINGS", AND SELECT "TRANSFER ALL PRODUCTS TO ANOTHER ORGANIZATION YOU ADMINISTER"

5. FOLLOW THE STEPS IN THE WIZARD

HOW TO DELETE AN ORGANIZATION

At the time of writing, you cannot delete an Organization. You will need to raise a ticket with Atlassian to do so (found in the "Transfer all products to another organization you administer" as seen in the "How to move products from one Organization to another" instructions)

Atlassian states that there will be a method of doing so by August 2022.

WORKING WITH SITES

ADD A NEW SITE TO AN EXISTING ORGANIZATION

1. OPEN THE **SWITCH TO** ⁝⁝⁝ MENU AND SELECT **ADMINISTRATION**
2. IN THE ATLASSIAN ADMINISTRATION VIEW, CLICK ON THE ORGANIZATION WHERE YOU WANT TO ADD A NEW SITE

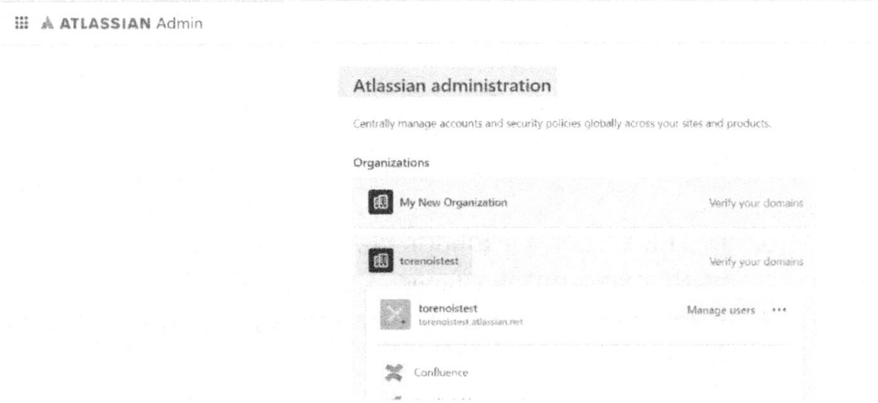

3. IN THE **ADMIN** AREA FOR THIS ORGANIZATION, CLICK ON THE **PRODUCTS** MENU

4. In the Products view for that Organization, click on **Add** product
5. In Select a site for your product, click on the **New Site** link

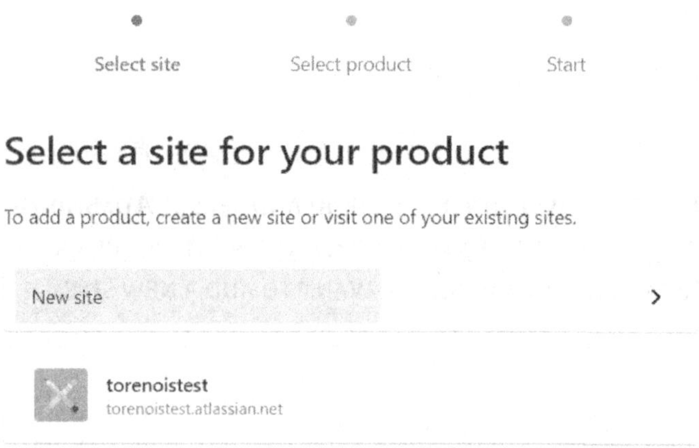

6. In the select a product view, select the **product** you want to include in the new site
7. In the Product page, enter a **site name** in **LOWER CASE** letters

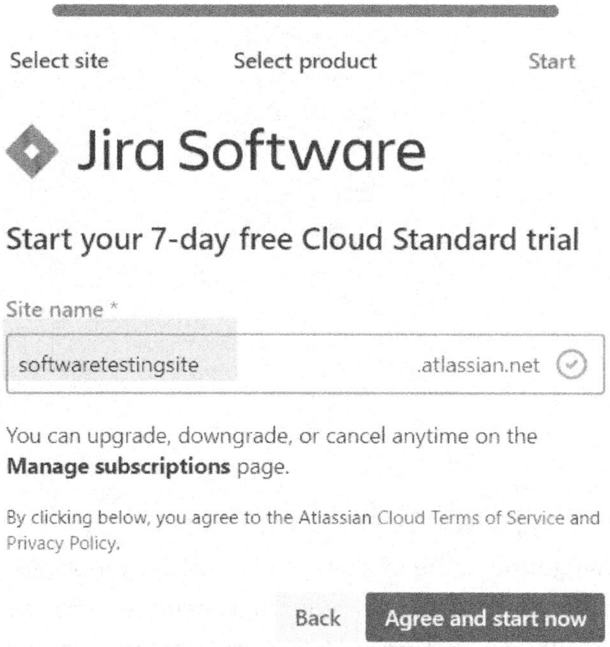

8. Click the Agree and start now button

It will take a couple of minutes for Atlassian to set up the site, but when finished it will take you to a view, where you can start setting up the new product in your new site.

9. To view the new site, go to the **Switch to** menu, and click on **Administration**
10. In the Administration view, you will see your new site

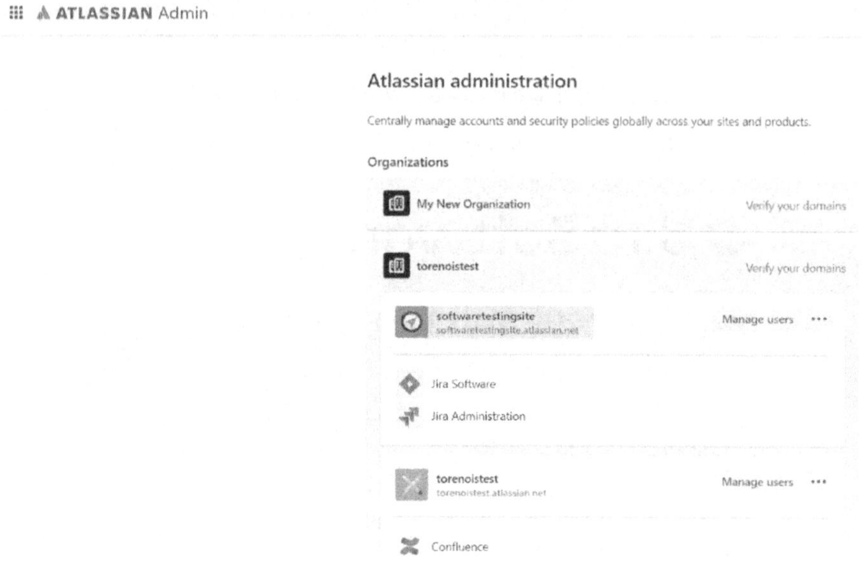

How to change the name of a site

To change the name of a site is somewhat complicated. In order to change the name of a site, you first need to change the URL. Changing the URL will, in turn, automatically create a new site name. Let's say you have a site named "product". The URL of that site will be "product.atlassian.net". You decide you want to change the name of the site from "product" to "productdesign". You must first change the URL from "product.atlassian.net" to "productdesign.atlassian.net". As soon as you change that URL your site name will automatically change to "productdesign".

It is important to note that once you change a site name, the old site name and site URL cannot be used again. Atlassian will retire them.

In addition, you can only change the name of a site three times.

Also note that you cannot change the name of a Jira Free site.

1. Open the **Switch to** ⠿ menu and select **Administration**

2. In the Atlassian Administration view, click on the **Organization** that includes the site whose name you want to change
3. In the Organization view, click on **Products** in the navigation bar

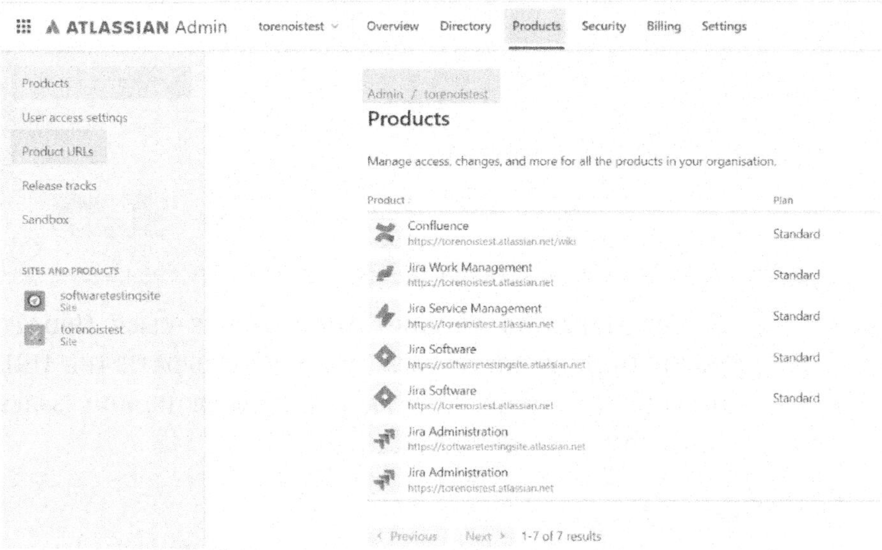

4. In the sidebar click on **Product URLs**
5. In the Product URLs view click on **Update URL**

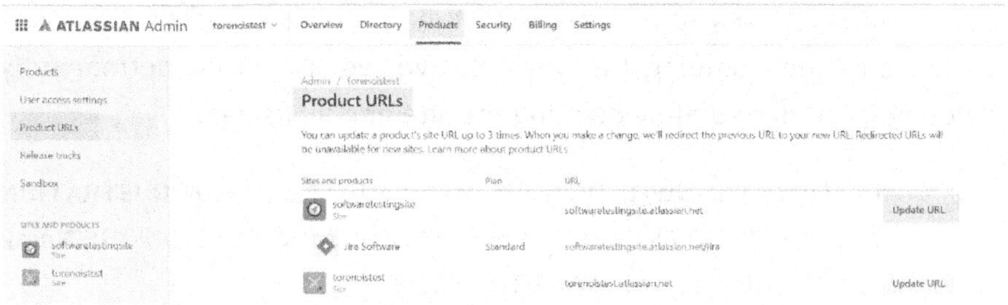

6. In the **Update URL** pop-up, change the URL name (remember to use lower case letters), and click **Continue**

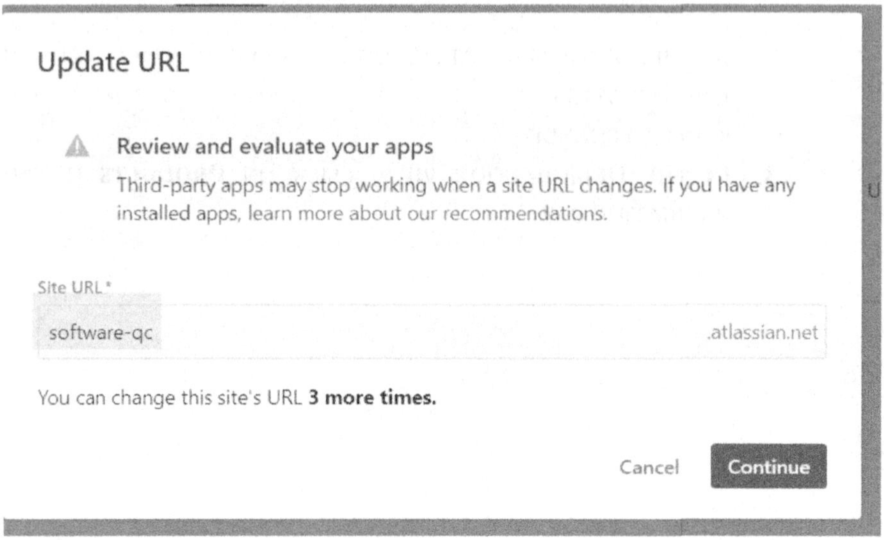

7. In the **Updating product URLs** pop-up click **Update** (note that it may take 5 minutes to update the URL depending on how many products, projects, and Issues you have).

How to delete a site

When you want to delete a site you must first cancel the product subscriptions for that site (even if using Free subscriptions). When you cancel all the subscriptions for the site, Atlassian will give you two options: allow you to work with the site till the end of the billing period and then holding the site for two weeks before permanently deleting it, or immediately deleting the site and all its data.

1. Open the **Switch to** menu and select **Administration**
2. In the Atlassian Administration view, click on the **name of the site** you want to delete
3. In the **Site** view, click on **Billing** in the navigation bar
4. In Billing preview, find the product associated with that site and click on **Manage subscription**

5. In the **Manage subscriptions** view click on Cancel subscriptions in the Active subscriptions area

NOTE: Though you clicked on the manage subscriptions link for one product, all active subscriptions for the site will appear in the active subscriptions view. Clicking on **Cancel subscriptions** will cancel ALL subscriptions for that site.

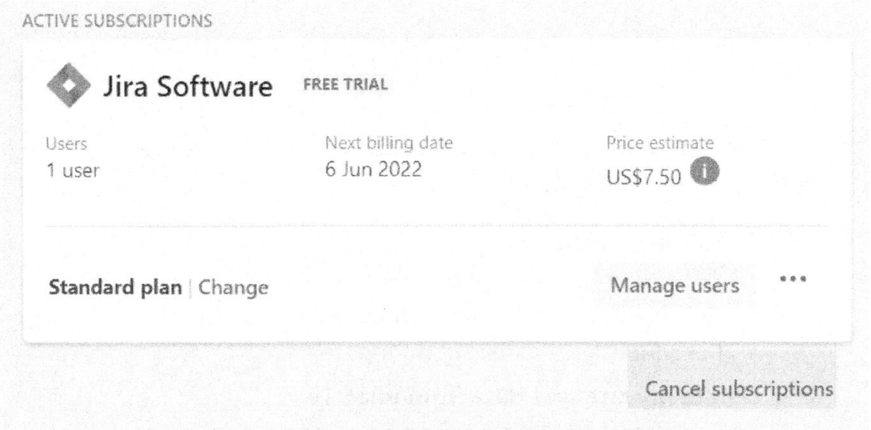

6. In the Cancel your subscription view, select either the **Cancel my subscription** or the **Delete my site and data immediately** option.
7. Enter CONFIRM in the "to continue" box

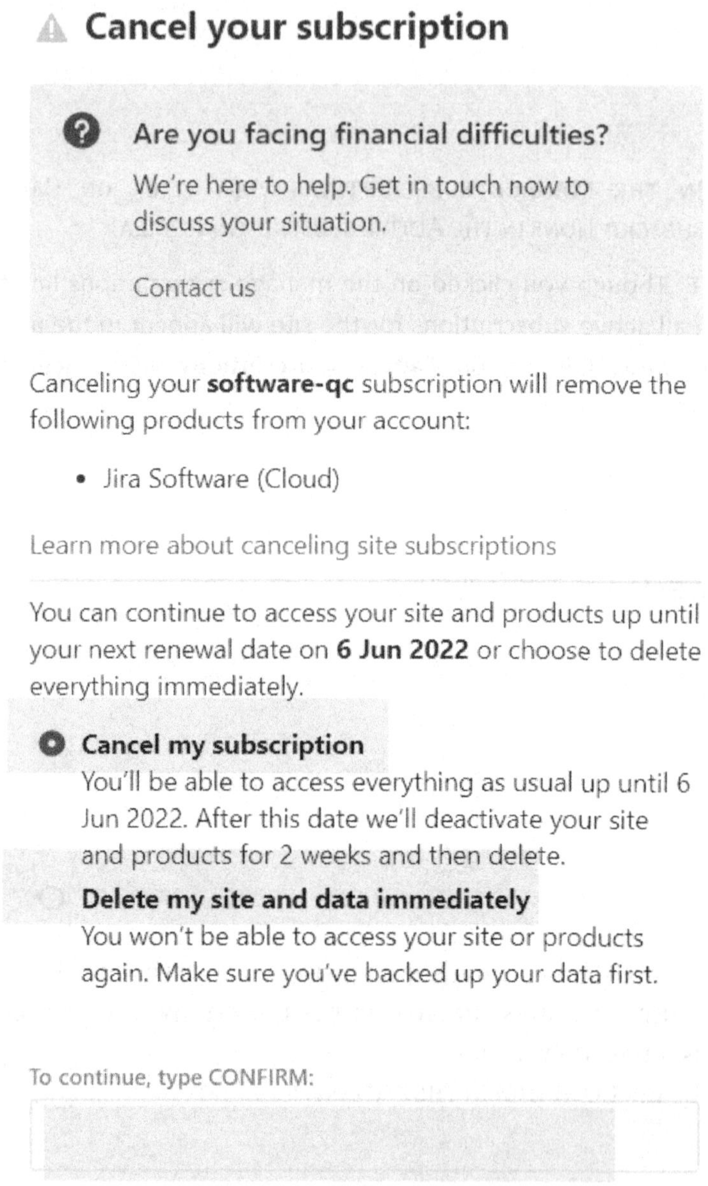
Cancel your subscription
Are you facing financial difficulties?
We're here to help. Get in touch now to discuss your situation.
Contact us
Canceling your software-qc subscription will remove the following products from your account:
• Jira Software (Cloud)
Learn more about canceling site subscriptions
You can continue to access your site and products up until your next renewal date on 6 Jun 2022 or choose to delete everything immediately.
Cancel my subscription
You'll be able to access everything as usual up until 6 Jun 2022. After this date we'll deactivate your site and products for 2 weeks and then delete.
Delete my site and data immediately
You won't be able to access your site or products again. Make sure you've backed up your data first.
To continue, type CONFIRM:

8. YOU CAN ANSWER THE SURVEY QUESTION AND THEN CLICK CANCEL SUBSCRIPTION IF YOU WISH, OR SIMPLY CLICK THE **CANCEL SUBSCRIPTION** BUTTON

WORKING WITH PRODUCTS

HOW TO INSTALL YOUR FIRST JIRA WORK MANAGEMENT PRODUCT

When you install your first Jira Work Management product you will at the same time set up your Atlassian account, create an Organization, create a Site, and install the product. All will, and must, happen in order for the Product to work.

Go to the beginning of this chapter and follow the steps for "How to install Jira Work Management."

HOW TO INSTALL ANOTHER JIRA WORK MANAGEMENT PRODUCT

If you want to install another instance of JWM in your Organization, you must first create another site. Remember that you cannot have two copies of the same product in one site.

Go to the "Working with sites" section earlier in this chapter and follow the steps for "Add a new site to an existing Organization". One of the steps in that script will ask you to select the product or products you want in that site.

HOW TO ADD OR DELETE LICENSES OF AN ATLASSIAN PRODUCT

IF YOU HAVE A STANDARD PLAN...

You don't have to do anything with the standard plan. Any time you add, or delete, a new User, Atlassian will change your monthly billing based on that change. You can have up to 10,000 JWM licenses in the Standard or Premium plan.

If you have a Free Plan...

If you have reached the limit of Users allowed in the free plan you will need to switch to the Standard plan. Remember that you need to be a Site Admin in order to change your plan.

1. OPEN THE **SWITCH TO** MENU AND SELECT **ADMINISTRATION**
2. IN THE ATLASSIAN ADMINISTRATION VIEW, CLICK ON THE **ORGANIZATION** THAT CONTAINS THE PLAN YOU WANT TO CHANGE
3. IN THE ORGANIZATION VIEW, CLICK ON **BILLING** IN THE NAVIGATION BAR
4. IN THE **BILLING PREVIEW** VIEW FOR THAT ORGANIZATION, FIND THE PRODUCT WHOSE PLAN YOU WANT TO CHANGE, AND CLICK ON **MANAGE SUBSCRIPTIONS**

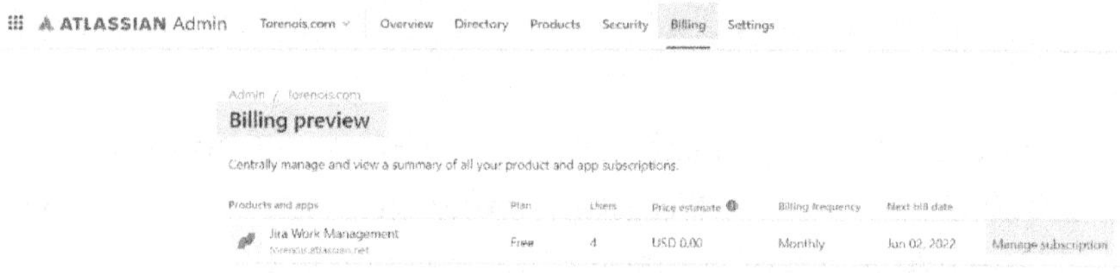

5. IN THE **MANAGE SUBSCRIPTIONS** VIEW FIND THE PRODUCT WHOSE PLAN YOU WANT TO CHANGE AND CLICK ON **CHANGE**

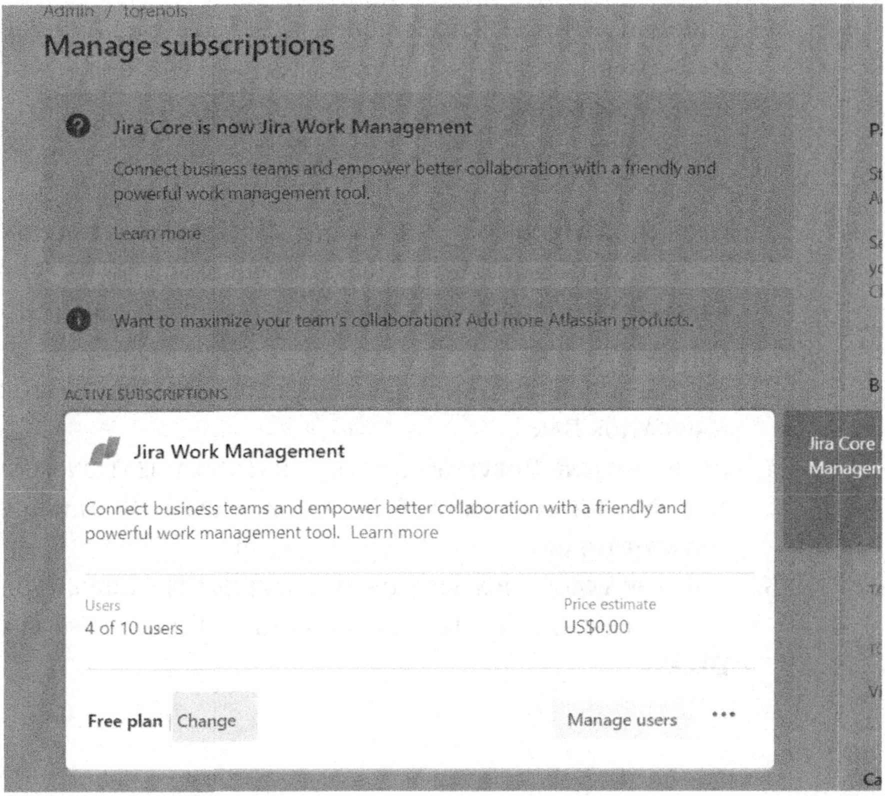

6. IN THE **PLANS** PAGE, CLICK ON **SELECT STANDARD**

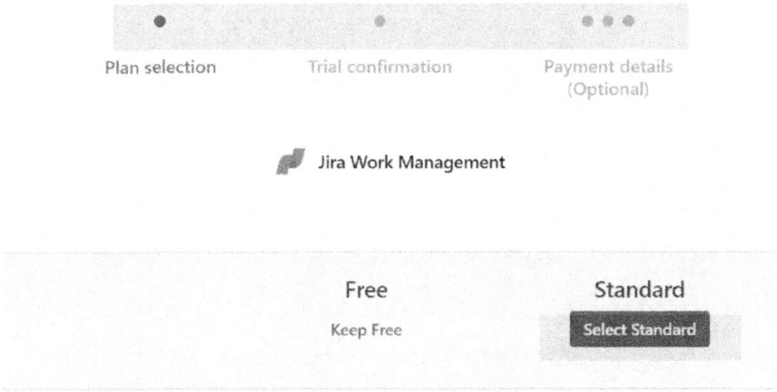

7. Once you click Select Standard you will be taken through a few steps regarding a trial period, and you may also be asked to add Payment details if you have not done so already.

How to Delete an Atlassian product

1. Open the **Switch to** ⠿ menu and select **Administration**
2. In the Atlassian Administration view, click on the **Organization** that contains the product you want to delete
3. In the Organization view, click on **Billing** in the Navigation Bar
4. In the **Billing Preview** view for that Organization, find the product you want to delete, and click on **Manage subscriptions**
5. In the **Manage subscriptions** view, find the product you want to delete and click on the **more** (**...**) link and select **Delete**

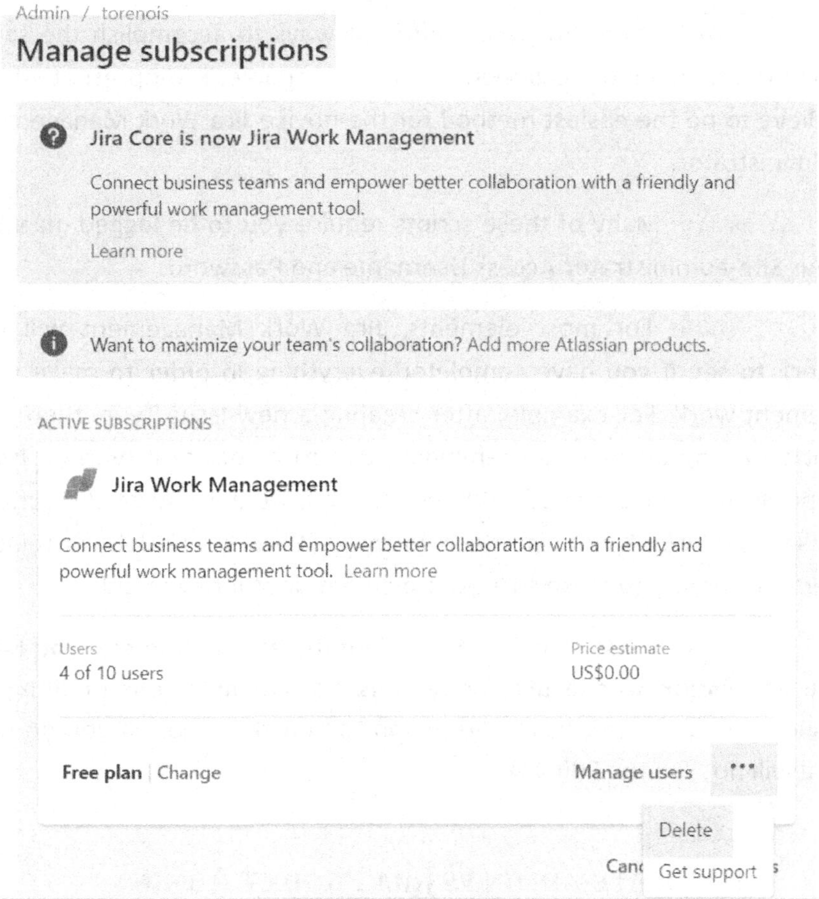

6. ENTER **DELETE** IN THE "TO CONTINUE…" TEXT BOX.

Note: If you have only one product in the site, you will be canceling the site along with the product. In this case the "To continue…" text box will ask you to enter "CANCEL" instead of Delete.

PART 2: "HOW TO" SCRIPTS

NOTE: There are often different ways to accomplish the same thing in Jira Work Management. To keep it simple, I will present what I believe to be the easiest method for the novice Jira Work Management Administrator.

NOTE: Many of these scripts require you to be logged on using your Site-administrator Access Username and Password.

NOTE: For most elements, Jira Work Management will not check to see if you have completed everything in order to make your element work. For example, after creating a new Issue Type, there will not be a pop-up message reminding you to associate it with an Issue Type Scheme or a Project. Where relevant, at the end of the script I included a "**What you also need to make it work**" checklist of related items necessary to make sure your element does indeed work.

NOTE: These scripts are based on the assumption that **you have the permission to execute the actions**. For example, when editing an Issue, it assumes you have permission to edit that issue. If you do not, you will not see the Edit link.

JWM SITE-ADMIN VS JIRA PROJECT ADMIN

This book is written for the JWM Site-admin (which includes Jira-admin and Org-admin). The Jira Project Admin may be able to do some of these scripts but only by accessing the administration area via a Project's Project Setting page. For example, a Project Admin can place a custom field on a custom screen, but only if the custom screen and custom field already exist (i.e. made by a Site-admin).

Of course, even if you can perform the script, you need to ensure you have the permission to do so (as defined by the relevant permission scheme).

Projects

Create a company-managed Project

NOTE: This script creates a full-function Jira Work Management project. Only a Site-admin may create a company-managed Project. Any licensed User can create a limited functionality Team-managed Project.

1. *Go to **Navigation Bar** > **Projects** > **Create Project***
2. In the Project templates view, select the **project template category** you wish to use
3. In the same view, Select the Business Project Type you want to use for your project
4. In the **Create project** view, enter the **name** of your Project

CAUTION: Project Names must be Unique as must Key names

5. Click the **Edit more details** drop down
6. In the Project Type drop down, select company-managed
7. Click the **Create project** button
   NOTE: it is critical to perform steps 5 and 6. If you don't you will inadvertently create a Team-managed project. Team-managed projects have limited functionality and cannot be converted to a Company-managed project

View Project (View Project's Issues)

1. Go to Navigation Bar > **Projects**
2. Choose the name of the Project from the **Recent** Projects sections and click on it; or click on **View All Projects** and select the project from the list that appears

Edit Company-managed Project Details

1. In the **project's sidebar**, click on **Project Settings**
2. In the Project settings **sidebar**, click on **Details**

3. In the **Details** pop-up you can change:
    i. The Name of the Project
    ii. The Key of the project

CAUTION: It is strongly recommended NOT to change the project key as it can cause severe database issues if not done correctly

    iii. The project URL
    iv. The Project type
    v. The Project Category
    vi. The Project Avatar
    vii. the Project Description
    viii. The project Lead
    ix. The Default assignee
4. Click the **Save Details** button

Delete Project

1. Navigate to ⚙ > **Projects**
2. In the **Manage Projects** view, find the Project you want to Delete, click on the More ••• link, and then click the **Move to Trash** link
3. In the **Move to trash?** pop-up, click **Move**

View Project Settings

1. Go to Navigation Bar > **Projects**
2. Select the Project from the **Recent** Projects sections and click on it; or click on View All Projects and select the project from the list that appears
3. In the **Project's** sidebar, click on **Project Settings**

Issue

Create an Issue

1. Go to **Navigation Bar**
2. Click **Create**
3. In the **Create Issue** pop-up, select the project that will be **associated** with the new Issue from the **Project** drop-down list
4. Select an **Issue Type** from the **Issue Type drop-down** list
    i. You must complete those fields having a red asterisk. They are mandatory. Other than that, complete the fields you feel are necessary to your project
    ii. **NOTE:** Occasionally, Jira Work Management does not have enough information to display a full Create Issue Screen. In those instances, only two fields might be appear: Project and Issue type. In such a case, select the Project and Issue Type, click the **Next** button and complete **all Fields**
5. Click the **Create** button

What you also need to make it work

- ✓ Project
- ✓ Issue Type *Note: Jira Work Management provides Issue Type defaults to select from. If you are not satisfied with them, you can create your own Issue Type*
- ✓ Issue Type Scheme

View Issue Details

1. On the Navigation Bar, click **Filters**, then select **Advanced issue search**

2. In the **Search** view, locate the **Issue** you wish to View
3. Click on the Issue's link
4. NOTE: You can also find your issues using the "Your work" drop down in the Navigation bar. However, this approach may not show the Issues you are following, but are not the assignee.

Edit Issue

NOTE: You will need to have the Edit Issues permission in order to edit the Issue

1. On the Navigation Bar, click **Your work**, and select **Go to Your Work page**
2. In the **Your work** view, locate the **Issue** you wish to edit
3. click on the selected Issue
4. In the **Issue Details** area click on any field and edit the data

Delete Issue

NOTE: You will need the Delete Issues Permission in order to delete the issue

1. On the Navigation Bar, click **Your work**, and select **Go to Your Work page**
2. In the **Your work** view, locate the **Issue** you wish to edit
3. click on the selected Issue
4. In the opened **Issue Details** area (on the right) click on the **MORE (...)** dropdown in the upper right corner
5. In the More drop-down list click on **Delete**
6. In the **Delete Issue** pop-up, click the **Delete** button

Issue Types

Add Issue Type

1. *Navigate to* 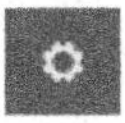 *> **Issues***
2. *In the Issues view, click on **Issue Types** in the sidebar*
3. In the Issue Types view, click on **Add Issue Type** button located in the upper right corner
4. In the **Add Issue Type** pop-up:
   i. Enter a **Name** for the Issue Type (Required)
   ii. Enter a **Description** for the Issue Type
   iii. Select the **Type** of Issue
      a. Standard Issue Type
      b. Sub-task Issue Type
5. Click **Add**

What you also need to make it work

- ✓ Project
- ✓ Issue
- ✓ Issue Type Scheme

Edit Issue Type

1. *Navigate to*  *> **Issues***
2. *In the Issues view, click on **Issue Types** in the sidebar*
3. In the Issue Types view, find the Issue Type you want to edit and click the **...** more link
4. In the More drop down menu select Edit
5. In the **Edit Issue Type** view you can:
   i. Change the **Name** of the Issue Type
   ii. Change the **Description**

   iii. Change the Issue Type **Avatar**

6. When done, click the **Update** button

Delete Issue Type

1. Navigate to  > **Issues**
2. *In the Issues view, click on **Issue Types** in the sidebar*
3. In the Issue Types view, find the Issue Type you want to Delete and click the **...** (More) link
4. In the More dropdown menu select Delete
5. In the **Delete Issue Type** view Click the **Delete** button

   CAUTION: a) the Issue Type cannot be deleted if there are open issues associated with that Issue Type (Jira Work Management will provide an error message). b) It is highly recommended you NOT delete an **Issue Type** if it is **associated with Workflow Scheme(s), Field Configuration Scheme(s), or Screen Scheme(s)**, as doing so will really, really, *really* mess up your project(s). If the Issue Type is associated with any of these schemes you will need to migrate them to a new Issue Type.

Issue Type Schemes

Add Issue Type Scheme

1. Navigate to > **Issues**
2. In the Issues view, Select **Issue Type Schemes** from the sidebar
3. In the **Issue Type Schemes** view, click on the **Add Issue Type Scheme** button located in the upper right corner
4. In the Add Issue Type Scheme view:
   i. Enter a Scheme **Name**
   ii. Enter a **Description** of the Scheme
   iii. Drag and drop all **Available Issue Types** you want to **associate with** this **scheme** from the Right Column (Available Issue Types) to the left (**Issue Types for Current Scheme**) column
   iv. Select a **Default Issue Type** from the drop-down list
   v. Click **Save**

TIP: If you need a new issue type for this scheme you can create one by clicking on the **+Add Issue Type** button at the top right of the view. If you use this feature, the Issue Type will a) appear in the left column (**Issue Types for Current Scheme**), and b) be added to Jira's Core database.

What you also need to make it work

- ✓ Project
- ✓ Issue Type

Copy Issue Type Scheme

See Add Issue Type Scheme

Edit Issue Type Scheme

1. Navigate to > **Issues**
2. In the Issues view, Select **Issue Type Schemes** from the sidebar
3. In the **Issue Type Schemes** view, click the **...** (More) link in the **Actions** column for the **Issue Type Scheme** you want to edit
4. In the Modify Issue Type Scheme view you can:
   i. Change the Scheme **name**
   ii. Change the **Description**
   iii. Change the Default issue Type
   iv. Change the **order** of the **Issue Types for Current Scheme** by dragging and dropping the Issue Types into the order you prefer
   v. Drag and drop issue types from one column to the other to **add** or **remove** an Available Issue Type from the Issue Type Scheme
5. Click the **Save** button

TIP: If you are not happy with any of your changes you can click the **Reset** button and your scheme will revert back to its original form. Reset will only work if you have not already clicked the Save button.

Associate Issue Type Scheme with Project

1. On the Navigation Bar, click > **Issues**
2. In the Issues view, Select **Issue Type Schemes** from the sidebar

3. In the **Issue Type Schemes** view, click the **...** (More) dropdown in the **Actions** column for the **Issue Type Scheme** you want to Associate, then select **Associate**
4. In the **Associate Issue Type Scheme** view, select the **project**(s) you want to associate with the Issue Type Scheme from the **Projects list**
5. Click the **Associate** button

Delete Issue Type Scheme

1. On the Navigation Bar, click  > **Issues**
2. In the Issues view, Select **Issue Type Schemes** from the sidebar
3. In the **Issue Type Schemes** view, click the **...** (More) dropdown in the **Actions** column for the **Issue Type Scheme** you want to Delete, and then select **Delete**
4. In the **Delete Issue Type Scheme** view, click the **Delete** button

CAUTION: If you have any **Projects associated with** the **Issue Type Scheme**, once you click **Delete** the projects will use the **Default Global Issue Type Scheme**.

NOTE: You cannot delete the Default Issue Type Scheme

Sub-Task Issue Types

Add Sub-Task Issue Type

1. On the Navigation Bar, click > **Issues**
2. In the Issues view, Select **Sub-Tasks** from the sidebar
3. In the Sub-Tasks view, click on **Add sub-task issue type** button in the upper right corner
4. In the Add Sub-Task Issue Type pop-up:
   i. Enter a **Name** for the Sub-task Issue Type (Required)
   ii. Enter a **Description** for the Sub-Task Issue Type
5. Click the **Add** button

What you also need to make it work

- ✓ Project
- ✓ Issue
- ✓ Issue Type
- ✓ Issue Type Scheme

Edit Sub-Task Issue Type

1. On the Navigation Bar, click > **Issues**
2. In the Issues view, Select **Sub-Tasks** from the sidebar
3. In the **Sub-Tasks** view, click the **Edit** link in the **Actions** column for the **Sub-Task** you want to edit
4. In the Edit Sub-Task Issue Type view you can:
   i. Change the **Name** of the Sub-Task
   ii. Change the **Description** of the Sub-Task
   iii. Change the Issue Type **Avatar**
5. Click the **Update** button

Delete Sub-Task Issue Type

1. On the Navigation Bar, click  > **Issues**
2. In the Administration Issue view, Select **Sub-Tasks** from the sidebar
3. In the **Sub-Tasks** view, click the **Delete** link in the **Actions** column for the **Sub-Task** Issue Type you want to Delete
4. In the Delete Sub-Task Issue Type view, click the **Delete** button

CAUTION: It is highly recommended you NOT delete a **Sub-Task Issue Type** if it is **associated with Workflow Scheme(s), Field Configuration Scheme(s), or Screen Scheme(s)**, as doing so will really, really, *really* mess up your project(s). If the Sub-Task Issue Type is associated with any of these schemes you will need to migrate them to a new Issue Type.

Workflows

Create a new Workflow

1. On the Navigation Bar, click ⚙ > **Issues**
2. In the Issues view, Select **Workflows** from the sidebar
3. In the **Workflows** view, click the **add workflow** button
4. In the Add workflow drop down, select **Create new**
5. In the **Add Workflow** pop-up enter:
    i. A **Name** for the workflow
    ii. A **Description** for the workflow
6. Click the **Add** button

What you also need to make it work

- ✓ Project
- ✓ Workflow Scheme

View Workflow

1. On the Navigation Bar, click ⚙ > **Issues**
2. In the Issues view, Select **Workflows** from the sidebar
3. In the **Workflows** view, click the ... Menu in the **Actions** column and select **View** for the workflow you want to see

Copy Workflow

1. On the Navigation Bar, click ⚙ > **Issues**
2. In the Issues view, Select **Workflows** from the sidebar
3. In the **Workflows** view, Click the ... Menu in the **Actions** column and select **Copy** for the Workflow you want to Copy

4. In the **Copy Workflow** pop-up enter:
    i. A new Workflow **Name**, *OR*, accept the default name which will be, "Copy of <name of original workflow>"
    ii. A **Description** of the new Workflow
5. Click the **Copy** button

Edit Workflow

CAUTION: When you edit a workflow that edit will affect all Issues using that workflow. I strongly suggest you **make a Copy of the original workflow and edit the copy**, rather than edit the working version. Next, test the new workflow with a test Issue. When satisfied with the results duplicate those edits in the original.

1. On the Navigation Bar, click  > **Issues**
2. In the Issues view, Select **Workflows** from the sidebar
3. In the **Workflows** view, click **...** Menu in the **Actions** column and select **Edit** for the **Workflow** you want to Edit
4. In the **Workflows Edit** view, Edit the workflow draft
5. When you are done and want to re-activate the workflow, Click the **Publish** button

Delete Workflow

1. On the Navigation Bar, click  > **Issues**
2. In the Issues view, Select **Workflows** from the sidebar
3. In the **Workflows** view, click the **...** Menu in the **Actions** column and select **Delete** for the **Workflow** you want to Delete

NOTE: You can only delete **INACTIVE** workflows.

4. In the **Delete Workflow** pop-up, click the **Delete** button

CAUTION: You cannot delete a **workflow** if it is **associated with** a **Workflow Scheme** or a **Draft Workflow Scheme**. You must first delete the Scheme (see Delete Workflow Scheme)

Workflow Schemes

Add Workflow Scheme

1. On the Navigation Bar, click > **Issues**
2. In the Issues view, Select **Workflow Schemes** from the sidebar
3. In the Workflow Schemes view, click the **Add workflow scheme** button located in the upper right corner
4. In the **Add Workflow Scheme** pop-up enter:
    i. A **Name** for the Workflow Scheme
    ii. A **Description** for the Workflow Scheme
5. Click the **Add** button

What you also need to make it work

- ✓ Project
- ✓ Issue Type
- ✓ Workflow

Copy Workflow Scheme

1. On the Navigation Bar, click > **Issues**
2. In the Issues view, Select **Workflow Schemes** from the sidebar
3. In the **Workflow Schemes** view, click the **Copy** link in the **Actions** column for the **Workflow Scheme** you want to Copy

CAUTION: Click **Copy** only once! As soon as you click 'Copy' a duplicate of the Workflow Scheme will be placed in the Inactive section of the Workflow Schemes view. In other words, a pop-up or new view will NOT appear.

Edit Workflow Scheme

CAUTION: It is highly recommended you **make a Copy of the original workflow scheme and edit the copy**, rather than edit the working version.

1. On the Navigation Bar, click  > **Issues**
2. In the Issues view, Select **Workflow Schemes** from the sidebar
3. In the **Workflow Schemes** view, click on the **Edit** link in the **Actions** column for the **Workflow Scheme** you want to edit
4. In the specific Workflow Scheme view you can…

…Change Workflow Scheme Name

5. To change the **workflow Scheme Name:** hover over the Workflow Scheme Name and click on it. In the Text box that appears make your changes

…Change Workflow Scheme Description

6. To add or change the **Workflow Scheme description** hover over the *Click to add description* and click on it. In the text box that appears make your changes

…Add another Workflow to the Scheme

7. To **Add** another **Workflow** to the scheme:
   i. Click the **Add Workflow** button
   ii. Select Add Existing or Choose From Marketplace
   iii. Follow the steps in the **Add Existing Workflow Wizard** that opens

...Remove a Workflow

8. To Remove a **Workflow** from the **Scheme** click on the **Remove** link in the **Actions** column

CAUTION: If you have only one workflow associated with your workflow scheme, then you must add the replacement workflow before you can delete the current one. In other words, **you must have at least two Workflows associated with the Scheme before you can delete one of them.**

...Add an Issue Type

9. To Add a new Issue Type to the Workflow assigned to the Workflow Scheme:
   i. Click on the **Assign** link in the **Actions** column for the **Workflow** to which you want to add an **Issue Type**
   ii. In the **Issue Type checklist** pop-up, check the **Issue Type(s)** you wish to add to the Workflow
   iii. Click the **Finish** button

...Remove an Issue Type

10. To **Remove** an **Issue Type** from a **Workflow** assigned to the Workflow Scheme click on the '**x**' beside the Issue Type's name in the Issue Types column

Associate Workflow Scheme with a Project

1. On the Navigation Bar, click the **Projects** menu
2. In the Projects Menu, click on the project that will receive the new workflow scheme
3. In the Project's view, select **Project settings** in the sidebar
4. In the project Settings sidebar, click on **Workflows**
5. In the Workflows view, Click on the **Switch Scheme** Button

6. IN THE **ASSOCIATE WORKFLOW SCHEME TO PROJECT**, SELECT THE **WORKFLOW SCHEME** YOU WANT FROM THE SCHEME DROP-DOWN LIST
7. CLICK THE **ASSOCIATE** BUTTON
8. FOLLOW THE STEPS IN THE **WIZARD**, WHICH WILL MIGRATE ANY **ISSUES ASSOCIATED WITH** THE **OLD WORKFLOW SCHEME** TO THE NEWLY ADDED SCHEME

TIP: If you want to delete a Workflow Scheme but it is associated with a project, then follow the steps above and switch the Project's workflow scheme to the Jira Work Management default workflow scheme as described beginning with step 5.

REMOVE WORKFLOW SCHEME FROM A PROJECT

A project must have a workflow scheme. A project can have only one workflow scheme. Consequently, if you want to remove a workflow scheme from a project you must replace it with another. Following the instructions in the "Associate a Workflow Scheme with a Project" will remove the workflow scheme you don't want.

DELETE WORKFLOW SCHEME

1. ON THE NAVIGATION BAR, CLICK  > **ISSUES**
2. IN THE ISSUES VIEW, SELECT **WORKFLOW SCHEMES** FROM THE SIDEBAR
3. IN THE **WORKFLOW SCHEME** VIEW, GO TO THE **INACTIVE** AREA AND CLICK THE **DELETE** LINK IN THE **ACTIONS** COLUMN FOR THE **WORKFLOW SCHEME** YOU WANT TO DELETE

NOTE: You can only delete INACTIVE workflows.

4. IN THE **DELETE WORKFLOW SCHEME** POP-UP, CLICK THE **DELETE** BUTTON

CAUTION: You cannot delete a Workflow Scheme if it is associated with a Project. To do so, you must associate a different workflow scheme with the project, this will then move the workflow scheme to the Inactive area. Of course, if your workflow scheme is associated with multiple projects you must remove the scheme from all those projects.

Screens

Add Screen

1. On the Navigation Bar, click ⚙ > **Issues**
2. In the Issues view, Select **Screens** from the sidebar
3. In **View Screens**, click on the **Add Screen** button
4. In the **Add Screen** pop-up enter:
    i. The **Name** of the Screen
    ii. The **Description** of the Screen
    iii. Click the **Add** button when done

NOTES: You cannot use a newly created screen unless:

i. It is **associated with** an **Issue Operation *and* Issue Type** (this is done by creating first a **Screen Scheme**, and then an **Issue Type Screen Scheme), or**
ii. It is **associated with** a **Workflow Transition screen (View).**

What you also need to make it work

- ✓ Project
- ✓ Fields
- ✓ For Issue Operation Screens:
    - Screen Scheme
    - Issue Type Screen Scheme
- ✓ For Workflow Transition Screens:
    - Workflow Transition screen (View)
    - Workflow Scheme

Configure Screen

1. On the Navigation Bar, click ⚙ > **Issues**

2. In the Issues view, Select **Screens** from the sidebar
3. In the **Screens** view, click on the **Configure** link in the **More (…)** menu for the Screen you want to configure
4. In the **Configure Screen** view you can:
    i. **Add fields** by selecting a field from the **Select Field** Dropdown and clicking **Add** button
    ii. **Rearrange** the fields order by dragging and dropping. Do this by clicking on the **hatch mark** to the left of the field name
    iii. **Remove** fields by hovering the mouse arrow over the field name and clicking the **Remove button** that appears
    iv. **Edit the Field Tab name** by clicking on the pencil icon
    v. Add additional tabs by clicking on the **Add Tab** link
5. When complete, simply exit the page, changes are made automatically

Copy Screen

1. On the Navigation Bar, click  > **Issues**
2. In the Issues view, Select **Screens** from the sidebar
3. In **View Screens**, click the **Copy** link in the **More (…)** menu for the Screen you want to Copy
4. In the **Copy Screen** view you can:
    i. Change the **Name** of the Screen, *or* accept the suggested name provided by Jira Work Management
    ii. Change the **Description** of the Screen
5. Click the **Copy** button

Edit Screen

1. On the Navigation Bar, click  > **Issues**
2. In the Issues view, Select **Screens** from the sidebar
3. In **View Screens**, click on the **Edit** link in the **More (...)** menu for the Screen you want to Edit
4. In the **Edit Screen** view you can:
    i. Change the **Name** of the Screen
    ii. Change the **Description** of the Screen
5. Click the **Update** button

Delete Screen

1. On the Navigation Bar, click  > **Issues**
2. In the Issues view, Select **Screens** from the sidebar
3. In **View Screens**, click on the **Delete** link in the **More (...)** menu for the Screen you want to Delete
4. In the **Delete Screen** pop-up, click the **Delete** button

CAUTION: You cannot delete a **screen** if it is **associated with** a **Screen Scheme** or a **Workflow Transition screen (View)**. You must delete the scheme or transition first.

Screen Schemes

Add Screen Scheme

1. On the Navigation Bar, click > **Issues**
2. In the Issues view, Select **Screen Schemes** from the sidebar
3. In View Screen Schemes, click on the **Add Screen Scheme** button
4. In the Add Screen Scheme pop-up:
   i. Enter the **Name** of the Screen Scheme
   ii. Enter the **Description** of the Screen Scheme
   iii. Select the Screen to be used as the **Default Screen** for the Screen Scheme (if not sure select the Default Screen)
   iv. Click the **Add** button

Configure Screen Scheme

1. On the Navigation Bar, click > **Issues**
2. In the Issues view, Select **Screen Schemes** from the sidebar
3. In Screen Schemes, find the Screen Scheme you want to configure and click on **Configure** in the More **(...)** menu in the **Actions** column
4. In the Configure Screen Scheme view:
   i. accept the **Default Issue Operation** (No action necessary), ***or***
   ii. Click the Associate an Issue Operation with a Screen button
5. In the Associate an Issue Operation with a Screen pop-up:
   i. Select the **Issue Operation** (**Create, Edit,** or **View**) from the drop-down list

   ii. Select the **Screen** to be **associated with** the **Issue Operation** from the drop-down list
   iii. Click the **Add** Button
6. Repeat steps 4 and 5 for the two other Issue Operations (Optional)
7. To **Delete** an **Issue Operation** associated with the **Screen Scheme,** or **Screen**, or both, click the **Delete** link in the **Actions** column

   CAUTION: You can only Delete an Issue Operation **if** a) it is **not the Default scheme**, and b) it is **not associated with any projects**

What you also need to make it work

- ✓ Project
- ✓ Screen
- ✓ Issue Operation (Create, Edit, View)
- ✓ Issue Type Screen Scheme

Copy Screen Scheme

1. On the Navigation Bar, click  > **Issues**
2. In the Issues view, Select **Screen Schemes** from the sidebar
3. In **View Screen Schemes,** find the screen scheme you want to copy, and click on **Copy** in the More **(...)** menu in the **Actions** column
4. In the **Copy Screen Scheme** view you can:
   i. Change the **Name** of the Screen Scheme, ***or*** accept the suggested name provided by Jira Work Management
   ii. Enter a Description

5. Click the **Copy** button

Edit Screen Scheme

1. On the Navigation Bar, click  > **Issues**
2. In the Issues view, Select **Screen Schemes** from the sidebar
3. In **View Screen Schemes**, find the screen scheme you want to edit, and click on **Edit** in the More **(...)** menu in the **Actions** column
4. In the **Edit Screen Scheme** view you can:
    i. Change the **Name** of the Screen Scheme
    ii. Change The **Description**
5. Click the **Update** button

Delete Screen Scheme

1. On the Navigation Bar, click  > **Issues**
2. In the Issues view, Select **Screen Schemes** from the sidebar
3. In **View Screen Schemes**, find the screen scheme you want to delete, and click on **Delete** in the More **(...)** menu in the **Actions** column
4. In the **Delete Screen Scheme** view, click the **Delete** button

CAUTION: You can only delete a **Screen Scheme** if it is ***not*** **associated** with an **Issue Type Screen Scheme**

Issue Type Screen Scheme

Add Issue Type Screen Scheme

CAUTION: This is a two-part operation, many people complete the first part, but exit before completing the critical second part. You must first Add and Issue Type Screen Scheme and then you must configure it. **Please follow the instructions** carefully

1. On the Navigation Bar, click > **Issues**
2. In the Administration Issue view, Select **Issue Type Screen Scheme** from the sidebar
3. In the Issue Type Screen Schemes' view, click on the **Add issue type screen scheme** button
4. In the Add Issue Type Screen Scheme pop-up:
   i. Enter a **Name** for the Issue Type Screen Scheme
   ii. Enter a Description
   iii. Select a **Screen Scheme** from the drop-down list
5. Click the **Add** button

Configure Issue Type Screen Scheme

1. On the Navigation Bar, click > **Issues**
2. In the Issues view, Select **Issue Type Screen Schemes** from the sidebar
3. In the **Issue Type Screen Schemes'** view, click on **Configure** link in the **Actions** column for the scheme you want to configure

NOTE: This will take you to the Configure Issue Type Screen Scheme view where you can...

...Associate an Issue Type with a Screen Scheme

1. In the Configure Issue Type Screen Scheme view, click on the **Associate an Issue Type with a Screen Scheme** button

2. In the Associate an Issue Type with a screen Scheme pop-up:
3. Select the **Issue Type** from the drop-down list
4. Select the **Screen Scheme** from the drop-down list
5. Click **Add** button

...Edit an Issue Type Screen Scheme

1. Click on the **Edit** link in the **Actions** column for the Issue Type Screen Scheme you want to Edit
2. In the **Edit Issue Type Screen Scheme Entry** view, select a new **Screen Scheme** from the drop-down list
3. Click the **Update** button

...Delete an Issue Type from the Issue Type Screen Scheme

1. Click o*n Delete link for the Issue Type you want to Delete*

CAUTION: You cannot delete the Default Issue Type

What you also need to make it work

- ✓ Project
- ✓ Screen Scheme
- ✓ Issue Type

Edit Issue Type Screen Scheme

1. On the Navigation Bar, click  > **Issues**
2. In the Issues view, Select **Issue Type Screen Schemes** from the sidebar
3. In the **Issue Type Screen Schemes'** view, click on **Edit** link in the **Actions** column for the scheme you want to Edit
4. In the Edit Issue Type Screen Scheme view:

    i. Enter a new **Name** for the scheme
    ii. Enter a Description
5. Click the **Update** button

Copy Issue Type Screen Scheme

1. On the Navigation Bar, click ⚙ > **Issues**
2. In the Issues view, Select **Issue Type Screen Schemes** from the sidebar
3. In the **Issue Type Screen Schemes'** view, click on the **Copy** link in the **Actions** column for the scheme you want to copy
4. In the Copy Issue Type Screen Scheme view:
    i. Enter the **Name** for the new scheme, ***or*** accept the suggested scheme name provided by Jira Work Management
    ii. Enter a Description
5. Click the **Copy** button

Delete Issue Type Screen Scheme

1. On the Navigation Bar, click ⚙ > **Issues**
2. In the Administration Issue view, **Select Issue Type Screen Schemes** from the sidebar
3. In the **Issue Type Screen Schemes'** view, click on **Delete** link in the **Actions** column for the scheme you want to Delete
4. In the Delete Issue Type Screen Scheme view, click on the **Delete** button

CAUTION: You cannot delete an **Issue Type Screen Scheme** if it is **associated with a Project**. See the note at the end of following **Associate Issue Type Screen Scheme with a Project** for details on how to 'disassociate'.

Associate Issue Type Screen Scheme with a Project

1. On the Navigation Bar, click **Projects**
2. In the **Projects'** dropdown click on the **project** you want to associate with the Issue Type Screen Scheme
3. In the Project, select **Project Settings** in the sidebar
4. In the **Project Settings** view, select **Screens** from the sidebar
5. In the **Screens** view, click on the **Actions** button in the upper right corner
6. Click on **Use a Different Scheme** from the Actions drop-down list
7. In the **Issue Type Screen Scheme Association** view, Select the Issue Type Screen Scheme you want to associate from the Scheme drop-down list
8. Click the **Associate** button

TIP: If you want to delete an **Issue Type Screen Scheme** but it is **associated with a Project**, then follow the steps above and in step 6 switch the Project's Issue Type Screen Scheme to the **Jira Default Issue Type Screen Scheme.** After that is done, follow the instructions for "Delete Issue Type Screen Scheme".

Custom Fields

Add Custom Field

1. On the Navigation Bar, click  > **Issues**
2. In the Issues view, select **Custom Fields** from the sidebar
3. In the **Custom fields** view, click on the **Create custom field** button located in the upper right corner
4. In the **Select a Field Type** pop-up, click on the **Field Type** you want to use
5. Click the **Next** button
6. In the **Configure Field** pop-up:
    i. Enter a **Name** for the Field
    ii. Enter a **Description** for the Field
    iii. Enter **Options** if requested:
        a. Enter an option and click **Add.** Options become the choice list from which you or your user(s) will select when using the custom field
        b. You can rearrange the order of the options by dragging and dropping them. Do this by hovering the mouse arrow over the hatch mark to the left of the option name. When your mouse arrow turns into a four-direction arrow you can drag the option up or down
        c. Delete an option by clicking the "x" next to the option name
7. Click the **Create** button

NOTE: When creating a custom field you may also be asked to associate the field with a specific screen or screens. If so, go to step 4 and 5 in the "Associate Field to Screens" script.

What you also need to make it work

- ✓ Screen

Associate Field to Screen(s)

1. On the Navigation Bar, click  > **Issues**
2. In the Issues view, select **Custom Fields** from the sidebar
3. In the **Custom Fields** view, click on **Associate to Screens** in the **... (More)** drop-down for the Custom Field you want to associate
4. In the **Associate Field to Screens** view, check the box in the **Select** column for each Screen you want to associate with this custom field

TIP: If a screen has more than one Tab, a drop-down list will appear in the Tab Column. Select the tab where you want the custom field to be placed

5. Click the **Update** button

Edit Custom Field Details

NOTE: Some system fields may be locked; meaning you will be unable to edit the field.

1. On the Navigation Bar, click  > **Issues**
2. In the Issues view, select **Custom Fields** from the sidebar
3. In the **Custom Fields** view, click on **Edit details** in the **... (More)** drop-down for the Custom Field you want to edit
4. In the Edit Custom Field Details view you can Change:
   i. The field name
   ii. The Field description

iii. Search Template Type

5. Click update when done

Change Custom Field contexts and default value

This segment deals with field data, if you are looking to change Field behaviour (e.g. making fields required, hidden, etc.) please see the Field Configuration section.

NOTE: Some system fields may be locked; meaning you will be unable to configure the field.

1. On the Navigation Bar, click  > **Issues**
2. In the Issues view, select **Custom Fields** from the sidebar
3. In the **Custom Fields** view, click on **Edit details** in the **... (More)** drop-down for the Custom Field you want to change

NOTE: There are a number of things you can do on the **Configure Custom Field** view depending on the type of custom field. For example, custom date field will have different configuration options than will a multi-select drop down list. In this script we will limit ourselves to changing the **Default Value** and **Field Options** for a "Select List (single choice)".

4. Click on **Edit Default value** link in the Default Value Field
5. In **Set Custom Field Defaults**, select a value (option) you want to use as the field's default value
6. Click on **Set Default** button
7. Click on **Edit Options** link in the **Options** Field
8. In the Edit Options for Custom Field view you can:
   i. Sort Options alphabetically by clicking on the link

ii. **Add a New Custom Field Option** by inserting a value (option) into **Add Value** field at the bottom of the view, and then Click **Add** button
iii. Rearrange the sequence of the options by clicking on the appropriate **arrow** in the **order** column, ***or*** by entering a value's position number in the **Move to Position** column and then clicking on the **Move** button
iv. **Edit** the name of the Value
v. **Delete** the Value
vi. **Disable** the Value (useful if you don't want to use it at the moment but want to keep a record of the value in the database)

9. Click **Done**

Translate a Custom Field

1. On the Navigation Bar, click ⚙ > **Issues**
2. In the Issues view, select **Custom Fields** from the sidebar
3. In the **Custom Fields** view, click on **Translation options** in the **... (More)** drop-down for the Custom Field you want to change
4. In the **Translate Custom Field** view, choose the **language** you want from the drop-down list
5. Enter the <u>Translated</u> **Name** into the **Field Name**
6. enter a <u>translated</u> **description** into the **Description** field
7. Click the **update** button

CAUTION: Jira Work Management will not translate the field name for you – you must do that yourself; however, it will store the translated field name for different screens. For example, you may have a default Screen where the fields are in English, but you may have another version of the Screen where the fields are in French.

MOVE A CUSTOM FIELD TO TRASH

1. ON THE NAVIGATION BAR, CLICK  > **ISSUES**
2. IN THE ISSUES VIEW, SELECT **CUSTOM FIELDS** FROM THE SIDEBAR
3. IN THE **CUSTOM FIELDS** VIEW, CLICK ON **MOVE TO TRASH** IN THE **... (MORE)** DROP-DOWN FOR THE CUSTOM FIELD YOU WANT TO DELETE
4. IN THE **MOVE TO TRASH** POPUP, CLICK THE **MOVE TO TRASH** BUTTON

CAUTION: If you delete a custom field, it will delete all the values for that field in all of your other issues. If you simply wanted to **remove** the custom field from the screen, follow the Instructions in the <u>Associate field to Screen</u> section and **uncheck** the box(s) in the **Select** column for the screen(s) you no longer want associated with the custom field.

Field Configurations

This Field Configurations section deals with Field behaviour within a project (e.g. Hidden field, Required field, etc.). For configuring data within a field please see "Change Custom Field contexts and default value" in the Custom Fields section.

Create a field Configuration

1. On the Navigation Bar, click  > **Issues**
2. In the Issues view, select **Field configurations** from the sidebar
3. In **View Field Configurations**, click the **Add field configuration** button located in the upper right corner
4. In the Add Field Configuration popup:
    i. Enter a **name** for the Field Configuration
    ii. Enter a description
5. Click **Add**

What you also need to make it work

- ✓ Fields
- ✓ Project
- ✓ Field Configuration Scheme

Configure Field Behaviour

1. On the Navigation Bar, click  > **Issues**
2. In the Issues view, select **Field configurations** from the sidebar
3. In **View Field Configurations**, find the Field configuration you want to change and click **Configure** in the **Actions** column

4. In **View field configuration** for that configuration, find the field(s) you want to configure and select the options you want (i.e. Edit, Hide, Required, screens, or Renderers) in the **Actions** column
5. Click on Field Configurations in the sidebar to exit this view and save your changes

---

What you also need to make it work

- ✓ Project
- ✓ Field Configuration Scheme

Create a Field configuration scheme

1. On the Navigation Bar, click  > **Issues**
2. In the Issues view, select **Field configurations** from the sidebar
3. In **View Field Configurations**, click the **Add field configuration scheme** button located in the upper right corner
4. In the Add Field Configuration scheme popup:
    i. Enter a **name** for the Field Configuration
    ii. Enter a description
    iii. Click **Add**
5. Back in **View Field Configuration Schemes**, click your browser refresh button if the new scheme does not show immediately

Configure Field Configuration Scheme

1. On the Navigation Bar, click  > **Issues**
2. In the Issues view, select **Field configurations** from the sidebar

3. In **View Field Configuration schemes**, find the field configuration scheme you want to change and click **Configure** in the **Actions** column
4. In the Configure Field Configuration scheme view, click on the Associate an issue type with a field configuration button located in the upper right corner
5. In the Associate an Issue Type with a Field Configuration popup:
    i. Select an **Issue Type**
    ii. select a field Configuration
    iii. Click **Add**

Associate a Field Configuration Scheme with a Project

1. On the Navigation Bar, click the **Projects** menu
2. In the Projects Menu, click on the **project** that will receive the new Field Configuration scheme
3. In the Project's view, select **Project settings** in the sidebar
4. In the project Settings sidebar, click on **Fields**
5. In the Fields view, Click on the **actions** dropdown field located in the upper right corner, and select **Use a different scheme**
6. In the Field Layout Configuration Association, select the Field Configuration Scheme you want from the Scheme drop-down list
7. Click the **Associate** button

What you also need to make it work

✓ Fields

- ✓ Field Configuration
- ✓ Field Configuration Scheme

Time Tracking

Change Default Time Tracking settings

NOTE: If you change the current Time Tracking settings, you will affect every Jira Work Management project in that site. So, if there are multiple Site-admins in your Organization, make sure you have consensus before making any changes.

1. On the Navigation Bar, click  > **Issues**
2. In the Issues view, select **Time Tracking** from the sidebar
3. Click the **Edit Global Settings** button located at the bottom of the screen
4. In the **Time Tracking settings** popup you can:
   i. Change **Hours** per day
   ii. Change **Days** per week
   iii. Choose the **Time format**
   iv. Change the default unit
   v. Copy **Comments** to Work Description
5. Click the **save** button when done

Log Time

1. Open an **Issue**
2. In the **Issue Details' View**, click the **... More** menu – located in the upper right corner) and select **Log Work**
3. In the Log Work pop-up, in the **Time Spent** field enter number of weeks, days, or hours spent working on the issue (make sure to use the W, D, H, M time format)
4. Click the **Save** button

Logging Work using the Remaining Estimate fields in the Log Work pop up

1. Open an **Issue**
2. In the **Issue Details' View**, click the **... More** menu – located in the upper right corner) and select **Log Work**
3. In the Log Work pop-up, in the **Time remaining** field enter number of weeks, days, or hours spent working on the issue (make sure to use the W, D, H, M time format)
4. Click the **Save** button

Create a Project Time Tracking Report

1. Open the **Project** for which you want a report
2. In the Project's sidebar, select **Reports**
3. In the All Reports' view sidebar, click on Time Tracking Report in the Forecast and Management area
4. In the **Configure – Time Tracking Report** view select options from the drop-down lists of the following fields:
    i. Fix Version Drop-down
    ii. **Sorting** Drop-down
    iii. **Issue** drop-down
    iv. Sub-task inclusion drop-down
5. Click **NEXT**
6. In the Time Tracking Report, you can either view the report, or export it in Excel View by clicking the Excel View link. Note: you need to have MS Excel or a compatible spreadsheet application to open the report in "Excel View"

Statuses

Create Status

1. On the Navigation Bar, click  > **Issues**
2. In the Issues view, select **Statuses** from the sidebar
3. In the **Statuses** view click the **Add status** button, located in the upper right corner
4. In the **Add status** pop-up:
    i. Enter a **Name** of the new status
    ii. Enter a **Description** (optional)
    iii. Select the status category (To Do, In progress, or Done)
    iv. Enter the Icon URL
    v. Click the **Add** button

Resolutions

Create Resolution

1. On the Navigation Bar, click > **Issues**
2. In the Issues view, select **Resolutions** from the sidebar
3. In **View Resolutions** go to the **Add New Resolution** area, located at the bottom of the screen
4. Enter a **name** and **Description** for the new resolution
5. Click the **Add** button

Priorities

Create Priority

NOTE: When you add a new priority level it will be automatically assigned to the default priority scheme, and will appear in all projects in your site using the default scheme. At the time of writing, Atlassian has no plans to add project specific priority schemes. Consequently, make sure to involve all stakeholders before making a change to the current list of priorities.

If it is critical for you to have separate and distinct lists of priorities, you must create a new Atlassian site within your organization, download a new instance of Jira Work Management, delete the default priorities and create your own new set of priorities.

1. On the Navigation Bar, click > **Issues**
2. In the Issues view, select **Priorities** from the sidebar
3. In **View Priorities**, go to the **Add priority level** area, located at the bottom of the screen
4. In the Add priority level area:

   i. Enter a **Name** of a new priority
   ii. Enter a **Description** (optional)
   iii. Select an **image**
   iv. Select **color**
   v. Click **Add** button

Edit Priority

1. On the Navigation Bar, click  > **Issues**
2. In the Issues view, select **Priorities** from the sidebar
3. In **View Priorities**, find the priority you wish to change and click on **Edit** link in the **Actions** column
4. In the **Edit Priority** view you can change:
   i. Priority **Name**
   ii. Description
   iii. Icon URL (**image**)
   iv. Color
5. Click the **Update** button

NOTE: When you edit a priority it will affect all projects and issues using that priority. Make sure to have agreement with all stakeholders before editing a priority.

Users

Invite Users

1. On the Navigation Bar, click > **User management**
2. Select **Users** in the sidebar
3. In the **Users** view, click the **Invite Users** button
4. In the **Invite Users** pop-up, enter the User's **email address**
5. Enter multiple email addresses by either separating the addresses with a comma, or entering the email addresses on separate lines
6. For the **product** you want the User to join, select the **Role** in the dropdown list you want the User to perform
7. Make sure to change the **role** to NONE in all other products (else you may be charged a license fee for that product)
8. (Optional) Add the User to a group
9. (Optional) Click the **Personalise invitation email** and write a personal invite
10. Click the **Invite people** button

Edit User

NOTE: These instructions relate to editing the User (e.g. assign the User to a role, suspend the User, Remove the User, etc.). Editing the User's Profile is done by the User clicking on their Icon on the far right of the Navigation Bar, and then selecting "Your profile".

1. On the Navigation Bar, click > **User management**
2. Select **Users** in the sidebar
3. In the **Users** view, find the user you want to Edit, and select **Show details** in the **...** (more) menu

4. IN THE **USER'S** VIEW CLICK ON THE **...** (MORE) MENU LOCATED IN THE UPPER RIGHT CORNER
5. IN THE **...** (MORE) DROP DOWN YOU CAN:
    i. ASSIGN THE USER TO AN ORGANIZATION ROLE
    ii. PROMPT A RESET PASSWORD
    iii. SUSPEND THE USER*
    iv. REMOVE THE USER**
6. YOU CAN ALSO ADD THE USER TO ANOTHER ATLASSIAN PRODUCT (WILL REQUIRE A LICENSE) IN THE **PRODUCTS** AREA
7. YOU CAN ALSO ADD THE USER TO A GROUP IN THE **GROUPS** AREA

* Suspending a User is useful for removing the User as a paid licensee but where you expect the User to return. For example, if a User goes on maternity leave, or goes on a year-long sabbatical.

**Removing the User will delete the User from the application.

DELETE USER

See **Edit User**

Edit Groups

1. On the Navigation Bar, click  > **User management**
2. In the **Users** view, click on **Groups** in the sidebar
3. In the Groups view, Click on the **Group** you want to edit
4. In the view for the selected Group, click on the **...** (more) menu, located in the upper right corner
5. In the **...** menu you can:
    i. Change the **description** of the group
    ii. **Delete** the Group (note: you cannot delete a default system group)
6. To add group members to this group click on the **Add group members** button located in the upper right corner of the view
7. To remove a member from this group, find the **User**, click on the **...** (More) menu in the **Actions** column, and select **Remove member from group**

Project Roles

Add Project Role

1. On the Navigation Bar, click  > **System**
2. In the **System** view, select **Project roles** in the sidebar
3. In the **Project Role Browser**, navigate to the **Add Project Role** section at the bottom of the view
    i. Enter a project Role in the **Name** field
    ii. Enter a Description
4. Click the **Add Project Role** button

Edit Project Role

1. On the Navigation Bar, click  > **System**
2. In the **System** view, select **Project roles** in the sidebar
3. In the **Project Role Browser**, find the **Role** you want to edit and click on the **Edit** link in the **Actions** column
4. In the **Edit Project Role** view you can:
    i. Change the **name**
    ii. Change the **Description**
5. Click the **Update** Button

Add Default Members

1. On the Navigation Bar, click  > **System**
2. In the **System** view, select **Project roles** in the sidebar
3. In the **Project Role Browser**, find the **Role** you want to manage and click on the **Manage Default Members** link in the **Actions** column
4. In the Edit Default Members for Project Role view, find the **Default User** you want to edit and click on the **Edit** link in the **Default Users** column next to their name

5. In the opened **Assign Default Users to Project Role** view, enter the **names** of the default Users for the project role in the **Add User(s) to Project Role** text box

TIP: Separate user names/groups with a comma

6. Click the **Add** Button

Edit Default Project Role members

1. On the Navigation Bar, click > **System**
2. In the **System** view, select **Project roles** in the sidebar
3. Click on In the **Project Role Browser**, click on **Manage Default Members** link in the **Actions** column for the **Role** you want to Edit
4. In the **Edit Default Members for Project Role** view, find the **Default User** you want to edit and click on the **Edit** link in the **Default Users** column next to their name
5. In the Assign Default Users to Project Role view, go to the Users in Project Role column
6. Click the **checkbox** next to the **name** of the User you want to remove
7. Click the **Remove** button

Delete Project Role

1. On the Navigation Bar, click > **System**
2. In the **System** view, select **Project roles** in the sidebar
3. In the **Project Role Browser**, find the **Role** you want to delete and click on the **Delete** link in the **Actions** column
4. In the Delete Project Role view, click the **Delete** button

CAUTION: Deleting a project role will delete it from **ALL** projects and schemes

Add User to a Role in a specific project

1. Go to Navigation Bar > **Projects** Select the Project from the **Recent** Projects sections and click on it; or click on View All Projects and select the project from the list that appears
2. In the **Project's** sidebar, click on **Project Settings**
3. In the **Project settings** sidebar, click on **People**
4. In the Project Settings' People view, click on **Add people** in the upper right corner
5. In the **Add people** popup, enter a name, group, or email address and then select the **role** you wish that User or Users to perform in that project

Remove User from a Role in a specific project

1. Go to Navigation Bar > **Projects**
2. Select the Project from the **Recent** Projects sections and click on it; or click on View All Projects and select the project from the list that appears
3. In the **Project's** sidebar, click on **Project Settings**
4. In the **Project settings'** sidebar, click on **People**
5. In the Project's People view, find the **User** you want to remove from the Role
6. In the **Role column** click the dropdown list for that User and **change their role** (note: a User must have at least one role in the project)
7. If you want **to remove the User from the Project**, click the **Remove** link in that row.

Groups

Create a Group

1. On the Navigation Bar, click > **User Management**
2. In the **Users** view, Select **Groups** from the sidebar
3. In the **Groups** view, click on the **Create Group** button located in the upper right corner
4. In the Create group popup:
   i. Enter a **Name** for the Group in the Group's name text box
   ii. Enter any **Users** you want for that group, using a comma to separate Users
   iii. Enter a group description
5. Click the **Create** button

Add Members to a group

1. On the Navigation Bar, click > **User Management**
2. In the **Users** view, Select **Groups** from the sidebar
3. In the **Groups** view, Find the Group you want to manage and click on **Show details** in the **Action** column
4. In the view for the selected group, click on the **Add group members** button located in the upper right corner
5. In the Add users to group popup, enter one or more **Users** names in the **Group's members** text box (separate Users with a comma)
6. Click the **Add users** button when done

Remove Members from a group

1. On the Navigation Bar, click > **User Management**
2. In the **Users** view, Select **Groups** from the sidebar

3. In the **Groups** view, click on the **Group** that contains the member or members you want to remove
4. In the Group's view, find the **User** you want to remove, click the **...** (More) link and select **Remove member from group**

Delete Group

1. On the Navigation Bar, click  > **User Management**
2. In the **Users** view, Select **Groups** from the sidebar
3. In the **Groups** view, click on the **group** you want to delete
4. In the **Group's** view, click on the **...** (More) link located in the upper right corner and select **Delete group**

CAUTION: It is highly recommended not to delete any default/system groups (e.g. administrators) as that may cause serious site management problems

TIP: You will not delete any Users if you delete a group

Giving a Group Global Permissions

1. Go to Navigation Bar >  > **System**
2. In the System sidebar click on **Global Permissions** in the Security section
3. Go to the Bottom of the **Global Permissions** view to the **Add Permission** area
4. Select the type of Permission you want to grant in the **Permission** drop-down list
5. Select a *Group* in the **Group** drop-down list

!IMPORTANT: do not select system-administrators

6. Click the **Add** button

NOTE: Giving a group a global permission will affect all projects.

Permission Schemes

Create a Permission Scheme

1. On the Navigation Bar, click > **Issues**
2. In the Issues Sidebar, Click on **Permission Schemes** (should be the last option in the Sidebar)
3. In the **Permission Schemes'** view, click on **Add Permission Scheme** button (in the upper right corner)
4. In the Add permission scheme view, enter a Name of the Permission Scheme in the **Name** field (required), and a **description** (optional)
5. Click **Add**

Change Permissions in a permission Scheme

1. On the Navigation Bar, click > **Issues**
2. In the Issues Sidebar, Click on **Permission Schemes** (should be the last option in the Sidebar)
3. In **Permission Schemes**, find the Permission Scheme you want to change and click on **Permissions** link in the **Actions** column
4. In the opened Permission Scheme, find the Permission you want to change and click **Update**.
5. In the Update permission popup:
    i. Find the Option you want to change
    ii. Either click the Checkbox to grant permission or unselect the check box to remove the permission

   iii. In some cases further dropdowns may show (e.g. If you select **Single user** a dropbox will appear where you will select a User)
6. Click **Update** when done

Associate a different Permission Scheme with a Project

1. Open a **Project**
2. Click on **Project Settings** in the Project Sidebar
3. In the **Project Settings** view, select **Permissions** in the sidebar
4. In the **Project's Permissions** view, click on **Actions** button (in the upper right corner)
5. Select 'Use a different scheme'
6. In the **Associate Permission Scheme to Project** page, select *your Permission Scheme* in the **Scheme** drop-down list
7. Click **Associate** button

Delete a Permission Scheme

NOTE: If you want to delete a permission scheme you must first remove that scheme from any project associated with that permission scheme. Follow the instructions in "Associate a different Permission Scheme with a Project" in order to change schemes.

1. On the Navigation Bar, click  > **Issues**
2. In the Issues Sidebar, Click on **Permission Schemes** (should be the last option in the Sidebar)
3. In **Permission Schemes**, find the Permission Scheme you want to change and click on **Delete** in the **Actions** column

4. In the Delete Permission Scheme view, click the **Delete** button

Dashboards

Create New Dashboard

1. On the Navigation Bar, click **Dashboards** > **Create Dashboard**
2. In the Create Dashboard popup:
3. Enter the **name** of the new Dashboard in the name field
4. Enter a brief **description** of the Dashboard (Optional)
5. In the Viewers drop-down list select Project, Group, My Organization, or Private
6. Depending on your selection, additional drop downs may appear, select the appropriate option(s)
7. When done with Viewers, click the **Add** button next to the **Viewers** fields
8. Repeat steps # 4-6 for the **Editors** fields
9. Click on the **Save** button when done

Copy Dashboard

1. On the Navigation Bar, click **Dashboards**, then select **view all dashboards**
2. In the Dashboards' view, find the dashboard you want to copy, Click on the **...** (more) button and Select **Copy Dashboard**
3. Follow steps 3 to 9 of the **Create new Dashboard** instructions.

Edit Dashboard

1. On the Navigation Bar, click **Dashboards**, then select **view all dashboards**
2. In the Dashboards' view, Open the dashboard you want to Edit
3. In the Dashboard you want to manage, click on the **edit** button located in the upper right corner
4. In the Edit view you can:

   i. Make the Dashboard a **favorite or unfavorite** by clicking the star
   ii. **Add** a **gadget** (see **Add a gadget to a Dashboard** instructions for more details)
   iii. Change the **layout** of the dashboard
5. In the ... (More) menu you can:
   i. Rename and share a dashboard
   ii. Make a copy of the dashboard
   iii. Configure the automatic data refresh timing
   iv. Delete the Dashboard by moving it to trash
   v. Create a new dashboard
   vi. Make, configure, and View a wallboard slide show
6. When done, click the **Done** button

Delete Dashboard

1. On the Navigation Bar, click on **Dashboards** > **View all Dashboards**
2. In the dashboards view, find the dashboard you want to delete, click on the **...** (More) menu and select **Move to trash**
3. In the **Move to trash?** pop up, click on the **Move to trash** button

Find Dashboard

1. On the Navigation Bar, click Dashboards > **View all Dashboards**
2. In the Dashboards view you can search for a Dashboards by:
   i. Using the Search box
   ii. Use the dropdown lists to narrow your search by Dashboard owner, project, or group

VIEW AS WALLBOARD

A wallboard will display a Dashboard's gadgets as a series of slides

1. ON THE NAVIGATION BAR, CLICK **DASHBOARDS**
2. OPEN THE DASHBOARD YOU WANT TO SEE AS A **WALLBOARD**
3. CLICK ON THE **...** (MORE) BUTTON LOCATED IN THE UPPER RIGHT CORNER AND SELECT **VIEW AS WALLBOARD**

SET UP WALLBOARD SLIDESHOW

1. ON THE NAVIGATION BAR, CLICK **DASHBOARDS**
2. OPEN THE DASHBOARD YOU WANT TO SET UP AS **WALLBOARD SLIDESHOW**
3. CLICK ON THE **...** (MORE) BUTTON LOCATED IN THE UPPER RIGHT CORNER AND SELECT **CONFIGURE WALLBOARD SLIDE SHOW**
4. IN THE CONFIGURE WALLBOARD POPUP:
   i. SELECT THE **DASHBOARD OR DASHBOARDS** YOU WANT IN YOUR WALLBOARD SLIDE SHOW
   ii. SELECT THE TRANSITION EFFECT
   iii. SELECT THE **DURATION** YOU WANT FOR EACH SLIDE
   iv. OPTIONAL: CLICK THE DISPLAY DASHBOARD IN RANDOM ORDER CHECKBOX
5. CLICK **SAVE** WHEN DONE

ADD A GADGET TO A DASHBOARD

1. ON THE NAVIGATION BAR, CLICK **DASHBOARDS**
2. OPEN THE DASHBOARD WHERE YOU WANT TO ADD A GADGET
3. CLICK THE **EDIT** BUTTON IN THE UPPER RIGHT OF THE DASHBOARD VIEW
4. IN THE GADGET'S EDIT MODE, CLICK THE **ADD GADGET** BUTTON IN THE UPPER RIGHT OF THE DASHBOARD VIEW
5. IN THE ADD GADGET SIDEBAR THAT APPEARS ON THE RIGHT SIDE OF THE SCREEN, SELECT THE GADGET AND CLICK ON THE **ADD** BUTTON NEXT TO THE GADGET
6. CLICK ON THE 'X" TO EXIT THE **GADGET SIDEBAR**

7. **Configure** the gadget's fields
8. When done click the **Done** button in the upper right corner of the dashboard

Edit a Gadget

1. On the Navigation Bar, click **Dashboards**
2. Open the dashboard whose gadget you want to edit
3. In the dashboard, click the **Edit** button in the upper right corner
4. To **move the gadget to another location**, hover the mouse arrow over the gadget's title bar, and drag the gadget to the new location
5. **To maximize the gadget** click on the box icon in the gadget's title bar
6. To **minimize** the gadget, click on the two facing arrows icon in the gadget's title bar
7. To **change the colour** of the band, **Configure**, **Rename** the gadget, or **delete** the gadget click on the **…** (more) icon and select one of those options

FILTERS AND REPORTS

QUICK SEARCH

1. ON THE NAVIGATION BAR, ENTER THE NAME OF A FILTER IN THE SEARCH BOX

SEARCH FOR ISSUES (BASIC SEARCH)

1. ON THE NAVIGATION BAR, CLICK **FILTERS** > **ADVANCED ISSUE SEARCH**
2. IN THE OPENED **SEARCH** VIEW USE THE **FILTER** MENU BAR TO NARROW YOUR SEARCH

NOTE: Jira Work Management builds searches in the order that the filters were selected, meaning **those filters in the filter menu bar are subsets of other filters.** Therefore, when building a multi-filter search, remember to build the search in the proper filter order.

ADVANCED SEARCH

1. ON THE NAVIGATION BAR, CLICK **FILTERS** > **ADVANCED ISSUE SEARCH**
2. IN THE OPENED **ISSUE NAVIGATOR (SEARCH)** VIEW, IN THE FILTER MENU BAR CLICK ON THE **SWITCH TO JQL** LINK
3. USE JQL LANGUAGE TO CREATE A JQL QUERY AND THEN CLICK SEARCH

SAVE SEARCH

1. ON THE NAVIGATION BAR, CLICK **FILTERS** > **ADVANCED ISSUE SEARCH**
2. IN THE OPENED **ISSUE NAVIGATOR (SEARCH)** VIEW, FIND YOUR ISSUE(S) USING THE BASIC SEARCH (THE FILTER MENU BAR) OR USING THE ADVANCED SEARCH
3. CLICK ON THE **SAVE AS** BUTTON
4. IN THE **SAVE FILTER** POPUP, ENTER A **FILTER NAME**
5. CLICK **SUBMIT**

Build Custom Filter

1. On the Navigation Bar, click **Filters** > **Search for Issues**
2. In the opened **Issue Navigator (Search)** view, find your Issue(s) using the Basic search (the filters menu bar) or using the Advanced search
3. Click on the **Save As** button
4. Type in a **Filter Name** in the **Save Filter** Pop Up
5. Click **Submit**

NOTE: Once you click the submit button your Search (really a filter) will be saved in the **Filters** sidebar

Create a filter subscription

1. On the Navigation Bar, click **Filters** > **View all filters**
2. In the Filters view, find the filter you want to manage, click the **...** (More) menu, then select **Manage subscriptions**
3. In the Subscriptions view, click on the **Add subscription** button located in the upper right corner
4. In the **Filter Subscription** pop-up, select:
    i. the **Recipients** from the drop-down list
    ii. the Schedule
    iii. the **Interval** from the drop-down lists
    iv. Check or leave "email this filter, even if there are no issues found"
5. Click Subscribe

Export a Filter's Results

1. On the Navigation Bar, click **Filters** > **View all filters**
2. Select the Filter that contains the results you want to export
3. In the Filter's view, click on the **Export** drop-down list in the upper right corner of the opened Filter's view
4. Select one of the **export options**:

i. Print list
ii. Print details
iii. Export XML
iv. Export RSS
v. Export RSS (with comments)
vi. Export Word
vii. Export HTML report (all fields)
viii. Export HTML report (current fields)
ix. Export Excel CSV (all fields)
x. Export Excel CSV (current fields)
xi. Create Dashboard gadget

Create a Project specific Report

1. Navigate Main Menu Bar> **projects**
2. Select The project where you want the report
3. Navigate to the project's sidebar and click on **Reports**
4. Select any report in the sidebar
5. **Configure** the Report (What needs to be configured will vary by report)

Source Material

The JIRA WORK MANAGEMENT User's Guide is an excellent source for technical instructions:

https://confluence.atlassian.com/alldoc/atlassian-documentation-32243719.html

Made in United States
North Haven, CT
10 November 2026

22091356R00264